RUN-THROUGH

A MEMOIR

BY

John Houseman

A TOUCHSTONE BOOK
PUBLISHED BY SIMON AND SCHUSTER
NEW YORK

Portions of this work have appeared in *Audience*.

Copyright © 1972 by John Houseman
All rights reserved
including the right of reproduction
in whole or in part in any form
First Touchstone Edition, 1980
Published by Simon and Schuster
A Division of Gulf & Western Corporation
Simon & Schuster Building
Rockefeller Center
1230 Avenue of the Americas
New York, New York 10020
TOUCHSTONE and colophon
are trademarks of Simon & Schuster
Designed by Irving Perkins
Manufactured in the United States of America

10 9 8 7 6 5 4 3 2
Pbk. 10 9 8 7 6 5 4 3 2 1

Library of Congress Cataloging in Publication Data

Houseman, John.
  Run-through.

  (A Touchstone book)
  Continued by the author's Front and center.
  Includes index.
    1. Houseman, John. 2. Theatrical producers and
directors—United States—Biography. I. Title.
[PN2287.H7A3 1980]   792′.0232′0924 [B]
80-36846
ISBN 0-671-21034-3
ISBN 0-671-41390-2 Pbk.

ACKNOWLEDGMENTS

To Joseph Barnes, without whose patient encouragement this book would not have been written; to Archibald MacLeish, Helen Wright and Sonia Orwell for permission to quote from letters and published material; to Martin Seiger and Denis Deegan for their research; to Louise Bernikow and Marian Fenn for their advice and help in preparing this manuscript for publication; to MGM, CBS, the Juilliard School and the Ford Foundation, which made possible its completion—my deepest thanks.

To Joan

CONTENTS

ILLUSTRATIONS

PICTURE SECTIONS FOLLOW PAGES 224 AND 416.

To say that our life is entirely what we make of it or entirely the data we are given is to say the same thing. . . . As far as freedom is concerned two things are certain: we are never predetermined and we never change; we can always find in our past the presage of what we have become.
—MAURICE MERLEAU-PONTY

OVERTURE

FOR

MAY HAUSSMANN

I

The Education
of a Chameleon

I WAS conceived in the second year of this century and legiti-
matized five years after that. By then I was speaking English with
my mother, French with my father and his friends, Rumanian
with the household and German with a visiting governess. Two
of my first four birthdays were celebrated on board the Orient
Express between Paris and Bucharest, the city where I was born
on September 22, 1902, of a Jewish-Alsatian father and a British
mother of Welsh-Irish descent.

He first saw her in the Bois de Boulogne riding a bicycle and
wearing a bright red blouse with black polka dots. A month later
they were living together at Maisons-Laffitte near the race track.
Six months after that, when he was sent off to manage his
family's grain and shipping interests in the Balkans, she accompanied him to the shores of the Black Sea, where they occupied a
large brick house on a hill overlooking the Danube.

Till I was four and a half my hair fell in long golden curls
over my shoulders: the day it was cut off I was photographed
twice—before and after. That same year my father's family

business collapsed as the result of a great-uncle's disastrous investment in the Marseilles streetcar system. As a result he was able to marry my gentile mother and I was registered at the French consulate under the name of Jacques Haussmann. Returning to Paris, he set up in business for himself as a broker and operator in commodities. He was a gambler; for the remaining ten years of his life he rode a series of speeding roller coasters (wheat, cotton, sugar, cocoa, coffee and various sorts of vegetable oils) up and down the "futures" markets of the world. They carried him from month to month, and sometimes from week to week, from riches to ruin and back again.

Our lives followed his fortunes in sudden moves from palatial suites to furnished rooms, from the favored corners of the Café de Paris to the dented aluminum tabletops of the Bouillons Duval. Lacking security, we lived in a whirling state of conspicuous extravagance. Chinchillas and pearls, a town house half-decorated but never occupied, two specially designed, custom-built automobiles (a Charron and a Delauney-Belleville, both bottle green with basket-weave cabins) were solemnly presented to my mother, then quickly resold to meet some critical margin call or to finance some new bonanza. My memory of my father—a composite of childish impressions and fading photographs—is of a short, pink-cheeked, bald, bearded, potbellied, elegant, smiling man with beautiful white hands and a striking resemblance to Edward VII of England.

When I was a child, before passports and police regulations and total wars, Europe was a garden through which the moneyed middle class journeyed incessantly in search of health and amusement. A few reckless eccentrics raced through clouds of dust along tree-lined highways, but the rest of them did their traveling in the swaying mahogany security of the Grands Expresses Européens. Beneath racks that strained under loads of label-covered cowhide luggage, leaning back on lace doilies pinned to seats of varicolored, dusty plush which, at night, were miraculously converted into beds by men in brown uniforms, they moved in well-ordered comfort between the capitals and resorts of Continental Europe: Biarritz, Deauville, Ostend, Baden-Baden, Aix-les-Bains, Nice, La Bourboule, Chamonix, St. Moritz and the Swiss and Italian lakes—these were their favorite playgrounds and, at one time or another, we visited them all. On various holidays, over the years, I was shown King Alfonso of Spain thundering by at dusk in his white Mercedes; the *Graf Zeppelin* rising from a bright-green German meadow dotted with tiny running figures; Max Decugis, the French lawn-tennis champion, demonstrating Diabolo on a hotel terrace to two Scandinavian princesses. But my most persistent memories are those of Lake Lucerne, where my mother and I spent seven consecutive summers until the World War put an end to our travels.

Here at the water's edge, with the snow-capped mountains all around us, we lived in an atmosphere of continuous and extravagant celebration: tennis tournaments, regattas and races succeeded each other in scheduled profusion, culminating in gala weekends that were filled with banquets, cotillions and fireworks. In these activities I participated only remotely. Coming out of our early table-d'hôte dinner while it was still light, Fräulein and I would pause to admire the translucent meringue castles topped with Swiss flags and the fabulous ice sculptures that rose glistening from long, crowded buffets at either end of the deserted ballroom. I was half-asleep when my mother came very quietly into my room at twilight, perfumed and rustling, to kiss me good night on her way down to her mysterious excitements. When I awoke with the sun in my eyes and Mount Pilatus rising steeply across the lake, there would be wrinkled balloons and tinsel favors and, usually, a scrawled note with crosses for kisses from her at the foot of my bed.

Summer was not the only time we traveled: I have memories of extended voyages undertaken for unknown reasons—to Vienna and Budapest, Berlin, Barcelona and Rome. It was the arrivals and departures that moved me—stations and hotels rather than landmarks and monuments. By the age of seven I had been in half the celebrated cities of Europe. Of this precocious Grand

Tour no clear recollection remains: I came away from Venice with a confused memory of dungeons and stagnant water and the walls of our rooms at the Danieli Palace red with blood from the crushed corpses of giant mosquitoes. In Rome the Sistine Chapel and the lobby of the Excelsior Hotel left me with identical impressions of grandeur.

My early education was erratic. At the age of six I made a brief appearance at the day school that my French cousins attended. The third time I vomited in class I was removed and resumed private instruction under a gentle, sallow, Catholic Mademoiselle with whom I made the rounds of the Paris museums and a sharp-eyed Fräulein from whom I learned to recite some of the shorter works of the German romantic poets and the words and music of *"Deutschland über Alles."*

Six months later (while my parents were in Istanbul) I made my second institutional experiment, this time as a guest in a celebrated Parisian girls' finishing school for the daughters of the English and American rich. Within that budding grove I spent eight amazing weeks in the company of two dozen nubile, spoiled and exuberant young women. I shared their meals, their entertainments, their French and German classes and, occasionally, their beds. To this brief, delicious sojourn and those unconsummated delights, I attribute many of my emotional problems in years to come including the deep shame of my superannuated virginity.

My third experience was less agreeable but more lasting. Soon after my seventh birthday I was sent to Bristol in the west of England to be brought up in the house of a schoolmaster with six children, the youngest of whom was exactly my age. After more than half a century Eric Siepmann recalled the appearance in his home of "a French boy known as Fat Jack who arrived from Paris with a beautiful Mama in a beautiful hat that actually had three storeys. As soon as she had gone he told us that he knew everything—for example that Eskimos live at the North Pole on a diet of candles. He was a spoiled only child and it never occurred to us, because he was plump and foreign and used to riches, that

18

he could be anything but a vulgarian. We set about him and I am surprised he ever recovered."

I was fortunate, in this my first confrontation with an alien society, to encounter so intelligent and humane a family as the Siepmanns.* Their persecutions were spontaneous, brief and almost entirely free of the calculated cruelties of the world's pecking orders as I came to know them later. During the four years I lived among them in their gray Bathstone house on College Road the struggle to be accepted by them remained the principal preoccupation of my life. Some of its most savage battles were waged in the bare room with striped walls which Eric and I shared and which was known from earlier times as the Nursery. It was here, after we had said our prayers and the lights were out, that I came to know loneliness in all its icy, corrosive horror and wept in panic as the doors of my lost happy childhood slammed shut behind me. And it was here that my first male relationship was formed—an intimacy rooted in inequality and fear: inequality since this was *his* house in which I was a stranger, *his* room in which I was an intruder; fear because it was through *him* that the hope of acceptance and the menace of rejection were kept in constant suspense. This created a pattern of insecurity that has persisted through most of my life and has permanently affected my relations with other men. It left me incapable of parity—a prey to competitiveness in its most virulent form. More than once, at some critical point in a working

---

* Otto Siepmann, as head of the Modern Language Department of Clifton College and the author of innumerable "primers," completely transformed the teaching of French and German in the British Isles. His eldest son, Harry, became one of the world's recognized experts on international currency and central banking and was deputy governor of the Bank of England for some years under Sir Montague Norman. The second, Charles, my oldest living friend, won the Military Cross at nineteen and an Oxford Blue two years after that. At twenty-four he became director of a Borstal Institute for Young Criminals, then head of Educational Broadcasting for the British Broadcasting Corporation before coming to the U.S. where, for thirty years, in various capacities, he has fought for his ideals of public service in radio and television.

relationship, I have had the uncomfortable feeling that I was following the emotional curve of that first ambivalent children's intimacy of long ago.

My mother believed that by combining the healthy austerity of my life in England with the glamor of her own cosmopolitan world, she was giving me the best of all possible lives. It didn't work out that way. Three times a year—for a month at Christmas and Easter and for seven weeks each summer—I was shuttled across the restless waters of the English Channel, from the cold reality of my days and nights at Clifton into the holiday sunshine of my childhood—back to that secret universe of fantasies and desires where my mother was queen and I was her only child. After these euphoric excursions no gradual decompression was possible; each holiday was followed by agonizing emotional bends and each return to school became a bereavement and a violation that left me frightened and sore for weeks to come. Divided between my two worlds, I belonged to neither.

At the age of nine, wearing a gray flannel suit with short trousers, a stiff Eton collar and a cap with blue concentric circles, I became a day boy at the Clifton Preparatory School and went on from there, after two years, in yellow radial stripes, long trousers and a top hat on Sundays, to become a junior. Since four of my eleven years at Clifton College were war years, mine was not a typical experience. The rituals and routines remained unchanged but much of the adolescent violence that normally fermented under the surface of British public school life was drained off and sublimated in the more immediate anxieties of the Great War. As a result I, who by nature and circumstance presented such an inviting target for persecution, was spared much of what, at another time, I would almost certainly have suffered. Yet this same war presented me with another, more grievous, problem.

Regularly, three times a year, as each holiday came around, I continued to make the long and sometimes dangerous voyage from Clifton to Paris and back again. Even for so skilled and experienced a chameleon as I had become, this constant alternation grew increasingly difficult as I found myself becoming a whipping boy for the rising resentments that divided the Entente Cordiale in those first, frightening years of the war. Arriving in France for the holidays, I was challenged by members of my own family as an emissary of *"perfide Albion."* When I proudly mentioned that a former Clifton boy (Sir Douglas Haig) had been named Commander in Chief of the British Army, I was asked bitterly where that army was. A third of France was still occupied by the enemy; two million Frenchmen had been killed, wounded or captured. What were the dirty English waiting for to come over and share the awful burden of the war?

When I returned to England (where I was an alien with a German name and had to register with the Bristol police under the Defense of the Realm Act) I faced the charge that Frogs were braggarts and cowards who expected the British to pull their chestnuts out of the fire. Also, more specifically, it was said that while Britons were tightening their belts and living on ever more stringent rations as their ships were sunk and their seamen drowned in their efforts to bring in essential foodstuffs and ammunition, the French—including me and my family—were gorging themselves on rich foods and wines. Year after year this whipsawing continued. Such was my capacity for rapid assimilation that, with each holiday and term, I was able to make a new and drastic adjustment to the prevailing mood—just in time to ensure my full distress at my next transplantation, when I again crossed the Channel and reappeared, full of the wrong loyalties in a strange and hostile world. As a result, in self-protection, I lost all sense of patriotism in my early teens and have not regained it since.

Except for the agitations of the war, my years in the Junior School were uneventful and undistinguished. I made the rugby fifteen, partly on account of my weight, but was poor at cricket, which I played without style or pleasure. Our academic life was conducted in an atmosphere that was predominantly Philistine, following a schedule that seemed to leave time for everything except reading. It was not until my last year that I encountered my first good teacher—a harsh, ascetic man with a beaked nose under whom I began the study of Greek. When I came to him my brain was clogged with a thick sludge of inertia and self-love; he scared, chivvied and finally helped me to achieve my first breakthrough into sustained and organized study. Later, at different times in my life, I sought refuge in a variety of lethargies. But I never quite forgot the satisfactions of the discipline he forced upon me and only once again reverted to the depths of torpor from which his rigor had saved me.

That summer, a few months after the sinking of the *Lusitania* by a German submarine, my parents decided to vary the routine of my cross-Channel holidays with a voyage to the United States, where my father had gone as head of a French Government purchasing commission. I arrived during a heat wave, ate my first grapefruit on the roof of the Biltmore Hotel, learned to fox-trot under the personal supervision of the celebrated Mrs. Vernon Castle, visited the Hippodrome, where I watched an entire regiment of chorus girls and a small herd of elephants disappear into a tank of water, and went riding in Central Park with a red-haired lady to whom my father sent roses. For added excitement, that burning August, there was the Black Tom explosion in New York harbor, a shark scare and a polio epidemic. We moved up to the Grand Union in Saratoga for the racing season, fished for black bass in Lake George, visited the dwarf genius of General Electric, Dr. Steinmetz, in his laboratory at Schenectady, where he and my father spoke in German of an electric car for the postwar European market, then continued north to Niagara Falls in our huge, double-clutching Packard Twin-Six, driven by a scowling Italo-American who had been chief racing mechanic to Ralphe de Palma and whom I worshiped. On our way back through the White Mountains we stopped at a great cream-colored caravanserai where, after my father had written his name in the register, we were politely but firmly refused admission. In Boston, that night, we read in the papers of the first German zeppelin raid on London;* the next day as we drove back to

---

* It was during this raid, as I learned more than thirty years later, that my wife Joan was born in Lady Ottoline Morrell's house on Bedford Square.

New York along the Post Road, the Twin-Six was suddenly and hideously transformed from a magic coach into a speeding hearse that was carrying me back to the grim realities of school and the war—out of the holiday brightness of the New World into a region of darkness and desolation and death.

Number 30 College Road, known in my day as "Mayor's House," was one of half a dozen buildings (each housing from fifty to sixty boys) set in an irregular cluster around the main body of Clifton College. Here we lived in a state of divided allegiance. We had our school patriotism, as prescribed by our own poet laureate Sir Henry Newbolt, whose "Clifton Chapel," "Vitae Lampeda" and "The Best School of All" we were expected to memorize and admire. But the basic unit and emotional center of our lives was The House. Here I spent the best part of four years, following the normal curve of the British public schools' "queuing up" system—from humiliation to power —under the watchful eye of our housemaster, Henry Bickersteth Mayor. He was a shy man of great vitality and goodwill with a large crimson nose and a walrus moustache overhanging a sensitive mouth. My relations with him were satisfactory but precarious. Throughout my first year, since I had recently returned from the United States, he held me directly responsible for America's shameful treatment of the Red Indian. Later he came to appreciate my resourceful work in the football scrum but was deeply aggrieved when, in my third year, on Otto Siepmann's instructions, I committed the unpardonable faux pas of switching from classics to modern languages as my principal study.

This was the last year of my father's life. He and my mother had returned from America during the darkest days of the war, following the disaster of Verdun, when the air was full of rumors of French Army betrayals and mutinies. But my father was confident that with America's entry into the war a quick Allied victory was certain. Soon after his arrival, he rented a large office on the Champs Elysées, where he had visions of himself and his son, one day, conducting vast and brilliant international affairs. In the meantime, he staffed it with a second cousin who had been invalided out of the army and an old friend who had fallen on evil days. Here, one morning, he suddenly felt weak and sent a boy out for a cup of chocolate and a brioche. Before they arrived he fainted, then quickly recovered. But by the time I left for school after the Easter holidays, my mother had been told by two specialists that her husband was suffering from Addison's disease and had only a short time to live.

Within three months this plump man whose face had been rosy and round under his beard was reduced to a sagging, copper-colored sack of bones and skin. He was dying and he knew it, but he tried to hold death off with a final spasm of financial activity —a last, frantic gamble in which he staked his whole new-won American fortune on a desperate chance that death would not call his bluff. He began by buying fifty thousand dollars' worth of Russian Imperial War Bonds (with which I was lighting fires in Rockland County forty years later), then invested hurriedly in a number of enterprises, including the controlling interest in an aircraft factory (which collapsed with the end of the war), and a trading corporation for supplying France's North African territories with American agricultural equipment (a large consignment of which was found rusting in warehouses in Algiers and Casablanca ten years after his death). But his main investment and highest hopes lay in a perfume factory, Les Parfums Sidlay de Paris. Considering the world-wide cosmetics boom of the twenties and thirties, this should have made my mother a millionairess. It never did. For the day came when my father had to give up. He lay in bed in his hotel off the Place Vendôme for a few weeks, then decided to move south. One July night, at Salies-de-Béarn, in the Basque country, my mother heard a dog howling mournfully in the street below. She went out onto the balcony for a moment. When she turned back into their room, she found my father stiff from a stroke. He died before morning at the age of forty-two.

When I reached Paris my mother was already there but the coffin, caught in a French wartime railway snarl, was still on its way. While we waited for it to arrive, the sitting room and bathroom at the hotel were filled with weeping members of my

French family spelling each other in a ceremonial sequence of mounting lamentations. The persistent moaning, nose blowing and gnashing of teeth, the hands that reached out and clutched me with possessive pity to heaving bosoms and groaning chests, the incessantly repeated commiserations and reminiscences—these all shocked and embarrassed me as I moved between the wailing figures and the bedroom in which my mother had taken refuge.

She did not attend the funeral, at which I wore black gloves and a bowler hat as I blindly shoveled the first spadeful of earth over my father's coffin in the Jewish section of the Montparnasse cemetery, under instructions from my Uncle Robert (in uniform) and a black-clad rabbi whose beard glistened in the sun. Afterwards relatives and friends drove back to the hotel, where they continued their wailing far into the night. Among the noisiest of the mourners was the second cousin, my father's associate in the perfume factory. Six months later, still weeping, he confessed to having embezzled the entire capital of Les Parfums Sidlay de Paris in a disastrous speculation in alcohol futures for which my father, over my mother's protest, had given him a temporary proxy shortly before his death.

The scenes at my father's grave (so different from the restrained ceremonial of Clifton Chapel) had disturbed and shaken me but they had not cracked the insulation which, for so many years, had enabled me to "pass," whenever it suited me, among Jews and gentiles alike, without the faintest feeling of betrayal or guilt. From the elaborate chameleon maneuvers which I found myself forced to perform throughout my childhood, I had developed a mechanism of adjustment so automatic and so complete that I was honestly unaware of the denials and deceptions that these transformations required of me. On a simple semantic level, phrases like "to jew down," "don't be a Jew!" "a fat Jew," even "dirty Jew" formed part of the standard vocabulary of that English middle class to whose customs I was so scrupulously trying to adhere. Yet I would have been surprised and hurt if I had ever heard them applied to my father while he lived, or to those cousins, uncles and aunts whose elegant Parisian apartments I visited during the holidays.* Unable or unwilling to make the distasteful connection, I remained blithely unaware of the problem.

Some of this duplicity accompanied my reception into the Church of England some months later. A letter had arrived in Paris during the Christmas holidays "reminding" my mother that I was approaching the age of confirmation and "assuming" that she would want me prepared for that event with the other boys of my group. We discussed the matter. "You never know," said my mother, "it might come in useful one day." (Years later, when I mockingly reminded her of this, she said, "Well, didn't it?" and I was not disposed to argue with her.) Some weeks later there was a second letter—from the Bishop of Bristol and Bath—asking for a copy of my baptismal certificate. Since I had never been baptized—in Rumania or anywhere else—this was an awkward request. The war saved us. Clearly it was impossible to obtain papers from a country that was under the iron heel of the Imperial German Army. I explained this to the ecclesiastical authorities and gave them a fictitious date which they accepted.

I recall my preparation for confirmation with the deepest distaste. It was conducted, first, in hollow, sanctimonious tones by our house tutor, a muscular Christian with high-church leanings, then, when he left to take a commission as chaplain in the RAF, by Henry Bickersteth in person. Both devoted far more time and thought to convincing us of the evils of masturbation and sodomy (neither of which I practiced) than to the salvation of our eternal souls. Intercourse with the other sex was an evil so heinous and unthinkable that it was never mentioned except in terms of profound revulsion.†

---

* Years later on a belated pilgrimage to the family vault in the Cimetière Montparnasse I noticed three plaques next to my father's. They were those of two aunts and one cousin—MORTS 1944 A AUSCHWITZ, ASSASSINÉS PAR LES ALLEMANDS.

† There was one boy in our House who boasted of intercourse with girls. We regarded him with incredulity and horror rather than admiration or envy—all the more since he was of low intellectual capacity and poor at games.

2 6

During the confirmation service in Clifton Chapel I was op-
pressed by such a weight of gloom that I hardly noticed the
strange sensation—something between a tickling and an ache in
my side—of which I first became aware as we moved toward
the altar and sank to our knees before the Bishop of Bristol and
Bath. While I crouched there, openmouthed, waiting to receive
my little strip of bread and the metallic sip of wine from the
hard edge of the silver chalice, I was suddenly pierced by a shaft
of pain so intense that it was all I could do to prevent myself
from rolling over at the Bishop's feet, and it came to me with
terrible clarity that this was God's punishment for my baptismal
fraud and that I was going to die. At two the next morning a
gray-faced army surgeon, hastily summoned to the school sani-
tarium, removed my distended, pus-laden appendix and left me
with three red rubber tubes dangling from what remains one of
the most gruesome incisions in the history of appendectomy.

It took me less than a month to recover from the surgery, more
than nine years to get over the emasculating effects of the obscene
and gloomy ritual that preceded it. If I retained my virginity
beyond the age of twenty-four it was not out of purity or from
any moral or religious scruples: it was from fear of violating the
taboos of a society to which I was desperately anxious to belong.
These inhibitions were implanted in me in various forms and at
different times during my eleven years at Clifton; they crystal-
lized during the six weeks of my hypocritical "preparation" and
have never been entirely dissolved.

No three more different human beings could be imagined than
the men under whose influence my last eighteen months at
Clifton were spent. Maurice Roy Ridley, scholar of Balliol, was
tall, aquiline, rhapsodic, vain and inordinately ambitious. It is to
him that I owe my first emotional contact with Shakespeare (of
whom he later became one of England's most prolific editors)
and my first meetings with Conrad, Meredith, and the metaphysi-
cal poets Crashaw and Donne. Monsieur Jaccard was a frail,
sophisticated Swiss—a scholar of the Université de Genève and
King's College, Cambridge. Modeling his behavior on that of

those seventeenth- and eighteenth-century authors whose *"noblesse et clarté"* he so admired, he wore gray suede gloves and his courtliest manner as he led us daily out of the stale air of our scaling schoolroom into the high mountains from which he invited us to look down upon the wonders of French civilization. From the formal splendor of the Sun King's palace at Versailles to the scientific naturalism of Zola; from Ronsard to Valéry and from Corneille via Victor Hugo to Feydeau; from the court gossip of his beloved Marquise de Sévigné to the Parisian notations of the brothers Goncourt—the life and literature of France were spread out before us in a pattern of astonishing variety and color. His love for the theatre was passionate and infectious. Most of my Paris holiday theatregoing, from the Comédie Francaise, Gémier and Copeau to the Boulevards was suggested by him and reported in detail for his vicarious appreciation. And a holiday reading of Emile Faguet's *Drame Ancien, Drame Moderne* so aroused my interest in the history of the theatre that it affected the whole course of my life.*

German was Otto Siepmann's personal domain, over which he presided in a hexagonal classroom on the top floor of Clifton's highest neo-Gothic tower. Here he propelled me through the entire range of German literature from Herder to Hauptmann by way of Klopstock, Lessing, Kleist, Goethe, Schiller, Heine, Sudermann and Hofmannsthal. From this formidable banquet such an indigestion resulted that it deprived me for the rest of my life of the pleasures to which my fluency in German would otherwise have entitled me.

I remember this final period of intense effort and continuous pressure as a time of fulfillment and satisfaction. As a prefect and a member of the school Rugby fifteen, I was more secure, mentally and physically, than I had been since childhood. I founded

* From childhood my theatrical experience had been mixed and extensive. Before the age of nine I had seen *Eighty Days Around the World, Carmen, Cyrano de Bergerac, Oedipus, Ne Te Promène Donc Pas Toute Nue, Chantecler, Peter Pan, The Bluebird, Pagliacci* and *Cavalleria Rusticana, Madame Butterfly, La Belle Hélène,* half of *Lohengrin* and the dancing of Pavlova and Nijinski.

the Clifton College Dramatic Society of which I was president and I became one of the editors of the *Cliftonian*, normally a bland, formal, pale-pink-covered quarterly, of which we devoted one whole devastating issue to reducing the Officers' Training Corps to what we considered its proper peacetime place in the life of the school. It was my first taste of the power of propaganda and I have never forgotten it. It was also my first act of subversion.

For my final vacation, in the summer of 1920, for the first time since the war, my mother and I visited Switzerland and went on from there, over the St. Gothard Pass, to the Villa d'Este on the Lake of Como. On the way home we stopped in Milan and saw trucks in the streets filled with men in workclothes and tattered uniforms with red flags flapping in the wind. The next morning when we came out from seeing Leonardo's *Last Supper*, there were more trucks, battered grayish wartime Fiats, lined up in the square outside, guarded by men in black shirts.

At Cova's, where we lunched on veal and white truffles, a middle-aged man came over to our table, kissed my mother's hand and asked if he might join us. He had been with my father in the grain business and spoke with feeling of the old days in Rumania. Over coffee he asked me about myself. I told him I was at school in England but that if I was successful in my examination for the University, I might leave at the end of the Christmas term and go traveling—possibly to Spain. Over cognac he suggested that I come instead to Argentina, where I could learn Spanish and the grain business at the same time. He gave me his card which I looked at after he had left and noted that his name was Señor Katz and that he was a member of the Jockey Club of Buenos Aires.

In the agitations of my final term this chance meeting was quite forgotten. Early in December I traveled with the rest of Clifton's Rugby team for our annual game against Wellington. I scored the winning try, spent the weekend in London and arrived in Cambridge the day before the scholarship examinations began. That night I was invited to a dinner party given by a famous University hostess, at which I sat silent, gauche and unnoticed among a dozen suave and mannered young men whose informed, sophisticated talk seemed to float, without strain or effort, far above my head. The effect of this exclusion, real or imagined, was to send me into the examination room the next morning in a state of furious determination.

For my English essay I chose, from among several alternates, to comment on a quotation that described opera as a bastard art, combining the worst elements of music and drama. Here was my chance and I took it. In two hours, as fast as my hand would write, I unloaded the knowledge and enthusiasm of my twelve years of theatre, ballet and opera going. With Faguet, Lessing, Wagner, George Bernard Shaw, and Aristotle on my side, my essay must have seemed like an opinionated but well-documented and surprising outpouring from a British public school boy of eighteen. It probably had something to do with my placement on the Cambridge scholarship list as it appeared in the *Times* of London on the morning of December 17th, 1920.

I had won one of the highest academic prizes of the year—the first major scholarship awarded for modern languages at Trinity College. For Otto Siepmann it was a glorious victory; even Henry Bickersteth was impressed. So was everyone except, possibly, my mother, who was delighted but entirely taken up with her preparations for my South American visit which seemed to have materialized without my knowledge during the autumn. On my last Sunday in Clifton, divided between pride in my success and suspicion of my incomprehensible voyage, Otto outlined the bright future that lay before me: four years of advanced studies under ideal cultural conditions with some of the world's greatest scholars; a few years of travel to the leading universities of France and Germany; then, a fellowship—and he said it with bated breath—at Trinity College, Cambridge: a life of dignity and honor, of ease and universal respect. At parting he gave me a long list of carefully selected reading for the months to come. I listened to him with attention, put the list in my pocket and never looked at it again.

Two nights later, in my blue-velvet School XV cap with its golden tassel jiggling about my ears, I sat with fourteen other heroes, high on the narrow ledge of the Big School gallery from which we looked down, like gods, at the hundreds of dark seated figures on the floor below. And when the concert was over, the prizes awarded and the speeches made, with a sudden rustling and scraping of benches and great swell of boys' voices and the organ roaring beneath us, we sang the school song—

> *We'll honour yet the School we knew*
> *The best school of all!*

—fervently, at the tops of our voices. And, afterwards, balanced on our perilous ledge high over the heads of the crowd, we led the singing of "Auld Lang Syne" with our hands tightly clasped and our crossed arms pumping up and down, over and over, faster and faster, setting the rhythm for those other hundreds of rocking figures below, till the whole building shuddered and heaved and swayed on its foundations.

*   *   *

I sailed for South America two days later in the R.M.S. *Almanzora*. My mother cried at saying goodbye and she was still crying and waving as the darkness swallowed up the swaying tender which was carrying her back to shore and the lights of Cherbourg and the French coast, which I was not to see again for thirty-five years.

I imagine, in the long, lonely hours of her train trip back to Paris, that my mother must have found comfort in the thought that against bitter opposition, through peace and war, riches and poverty, separation and death, she had achieved her goal: her son was tall, blue-eyed, and multilingual, with a pleasant manner and a completed British public school education. From here on, with such advantages, it was up to him to make his way in the world, and she never had the slightest doubt that I would.

For my part, while the *Almanzora* moved out of the Channel into the full fury of the Atlantic, I might have reflected—if a sudden, violent wave of nausea had not banished all other thoughts from my mind—that at eighteen and a half I still had not the faintest notion of what I wanted to do with my life, that I had a little less than five hundred francs in my pocket, a modest but elegant wardrobe and no return ticket.

The Argentine Republic, when I arrived there in 1921, was still a colony—no longer of Spain, but of half a dozen of the great industrial powers of the Western world. Its army and police were trained by Germans; its culture was imported from France; its films and automobiles came mostly from the United States; its latest immigrants were Italians and Spaniards; while all its railroads and a great part of its industry and banking were run by Europeans—principally British. Agricultural production was native but its export was in foreign hands: the packing plants were American and grain shipments were controlled by international firms, of which Señor Katz's was one.

My first home in Argentina was the *hotel particulier* which he occupied on the Avenida Alvear. He was a pleasant, shrewd, extravagant, domineering and moody man (with a curiously bent middle finger on his right hand), with whom, since we had nothing in common except his former association with my father, I found it difficult to communicate. Yet, it should soon have become apparent (if I had been in a state to use my brain for a moment) that this South American voyage was the subject of a total misunderstanding between us. My host was under the impression that he was helping his friend's son on the first step of a career in the international grain business, which he assumed I was impatient to embark on. For me the trip was nothing more than a holiday, a reward for three years of good work, a pleasant and instructive interlude between Clifton and Cambridge. This delusion was encouraged by the dream life which I led as his guest that first month, in a lotus land whose temptations I was not disposed to resist. While my former companions at 30 College Road were being awakened by the clanging of the bells, washing in ice water, answering roll calls and undergoing the horrors of cross-country "runs" and open-order drills, I was lying in bed until noon every day, breakfasting from a tray on which, once a week, I would find an envelope thick with spending money, which I had no compunction in accepting. Around noon I would rise, bathe and dress in time to be driven downtown in a long, open, maroon Minerva, either to Señor Katz's office or directly to the echoing marble Exchange, where I was introduced to a number of middle-aged men who claimed to have known me as a baby on the shores of the Danube. After lunch I would accompany Señor Katz to the races at the Palermo track, where flamingos flew in orange clouds over the jockeys' heads. Later in the afternoon, while Señor Katz returned to his business, I attended chaperoned tea parties with my shipboard friends on the top floor of Harrod's department store, where society debutantes, accompanied by their mothers or older sisters, sat with their brothers, cousins and fiancés in shrill, trivial, interminable chatter. Later, I accompanied those same brothers, cousins and fiancés on their regular evening rounds of the bars and brothels of the Calle Florida, where I would exhaust myself in endless tangos with the native call girls (*pour apprendre l'espagnol*) to the pumping rhythms of long, flexible concertinas, while my friends went upstairs with the newly arrived French and German girls who had been reserved for their sampling.

Known as the *niños bien* (the sons of good families), these young men were the accepted leaders of the city's night life, from which they seldom absented themselves, except when they were off doing the same thing in Paris or exiled to a distant family *estancia* following some especially unsavory scandal or racing up and down the Avenida del Cinco de Mayo in their Hispanos and Bugattis, charging into processions of protesting workers or marching strikers. Spoiled, ignorant and dangerous, they were consistently pleasant to me—so pleasant that I thought it wise to conceal three vital facts from them: a) that I was penniless (which was not apparent, with my O'Rossen suits and my Sulka haberdashery); b) that I was the houseguest of a Rumanian-Jewish grain merchant; c) that I was a virgin.

This dream life ended suddenly one February night when I left with Señor Katz for the larger of his two *estancias*—in the northwest of the province of Buenos Aires. In an airless compartment of the Central Argentine Railways (he in the lower berth, I in the upper), just as I was falling asleep, Señor Katz began to talk to me out of the darkness. He spoke of my father: what a great gentleman he was and what a wonderful couple he and my mother had made in those happy, far-off days in Bräila. This led him, after a while, to talk of my mother's present financial situation. It was common knowledge among my father's friends, he told me, that she could not last much longer on what my father had left her—not living the way she did. When that was gone, what would she do? Had she ever discussed her situation with me? Had she talked of remarrying, ever? Soon after that he fell asleep and I could hear his peaceful breathing through the racket of the train wheels and the moaning of the racing locomotive. There was nothing surprising in what he had told me—nothing I had not been aware of for years. But now it had been said—and nothing would ever be the same again. I lay in the dark, frozen with fear, clutching at the sides of the narrow berth and hanging on for dear life while great waves of guilt and panic came sweeping over me in such a flood of anguish as I had not known since my first nights in the Nursery at Percival House. Once again a door had swung shut behind me; I had heard the click of a trap from which I knew there was no escape.

The train made a special stop for us at Arribenos around four in the morning. There was no one at the station to meet us, and a small, bitter wind swept the empty tracks and tore at the kerosene lamp in the stationmaster's deserted office. Ten minutes later two dust-caked Model T Fords came roaring over the level crossing and stopped at the loading platform. A harried-looking man with a broad face and glasses and leather leggings jumped out and started shouting in broken Spanish at the driver of the second car to take charge of our luggage, while Señor Katz yelled at him in a shrill combination of Rumanian and German. The man answered in Yiddish that one of the Fords had blown a tire.

After we cleared the village, the night closed in on us, except where the flickering yellow stripes from the headlamps of our swaying cars lit the road ahead—the wide corridor of rutted earth between wire fences that ran in endless parallel lines before us into the darkness. Twice we had to stop with screaming brakes to avoid running into herds of sleeping horses that rose suddenly out of the ground as our lights hit them and went galloping off heavily into the night, past the wagon trains to which they belonged—towering, six- and eight-horse carts with iron-rimmed wheels twelve feet high, their long, narrow bodies loaded with grain sacks and their drivers asleep around their dying fires.

It was hard to tell, at first, when the late-summer dawn began to come up behind the wire. There was nothing to catch the light —only the slowly hardening line between the long, flat stretch of the earth and the cloudless, slowly brightening sky. Then, gradually, as color was added to the light, the varying textures of the pampa became visible—gray stubble and standing grain, sunburnt pastures and the green of young maize and, sometimes in the distance, a small island of young, straggly trees or the thin outline of a steel windmill whirring above the mud shack and the accumulation of refuse that marked a sharecropper's place.

After a while, through the roaring of our Model T's, we began to hear the lowing of cattle and then, suddenly, rising out of the earth ahead of us, shimmering in the sun, we saw trees, taller and fuller grown than any we had seen till then, and the outlines of the buildings and windmills and water tanks of the Estancia Santa Maria. As we turned into the driveway, we could see a herd of cattle being moved slowly through a lake of green clover by four dark-skinned men sitting hunched on small horses, with what looked like bowler hats on their heads. These, said Señor Katz, were his "gauchos," and when we came through the outer yard with its sheds and mud shacks, dogs began to bark and children with Indian faces stared at us from open doorways as we came to a stop before a long, dirty-white building in which two naked light bulbs were still burning.

The Estancia Santa Maria, where Señor Katz never stayed for more than two days at a time, was a large commercial ranch he had acquired out of his wartime profits. Its main structures, beside the native shacks that seemed to grow out of the earth of which they were made, included the gray-white, brick admin-istration building and a pink stucco bungalow with modern plumbing set in a struggling eucalyptus grove. Here I lived with my benefactor's half brother, a recent arrival from Rumania, whose resentment of me was exceeded only by his raging envy of his more successful brother. Though he was titular administrator in his brother's name, the Estancia Santa Maria was, in fact, managed by his bitter enemy—an ambitious, khaki-clad Palestin-ian agricultural expert named Edelstein. Working in the office were two clerks in their twenties: one local—a Galician with a moustache and bad teeth (an animal torturer) ; the other a quick, intelligent city Jew sent out from Señor Katz's office in Buenos Aires to recuperate, in the country air, from threatened tuberculosis. They sat all day and half the night working over piles of tallies and bills of lading wearing eyeshades under the naked bulbs.

These four were my trapmates. They detested each other and were in turn resented and mocked, behind their backs, by the natives—the Indians and Mestizos, cowhands and peons, who did the physical work of the *estancia*. Chief of these, captain of gauchos and father of seven sons, was Don Bernardo—a dark, massive, bowlegged man in a stiff black felt hat and stained leather apron, silent, slow and awkward on the ground but agile, eloquent and formidable in the wide sheepskin saddle on which he bestrode his string of horses—six shaggy work ponies, one for each day of the week, and a gaited Arab stallion which he rode with a silver-studded bridle on Sundays. In his charge were several thousand head of cattle—Durham and Hereford—ser-viced by two huge, ill-tempered and dangerous bulls, whose stalls occupied the other half of the windowless, smoke-filled shed in which Don Bernardo slept on the earth floor with his sons, his two wives and half a dozen black-haired girl-children.

Running through the estate, a few hundred yards behind the building, was a wide, shallow creek into which great flocks of flamingos descended at dusk and stood, all night, balancing themselves on one leg in the shallow water. Beyond it were fields of alfalfa, alive with thousands of squirming, grunting, screeching, cannibalistic black pigs, which were bred according to the latest American methods in individually movable pigpens. One of the first of the bucolic duties to which I was assigned was the castration of four hundred and eighty-seven young porkers— emasculated between lunch and dinner, then dropped squealing into a strong solution of creosote. But it was in the grain operations of the *estancia* that I was expected to serve my apprenticeship, for which I received a salary of twenty pesos a week.

All through the late summer and fall, as the threshing crews moved in clouds of dust from farm to farm and the straw rose in gray-gold mounds above the stubble, we drove out in our earth-caked Model T's to acquire what was left of the sharecroppers' grain. Unskilled, ignorant and recently arrived from the poorest farmlands of Europe, they regarded us with mute, resentful suspicion. Finally, rather than let their grain rot in the late-autumn rains, they were forced to sell us their wheat, barley and oats well below market price. This meant more paper work, and night after night I found myself sitting with the two clerks at their cluttered table checking contracts and bills of lading against the scrawled piles of wagon receipts. (It was here that the station-master from Arribenos called us one night to announce that Firpo, the Wild Bull of the Pampas, had just knocked Jack Dempsey out of the ring in Panama City, then called back sadly twenty minutes later with the grim news of the national hero's defeat.)

Some nights, after we were done, the clerks would invite me to accompany them on their excursions to the neighboring villages —sad, hideous places, with wide streets ankle-deep in dust and mud and, invariably, off to one side (with its red light, dirt floor and scratchy gramophone) the local brothel with its changing personnel of dark, unwashed country girls and an occasional European derelict, shipped here from the Buenos Aires water-front to die or recover in the country air. It was late when we got back from these forays, of which I was never more than an embarrassed and frightened spectator. Approaching Santa Maria, we could hear the dogs barking a long way off; they were still barking as we roared in between the silent buildings, all dark except for the red glow of Don Bernardo's eternal corncob fire and the light in the window where Señor Katz's brother sat playing solitaire on the bare dining-room table. He was devoured by loneliness, as by a cancer, and as soon as his brother had left for Europe, we were joined in the bungalow by a middle-aged German blonde whose amorous moanings were clearly audible through the beaverboard that separated our rooms. She stayed a little less than two months—exactly the time it took Edelstein to report her presence by letter to Señor Katz in the South of France and for Señor Katz, by cable, to order his brother to get rid of her or leave Santa Maria immediately. After that, since he and Edelstein were not speaking and the clerks were not allowed in the bungalow, we returned to two-handed card games and the reading of last month's papers from Europe.

I lived on the Estancia Santa Maria for eight and a half months in a state of deep mental torpor. Within a few weeks any excitement or curiosity I may have felt at the novelty of my situation had worn off. What was left was boredom, fear and a slowly accumulating desperation. The disciplines I had formed at Clifton proved entirely useless outside the limited frame for which they were intended. With nothing to put in their place, separated by eight thousand miles from encouragement or counsel of any sort, I found myself hopelessly adrift. And as the cold wind began to blow across the bare, treeless plains I looked on with idle indifference while the frail structure of self-confidence I had so painfully acquired during my last years in England was frayed, torn apart and scattered over the dark, rain-soaked earth.

I do not recall a single book that I read during those months, and since I was neither willing nor able to give a true description of the abominable wilderness in which I found myself, I soon stopped writing any but the most perfunctory letters. In the limbo in which I was living, news from Europe reached me as a faint, meaningless echo from a world to which I had ceased to belong. For if I was unmoved by the latest gossip from my companions at the Best School of All, how could they, on their part, be expected to thrill to reports of how two weeks of steady rain had benefited the winter wheat but damaged the pastures; that Verdun, our Negro cowhand from Paraguay, had run amok after drinking a bottle of wood alcohol and knifed two of the foreman's sons before being shot in the left thigh by Edelstein's .38; that a bright-green venomous toad the size of a soup plate with teeth like fishhooks had appeared in the bottom of our well; and, finally, that on the night of the first heavy frost thirty-seven calves had been trampled or crushed to death around the water tank in pasture number three?

Sometime in June a letter with an English stamp was delivered to me in the office of the Estancia Santa Maria, where Edelstein and Señor Katz's brother were going over the monthly inventory—each hoping to catch the other in some error or, better still, in some petty theft. The letter, which had been forwarded by my mother from Paris, bore the crest of Trinity College, Cambridge—of which no one in that room had ever heard. It was from the man who was to be my tutor and contained a number of practical and academic questions and suggestions relating to my arrival at the University in October.

I put the letter in my pocket, where it stayed for several days, then laid it away in a drawer among my carefully folded Sulka shirts. Some weeks later a second letter arrived, in which my tutor expressed surprise at my failure to answer his first. Also a letter from Otto Siepmann, which I never opened. That afternoon I drove over to Arribenos in one of the Model T's and sent off a cable to Trinity College, Cambridge, informing them that "due to financial reverses and family problems" I had reluctantly decided not to attend the University. Then, feeling vaguely noble, I returned to the Estancia Santa Maria, where I spent the evening playing cards with Señor Katz's brother.

Sometimes, looking back, I am inclined to think that I never really had a free choice: that my decision was the logical, necessary and mathematical consequence of my birth and upbringing —an instinctive and hereditary imperative, which it was impossible for me to deny. At other times I tend to believe that if I had

had a return ticket to Europe in my pocket I would probably have used it and presented myself at Trinity for the start of the academic year.

I remained four months longer on the Argentine pampa—paralyzed, self-pitying and desperately waiting for someone to tell me what to do. No one did. Then, late in November, just as the new wheat was beginning to show green in the fields, I woke up one morning, got my bags out of the storeroom and packed my things. I arranged for one of the clerks to drive me over to Arribenos, said goodbye to everyone in fluent Argentine Spanish and caught the noon train to Buenos Aires.

Señor Katz was still in Europe. His manager, a gentle Hungarian with velvet-brown eyes, found me a job as a junior clerk in the foreign exchange department of a bank. Here, for the next five months, I pursued my education behind a calculating machine at a high desk in the international arbitrage department of the Banco Hollandes de la America del Sud. I was sitting there when a letter arrived from England which informed me that, on the recommendation of M. Katz, Esquire and other former associates and friends of the late Georges Haussmann, I had been accepted as an apprentice to the firm of Wm. H. Pim, Jr. & Co. Ltd. of Bury Street, Saint Mary Axe, London, E.C.3 and that a reservation had been made for me aboard the R.M.S. *Avon,* sailing in mid-August from the River Plate to Southampton.

* * *

My mother, whom I found waiting for me at the Savoy Hotel in a room overlooking the Thames, had two gifts for me. The first was a visit to Savile Row, where she ordered two business suits, a dinner jacket, a set of tails and a silk hat the total cost of which, added to my scholarship, would have gone a long way toward the expenses of a year at Cambridge. The second was less welcome: it was a mobilization order inviting me to report within the month to the military authorities at Besançon in the department of Doub for induction into the French Army. This summons, which

I had not the slightest intention of obeying, meant that I would now be listed as a deserter and exiled from the territory of the French Republic for the rest of my natural days; it also meant that for the next eighteen months, until I could become a British citizen by naturalization at the age of twenty-one, I would remain in a state of perilous vagrancy without nationality or papers of any kind.

Two days later, at a starting salary of four guineas a week, I went to work in a shabby second-floor office overlooking the Baltic Exchange for the firm of Wm. H. Pim, Jr. & Co. Ltd. By operating as a confidential agent between the exporters of North and South America, India, Australia and the main importing centers of Continental Europe and the United Kingdom, it had become the most successful grain-brokerage house in the world. Through its crusted telephones and battered ledgers passed orders and shipping papers for millions of bushels of grain, stowed in the holds of dozens of ships bound on never-ending voyages along the trade routes of the globe. Yet its employees numbered less than two dozen—including partners, traders, freight experts, clerks, secretaries, office boys, a sultry, multilingual switchboard operator and a one-armed veteran porter-commissionaire.

Pim and his heirs had long since vanished. The firm was now controlled by a florid vulgarian of enormous energy, charm and guile named George Howe. He and my father had known each other in London as apprentices, and, later, in Paris as bons vivants. He combined shrewd judgment with an almost limitless capacity for drink and a persuasiveness that led clients of sharply contrasting interests to believe that he was sincerely and wholeheartedly on each of their sides. When he died suddenly of uremia on the Riviera near the end of my first year with the firm, a prominent Japanese client for whom he had made a fortune through a long-term purchase of Canadian wheat refused to realize his profits until he had journeyed to the edge of the new-turned earth and received George Howe's personal advice from beyond the grave.

He had a house on the Thames at Maidenhead, to which he

invited me for several gay weekend business parties which, in my continuing state of virginity, I found mildly embarrassing. But throughout the office, these visits and the knowledge that I was connected with important figures in the international grain world marked me as a favored apprentice destined for quick advancement.

My first year was spent acquiring the vocabulary and syntax of the mysterious language in which the international grain trade was conducted. This instruction took place in an airless inner room filled with high, old-fashioned wooden desks and bursting cardboard files. Here, like a gray spider at the center of his web, sat the office manager, "Mister" Newsom, in his faded alpaca jacket. He was a celebrated figure in the trade, and Pim's paid him handsomely. Bald, pale and stooped, full of shrewd saws and shady precedents, with a cockney-drawling slit of a mouth from which four-letter words flowed incessantly past a false, vacuous smile, he chose to maintain a perverse humility that never for a moment concealed his profound contempt, not only for his peers (the office managers of other firms) but also for his superiors—the sharp, successful, well-tailored traders who made the deals that ended up on his desk for processing.

To assist him in his complicated functions, "Mister" Newsom had a crew of three horribly overworked clerks. Half-buried under piles of papers, they complained incessantly and rejected all offers of additional help. First, in order of seniority, was a gentle, purple-faced giant with huge front teeth, named Bill. Next came a potbellied sycophant with a soapy yellow moustache under a greasy, bald skull that drooped on a scrawny neck over his ash-littered desk. To an accompaniment of wheezy cackling, he would regale us with a collection of jokes, in which food, excrement and sex were obscenely and inextricably mixed. Far behind these two in age and experience came a frail, sandy-haired clerk known as "Young Coppins." He had been an office boy at Pim's before the war, from which he returned with one side of his face paralyzed and a shattered hand. When he felt ill or tired, which was quite often, he would drift back to the war—

to one particularly savage incident of Hun prisoners shot in cold blood.

These were the constant and intimate companions of my first year at Pim's. They treated me with indulgent contempt, amazingly patient under a system that required them to share their specialized, painfully accumulated professional knowledge with a privileged amateur soon to be elevated, through no merit of his own, to a world of wealth and power that they themselves could never hope to achieve. When after nine months, I followed my predestined promotion to the Wheat Room, they accepted the move without surprise or resentment—but our intimacy was at an end.

With my return to England I had reverted to the emotional habits of my childhood and adolescence: once again I found myself seesawing between the realities of "work" and the fantasies of my secret "holiday" world. The circumstances were changed but not the mechanism: my pattern of escape remained the same. Once again my life was sharply divided into two parts. Every morning a red bus carried me eastward to my servitude, past the Inns of Court, St. Paul's and the Royal Exchange deep into the City. And every evening amid grinding gears and the stench of petrol, somewhere between the Strand and Pall Mall, the same red bus carried me back through the magic looking-glass that separated my two worlds—out of the fetid penumbra of Mister Newsom's domain into the shining region of my fantasies and desires.

In reality, few lives could have been less glamorous or adventurous than the one I led, after office hours, during my first months in London. For a few weeks following my return from exile, I had made determined attempts to resume the relationships of my eleven years at Clifton. Of my companions from Mayor's House two were in the army, others at Oxford or Cambridge, where I was reluctant to visit them; still others (so drastically had British life changed since the war) were working for industrial and commercial concerns in the provinces and overseas.

4 3

When we met finally in carefully arranged reunions we found, after our first sentimental effervescences, that we had absolutely nothing to say to each other.

In my loneliness and from a desire to salvage some residue of human value from those wasted, detestable months, I began to record my impressions of that dark, brutal world in which I had lived for close to a year on the Estancia Santa Maria. I wrote compulsively, in response to an urgent emotional need—without any of the literary fantasies that plagued me later for so many years—slowly and painfully at the rate of fifty or a hundred words a night, deriving a sharp, pure pleasure from this secret and hopeless labor. As the months went by and the tide of loneliness receded, the necessity to write became less pressing. I still wrote on one or two nights each week but without my former urgency, almost as though I were fulfilling a commitment on which I was reluctant to default. And as the pages accumulated in my drawer they changed gradually from a consolation and an escape into that concrete and alarming object—a book to be completed and shown, one day, to others.

Slowly I was beginning to make a life for myself. In the company of Alan Napier (who had fled his family's hardware business in Birmingham* to try his fortune as an actor and who, alone of my contemporaries in Mayor's House, became my friend in the adult world), I began my education in the theatre, which we attended undiscriminatingly as often as two or three times a week at prices ranging from one shilling to half a crown.

In my second year in London, Eric Siepmann appeared. He had left Oxford suddenly in one of those inexplicable breakdowns that marked the entire course of his life: now he too was living on Ebury Street two hundred yards east of me (with George Moore on one side of him and Noël Coward on the other) but we moved in different spheres and our paths seldom

---

* Alan Napier, who after a distinguished theatrical career achieved his crowning fame as Batman's butler on TV, was descended on his father's side from General Napier of the Napoleonic Wars and, on his mother's, from a distinguished tribe of Birmingham Unitarians that included Uncle Joseph and cousins Austen and Neville Chamberlain.

44

crossed. Through his friendship with Puffin Asquith at Win-
chester he had been adopted into the brilliant world that revolved around the ex-prime minister and his wife Margot at The
Wharf and in their townhouse in Cavendish Square. My own
social associations were more modest; they were formed among
the less extravagant elements of what the newspapers of the day
insisted on calling "The Bright Young People." I met a pair of
sisters about whom I made the astounding discovery that they too
were alumnae of that finishing school for young ladies in which I
had spent the most blissful weeks of my life. (I was of the class of
1907, while they belonged to a much later era during the War,
when the establishment was moved from Paris to the South of
England.) Eileen, the elder, with the high color and wide-set
green eyes, was the bohemian of the family—a painter of talent
who left her parents' home in Mayfair to live in sin, first in
Pimlico and then in Paris, where she became one of the earliest
and best of the British surrealists. Winifred, the younger, with
the red hair, was the "literary" one—a protégée of Michael
Arlen. She lent me books by authors of whom I had never
heard—D. H. Lawrence, Lewellyn Powys, E. M. Forster and
Katherine Mansfield; she gave me *Crome Yellow, Howard's
End, South Wind, The Purple Land, The Criterion* and *The
Adelphi* to read, presented me with *Lady into Fox* for Christmas
and a thin orange book—*Jacob's Room* by Virginia Woolf—for
my birthday. It was through her and her friend Bea Howe, who
lived in a flat above Harrod's department store and with whom I
thought I was in love for a year, that I entered the magic region
that was coming to be known as Bloomsbury, from which I returned to my bed-sitting room on Ebury Street—having laid eyes
on Keynes and Lopokova, Roger Fry, Clive Bell, Lytton Strachey,
Elsa Lanchester, Aldous Huxley, the Meynells and the mythical
sisters, Virginia and Vanessa—with the pleasantly dizzy feeling of
having been on the heights among the Gods.

(Two evenings stand out in my memory: one was the first and
only performance of a play by Lytton Strachey in which Julia
Strachey played the last Manchu empress and I sat stiffly between
Komisarjevsky and Raymond Mortimer while a number of young

men in the rented dress uniforms of the Western Colonial Powers ran across the stage at the finale to crush the Boxer Rebellion. The other was a party given in a house off the Fulham Road by two American girls whose beauty, energy and wealth were causing something of a stir in London that winter. David Garnett was believed to be in love with them both and had just dedicated his latest book, *A Man in the Zoo,* to them. Later, in different ways, both came to play important parts in my life, but of that night I remember only that Mina Kirstein, the elder and more serious one, spoke to me about *The Education of Henry Adams* while the other, Henrietta Bingham—known in Bloomsbury as "The Kentucky Heiress"—sat on top of a piano in a purple velvet dress and played the saxophone.)

The day following my twenty-first birthday, armed with a note from Harry Siepmann on Bank of England stationary to a Home Office official, I filed my naturalization papers. I hoped for prompt action. I was disappointed. Four months were to pass before I was summoned for formal questioning and seven more before I was finally accepted as a citizen of the country in which I had spent more than twelve of the twenty-one years of my life. This was maddening for several reasons. After ten months in the Wheat Room at Pim's assisting the partners in duties that ranged from holding a client in patience at the end of a long-distance line, checking calculations, coding an urgent cable and mixing a drink, I was nearing the end of my apprenticeship. The next step was for me to become an assistant trader on the Baltic Exchange, which admitted only British citizens to its floor. Until my papers went through I could not even apply for membership.

I was stuck in other ways too. For more than two years now I had been a man without a country, incapable of movement in a world that lived by passports and visas. When my annual holiday fell due it was my mother, who, reversing the rhythm of so many years, crossed the Channel to visit me. We spent a quiet, pleasant fortnight at Clovelly in Devonshire, where I finished the last and longest of the nine stories that were to make up my book. I had written around forty thousand words by now and I could not force myself to write another line. I made nervous, meaningless last-minute revisions and tried out several title pages, of which my final choice was:

THE PLAINS
by
John Houseman

Then I wrapped the manuscript with great care and sent it off by registered mail (receipt requested) to a lady typist in Bristol.

When I got back to Ebury Street, the receipt was waiting for me together with a summons from the Home Office to appear for my final naturalization proceedings. Within a month I was able to present the partners of Wm. H. Pim, Jr. & Co. Ltd. with a certificate of British nationality to be submitted with my application for membership to the directors of the Baltic Exchange. While I anxiously awaited their verdict two things happened that made it irrelevant.

In the three years since I had started work on the book, less than half a dozen people had known of my nocturnal writing habits and only one had read more than a few pages of what I had done. This was Flora Mayor, the sister of my Clifton housemaster, Henry Bickersteth, one of the very few to whom I kept writing during my South American exile. Plain, delicate and pathologically timid, she had poured most of her life into a novel that had been published while I was away and had been favorably received with reviews in which she was frequently compared to Trollope. It was to her, rather than to my Mayfair friends, that I brought the manuscript of *The Plains* and, on the following Sunday, under the trees of Richmond Park, received her approval. She added (and she hoped I would not mind) that she had sent it on to her friends Leonard and Virginia Woolf at the Hogarth Press. I was appalled.

In the successive emotional stages I had gone through with the book I had only remotely considered the possibility of publication. This sudden, irrevocable exposure of my work to the publishers of Katherine Mansfield, T. S. Eliot, E. M. Forster, Sigmund Freud and Virginia Woolf herself shocked and terrified me. Within ten days a note arrived from Leonard Woolf saying that he and his wife had both read my book and would like to talk to me about it. He understood I worked in the City: how would Saturday tea suit me? I replied that Saturday tea would suit me very well, gave my blue suit to be pressed and carefully combed my hair for my visit to Tavistock Square.

I was received by a dark, slender, soft-spoken man who led me upstairs to a front room, where a lady whom I recognized as Virginia Woolf was seated at the tea table with a schoolboy of twelve or thirteen—a nephew, I gathered. During tea, I became aware of the incessant trembling of Leonard Woolf's hands and of the faint rattle of his cup and saucer, but it was on Mrs. Woolf that my attention was fixed. I had read *Jacob's Room, Kew Gardens* and *The Voyage Out* and I had seen her from afar, at night, tall, rustling and brilliant, at Bloomsbury soirées. I had heard of her wit and malice, of her shyness and melancholy. Here at home, behind her teapot, in the afternoon light, she was less formidable, with her hooded eyes and noble features, beautiful in a prematurely faded way, talkative, humorous and domestic.

Like film fogged by the brightness of the sun, my memory of that enchanted tea party is blurred and incomplete. I recall the boy asking some question about H. G. Wells, which Virginia Woolf, smiling, passed on to me and to which I replied, flustered and unprepared, that in my opinion, if Mr. Wells was remembered at all, it would be for his prophetic and pseudo-scientific works. Mrs. Woolf disagreed categorically. She maintained that Wells's early novels such as *Mr. Polly, Kipps* and *Tono Bungay* were works of originality and merit and the rest journalism of no interest whatsoever. Mr. Woolf shared her opinion, though less emphatically. After that the conversation became personal: I was asked questions about myself to which, in my desire to shed a more interesting light upon my writing, I gave answers that were only partially true. It was not until tea was over and the nephew had gone back to his homework that my book was mentioned. After nearly fifty years I can still feel myself in that small book-lined room, sitting breathless with delight, hardly hearing the quiet words of praise, spoken first by Mrs. Woolf and then by her consort—conscious only of the incredible and overwhelming

4 8

fact that they liked my book and actually wanted to publish it!*

Like most ecstasies, it was short-lived. At my second meeting with the Woolfs, Leonard did most of the talking. He confirmed their liking for the work and repeated that he and Virginia would like to publish it at the Hogarth Press. However, as a small house of very limited resources, they were in no position to assume the financial risk that a commercial publisher would normally take with the first work of an author of promise. In the six years of its existence, the Hogarth Press had achieved a unique position among British publishing houses and a total net profit of less than one hundred pounds. This was just about what it would cost to print and publish *The Plains*. The Woolfs offered to assume one third of the cost of publication if I could supply the rest.

It must have been my sudden look of dismay that caused Mrs. Woolf to break in and explain that all her own books had been published in this way, including *Mrs. Dalloway,* which was about to appear. On the other hand, she could understand my reluctance at having to raise money for the printing of my first work—all the more since she felt I would have no trouble finding another publisher for it. Both she and Leonard suggested that I think it over; meantime they offered to pass the manuscript on, with their recommendation, to Heinemann's, of which their close friend Desmond MacCarthy was chief editor. The weeks during which I waited for his reply were also those in which I continued to await the verdict of the directors of the Baltic Exchange. His came first—in longhand under the Heinemann letterhead: "I have just finished your manuscript. It is a pleasure to read what is so well written."

I lunched with Desmond MacCarthy at Boulestin's and found him charming and kind. He had reached the middle stage of his

---

* It was not until many years later, when I read Leonard Woolf's autobiography, that I became aware of the similarity between *The Plains* and his own first book, written as a young man on his return from Ceylon. ("The people who lived in the jungle villages fascinated, almost obsessed me . . . In *The Village* I tried somehow or other vicariously to live their lives.")

life—no longer the "superb young eagle who with one sweep of his wing could soar to any height he chose" but not yet the "asthmatic, shattered, dying rook" of his latter days. He told me over brandy that he shared the Woolfs' good opinion of my book and was reporting favorably on it to Heinemann, but added that there were others to be consulted and that this would take time. As we were walking back to his office at the *New Statesman,* of which he was literary editor, I asked him on a sudden impulse if, in his opinion, I should adopt writing as a career. It was a foolish question, to which he gave me a sincere, sympathetic and realistic answer based on the experience of his own creative failure. One wrote out of necessity he told me, not by choice. Then, as I was leaving, he suggested that I take one of the dozens of new books that were piled high on his table and chairs and try to review it for the *New Statesman.* I chose *A Story Teller's Story,* the autobiography of Sherwood Anderson, whose *Winesburg, Ohio* I had read and loved the year before. Utterly inexperienced in critical writing, I took more than three weeks to do the piece, working three or four nights a week. When it was finished it was more than double the length Mr. MacCarthy had requested and included most of what I knew and felt about contemporary American writing. He never acknowledged receipt of it, but when I received proof sheets some days later I found it uncut and almost unedited.

Four more pieces of mine were published in the *New Statesman* that autumn, including a rather morbid short story over which the name John Houseman appeared in print for the first time.* Reading and rereading them at my desk in the Wheat Room, I found myself encountering thoughts and phrases that I recognized as having been written by someone very close to me— but not myself. Which indeed they were; for it was during those last few months of my time in London that the rift which had been widening so long under the surface finally broke open and

* Viz.: O'Brien's *Best Short Stories of 1926,* where *The Ghoul* by John Houseman is listed among the hundred best British and Irish stories of the year.

that I found myself inhabited by the two warring and irreconcilable fantasies that continued to wage their dubious battle inside me for the next ten years.

As Jacques Haussmann, I continued to live in my mother's image of me—a blend of English gentleman and Continental merchant prince, a chosen member of the world's international élite. So vague and grandiose were my expectations in this role that they made it almost impossible for me to face reality in any form. Hence the alternating waves of aimless megalomania and passive despair which formed the enervating pattern of my years in the international grain business.

As John Houseman, the younger brother who had only recently acquired the dignity of a name, my dreams were no less wild, but at least they were my own. From the day of my arrival at Clifton among the Siepmanns, throughout the eleven years of my middle-class, anglican, public-school education, I had developed vague cultural yearnings to which were added a deep, unreasoning distaste for the sordid activities of the mercantile world into which I had been born. Repressed or dormant during my Argentine exile, this fantasy had gained strength during my years in London till, in the months following my first small literary successes, it had become the dominant influence in my life. Like my Trinity scholarship, with its vision of a distinguished academic career, this was a deceptive and temporary triumph. At the first real test of strength, it was, once again, the deep-rooted, inherited image of the merchant prince that prevailed.

While the directors of the Baltic Exchange were still arguing over my case—whether trading privileges should be granted to all British citizens or only to the British-born—I received a call one morning to come to the Ritz Hotel to the apartment of Monsieur Fribourg of Paris. As I followed the familiar bus route—past St. Paul's up Fleet Street and the Strand and across Trafalgar Square—I knew precisely what he was going to say to me and what my reply would be.

René Fribourg, a dapper man with a fuzzy moustache, received me cordially, inquired after my mother and then asked me how I would like to go to the United States where his company needed executive personnel for its rapidly expanding operations. I said yes before he had finished speaking and, in that instant, slammed the door shut on everything I had most desired during the past year.

My roots in London lay loosely in shallow soil and my farewells were sentimental but painless. Among my colleagues at Pim's, Jim Mitchell (a thin-lipped, ambitious Scot with a fleshy nose and a bulbous forehead), whose assistant I had been in the Wheat Room, expressed the hope that we would work together again someday. Desmond MacCarthy, when I called upon him to thank him for all he had done for me, admitted what I had long suspected—that he had lost the script of my book before showing it to anyone at Heinemann's.* He asked if I had another copy and I said yes and he urged me to send it to him. I never did, for I had other things on my mind.

*   *   *

I sailed on the *Mauretania* with my new British passport and a special commercial visa issued to Jacques Haussmann under the Anglo-American Treaty of Commerce and Navigation. I arrived in New York dreaming of adventures and triumphs that had not the faintest relation to the realities of my situation. I spent the weekend with one of my mother's friends in his Park Avenue apartment, was driven through the flaming Indian summer of the Hudson Valley, lunched at Voisin's under the hanging canary cages and dined with my aunt, looking out over the East River and Brooklyn Bridge, in the apartment she occupied on the top floor of the Beekman-Downtown Hospital, of which she had just been made superintendent. Then, on Monday morning, in pouring rain, I set out for the offices of the Continental Grain Corporation in the Produce Exchange at 1 Broadway.

In the next five years that vast, low, red-brick building became hatefully familiar to me: I can see it still (through the towering

---

* It was not unusual for Desmond MacCarthy to mislay manuscripts— his own and others. I never found out if he had already lost mine at the time of our first luncheon and, if so, whether he was aware of it.

52

structure of glass, steel and tile that has long since taken its place) as I first looked upon it in fear on that gray November morning on which my dream of America ended and reality began.

The ground floor of the Produce Exchange—which served as a tunnel, in bad weather, between Wall Street and Battery Place—looked, sounded and smelled like something between a railroad terminal, a midway and a monkey house. The trading floor was on the mezzanine; shipping and grain companies' offices occupied the remaining three floors. The Continental's was on the second, and it was there, in the sweet-stale stench of rotting grain samples, wooden partitions, dried ink, glue and rubber stamps together with various kinds of paper (ledgers, carbons, ships' manifests, bills of lading, insurance certificates and warehouse receipts) and the tired bodies and sour breath of sedentary clerks, that I was interviewed by my new employers, who sat at a double desk in a small glass-enclosed room under a rain-streaked window overlooking the river. The senior director, Joseph Feuer, who said he had known me as a child in Rumania, was short, bald and potbellied with red-rimmed eyes and a duck-bill nose overhanging thick, dry lips, through which issued a strong Eastern-European accent that remained constant in all of his many languages. He was also—as I discovered later when I was less completely blinded by disappointment and loathing—a man of great charm and culture, a strategist with a fertile imagination, which had enabled him, in less than five years, to build the Continental Grain Company into one of the most active and progressive grain-handling firms on the North American continent. His associate, Mr. Isaac, was a somber, plodding German with an elephantine memory and a passion for detail. Between them, while I listened, nodding and smiling, staring past them at the dirty, wrinkled water of New York harbor and the Statue of Liberty beyond, they outlined a future that in no way resembled the glamorous fantasies that I had come trailing across the Atlantic. Beginning the next day, I was to go to work in the office at a starting wage of fifty dollars a week, learning the business once again "from the ground up." In the spring, if they felt that I was ready, I would be sent to Chicago and from there to Kansas City, Winnipeg and the Pacific Coast. What I was being offered, I knew, was the opportunity to advance rapidly, along the accepted nepotistic route, to the top of the fastest growing company in the international grain trade. But all I could hear, as I sat sunk in self-pity in the stale air of that cramped and squalid office, was the snap of the trap which I had myself baited with false dreams and megalomaniac fancies.

On the advice of an English actor friend, I had moved into a monolith known as the Shelton Tower. With its thirty-two floors of identical cells, this was a new kind of hotel—antiseptic, impersonal and functional. At seven each morning the phone rang. Through the single window of my overheated cubicle I could see the astonishing variations of New York's winter sky; leaden clouds full of rain and snow alternating with a pure, icy blue such as I had never seen anywhere before. And through the glass I could hear sounds that were different: to the familiar big-city noises and deep rumble of traffic were added the crash of falling masonry, subterranean explosions and the hysterical screams of riveters and hydraulic drills. At 7:15 A.M. a soughing elevator plunged me down to the Olympic pool in the basement where I swam in hot, chlorinated water before returning to my cell to dress. Then I was whirled up to the cafeteria on the roof, where I joined the jostling herd of men and women—their eyes frozen in their sockets, their skin stiff with sleep under the skin lotions and cosmetics—who stood tensely in line with their aluminum trays before gleaming counters, from which young men in the uniforms of hospital orderlies dispensed rustling cereals, canned fruit juice, stewed prunes, and pale-yellow mounds of dry scrambled eggs. Then down again and along the freezing corridor of Lexington Avenue into the stale warm mouth of Grand Central Station and the exhilarating rush-hour frenzy of the IRT's South Ferry downtown express.

My cell at the Shelton was on the twenty-third floor and here, in the evenings, John Houseman made a few vain attempts to resume his literary activity.* But it soon became apparent that the Tower was unsuited to creative work—especially after dark. For with the coming of night those same men and women with whom I had stood in line on the roof at dawn—constipated and separate, sullen from forced awakenings and rigid with apprehension of the day ahead—seemed to become liberated and transformed. Filled, now, with a feverish awareness of each other's presence and a collective lust that spread like wildfire through the thin walls, across air wells and corridors, from cell to cell and from floor to floor, they began to communicate with each other by phone or—if they faced the inner court of the building as I did—by signs, grimaces and gestures, through the brightly lit windows, from one face of the tower to the other. These salutations went through various stages, from preliminary approaches and rejections to smiles and assignations. And as the evening wore on, the corridors and safety stairs of the Shelton Tower became alive with furtive migrants, each making his cautious but determined way, in defiance of floor supervisors and house detectives, to or from the cell of a fellow resident. I observed this mating dance with fascination, but since there was only one logical end to these maneuvers—one that I was still incapable of consummating—my participation remained that of an enervated voyeur.

In England, where sexual backwardness such as mine was not exceptional, I had succeeded, without too much embarrassment or difficulty, in finding intellectual and sentimental palliatives for my chastity. In puritan, immigrant America, where sex seemed to play a more direct and aggressive part in the national life, my nagging concern with my condition was harder to bear. Aggravated by boredom and loneliness, it became my main preoccupation and involved me in romantic sublimations and senti-

---

* Soon after my arrival I sent a short story, hurriedly transplanted to U.S. soil, to *The Dial* which returned it with a note from Marianne Moore in which she regretted that it was "not that of which we are in search." I switched envelopes and sent it off to the *New Masses*, which printed it opposite a cartoon by William Gropper but did not pay me. It was the last thing of mine to be printed for eleven years.

mental obsessions which have no place in a factual narrative such as this. (At their center stood the figure of a tall girl with blue eyes—or, rather, the image of her I had formed to suit my own urgent emotional needs. For the next two years, during most of which we were thousands of miles apart, there was hardly an hour of my days and nights that was not permeated and colored by dreams of her. Looking back through the mists of hope, ambition and frustrated yearning with which I surrounded her, I find it impossible to separate the memory of the real Henrietta Bingham, with whom I fell in love my first Christmas in America and with whom I finally lost my virginity in a seaside hotel with a crystal chandelier and red damask walls sixteen months later, from the fantasy of her that I created in the loneliness of my first wander-years in America.*)

I left New York in mid-March of 1926 on the Twentieth Century Limited. In my parting interview with Joseph Feuer he had outlined my new assignment: Chicago was the first stop in a journey that would, in time, cover most of the North American continent. As a traveling representative of the Continental Grain Corporation and one of its future directors, I was to familiarize myself with the workings of the two great wheat markets—Chicago and Winnipeg—and their relation to the flow of grain from the Western prairies through the elevators of the interior to the main coastal shipping points—Montreal and New York in the East, New Orleans and Galveston in the Gulf of Mexico and the Northern Pacific ports of Seattle, Portland and Vancouver. I was no longer an apprentice: my salary was doubled and I was given a generous living allowance.

* In a nostalgic memorial to an infatuation of his youth, an aging British novelist described her as "a lovely girl of twenty, her face the perfect oval of a Buddha . . . her straight, dark hair was parted in the middle; long black eyelashes shaded her brilliantly blue eyes. She spoke with the warm, caressing voice of the South, drove a car really well and understood its mechanism, sang Negro spirituals and never at any time read a book unless forced to do so." *The Familiar Faces* by David Garnett (Chatto and Windus, London, 1962) .

Yet so deep was the division inside me that, as the train carried me through the night, following its vaunted water-level route along the Hudson, the Erie Canal and the southern shore of the Great Lakes, it was still unclear whether it was the exciting prospect of a brilliant career in the grain-export business that kept me awake in my lurching lower berth or the exhilaration of being once more in motion, about to enter that vast, enchanted land—the America of Whitman and Sandburg, and Dreiser, Sinclair Lewis, Frank Norris and Sherwood Anderson—of which I had already formed such a vivid literary image and which I was now impatient to discover for myself.

At dawn, through the dining-car window, I watched the gray, sprawling steel mills of Gary, Indiana, sliding by and, soon after, as we clanged slowly through the yards, the littered desolation of the Chicago slums. I first saw the Loop, deserted on that Sunday morning—the air tainted with a faint, sickening smell of putrefaction from the stockyards. There was a motion-picture convention at the Drake Hotel when I arrived and the lobby was jammed with men with Western hats and cigars and girls who looked like Clara Bow, with pillboxes on their shingled heads. When I got to my room I could see the vast expanse of Lake Michigan through my window, its shimmering, wind-swept water stretching out beyond the breakwater for what seemed like an infinite distance into the sky.

The Continental Grain Corporation's Chicago office occupied two small, crowded rooms in an annex of the Chicago Board of Trade. It was run by a slender, serious, opinionated man with dark, sharp eyes and prematurely white hair named Simon Mayer. It was he who gave me my first vision of the Chicago Wheat Pit.

I had been aware of the Pit's existence and felt its remote power in the Wheat Room at Pim's; I had read Frank Norris' account of it. Looking down on it for the first time from the visitors' gallery, confused by the reverberating howl that filled the building, I was aware only of a dark, circular motion below me—as of a huge pot boiling. Then as I grew accustomed to the movement and the continuous roar, I came to realize that this seething mass was the sum of the movements of hundreds of human beings—of waving arms, struggling bodies and, occasionally, an upturned face distorted in a grotesque expression of passion. For five hours, each day, in this bowl of heaving flesh, furious battles were fought by men in business suits, alpaca jackets and shirtsleeves—deadly single combats in which opponents sought each other out, slashing their way through the struggling mass as they moved toward each other with threatening gestures, one sweeping his hands forward and down in a violent, repeated, thrusting motion, the other working his outstretched arms in a frantic gesture of beckoning—moving closer and closer till finally they stood face to face, straining for each other's throats, grappling, grabbing, tearing at each other's clothes, their mouths twisted, screaming inaudible words which they punctuated with wild, spastic gestures that indicated to those who were familiar with the Pit's mysterious sign language the price and delivery date of imaginary masses of wheat, bought and sold in lots of between five and five hundred thousand bushels.

Multiply this action by hundreds and you had a normal morning's activity in the Chicago Wheat Pit. And over it hung that cloud of sound—the roar of hundreds of human voices which, combined, expressed the collective emotion of the moment: the sharply rising modulation that goes with a Bull market and the barking, descending tone which indicates that the Bears are in command—so that even an outsider like myself could soon tell by ear, from the sound that rose out of the Pit, whether the wheat market was, at that moment, rising or falling.

In my second week Simon Mayer got me a pass to the floor of the Board of Trade. From this angle the Pit had a wholly different look: you realized what you had not been aware of from above—that the Pit was the dramatic climax of an infinitely greater and more complex operation in which the Pit traders, with their furious challenges and heroic encounters, were no more than mercenaries in the service of forces of which they had no control and often no understanding. Long after the first physical thrill had worn off and I had begun to understand the inner workings of the international wheat-futures markets, I continued to derive excitement and pleasure from the action of the Pit itself and from the realization that its fluctuations occurred in response to influences that went beyond immediate considerations of supply and demand and included the meteorology of four continents, national and international politics, greed, fear, money power and sometimes, nothing more than collective hysteria.

New York had overwhelmed me with its violence; in Chicago it was the extremity of the contrasts that fascinated me. These began with the weather and included every aspect of the city:* the old and new side by side, the beautiful and the indescribably hideous, the sickening poverty and the exaggerated, flaunted wealth—all in a state of rapid and continuous flux. Close by my hotel, along the luxurious Lake Shore Drive, stood the great houses of the very rich. And here, each Sunday, in the first exploding heat of that Middle-Western spring, I watched the proletariat take over. They came in their thousands—Italians, Jews, Czechs and Poles, gray from their long hibernation in their dark crowded tenements—an untidy flood darkening the sidewalks, flowing past the locked doors and shuttered windows of the millionaires' mansions, irresistibly drawn to the waters of the lake, where they lay all day on the narrow public beaches, devouring huge Old World meals and washing their pale, hairy bodies in its dark-green, restless waters.

My memory of Kansas City, where I arrived in early June, in time for the start of the wheat harvest in western Kansas, Okla-

---

* Chicago, in the mid-twenties, was still the railroad terminal of the United States; it was also its gangster capital and one of its recognized cultural centers, with an artistic life that seemed surprisingly independent of the East. In 1926, at the time of my first visit, Chicago had more than a dozen theatres, a repertory company and three celebrated drama critics; it had two opera houses, a first-class symphony orchestra, a ballet troupe of its own, a number of advanced literary and poetry magazines, several of the world's leading architects and an Art Institute that was years ahead of any other museum in the country in the acquisition and exhibition of contemporary art.

homa and the panhandle of Texas, is colored by two dominant impressions—loneliness and heat. Nowhere else had I experienced such unbearable heat—harsh and dry like the blast from an open furnace, the air radiated from the brick and concrete walls of buildings, rose trembling from the pavements and melting asphalt of the streets and lay over the mouth like a blanket, drying the saliva and forcing the breath back into the throat. Much of the city's life during July and August seemed devoted to finding ways of defeating or evading the heat. The surest refuge was to be found in the newly constructed movie palaces: vast, freezing, red-carpeted caverns of marble and gold which, in addition to the icy ecstasy of excessive refrigeration, offered three hours of variegated entertainment. Those were the last years of silent films: floating up through the mists of half a century are visions of Negri, Bow, Swanson, Gilbert, Laurel and Hardy and Keaton, Valentino, Mae Murray, Doug Fairbanks and Billie Dove,* supplemented by swooping and trilling performances on the Wurlitzer and, in the larger theatres, by massive, ineffably tedious "stage shows." Other places of refuge were the basement of the Muehlbach Hotel, the Fred Harvey restaurant in the Union Station and the several "roofs" atop Kansas City's newer hotels where couples left their thin, tepid jellied consommé, limp lettuce smeared with creamy dressings and melting ice cream to shuffle around in dank, joyless circles in the mistaken belief that they would feel the heat less if they moved. This same craving for motion motivated the hundreds of thousands of miles of driving that took place in and around Kansas City throughout the summer nights. For some it was a prelude to love-making; with others it led to roadhouse crap games and the spiked-beer joints on the Kansas side of the river. But for most of them it was a hopeless attempt to postpone the insomnia that played such an essential part in Kansas City's summer life. I, whom war, bankruptcy and

* Here as usual, memory and the records are far apart. According to *Variety*, films shown in Kansas City during the summer of 1926 include *When Husbands Flirt, Fascinating Youth, Footloose Widows, Tony Runs Wild, Mantrap, The Wise Guy, Volga Boatman, Son of the Sheik,* and nothing else anyone ever heard of.

the preoccupation of sex have seldom prevented from falling asleep within thirty seconds of my head's hitting the pillow, would lie trapped hour after hour in my creaking, rumpled, sweat-dampened Murphy bed on the seventh floor of the Ambassador Hotel, caught between the lights of the streaming traffic in the street below and the muted, persistent pounding of the dance bands on the roof above. And when the bands were finally still and most of the cars were off the streets, a new sound would take over—the dry crackling and rolling thunder of the endlessly circling electric storms that nightly shook the overheated Missouri River bottoms and, far from relieving the heat, seemed to aggravate and intensify it.

Loneliness was nothing new. I had known it for much of my life—in its most painful form in my early years at Clifton, in its most dismal and damaging shape on the Estancia Santa Maria. In Kansas City, from the time I left the office in midafternoon till the next morning when I took a green Broadway bus to work, I was almost always alone; over the weekends I would go for sixty hours without speaking a word to anyone except a waitress or a bus driver. It was at such times, in the past, that my fears (the old paralyzing terrors of death, of poverty and of never really belonging anywhere) were likely to proliferate with paralyzing effect. But there was something in the Midwestern American air that seemed to protect me from such inertia. My work with the Continental, which I continued to do conscientiously but with ambivalent feelings, occupied only part of my time and none of my emotional energy. To fill the void of my days and nights I wrote endless yearning letters to Henrietta wherever she happened to be and engaged in curious activities of my own: I found myself singing "Brighten the Corner Where You Are" one night with ten thousand of Billy Sunday's adherents in one of the last of his monster revival meetings; I attended the dog races, walked for hours in the railroad yards, paid weekly visits to the Columbia Burlesque Wheel and to the Wednesday evening testimonies at the Christian Science churches that abounded in Kansas City. When these palled I found myself resuming my interrupted education: I began to read compulsively in English, French and occasionally in German with an appetite that grew with the months, following no organized plan or order but letting one book lead to another, one writer suggest another, one area of interest bleed into another and create the desire and the necessity for further reading.

Chicago and Kansas City were the first stops in the chain of travel which, for the next two and a half years, carried me back and forth across the North American continent to such places as Kansas City (three times), Winnipeg, Duluth, Calgary, Vancouver (three times), Seattle, Portland, Minneapolis, Wichita, Enid, Fort Worth, Galveston (four times), New Orleans and St. Louis (twice).

I made few friends on my travels: a fifty-year-old Mormon in Vancouver, B.C.; an anarchist hobo from New York, who followed me from Kansas City to the Coast and taught me IWW songs; a nigger-hating shipowner's son in Galveston, Texas— these were the temporary associates with whom I ate and talked and went for walks. They remain vague figures on the edges of my memory: my constant companions of that time—besides my own dream-figures and fantasies—were the ideas and the characters in the pages of the books I was reading.

Certain clear memories persist of the places that I passed through; they are always related to what I was reading while I was there and form a strange emotional geography of their own. I discovered the wonders of *The Golden Bough* on a hill of tall grass and yellow daisies in a public park overlooking the Missouri River, *The Brothers Karamazov* on a peeling green bench in a Kansas courthouse square on which I sat waiting all afternoon for a bus. I read the first five volumes of Proust in a maroon Pullman car of the Canadian Pacific Railroad crossing the snowwhite prairie from East to West; the first hundred pages of *Das Kapital* in a sand- and soot-filled lower berth close behind a wood-burning Southern Pacific locomotive speeding at night along the Gulf Coast; Rilke and *Bateau Ivre* in the cabin of a camp in the Ozarks, which I shared with an insurance salesman from St. Joseph, Missouri; Michelet's *Histoire de la Révolution Française*, *Tom Jones*, *The Possessed*, *War and Peace* and the

Revelations of St. John the Divine under the rain-laden winter skies of the Pacific Northwest; *The Conquest of Mexico* in a hotel room on the main street of Joplin, Missouri, where, through a missed connection, I found myself spending the night of the Fourth of July, 1926. The agonies of Hernán Cortez and his men, beleaguered on the causeways of Tenochtitlan, are forever related in my mind to the stained carpet of that high-ceilinged, ill-lit second-floor room and to the boys' voices and the patriotic explosions of torpedoes and crackerballs in the street below.

*　　*　　*

Halfway through my twenty-fifth year some inherited, long-buried Alsatian trader's instinct suddenly and violently asserted itself. Leaving John Houseman to his books, I became, almost overnight, one of the most successful young men in the North American grain-export business. It began with the campaign I conducted that winter for the Continental Grain Corporation in the Pacific Northwest. As a direct result of my strategy, our sales and shipments from the port of Vancouver almost doubled and greatly exceeded those of our competitors—the giant international firms of Dreyfus and Bunge. This first success filled me with childish exultation: after so many years of passive indifference and vague resentment, I had suddenly found in the international grain business a short cut to wealth and power of which I was determined to take full advantage. The merchant prince was coming into his own.*

The following summer, on my second visit to Kansas City, I showed energy and skill in anticipating and exploiting an unusually early movement of American winter wheat to the Gulf of Mexico. Once again we overwhelmed the competition and made a killing. The Continental, surprised and delighted at this

---

* Many years later, in California, Alan Napier showed me a postcard with a Vancouver postmark dated January, 1928. "Now indeed am I the Meteor of the West! Verily I pull the strings of the Pacific! Riches are mine and the glittering prizes of Ashteroth!" is, literally, what it says.

change in me, redoubled then trebled my salary and I received personal congratulations from Paris.

It was not enough for me. During my years of frustration I had built up a head of steam that was now driving me forward at a speed I could no longer control. For years I had felt not the slightest material ambition; I made up for it now with a ravenous hunger that I made no attempt to curb. From an insecure, reluctant apprentice I had been transformed in twelve months into a confident, arrogant young proconsul moving from one provincial victory to another. Now I was becoming impatient for my triumphal entry into the capital.

I spent the last part of that summer in St. Louis, supervising our shipments of wheat down the Mississippi to New Orleans, having an affair, on the rebound, with an Olympic swimming champion whose appetite and energy almost equaled my own and preparing for my next move. One evening, while I was listening to the start of Al Smith's presidential campaign on the radio, I received a long-distance call from Winnipeg. It was from Jim Mitchell, the shrewd, thin-lipped Scot with whom I had worked in the Wheat Room at Pim's, who, for two years now, had been running a successful grain-brokerage business of his own. He said he would be in New York the following weekend and needed to talk to me on a most urgent matter before returning to London.

We met secretly in his suite at the Plaza Hotel. He had just concluded a deal with one of the leading grain-elevator chains in Western Canada; now he was looking for someone to set up a New York office and to run the North American branch of his firm. Two days later I was president and managing director of the Oceanic Grain Corporation (a name I had thought up while lying sleepless with excitement in a lower berth of the Broadway Limited) at a guaranteed salary of $20,000 a year plus five per cent of the profits.

My parting from the Continental was traumatic. When I first handed in my resignation the directors figured it was a maneuver to get more money out of them and offered to match whatever I was offered elsewhere. When they realized that I really intended

64

to leave they were hurt and furious. They had every right to be. I had received the full nepotistic treatment; they had been patient and generous during my two years of apathy; I had learned their trade secrets, which I was now intending to use against them in the service of the enemy. In their eyes my desertion was more than a commercial infamy: it was a personal and racial betrayal.

In the days that followed, great pressure was put upon me. I received cables and phone calls from Paris, Antwerp and London. My mother wrote to ask what was happening, and I was taken to lunch by several emotional, gray-haired gentlemen— former friends of my father—who pointed out, more in sorrow than in anger, that in leaving the security of the Continental I was about to make the most serious mistake of my life. I listened politely, unable to explain to them that the more reckless and irrevocable my action appeared, the more irresistible and exhilarating I found it.

The Oceanic Grain Company was incorporated in the State of Delaware with a paid-up capital of two hundred and fifty thousand dollars—most of which was also being used to finance Mitchell's European operations. (I personally subscribed twenty thousand, of which three were my own and seventeen were borrowed.) We decided to start slowly and cautiously: our opening offensive would be launched during the winter from the Canadian Pacific coast, where I had already demonstrated my skill. The Vancouver season did not start till December, when the Eastern waterways froze over; this gave me time to start setting up my New York organization. It also gave me time to fall in love.

I had been surprised, on my return to New York, to find my foster-sibling, Eric Siepmann, living on Twelfth Street, three blocks from the Brevoort where I was staying. He had come to the United States as a correspondent for the London *Times,* thrown up his job on an alcoholic caprice but remained in New York as an editorial writer for the New York *Post.* For years he had paralyzed me with his superiority; now the balance was re-dressed and I was delighted to see him.* He was in love with a girl named Magda—a painter who made her living doing draw-ings of children's clothes for Macy's and whom Eric had de-scribed to me as "a catlike beauty with a small round head, huge black eyes, little hands like claws and thin legs of the American kind though she was brought here from Hungary at the age of six."

They led an uneasy and fascinating life on the margin of Greenwich Village; and most of my evenings—after so many months of provincial solitude—were spent in their company and that of their friends: Sally and Philip Wylie (whose first novel had just appeared), Jimmy Light from the Provincetown The-atre, Edmund Wilson, e. e. cummings and Ann Barton, Hans Stengel (until he hanged himself at a party), Elinor Wylie, Lois Long, Maury Werner, occasionally Heywood Broun, Marcus Aurelius Goodrich (who had just ended a three-month retreat in a hair shirt) and Magda's sister Zita, who was seldom around because she was rehearsing a new play.

It was to see her that I went one night, with Eric and Magda, all dressed up, to the Plymouth Theatre to my first Broadway opening. *Machinal*, by Sophie Treadwell, was a sentimentalized, expressionistic version of the recent Snyder-Gray murder case which exploited, in obvious theatrical terms, the revulsion and pity aroused by the yellow press's lurid coverage of the trial and electrocution of the murderess—Ruth Snyder. It was sensitively directed by Arthur Hopkins and dramatically lit by Robert Edmond Jones. But the evening really belonged to a dark, slen-der, totally unknown girl by the name of Zita Johann, who illuminated the play's feminine clichés with a deep, tragic ten-derness of her own. (It also belonged, in a lesser degree, to a tall, dark, relaxed, sexy young man with big ears who was making his

* In writing to his brother in England, Eric reported: "Fat Jack, no longer fat, is a magnate. Singlehanded he undertakes enormous specu-lations from which he expects to make a fortune and retire at the age of thirty."

Broadway debut that night under his stage name of Clark
Gable.)

We went backstage after the show and took Zita out to supper
while we waited for the reviews. I found her beautiful and exciting and vulnerable, with glowing dark eyes and a smile which,
on that first evening, when she was flushed and bewildered by
her sudden success, I found irresistibly moving.

Five days after the opening of *Machinal*, Zita and I became
lovers. She was living in an apartment hotel on West End
Avenue in a room with a studio couch. I moved into an identical
room on the floor below which I used for dressing in the morning. It was the first time in my life I had lived with a woman,
spent each night with her—our bodies restless and intertwined in
that narrow bed—made love half-asleep in the dark and awakened beside her at dawn. We were apart during the day and met
again at dusk—almost always alone. Since she insisted on being
in her dressing room by seven, we ate at strange hours in curious
places. After the performance she was completely wrung out and
wanted only to be taken home. But several times, after the
Saturday night show, we took a late train to Long Beach and
spent the night and the next day in a curious and awful hotel
(under the name of Mr. and Mrs. John Wolf) overlooking the
deserted boardwalk and the beach and the gray, rolling Atlantic
breakers.

In mid-November, while *Machinal* was still running, I left for
Vancouver. I was to be gone for three months and, when her play
closed, Zita was to join me on the coast. It did close early in
January, but she went off, instead, to California—to the MGM
Studio in Culver City where Irving Thalberg, then at the height
of his inflated fame, was courting her with golden promises. In
February, on my way East, I spent two days with her in Santa
Monica, where she had taken a small house and had acquired a
Russian wolfhound. There was no film in view, but she was
enjoying the sun and the beach and living in reasonable luxury
for the first time in her life. We talked vaguely of our future, and

when I got back to New York I began to search for an apartment for us. In a bare penthouse on the roof of 66 Fifth Avenue, where an old man lay dying, I found what I was looking for.* I signed a two-year lease and asked Jeanne de Lanux, a French girl who was working with the architect William Lescaze, to decorate it. She assumed I wanted it "moderne" and I made no objection.

My first Pacific Coast season for the Oceanic had gone well. With the Manitoba wheat available to us through our grain-elevator association, I had succeeded, once again, in dominating the field. And by supplying Mitchell in London with a continuous flow of salable cargoes, we had helped him to build up his sales organization into one of the finest in Europe. As a result, when the Oceanic opened its New York office in March in a half-furnished, newly painted office on the third floor of the Produce Exchange and we started cabling our first offers of open-water Canadian wheat from the Eastern seaboard, we found ourselves almost immediately doing a huge business in that, too. I had designed the Oceanic as a flexible, streamlined organization capable of operating with a lower overhead and at a smaller profit margin than our competitors. The system worked even better than I had expected. To our rivals' resentment of our upstart presence was now added their bitterness over what they considered our price-cutting tactics and our rapidly growing share of the wheat-export business to Europe. This took a further jump in June when the American winter-wheat crop began to move to market and we once again outpaced the field. By the end of July I was becoming seriously concerned over the extent of our success.

There was nothing speculative about our operation. Each of

---

* 66 Fifth Avenue was an interesting building. Among its varied tenants were the great international publishing house of Macmillan, one of New York's first movie art houses in the basement, and one of its oldest book stores at street level. On its upper floors Martha Graham had her dance studio, the Boni Brothers ran their small but distinguished publishing firm, Carl Van Doren had a *garconière* on the roof, and a well-known author of travel books was reputed to keep his mistress manacled and chained to a post.

our trades was made at a profit and each purchase and sale was instantly and automatically covered in the futures markets of Chicago and Winnipeg. By year's end, when all our shipments had been made and paid for, the Oceanic Grain Corporation should be showing a clear profit of a quarter of a million dollars or more. It was the sheer mass of our business that worried me in a market that I knew to be unsound. This was the mad summer of 1929—the last feverish spasm of the great boom of the twenties. Inevitably, spiraling stock prices had affected commodities. Speculators were pouring their easy money into anything they could find—including grain. From being an international market in the service of the world's producers and consumers, wheat futures had become part of the national crap game.

I called Mitchell in London and told him that according to my best information, the two major American wheat-futures markets were in dangerous condition, honeycombed with margin purchases and stop-loss orders. He agreed, and we decided to rest on our laurels and not to press sales in the weeks to come while we sat tight and hoped for an orderly execution of our existent commitments, which were already enormous. One morning in mid-August, Mr. Weaver, our office manager—his jowls gray and flaccid from sitting all night over his calculating machine—walked into my office, closed the door and pushed a slip of paper across my desk. It indicated that within two months, with the bulk of our wheat shipments in transit, our loans would have reached the astounding total of over eight million dollars—more than thirty times our declared capital of a quarter of a million.

Late in August Zita returned from California. In her six months with MGM she had made a lot of money but no pictures. Thalberg, after all this wooing, had offered her two small parts, neither of which she had accepted. (The second was given to a promising contract girl named Myrna Loy.) She arrived—with the Russian wolfhound and a Croatian cook—just in time to move into the penthouse, which, though far from finished, was becoming habitable. We never succeeded in recapturing the wonder of those first weeks on our studio couch on West End

Avenue, but we were pleased to be together again and fascinated by the strange new world that was forming around us—the sheer white walls, the gray-and-black built-in cabinetwork, the black glass-and-chromium tables, the tubular metal chairs and the vast, shiny cork surface of the outer terrace.

Living in sin among all these gleaming and costly belongings required more nerve than either of us possessed; so in mid-September, a few days before my twenty-seventh birthday, we went down to City Hall one morning and got married, with my aunt and one of her ambulance drivers as our witnesses. Early in October we gave our first party: Marc Connelly was there doing magic tricks, Pepe Schildkraut came with Henrietta Malkiel, Billy Kirkland, Hortense Alden, Polly Damrosch, Nazimova (who arrived late from the Civic Repertory around the corner, where she was playing in *The Cherry Orchard*) and Philip Goodman with Red Lewis and Dorothy Thompson.

Two weeks later, on the morning of what came to be known as Black Thursday, I stood on the floor of the Produce Exchange and saw the market collapse—saw it first, with fascinated, incredulous horror, on the overhead blackboards where the Chicago and Winnipeg wheat-futures quotations were posted, sharply lower at the opening and falling so fast that, within an hour, trades were no longer being recorded. After that we huddled around the grinding ticker tape, and when that too fell hopelessly behind, stood leaning across the telegraph counters listening to the dry clacking of the keys and the flat voices of the operators reporting orders executed at prices that could not be believed. Most clearly of all it was to be seen on the faces of the men who rushed to answer the constantly ringing bells in their private phone-booths and who came out, seconds later, blind and shaking and looking suddenly as though they wanted to die.

Nothing like it had ever been seen or imagined. Infected by the stock-market panic, wheat futures, whose normal fluctuations seldom exceeded a fraction of a percentage, lost more than a tenth of their value in two hours and double that in the days to come.

At the height of the first day's panic Mitchell called from

London on the overseas phone. There was not much I could tell him except to assure him that we were all right. At the time I believed it. Holding no speculative position on the market, the Oceanic was not directly or immediately affected by the crash. It was its aftereffects that were fatal.

I was like the captain of a heavy-laden ship that has come through a hurricane. His first feeling is one of relief at finding himself still afloat; it is only gradually that he realizes that, with his plates smashed and the sea pouring into his hold below the water line, he will never make port. Our huge wheat sales had been made at pre-crash prices to various parts of Europe with delivery dates that extended over a period of three months. This meant that until we got paid, we had to carry several million bushels of wheat, financed at prices so far above their present value that we were being pressed on all sides to make up the difference. This was one of the regular risks of the trade; in normal times, with fractional fluctuations, it would have presented no particular problem. For the Oceanic, overextended, undercapitalized, precariously balanced on its frail pyramid of shrinking credit, it became a catastrophe.

All through November and early December, still only partially aware of our situation, I continued to navigate a vessel whose decks were already awash. Every morning, with my assistant Matt Ryan, I would go down to the floor of the Exchange, where we would act jovial and unperturbed until closing time. The rest of the day and far into the night I would sit at my desk signing checks which I hoped were good and listening to bad news that grew steadily worse. Mr. Weaver, gray and glassy-eyed, was fighting desperately to keep us afloat—juggling collateral, postdating checks, ignoring calls, acting dumb, using every technicality to put off the inevitable moment when a note would be presented or a loan called and we would have to admit our inability to meet it. I asked Mitchell for help, which he was unable to give us.

Just before Christmas the last of the imported furniture—a gray fur-lined armchair—was delivered to the penthouse at 66 Fifth Avenue. That same day, in midafternoon, I locked the door of my private office, called Mitchell in London and told him I was coming over. He asked what I had to tell him that could not be said over the phone. I repeated that I was sailing that night on the *Bremen*. I called Zita and asked her if she cared to go with me; she had exactly three hours to pack and she said she'd be ready.

Within a few hours of my arrival in London, it had become evident that our collapse, aggravated by the multiplying losses of a forced liquidation, would engulf not only the Oceanic but also the parent company of J. W. Mitchell, with serious repercussions in Canada. Any day now the news would be out and I had better be in New York when it broke. The *Bremen* was leaving the next day on her return voyage. I called Zita, who was still in the hotel, and told her our honeymoon was over.

Ryan was at the dock to meet me. Among other tales of disaster he reported that our Mr. Weaver had left his desk one afternoon and had spent the rest of that day and the next visiting the nation's leading manufacturers of office equipment and ordering half a million dollars' worth of calculating machines in my name. He died of a brain tumor three weeks later.

And a few weeks after that—wearing an appropriately sober suit and a black knitted tie—I appeared in the Arbitration Room of the New York Produce Exchange before the assembled creditors of the Oceanic Grain Corporation. These included three New York banks, a grain-elevator outfit, a barge and towing concern, two railroads, the telephone company and several members of the Exchange.

The meeting, which was held with the lights on in an atmosphere of stale grain-dust and varnished wood, was brief, humiliating and dull. First, the accountants revealed what everyone had known for a month: that the Oceanic's liabilities greatly exceeded its assets. To the questions that were put to me as president of the stricken corporation I gave sincere and straightforward answers in a voice that was muted with remorse. Since blood cannot be squeezed out of a stone, the creditors were reproachful but lenient. It had already been determined that there was no ground for criminal action and no material advantage to anyone in a forced bankruptcy. So they lectured me on my folly, then excused me while they made the final tally of their losses (which amounted to between two and three hundred thousand dollars, mostly to the banks) and settled the details of the liquidation. I thanked them with hatred in my heart and left the room—a picture of modesty and repentance.

I walked down the long, overheated corridor with the faint, familiar rumor of the Exchange floor on my left and went on down the steps that wound around the antique iron elevator shaft to the street level, past the newsstand, the telegraph office, the spittoons and the shoeshine stands, on through the swinging doors into the cold air of Battery Place, past the Customs House, through the early afternoon traffic into Battery Park with its bare winter trees, across the burnt grass, among the fluttering pigeons, sandwich wrappings and paper cups—the lunch-hour leavings of secretaries and office boys.

Seated on a bench, looking past the Aquarium across the river to the Jersey shore, as the exhilaration of disaster slowly ebbed away, I held a small, private liquidation meeting of my own over the affairs of Jacques Haussmann and concluded that there, too, the liabilities greatly exceeded the assets. He had had his big chance and muffed it; at twenty-seven he was thoroughly discredited in the only activity in which he had any training or experience or connections. His cash position was deplorable: against the few thousand dollars he had managed to salvage, he had personal debts of over twenty thousand dollars including the seventeen thousand he had borrowed from one of his father's friends to acquire his now worthless stock in the Oceanic. His emotional situation was little better: involved in a marriage that he had never really desired, he found himself committed to a way of life that he could no longer afford but from which he saw no way of disengaging himself. Other liabilities included his mother in Paris, to whose support he had been contributing for the past two years and who, by her own account, was once again down to her last few thousand francs. Last, and by no means least, was the disturbing realization that with the dissolution of the Oceanic Grain Corporation and the consequent loss of his commercial visa, Jacques Haussmann was, as of this moment, an illegal resident of the United States of America, subject to arrest and expulsion, and with little likelihood (as a native of Rumania, whose immigration quota was filled for years to come) of ever achieving legal entry to the only country in the world to which he had any sense of belonging.

It was a dismal catalogue of defeats—one that filled him with a sudden sense of overwhelming despair. In spite of the cold, he remained seated on his bench for more than an hour, while the red mass of the Produce Exchange darkened behind him. Finally, after the street lights had been turned on, he got up and moved slowly through the small, deserted park, between the bare trees and the pigeons, back toward Battery Place and the Bowling Green subway station of the Broadway IRT. It was midafternoon and the rush hour was just beginning. At the head of the stairs he hesitated for a moment and turned to look for a cab. Seeing none, he went on down the steps and, once and for all, out of the pages of this history.*

---

* Legally Jacques Haussmann survived for thirteen years, signing checks, leases and contracts, being investigated on various occasions by the Civil Service, the U.S. Army's G2 and the FBI. He finally ceased to exist "on the first day of March in the year of our Lord nineteen hundred and forty-three and of our Independence the one hundred and sixty-seventh," when, under Naturalization Certificate #5312366, before the Southern District Court of the State of New York, I was formally and permanently transformed into John Houseman.

ACT ONE

FOR

VIRGIL THOMSON

II

FROM Haussmann, the merchant prince, I inherited five business suits, a black Auburn convertible, a penthouse with sixteen months of its two-year lease still to run, four languages, perfect health, a beautiful and talented wife, and an extensive collection of fantasies, the most persistent and dangerous of which was the notion that I was a long-repressed creative artist who would now, at last, have a chance to follow his true vocation as a writer. The three years I spent trying to reconcile this yearning with the realities of the world were among the worst of my life.

Seated on my imported tubular metal chair at my black glass-and-chromium table, faced with the necessity of transforming my accumulated dreams into some sort of communicable expression, I soon made the horrifying discovery that I had absolutely nothing to write about. I sat there day after day and then week after week, through the spring and early summer of 1930, with a pile of crumpled paper at my feet, darkening sheet after sheet with words that only vaguely reflected my own confused private fantasies and could be of no conceivable interest to anyone else.

And all this time my money was running out and my personal situation was getting worse by the hour.

My relations with my wife—even in the days and nights of our first romantic and physical ardor—had been based on the mutual assumption that we were a unique and glamorous couple, wonderfully and peculiarly suited to each other. Lovely, sensitive, much admired and publicly acclaimed, Zita Johann was the perfect mistress for a successful, sensitive young executive at the height of his powers; she also supplied a vicarious outlet for my frustrated artistic aspirations. I offered equivalent attractions: a young man of a kind she had never known, handsome, self-confident, cultivated and rich, performing mysterious miracles in the international markets of the world; I also represented security—her permanent protection from the hazards of a notoriously precarious profession.

Now suddenly I had broken my part of the contract. In place of the glamorous merchant prince she had married, she woke up to find herself in bed with a frightened, ruined man in his early thirties who seemed intent upon groping his aimless and anxious way into a new way of life for which he had no apparent qualifications. What was worse—he seemed quite content, after his savings were gone, to live indefinitely on her earnings.

Yet it was Zita who broke up the inertia into which I was sinking and who first brought up a possibility that I had never even considered: that my future might lie in the theatre. She suggested one night that we try writing a play together.

It happened quickly and it came out surprisingly well, flowing free and easily out of our combined subjective experience. It was a story of unrealized love between two insecure, ill-suited young people—a lonely girl and a boy with a frightened, possessive mother—and it took place in a small hotel by a lake that blended some of the nostalgic elements on my own Swiss holidays with Zita's memories of the times when she had waited on the tables of summer resorts in her teens. It was derivative, low in energy and quite European (somewhere between Katherine Mansfield, Lenormand, *Grand Hotel* and *The Seagull*), but it had a depth of personal feeling that makes it unlike anything I ever wrote before or since. We finished it in six weeks and Zita typed it—under the name of Joan Wolf. For my own part I used what I now considered my true name—John Houseman.

Zita had a friend, Alexander Kirkland, who with his partner, Cowles Strickland, ran the Berkshire Playhouse at Stockbridge, Massachusetts. They agreed, if she would appear in it, to present *The Lake* during their summer season, between *Romeo and Juliet* and *The Admirable Crichton.** Kirkland directed it and played the boy. Leo Carroll was in it; so was George Coulouris in his first good American role—that of a sad, lecherous guest in the hotel. I watched rehearsals—the first I had ever followed—and found them altogether absorbing. After the first dress rehearsal, Aline MacMahon told me that the play made her feel as though she had grown hair on her teeth during the evening. But, once again, Zita was much admired, and we got sympathetic reviews from one New York critic who was vacationing in the neighborhood.

While we were in Stockbridge a call came from Jed Harris, then at the height of his sulphurous fame. He wanted Zita for the part of Sonya in his production of *Uncle Vanya*, which had been a success on Broadway the previous season and which he was now sending on tour. She was dying to play it but reluctant to follow another actress in the role; and she felt that Jed must be punished for not having thought of her in the first place. There followed three weeks of skullduggery: Jed wooing, Zita fleeing; Zita relenting, Jed cooling then pursuing again. (Ben Hecht in *A Jew in Love* has described the mixture of deadly cruelty and ineffable charm of which Harris was capable; when he really wanted something or somebody—and even when he did not—no effort was too great, no means too elaborate or circuitous if it helped to satisfy his craving for personal power.) In the midst of

---

* At a run-through of *Crichton*, in the secondary part of Agatha, I watched a very young, inexperienced girl with a large mouth, wonderful bones and an impossible voice take over the stage. It was Katharine Hepburn two years before she appeared in *The Warrior's Husband* and became a star.

their ballet it occurred to Jed that one way to get at Zita was through me. He summoned me to his office. Having learned from Joseph Schildkraut (whom he had on a string for another project) that it was one of my favorite plays, he told me that he was thinking of producing Crommelynck's *Le Cocu Magnifique** and suggested that I do a translation for him. I asked how soon he wanted it. Could I do it in two weeks he asked, smiling.

I worked on it day and night with intense pleasure. I was not paid and I doubt if he ever read it. For by then Zita had signed her contract and he was making her pay for his wooing: he left rehearsals to a stage manager and, when he finally came to a run-through, pointedly ignored her while he gave notes to every member of the cast, which included Lillian Gish, Walter Connolly and Osgood Perkins. But I was glad to have done it. It gave me self-confidence and it sharpened my appetite for the theatre. Having lost all faith in my own inspiration, I was finding in translation a satisfying outlet for my creative energy. I spent a month on an adaptation, for my wife, of Jean-Jacques Bernard's *Martine*, only to discover that it had already been done. And I started looking around for a congenial collaborator to work with while she was away.

I found him in the person of Lewis Galantière whom I had known for some years and with whom I had occasionally lunched downtown when I wanted to get away from my colleagues in the Produce Exchange. He was a multilingual Franco-American, a few years older than myself, who worked for the Federal Reserve Bank and had acquired some reputation for his translations and critical writings. Erudite, myopic and gregarious, he saw himself following the great European literary tradition of the bureaucrat-intellectual man about town. After some conversation we decided to write a play together: something between a Restoration comedy and the best kind of Parisian boulevard farce. We both

---

* First produced by Lugné-Poë in Paris, where I saw it on one of my last school vacations, it became one of the great European successes of the twenties: its most celebrated performances are those of Max Reinhardt in Germany and Meyerhold's "constructivist" production in Moscow.

knew and admired Sacha Guitry's *L'Illusioniste,* from which we
purloined the basic idea for our play: that of a man so charming
and persuasive that he can talk any woman he desires into loving
him and, when he is tired of her, instead of leaving her, talk her
painlessly out of love under the impression that she is leaving
him. It was all very Gallic and we took our title *Lovers, Happy
Lovers* from the last stanza of La Fontaine's fable *Les Deux
Pigeons.* The structure—the least interesting part of the work—
was mine: the dialogue and the style were mostly his. We worked
with interruptions (for Lewis led an active social life) during
weekends and hours when he was free from the bank, either at
my glass-and-chromium table or at the Royalton, where Lewis
was living—part of the time in Robert Benchley's apartment.
Lewis protested periodically that such foolery was not for him,
but he was having a good time; as a small fastidious man with
thick glasses, he found vicarious satisfaction in the gambits of our
philandering hero.

We progressed slowly, and we were barely halfway through the
second act when Zita returned from her tour in a mood of angry
depression. In her loneliness she had had time to brood over her
personal and professional situation. Since her sudden triumph
in *Machinal* nothing had been offered her in the theatre that she
considered worthy of her; her experience with Irving Thalberg at
MGM had been profitable but disturbing. Convinced, like all
theatre people, that each engagement was the last, she was filled
with growing resentment over my fecklessness—especially when I
admitted that, during her absence, I had been unfaithful to her
and had been offered a job on the Produce Exchange at ten thousand dollars a year which I had turned down. We had scenes
that alarmed even our savage Croatian cook. Then suddenly, out
of the blue, she was offered the starring role in Philip Barry's
new play, *Tomorrow and Tomorrow,* to be produced and directed by Gilbert Miller, opening on Broadway early in the new
year.

Rehearsals began almost immediately and Zita was able to
transfer some of her rage from me to her producer-director, who

never for one moment concealed the fact that he had cast her at the author's insistence and that he himself felt she was all wrong for the part. Spoiled by the loving permissiveness of Arthur Hopkins' direction in *Machinal*, she reacted to Miller's bellowing coarseness with sullen Hungarian fury.

For his part, accustomed to the smooth professionalism of the expensive English drawing-room actors he normally employed, he found her gauche, inept and rather "common," and said so daily during rehearsals. His opinion was shared by her British leading man, Herbert Marshall, who considered her woefully deficient in social and theatrical savoir-faire. Philip Barry remained loyal. To give her the polish she lacked he invited her—and me—during the Christmas and New Year holidays to some of the fanciest homes in New York—the Gates's, the Lovetts', the two Whitneys' and his own.

Tomorrow and Tomorrow was not one of Barry's brightest successes. One critic wrote of it that "a man of one expert minor gift in the theatre has tried without equipment to go beyond it." According to *The New York Times*:

> Clarity is not one Mr. Barry's virtues and when he mixes rueful romance with a dash of psychoanalysis his thought is more attenuated than ever . . . But whatever it is, he has managed to make it beautiful and *Tomorrow and Tomorrow* is a profoundly moving play to which Zita Johann brings distinction with the fragility and radiance of her personality.

It ran through the spring into early summer, and it was still running when Lewis Galantière and I finally finished our comedy. I gave it to Adrienne Morrison, mother of the famed Bennett sisters (Constance, Barbara and Joan) and wife of the head of the American office of the Pinker literary agency. Within a week, to our stupefaction, three major Broadway producers had offered by buy it and it had been sold to Gilbert Miller as a vehicle for New York's leading romantic star and matinee idol, Leslie Howard. Under the Dramatists' Guild contract the standard price for a six-month option was five hundred dollars. With what I had made on *The Lake* and after deducting the agent's commission, my total earnings for the year amounted to two hundred and seventy-five dollars.

My situation was desperate, but I was not dissatisfied. In twelve months I had worked on four plays and now I was starting on a fifth—another collaboration. I had made the acquaintance, soon after my arrival in New York, of a former newspaperman, A. E. Thomas, the author of several successful, conventional Broadway comedies. He was no longer young and, shaken by the convulsions that were changing his world, he was looking for a partner with a contemporary idea for a play. He felt he had found it in a notion I suggested to him after borrowing it from Jules Romains, who had used it in two of his plays—first in *Dr. Knock* and then again, more recently and elaborately, in *Donogoo Tonka:* that with the multiplying means of publicity in our modern world almost any idea or personality can be sold to a sufficient number of people to make it seem real. My plot—by no means a brilliant or original one—showed an aging, indigent and alcoholic trombone player being taken from a street band and elevated through human credulity and corruption and the machinations of a high-powered publicity agent to the status of an international celebrity—somewhat after the manner of Professor Einstein, whose photograph, with his fuzzy hair falling over his violin, had appeared in every newspaper and magazine in the country, though no one but a handful of scientists had the faintest notion of what his real accomplishment was. We talked about it through the late spring—mostly in the bar and library of The Players' club on Gramercy Park. Then he went off to his house at Narragansett, where I visited him twice and where, in a surprisingly short time, he turned out a well-crafted mechanical comedy of mediocre texture, complete with stock characters and standard comic situations.

I remember our collaboration with some embarrassment. With incredible arrogance I set about correcting this veteran playwright's work. When he had the temerity to question some of my amendments, I snatched the script from him and proceeded, without consultation or permission, to rewrite whole sections of it before sending it off to the agent, who immediately sold it to Frederick McConnell for production at the Cleveland Play House during the following season.

With the sale of *A Very Great Man* my earnings had risen to four hundred and ten dollars in fifteen months—hardly enough to justify renewing the lease on the penthouse, which, besides, had been the scene of too many miseries and disasters. Still, it was saddening to watch all that costly, built-in cabinetwork ripped out and carted off, together with the glass-and-chromium table and the fur-lined armchair, to a warehouse, where they remained until they were sold at auction for nonpayment of storage two years later.

We moved for the summer to a small house in New City in Rockland County on the west shore of the Hudson River, from which Zita was driven at dawn each day to the studio where she was working on her first film—for D. W. Griffith. The great man had sent for her during the run of *Tomorrow and Tomorrow,* interviewed her in his New York hotel room (in a fine, old-fashioned way, with the lights so arranged that she sat in brightness while he remained concealed in the shadows) and announced to the world that he had chosen her above all other young actresses in America to star in his latest picture—*The Struggle.*

His fortunes were at the lowest possible ebb. No major Hollywood studio would touch him. From somewhere he had raised not quite enough money to make this, his last film, in a small ill-equipped studio in the Bronx. The screenplay was melancholy—the drab, maudlin saga of an incurable alcoholic (played by Hal Skelly, who had made his name—also with Arthur Hopkins—in *Burlesque*) and his loyal, long-suffering wife. But the Griffith name was still magic, and Zita had signed without hesitation for a fraction of what she had earned with MGM two years earlier.

It was an unhappy engagement, during which she found herself working in outrageous conditions with none of the charismatic inspiration that Lillian Gish and so many others had found in earlier films with the Old Master. She would return late at night, green with exhaustion from chasing Skelly from saloon to saloon in pouring rain—drenched, shivering, wind-whipped and deafened by the old-fashioned wind machines—and sit hunched before our midsummer fire, drying out and mumbling bitterly through her tears as she chewed her cold supper that she should never have done the lousy picture and that she was ruining her career and her health to hold our marriage together. She was still trying to hold it together in the fall when she insisted that I accompany her on the tour of *Tomorrow and Tomorrow,* which Miller was sending out through the Theatre Guild to the principal cities of the East and Middle West. I resisted. I wanted to stay quietly in the country where it cost me almost nothing to live and work. By the time she got back we would both have had a chance to test our crumbling relationship and, possibly, with one or more of my plays in production, to redress my ignominious financial situation. Zita refused: she would not go on the tour unless I went with her. After days of bitter argument I gave in. But, before leaving, we set up a bookkeeping system under which all living expenses on the tour (except travel, which was absorbed by the company) would be divided by two and entered in my debit column, which was already considerable. As a protection for her and to outwit any Oceanic creditor who might, one day, following the triumph of *Lovers, Happy Lovers* (on which Miller had just renewed his option) take it into his head to bring a belated personal suit against me, I gave her a note for twelve thousand dollars, payable on demand.* With these domestic arrangements completed and no new work in progress, I set out on our melancholy winter journey.

I have always found travel exciting. For all my loneliness and frustration, my three years of wandering for the Continental had been rich in personal discoveries. This tour was a nightmare: Boston, Cleveland, Detroit, Chicago, Minneapolis, St. Louis and Cincinnati—in that order and all equally deadly. For Zita there was the stimulation of facing new audiences eight times a week. For me there was nothing but the tedium of sitting in identical,

* The demand was met with interest computed at six percent, nine years and two marriages later, soon after the production of *Native Son.*

overheated hotel suites, pretending to work but, in fact, reading the papers and sleeping and, when I could stand it no longer, walking the frozen streets.

My gloom was not entirely personal. On my earlier visits to many of these same cities in the twenties I had breathed an air that was vigorous and lively and rich with hope. Now all that was changed. The Great Depression had the country by the throat. Everywhere in the streets, in that winter of 1931, there was the bitter, pervasive smell of fear and despair.

Then one morning we woke up in our drawing room aboard the Santa Fe Superchief and saw the orange groves and palm trees of the San Bernardino Valley racing by. An hour later, with flashbulbs popping, we were basking in the bright sunshine of Hollywood. Zita had signed a new contract, this time with RKO, which had promptly loaned her out to Howard Hawks for a picture called *Tiger Shark,* in which she was to appear, as a tuna fisherman's wife, with Richard Arlen and Edward G. Robinson. We lived for two weeks in the tower of a Norman castle known as the Chateau Elysée, then moved to San Diego for location work with the tuna fleet. I followed and, for a few days (through the influence of Zita's agent, Leland Hayward), became one of five writers whom Hawks kept in various hotel rooms writing different versions of the script, from which he would, each morning on the set, extract the lines that took his fancy. Not one word of mine was ever used and I soon stopped trying and spent all day on the pier watching him shoot.

Ten days later the corpses of the two eighteen-foot tiger sharks that had been caught off the coast of Baja California, were hauled out of the deep freeze and wired for action. The company moved across to Catalina Island, where we lived in bungalows at the water's edge. There was another film shooting at the Isthmus—a new version of *Rain* which Lewis Milestone was making with Joan Crawford. As a result the harbor was filled with yachts and the nights were gay with parties. I continued to spend my days on the set, learning what I could about the making of motion pictures, until one day, in the Catalina Channel, while Robinson was playing his final sequence on the deck of the tuna boat (after the tiger shark had chewed off his remaining leg), he refused to continue his death scene with Zita until I had been removed and rowed to shore.

When we returned to the mainland we moved into a small beachhouse we had rented from Alexander Kirkland in Malibu. It was elegantly decorated in blue and white with nautical motifs and had been used by Joan Crawford for her honeymoon with Franchot Tone. From here Zita was driven to work each morning, across the mountains to Burbank, in her secondhand, sixteen-cylinder Cadillac, while I chugged along the coast to Culver City in the Chevrolet roadster I had bought for two hundred dollars. This represented my first week's salary at MGM, where I had been engaged to work on a film about the Kansas wheat fields, on which Heyward had assured them I was an expert. I sat in my cell in the Writers' Building and no one came near me or told me what the movie was about. After three weeks, Hunt Stromberg, the producer, summoned me and told me it was off.

I sat on the sand at Malibu making final revisions on *A Very Great Man,* watching the gulls and the pelicans make their regular flights up and down the coast, and waiting for Zita to come home. On weekends or when she did not have to work the next day, we dressed up and went to openings on Hollywood Boulevard and to parties which I attended as the Star's husband. She was having her usual fights with the Studio: unable to find a film that was mutually acceptable, they had loaned her out again—this time to Universal for a picture called *The Mummy,* in which she appeared as a reincarnated Egyptian princess pursued by Boris Karloff.

Our last months in Hollywood were spent at the Garden of Allah, where we occupied the suite with a black marble bathroom that had been designed for Nazimova when this was her home. Neighbors complained that we kept them awake with our nocturnal quarrels. Twice I started to leave and twice Zita begged me to stay with her until she had finished her film. Finally, in late October, we set out for New York in the Cadillac with a platinum cocker spaniel replacing the wolfhound and a White Russian couple whom Zita had found at the studio and engaged as her maid and chauffeur. It took us eight days to cross the continent, including the detour we made in Ohio, from Columbus to Cleveland, to catch the last performance of *A Very Great Man* at the Play House. Al Thomas had sent me the reviews, which were better than I expected, together with the news that the play was about to be optioned for Broadway. We arrived halfway through the second act and the audience seemed to be amused. The next day we crossed the Appalachians in driving rain with four of our sixteen cylinders out of commission and the transmission barely holding together as we crawled through the Holland Tunnel into New York. Three weeks later when RKO summoned Zita back to the Coast, I did not go with her.

I spoke to her twice in the next ten months. The first time was when I saw her photograph one night on the front page of the bulldog edition of the *Daily News* under the headline BEAUTY MARRED and read that she had been injured by flying glass in an auto crash with John Huston in the Hollywood hills. I called the hospital and she said it was nothing and thanked me for calling.

*   *   *

New City, where I spent five months of that winter and spring (and thirty-seven years, on and off, after that) is the only place in the world I have ever thought of as home. At that time, before the George Washington Bridge was open, it was a remote village with a courthouse, an inn, half a dozen stores, two churches and one garage. Three miles north, running along the foot of a low mountain that ended at the edge of the Hudson River in a bluff known as High Tor, was the South Mountain Road, where, among the farms and broken-down houses of the original settlers, a so-called artists' colony had sprung up after the war.*

---

* Among those who were attracted by the beauty of the countryside and the cheapness of the land were Rollo Peters, the actor; writers like Maxwell Anderson, Bessie Breuer and John Howard Lawson; Edna Millay's sister, Norma; Amy Murray, the folk singer; a Chaucerian scholar Frank Hill; the architect, Herman Rosse and a group of artists—Ruth Reeves, Millia Davenport, the Kantors and Henry Varnum Poor.

I had fallen in love with the Road during the difficult summer I had spent there with Zita. Now I returned to it in the dead of winter in search of peace. The house I lived in was a former farmhouse with a shingle roof, faded blue shutters and huge trees all around it, which I had persuaded my aunt to rent (for a few hundred dollars a year) as a refuge from the pressure of the great downtown hospital of which she was superintendent. That winter, except for an occasional weekend visit when she arrived, loaded with huge steaks and bottles of Canadian Rye, I had it all to myself.

I had never lived in the country or in a house alone. In New City, surrounded by snow and silence (the silence of the day and the deeper silence of the night), liberated from the last of the traps I had built for myself, I found some of the peace I was looking for. It began with simple, immediate things. For years, ever since my nights in the Nursery at Clifton, I had been afraid of the dark. In the freezing darkness of that isolated house, with my nearest neighbor a quarter of a mile away, these child's night fears grew to such an unbearable pitch of violence that I knew I had to break through them or go mad. When they finally scattered and dissolved, they drained away some of those other, deeper terrors—of rejection, poverty, death and annihilation—that had haunted me for so many years of my life.

No miracle took place during those five lonely months; no sudden vision came to me of what I was going to do with my life. But with the ebbing of my fears it became easier, as the weeks went by, to adapt my fantasies (in which I continued to indulge) to the realities of the world around me.

I was helped in this adjustment by the friends I made that winter on the South Mountain Road. The house I was living in was owned by Bessie Breuer, who had left it when she married Henry Varnum Poor and moved to the stone house he had built with his own hands two miles up the road. Henry was a strong, gentle man, an athlete who retained his physical grace and power in his work and in his life. Born in Kansas, educated in California and in Paris, he began as a painter; then, discovering that he could make a more secure living as a potter, he became one of the great American ceramists of his time. He continued to paint, wrote books and designed and built several beautiful and original homes (including the one in which this is written) along the South Mountain Road. With his soft-spoken, blond craftsman's serenity, he was the exact opposite of Bessie, who was dark, garrulous, loving, impulsive and acutely sensitive to the vibrations of those around her. She had been a successful journalist and feature writer; after her marriage she became a short-story writer and a novelist. With her daughter Anne and their son Peter, the Poors became, after the Siepmanns, the nearest thing to a family I had known. Every day, in good weather and bad, I walked the two miles that separated our two houses, sometimes for a brief greeting if Henry and Bessie were both at work, sometimes for a meal or a drink by Henry's big fireplace before starting back on my long walk home.

With the last of the snow, from what was left of my option money, I bought a battered Model A Ford and used it to get in and out of New York. On the nights when I stayed in town, there was a small circle of friends (the Mielziners, the Malkiels, the Lights) on whose hospitality I could count and in whose apartments I billeted myself in rotation as I began to pick up the threads I had left dangling during my retreat. *A Very Great Man* had been sold to a producer who was planning to try it out in one of the summer theatres before bringing it into New York. *Lovers, Happy Lovers* was still owned by Gilbert Miller, but both his stars were otherwise employed. Next on the buyer's list was Brock Pemberton who, with his partner, Antoinette Perry, was looking for a chance to repeat the Broadway success they had had with Preston Sturges' *Strictly Dishonorable* the year before. There were certain changes they wanted made and, to save time, Lewis and I set about rewriting the play to their specifications even before they owned it. Some of our original elegance was lost in the process, but they had the reputation of being shrewd producers and we were tired of waiting for a production. Miller's option lapsed at the end of February. Our contract with Pemberton was ready to be signed when all the banks closed, then reopened after two days. Still no check arrived. By this time I badly needed my share of the five hundred dollars and I was aggrieved at having done so much work without compensation. Besides, we had another producer waiting—the English team of Maurice Colbourne and Barry Jones (known for their productions of the plays of George Bernard Shaw), who were prepared to guarantee us a London production within six months and whose certified check was lying in an envelope on the agent's desk. We gave the Pembertons a week's grace. When nothing happened, we cabled our acceptance to London and cashed the check. Neither Brock Pemberton nor Antoinette Perry ever spoke to us again, and we later discovered that, in our haste, we had made an irreparable mistake. But at least I had my advance, on which I could live for the next few months.

During these negotiations two new projects had come up. One was a German theatre piece called *Gallery Gods,* which Pepe Schildkraut had seen abroad and sent to his friend Henrietta Malkiel as a possibility for the U.S. market. She asked me if I would like to work on it with her and I said yes, of course. It was very European and we made no attempt to transpose it to the American scene. I was delighted when Harold Clurman, one of the directors of the Group Theatre, saw in it an opportunity for ensemble acting for the company and a contrast to the Group's first production for the coming season—Sidney Kingsley's *Crisis,* later known as *Men in White.* The other was a French farce, *Trois et Une,* a Paris success of which William Harris, Jr., needed a quick adaptation. He was one of Broadway's leading commercial producers, specializing in sex comedies, of which Zoë Akins' smash hit *The Greeks Had a Word for It* was the latest. He was notoriously parsimonious: for $250, against one percent of the gross, Lewis and I did a hurried job for him, without pride or pleasure, in the hope that with seven characters and one set *Three and One* might, in its meretricious way, achieve some sort of a run.

In July Harold Clurman called from the Adirondacks, where the Group Theatre was spending the summer in an adult camp known as Green Mansions. In exchange for entertaining the guests four nights a week and on weekends, members of the

Group, including dependents, designer, choreographer, voice teacher and other associates to the number of fifty, received board and lodging during the months of July and August. Harold said there were still a few places open and suggested that Malkiel and I come up, follow rehearsals of *Gallery Gods* and make whatever textual changes seemed desirable after hearing the scenes played. I leapt at this chance to extend my theatrical education and spent two enthralling weeks in a world that was unlike anything I had ever known. I was familiar with the Group's artistic and social attitudes and beliefs. It was another thing to see them at work and in their collective life.

It was a summer (the third since their formation) which, according to Clurman, was full of personal upsets and dissension. I watched their rehearsals, sat with them at meals and attended their meetings, which all were highly emotional and conducted with a curious combination of communal spirit and arbitrary authority. I was there when Max Gorelick had his annual outburst against the tyranny of the directors and was answered by Lee Strasberg, who spoke for two and three quarter hours at the top of his voice. And I was present at the first reading of a new play, *I've Got the Blues,* by one of the Group's younger members—Clifford Odets. Clurman has reported that when he first read it he liked the second act but found the first "cluttered with some rather good Jewish humor and a kind of messy kitchen realism" and the last "masochistically realistic."* The Group's initial reaction to the play, which, later, under the name of *Awake and Sing,* ensured their place in theatrical history, was, as I remember it, even less favorable, with Stella Adler declaring, at one point, that she would never, under any circumstances, appear in such an anti-Semitic piece.

The Group's principal activity that summer (aside from the sketches and one-act plays with which they entertained the campers) was devoted to preparing *Men in White,* which Strasberg was directing, with Alexander Kirkland, who had returned

* *The Fervent Years,* by Harold Clurman (Alfred A. Knopf).

from California, in the leading role. They did not like that either; several of them felt that "it would surely ruin the Group." But there was money available for its production and they could not afford to turn it down. *Gallery Gods*, of which Clurman was the director, had in its cast some of their most experienced actors, including Luther and Stella Adler, whose presence with the Group constantly perplexed me. A young woman of striking presence and keen intelligence, a scion of one of the three great Jewish acting dynasties (the Schildkrauts, the Adlers and the Tomashevskys), she had been the leading ingenue of the international Yiddish theatrical circuit that existed in the main cities of Europe and North and South America until the Great Depression and the emancipation of the younger generation finally destroyed it. (Stella still referred to it fondly as "the professional theatre.") Harold Clurman, who was deeply in love with her, had brought her into the Group, of which her acquaintance with Stanislavski made her an honorary member but to which she never really seemed to belong.

To justify our presence at Green Mansions, Malkiel and I made minor changes and textual corrections during rehearsals, but it was sadly evident that *Gallery Gods* was Harold's personal project and that it was unlikely to be produced unless something went wrong with *Men in White*. Watching rehearsals this seemed improbable: Kingsley's play had the sort of superficial realism which Strasberg, for all his pontifical "method" talk, was particularly fitted to bring to the stage.

From the Adirondacks I moved to Provincetown on Cape Cod, where *A Very Great Man* was being tried out by the alcoholic young millionaire who had it under option. No two worlds could have been more widely apart than that of the Group, with its contentious, obsessive dedication, and this cheerful band of summer theatre actors, who laughed and made love and smelled of salt from continually diving off the pier for a swim between scenes. Richard Whorf, who was directing the piece, had cast himself in the part of the publicist, created by K. Elmo Lowe in Cleveland; his wisecracking secretary was played by a vivacious beauty of Armenian descent who called herself Arlene Francis. Whorf gave the play the kind of energetic, slapdash treatment it deserved and it turned out to be one of the summer's most popular shows. On the day of the opening, I received a registered letter from Zita, forwarded from New City. It contained some enclosures in Spanish—applications for a Chihuahua divorce—which she asked me to sign right away because she was anxious to get married again.

Soon after Labor Day, at Lewis Galantière's suggestion, I moved into the building in which he was living at 125 East Fifty-seventh Street. With its grand staircase, scarlet carpet, mahogany paneling and brass elevator cage, it had once been one of Manhattan's most elegant apartment houses. In what had been the servants' quarters, on the top floor, I occupied a cell with a washstand, a table and chair and a bed just wide enough to make love in. Down the hall Lewis had a larger room with an alcove, a bath, a telephone and some Schnabel recordings which he allowed me to use by day while I waited for my theatrical ships to come in.

Whorf confidently predicted a Broadway opening for *A Very Great Man* before Christmas. I doubted that and I did not really desire it. I had no great hopes for *Gallery Gods. Three and One* was already in rehearsal. I went to the theatre and watched William Harris at work and was filled with irritation and gloom. My only stimulation came from a pale-faced, garrulous, exhaustingly eager and ambitious young lighting expert just out of Carnegie Tech. He was called Abe Feder—professionally abbreviated to Feder.

Three and One opened in mid-October, got mediocre reviews and ran to modest business for one hundred and twenty performances. It made a minor movie star of a luscious, sluggish young Englishwoman named Lillian Bond and launched a muscular male by the name of Brian Donlevy. Lewis and I made less than four hundred dollars apiece from it.

So now my hopes were fixed on *Lovers, Happy Lovers,* which

was touring the British provinces before coming into the West End of London. I rose before dawn after a sleepless night, went down with my coat over my pajamas to the newsstand on the corner, then burst triumphantly into the darkness of Galantière's room and read him the brief cabled report of our play's successful London opening. Lewis took the news more calmly than I did and was less disappointed three weeks later when the first box-office statements arrived and it became evident that London had not taken Mr. Jones and his company to its heart. They closed after five weeks, but in a note that accompanied their final box-office statement, Maurice Colbourne assured us that he and Barry were in no way disheartened; they were renewing their option and would be bringing the play into New York after a short Canadian engagement soon after the turn of the year.

In a letter to my mother in Rome I wrote hopefully of their coming as the possible solution to all my problems. I doubt if I really believed that, but while I waited for them to arrive, I found myself using the faint hope of their success to stem the tide of fear I felt rising around me again. In a time of general panic I had my own personal reasons for anxiety: the more calmly I examined my situation the more precarious it seemed. Through luck, shrewd associations and my knowledge of languages I had managed to gain a slippery toe hold in the theatre and to earn the few hundred dollars of option money and advances on which I was managing to subsist. But it was not a way of life and I knew it. Quite soon now I must find regular work in a profession in which I had a vague accretion of superficial knowledge but no training, no craft, no special skill or experience of any sort. In normal times there would have been little reason for anyone to employ me; in mid-depression with so many thousands of theatre people out of work, it was unthinkable—all the more since I myself seemed to have no clear notion of the capacity in which I was preparing to offer myself for hire.

Yet, for all my anxiety, I was leading a fairly agreeable and gregarious life in New York that fall. To eke out the last of my option money I had rationed myself to twenty dollars a week, on which I managed to subsist without humiliation or hunger. Most of my social activity seemed to take place after dark; much of it was theatrical—evenings that were cool and professional at the Gershwins'; intimate and intellectual in Rosamond Gilder's apartment on Gramercy Park; turbulent and alcoholic in Cleon Throckmorton's studio in the Village; soul-searching, very personal and argumentative with members of the Group Theatre in Stewart's Cafeteria after the show. There were weekends at Sneden's Landing, where I listened to Pare Lorentz, Jack Ratcliffe and Charles Wertenbaker (all working for national magazines) arguing over the New Deal and the State of the Union; all-night poker games for negligible stakes in Lee Miller's apartment to which I was drawn less by passion for gambling than by an unrequited lust for my hostess.

Lee Miller was a handsome blonde from Poughkeepsie, N.Y., with deep-set eyes and a mouth that had been immortalized by Jean Cocteau in his film *Le Sang d'un Poète*. She was taken up by the Paris surrealists, became Man Ray's assistant, sued *Time* magazine for printing an unauthorized close-up of her navel, collected, and returned to New York in the early thirties as a successful fashion photographer for the glossy magazines. She had a constant companion—the best of the poker players—of whom I was bitterly jealous. In a reckless and vain attempt to take her from him, I escorted her one night in a long white satin evening dress to the Casino in the Park, where we danced to the music of Eddie Duchin. The next morning, poorer by three quarters of my week's budget, I was back in Lewis Galantière's room, listening to Schnabel's Beethoven sonatas, waiting for a new wind to fill my sails.

It came—quite soon, from an unexpected quarter. One day in mid-November Lewis asked me to go with him to someone's house for a drink the following Sunday afternoon, to meet his friend Virgil Thomson, who had recently arrived from Paris with an opera he had done with Gertrude Stein, on which he needed theatrical advice. I almost did not get there. I had arranged with my aunt to drive to New City for the weekend. At the last moment some crisis at the hospital changed her plans and I accepted

Lewis's invitation—nervous, as always, at the prospect of entering a world I did not know.

I had read Gertrude Stein's *Three Lives,* some of *Tender Buttons* and more recently *The Autobiography of Alice B. Toklas;* I knew nothing about Virgil Thomson except what Lewis told me as we walked the four blocks to Sixty-first and Third Avenue. Born in Kansas City, he had been to Harvard, then to Paris during the twenties, where Galantière had known him as an associate of the poets, painters and musicians of the neoromantic movement. And I had never heard of the Askews, at whose brownstone house we arrived shortly before six. From the small, cork-lined library in which we were invited to shed our coats I could hear, through the half-open door of the next room, the modulated hum of three or four dozen cultivated voices.

The Askews' Sunday "at homes" were not parties: they were a continuing, well-organized operation with a clear and consistent objective. This weekly gathering, known to its habitués as "The Askew Salon," conformed to the dictionary's definition of that word as "a reunion of notabilities in the house of a lady of fashion." The lady, Constance Askew, was a New England woman of means, of broad cultural experience and striking beauty. With her generous, unfashionable bosom and coils of light hair that were just beginning to turn gray, she gave a splendid, Junoesque solidity to a world that might easily have seemed effete. Her consort, Kirk Askew, small, bright-eyed, with carved ivory features, was one of a band of young men—art dealers, historians and museum curators, most of them trained by Paul Sachs at Harvard—for whose artistic and professional benefit the Salon existed and functioned. This group, which came to exert such a dominant modernistic influence on the art fashions of its time, included Alfred Barr and Jere Abbott, directors of the new Museum of Modern Art, John McAndrew and Agnes Rindge of Vassar, Russell Hitchcock of Wesleyan, Philip Johnson, A. E. (Chick) Austin, director of the venerable Wadsworth Athenaeum in Hartford, Connecticut, Kirk Askew, our host, who represented the London firm of Durlacher Brothers, and Julien Levy, in whose small gallery on Madison Avenue, Dali, Tchelitchew, Campigli, the two Bermans (Eugene and Leonid), Juan Gris, Kandinsky and Magritte had their first New York showings and their first modest American sales.

These "reunions" were held each Sunday afternoon (during the R months, like oysters) from five o'clock on in a large drawing room with tall windows overlooking a garden. Leading off this drawing room and serving as a cloakroom and a place for serious artistic or personal dialogue was the small library which the hostess used as her study on weekdays. Its cork walls, where they were not covered with books, were hung with original drawings and historic photographs. Through these two rooms circulated the "notabilities,"* some four or five dozen each Sunday, evenly divided, as a rule, between the sexes. They flowed in

* Of the notabilities I encountered during my three years of fairly regular attendance at the Askew Salon I recall that music was represented by Aaron Copland, Nicolas Nabokov, Roger Sessions, Virgil Thomson, George Antheil, Elliot Carter and a very young Leonard Bernstein; fiction by Carl Van Vechten, Emily Hahn, John Mosher of *The New Yorker*, Glenway Wescott and Elizabeth Bowen; poetry by e. e. cummings, Archibald MacLeish, Charles Henri Ford and Lincoln Kirstein; photography by George Lynes, Hoynigen-Huhne and Lee Miller; criticism by Gilbert Seldes, Henry McBride and Hyatt Mayor; Wall Street by Douglas Parmentier; Oriental art by Alan Priest of the Metropolitan Museum; fashion by Elizabeth Hawes and Muriel King; the dance by Agnes De Mille, Edward Mahoney and Georges Balanchine, and politics by Esther Murphy, recently divorced from John Strachey. Among the art dealers present were Marie Harriman, Pierre Matisse, Val Dudensing; painters, in addition to Julien Levy's artists, included Masson, Louis Bouché, Jean Lurçat, Alexander Brook, Maurice Grosser, Louis Marcoussis and Leonore Fini. Show business was sparsely represented by Fania Marinoff, Elsie Houston, the Brazilian singer, Tonio Selwart, two very young actresses named Ruth Ford and Olive Deering, a novice costume designer, Irene Sharaff (assistant to Aline Bernstein) and two embryonic directors, Joseph Losey and myself. Other ladies distinguised for their elegance, their wifely position or their creative talent were Muriel Draper, Amanda Seldes, Edna Thomas, Helen Simpson, Joella Levy, Lucia Davidova, Marga Barr, Helen Austin, the three Stettheimer sisters, the Duchesse de Clermont-Tonnere, Iris Barry (founder and director of the Film Library of the Museum of Modern Art) and a tall, dark lady with protruding eyes known to me only as La Belle Uruguayenne. There must have been dozens more, regulars and occasional visisors, whom I have forgotten or never encountered.

slowly revolving eddies over the brown-purple carpet, between the massive Victorian furniture. From time to time this human stream seemed to get caught against some physical object—the tail of the piano or the curve of a love seat—or it would become congested around some particularly eloquent or glamorous guest. Then Kirk Askew would appear, smiling and efficient, and start the traffic back into its normal flow. Tea was served, also cocktails and whisky, though never in quantities that would interfere with the serious business of the gathering. Shoptalk was permitted up to a point; so were politics, if discussed in a lively and knowledgeable way. Flirtation (homo- and heterosexual) was tolerated but not encouraged. If it threatened to hold up traffic or disrupt the interchange of ideas it was soon ferreted out and broken up by the smiling, relentless and faintly malicious host.

Such was the new world I entered that Sunday in November, nervously, as I had entered Bloomsbury ten years before. I did not see much of it on my first visit; I met my host and hostess and received a drink. There were a few familiar figures in the room, but before I could join them I was led toward a small, vivacious man several years older than myself, with a pale face, a piercing voice, precise articulation and a will power that became evident within thirty seconds of meeting him, who immediately propelled me through the crowd toward a free spot in the curve of the piano, from which we moved after a moment to a sofa in the library under a photograph of Sarah Bernhardt in the role of Phèdre. Here we talked, or rather he talked, for close to an hour about the opera he had written with Gertrude Stein which was to be performed in Hartford in ten weeks' time.

Virgil Thomson in his autobiography has described the various stages which *Four Saints in Three Acts* went through between its composition in Paris in 1927 and its premiere in Connecticut on February 7, 1934. Miss Stein has given her own account of its conception:

> Virgil Thomson had asked Gertrude Stein to write an opera for him. Among the saints there were two saints whom she had always liked better than any others—St. Teresa of Avila

and Ignatius Loyola and she said she would write him an opera about those two saints. She began this and worked very hard at it that spring and finally finished *Four Saints* and gave it to Virgil Thomson to put to music. He did. And it is a completely interesting opera both as to words and music.*

For the next five years Thomson performed it, singing all the parts himself, first in Paris and then in a succession of New York drawing rooms including that of Carl Van Vechten, who found it "as original in its conception as *Pelléas et Mélisande."* But it was not until 1933 that the leaders of the rising group that frequented the Askew Salon finally rallied behind the opera and decided to ensure its production. Barr and Hitchcock had heard it in Paris and approved it; Austin undertook to present it in the small theatre he was building into the wing he had just added to Hartford's Wadsworth Athenaeum to house his considerable acquisitions of baroque and modern art. The opera would be its inaugural presentation to coincide with the Museum's opening show—the first retrospective Picasso exhibition ever to be held in this country. With a budget of ten thousand dollars guaranteed by a Hartford organization known as The Friends and Enemies of Modern Music, it was, for the composer, "the ultimate in dream fulfillment—a production backed by enlightened amateurs and executed by whatever professional standards I chose to follow."

By the time I arrived at the Askew Salon, Thomson had already set most of the elements of his production, but he still lacked a director. A number of professionals had shown little interest or faith in the work since it resembled nothing they knew. Besides, the composer had very clear and positive theatrical ideas of his own, which he outlined to me as we sat on Mrs. Askew's couch. He was pleased to discover that I was "a European, a product of French lycées and an English public school." He asked me what I had done in the theatre and I told him the truth, which did not seem to disturb him. Anxious to make an impression of sophistication, I observed that from his description

* *The Autobiography of Alice B. Toklas.*

of the opera it sounded like something that might have been presented by Etienne de Beaumont at one of his Soirées de Paris in the twenties. Virgil agreed and invited me to come and hear it the next morning at the Hotel Leonori, where someone had lent him a room with a piano.

> To know to know to love her so.
> Four Saints prepare for Saints
> It makes it well fish.
> Four Saints it makes it well fish.

So sang Virgil Thomson, banging away at the piano and filling the small room with his thin, piercing tenor voice. He sang for close to two hours—arias, recitatives, choruses, stage directions and all. And I sat there trying to look intelligent and appreciative and hoping with all my soul that he would invite me to work with him. He did so two days later, and I accepted. He explained there was no money in it and asked me when I could start. I said immediately, and so began the busiest and most decisive weeks of my life.

I soon discovered that what Virgil needed was not just someone to stage his opera but some sort of director-producer-impresario who would combine, coordinate and regulate the various artistic elements he had already selected. I accepted the assignment without diffidence and without question. We had ten thousand dollars and nine and a half weeks in which to find a cast, coach and rehearse them in two hours of unfamiliar music and complicated stage action, execute scenery and costumes, rehearse a new score, move to Hartford into an unfinished theatre with an orchestra of twenty and a cast of forty-three, set up, light, dress rehearse and open cold before one of the world's most sophisticated audiences. With the slightest theatrical experience I would have realized the impossibility of our task. In my total ignorance I assumed the job in a mood of irresistible euphoria.

The first thing I must do, I decided, was to find out what the opera was about. I had heard it three times by now and read it zealously; the text was becoming familiar but not intelligible. So

I asked Virgil to help me, and he gave me this outline of a scenario that had been jointly developed by his friend Maurice Grosser and himself and accepted by Gertrude Stein:

Imaginary but characteristic incidents from the lives of St. Teresa, St. Ignatius and their followers constitute the action of the opera, which is laid in sixteenth-century Spain. The first part of Act One is a series of *tableaux vivants* taking place in front of the Cathedral at Avila with the Saints and pupils assisting, and the Compère and Commère (characters created by the scenarist and composer) acting as master and mistress of ceremonies. St. Teresa is seen in various guises—with the Holy Ghost in the form of a stuffed pigeon, painting Easter eggs, rocking a baby, shaking hands with herself and posing for photographs. St. Teresa "half in and half out of doors" is divided in two—St. Teresa I, a soprano, and St. Teresa II, a contralto. Toward the end of the act St. Ignatius makes an entrance as a visitor to St. Teresa and her establishment. The act ends with comments, congratulations and general sociability.

Act Two begins with a picnic attended by St. Ignatius, St. Teresa and their male and female followers. At one point there is a ballet in which small angels learn to fly under the curious gaze of the Saints. Night falls and the Saints and sisters, carrying long candles, play games and move about. St. Ignatius appears with a telescope through which he sees the Heavenly Mansions (looking rather like the Capitol of the United States of America) and the question is asked "How many doors are there in it?" St. Teresa badly wants the telescope but St. Chavez explains that it belongs to the men. "I will try. Theirs and by and by," she says as she leaves and the curtain falls.

In Act Three the male Saints sit mending their nets by the seashore while the ladies observe them from behind a wall. As their work ends the Saints are vouchsafed a vision—the Holy Ghost in the form of a magpie. St. Ignatius sings:

Pigeons on the grass alas . . .
If they were not pigeons what were they.

The ladies are skeptical but the male Saints are disturbed. A storm develops, the light dimming and the solemnity of the occasion growing until it develops into a vision of the Last Judgment. The ladies are now thoroughly convinced. A religious procession is formed. Solemnity and grandeur.

After a short instrumental intermezzo, the Compère and Commère, before the curtain, discuss whether there is to be a Fourth Act. When this is decided the curtain rises on the Saints, happy in Heaven, with rivalries all forgotten, reminiscing about life on earth. The opera ends with a hymn of communion, "When this you see remember me," after which the Compère calls, "Last act" and the chorus shouts, "Which is a fact," as the final curtain falls.

Thomson also explained that the relations of St. Ignatius and St. Teresa in the opera had their counterpart in the literary and artistic life of Paris in the twenties—St. Teresa being Gertrude Stein and St. Ignatius being James Joyce (or possibly André Gide) surrounded by disciples. "They would be very courteous but they couldn't hand over the stage to each other at any point." With this added clarification I was ready to move on to the next step, which was to find out what the opera was going to look like.

Florine Stettheimer, whom Virgil had chosen for the task, was one of three daughters of a distinguished and wealthy New York family. She had been painting for years, mostly family portraits of her sisters, her mother, herself and her friends—canvases titled *Heat, West Point, Lake Placid, Asbury Park South* and *Russian Bank*—in colors of a clean and extraordinary brilliance. She also painted pictures of New York City—including a photographic likeness of Mayor Walker—in which she anticipated many of the elements of Pop Art. (Proud and retiring, she refused to sell or exhibit; her painting was little seen by the world until after her death, when she was honored with a special exhibit at the Museum of Modern Art.) She had heard Virgil sing the opera and admired it. When he invited her to design it she asked for time to consider the idea. Some months later she consented and began her research. She looked into history and art books and one of the elements that struck her was the portal of the Cathedral at Avila with stone lions chained to a stone cathedral. The following year she painted a portrait of Virgil Thomson which has, in the background, an arch made of tulle and a lion chained to a rainbow sitting on a cushion like a poodle dog. There is a toy theatre floating in the air, a bird bringing a bouquet, a big black flower in an upper corner, the Holy Ghost in various forms and a shaft of light pouring down on St. Virgil. Much of this imagery found its way into her designs for the opera, of which I got my first glimpse when Virgil conducted me one afternoon to her studio overlooking Bryant Park. Its windows were hung with cellophane curtains and the chairs and tables were all white and gold. The tables were glass and gold and there were lamps streaming with white beads and gilt flowers in vases. The windows of the little balcony that looked down on the studio were hung with Nottingham lace.

Florine herself, frail and elegant amid all this elaboration of gold, crystal and lace, proved formidable but enchanting. From a closet she brought out three boxes swathed in shawls and gauze, and when she had removed these, I saw that they were cello-phane-lined models of the three acts of *Four Saints* and that they were inhabited by tiny dolls draped in Cardinals' and other religious costumes—all in primary and secondary colors: red, purple and green for the first act; white for the second; yellow and Spanish black-and-white for the third. With slender fingers she set in place an arch of crystal beads, a golden lion with a cellophane chain around its neck, an emerald grass mat and palm trees of white and pink tarlatan.

Over tea and a homemade Viennese cake she listened while I expressed my admiration and tried to indicate (out of the depths of my inexperience) some of the problems we might encounter in translating her delicate, diminutive models and special materials to the theatre. I suggested as a suitable executant my friend Kate Drain Lawson, for many years technical director of the Theatre Guild. It was, from the start, an uneasy collaboration: Florine, "willful, unconcerned with precedent and as unpredictable as a butterfly in a garden of flowers"; Kate, solid, professional, devoted, bossy and harassed. But without her, Florine's designs might never have reached the stage.

Long before we met, Virgil had decided to have his Spanish Saints played by black singers. His reasons were simple and basic: quality of voice, clarity of speech and an ability to move with dignity and grace. As to the circumstances of this choice two versions exist: according to Carl Van Vechten it was made during an intermission of Hall Johnson's revivalist play, *Run Little Chillun!*, to which they had gone together. "Virgil turned and said to me, 'I am going to have *Four Saints* played by Negroes. They alone possess the dignity and the poise, the lack of self-consciousness that proper interpretation of opera demands. And they are not ashamed of words.' " According to Virgil the idea occurred to him late one night in Jimmy Daniels' Harlem night club. He was struck by the clarity of Daniels' speech and remembering his own happy experiences with Negro church choirs, suddenly asked himself why they would not be the right persons to sing in his opera.

When Miss Stein was informed of his design she was shocked, "assuming there would be some sexuality inherent in the opera's being done by Negroes." Miss Stettheimer was pained on the simpler ground that brown faces and hands would interfere with her color scheme; she suggested they be painted white. But Virgil's mind was made up. Years later he wrote of his Negro performers that "they took on their roles without self-consciousness as if they were the Saints they said they were. They moved and sang with grace, gave meaning to my music and made the Stein text easy to accept."

Thomson had already chosen as his musical director Alexander Smallens, assistant to Leopold Stokowski in Philadelphia. Now he came up with one final artistic suggestion which he had been reluctant to express until he had a director. In our first interview he had told me, "I don't really want them to act. I want them to be moved." Since I had never staged a play, let alone an opera or a musical, he suggested that I might welcome the aid of a choreographer, to which I immediately agreed. He had first considered

Agnes De Mille, then switched to a young English dancer whom he had met with the Askews in London and whose work at Sadler's Wells he had never seen. His name was Frederick Ashton;* he knew the opera and was eager to work on it. With my approval a cable was sent to London by the Askews inviting him to come over immediately. He arrived within ten days, third class, and moved into the guest bedroom that had just been vacated by the Irish novelist Elizabeth Bowen. That and the ten dollars a week pocket money he received during rehearsal were his only remuneration. He was a delight to work with: except for occasional brief spasms of homesickness, he was gay, free, self-confident, infinitely resourceful and imaginative and dearly beloved by everyone with whom he worked.

Our next urgent task was to assemble singers and chorus. To advise us in this we engaged an elegant, soft-spoken, very thin young Negro named Edward Perry. He was a member of Edna Thomas' sophisticated circle in Harlem and, besides, knew something of show business. It was Perry who pointed out that the famed Hall Johnson singers, whom Virgil had so admired in *Run Little Chillun!*, rehearsed and sang mostly by rote. Virgil felt this would delay us unduly. Perry then suggested a lady named Eva Jessye, whose group was small but of high musical standards. Virgil met her, interrogated her, heard her singers and approved. From then on, daily auditions were held—for the chorus uptown by Miss Jessye, for the principals in the Askews' living room.

Our first and easiest casting was for the part of St. Ignatius. Edward Matthews was a short, light-skinned baritone, a concert singer of some reputation whom Virgil engaged immediately. Most difficult to find was the soprano—St. Teresa I. We interviewed a diva named Caterina Jarboro who had recently sung *Aïda* at the Hippodrome and in Rome. She received us in her apartment with her agent, voice coach and accompanist present and, after much conversation, sang for Virgil, who thought she had a fine voice. But about that time someone discovered, in a

* Sir Frederick Ashton, C.B.E., for seventeen years director and principal choreographer of Britain's Royal Ballet.

church in Brooklyn or Queens, a high soprano named Beatrice Robinson-Wayne. She was a plain middle-aged lady, pug-nosed and pigeon-toed; but her voice was sensational and she had all the things Virgil was looking for—the clear speech and the rapt, simple, dedicated quality of a Saint.

We engaged her and never regretted it. And we teamed her with a contralto St. Teresa II, a voluptuous, lethargic girl whose lover, a liveried chauffer, used to collect her at rehearsals and beat her from time to time. Our Saint Settlement sang like an angel, and for St. Chavez, the saintly intermediary, we found a brilliant high tenor who could not stay on pitch and had to be replaced. The Commère and Compère, being constantly on stage, required presence, variety and charm, which we found in the persons of Abner Dorsey, a former small-time vaudeville performer, and Altonnell Hines, a lovely, slender honey-colored girl —very dignified and very chic in the red paillette evening dress which Florine designed for her in the first act, white tulle ruffles in the second and black paillettes for the third. The Compère wore a stiff black Spanish hat and tails.

Rehearsals started in mid-December in an atmosphere of love in the basement of St. Philip's Episcopal Church on 137th Street. It was the first time I had worked in Harlem—almost the first time I had seen it by day. Every morning I rode north on the Lexington Avenue express; twice each day I made the underground transition from white to black and back to white in the evening. North of 125th Street I found another world, a world of poverty and desolation and fear where the winter winds seemed to blow twenty degrees colder than downtown and one could smell decay and despair in the uncollected garbage in the streets. But in our clean, stuffy church basement, all through Christmas and into the New Year, we were crowded and warm and secluded and busy. Visitors came up from time to time: Kate Lawson would arrive with cutters and fitters from Helene Pons, who was making our costumes at cost to keep her shop open during that Depression winter. Alexander Smallens appeared periodically, listened, consulted his score and departed. Feder, the passionate lighting expert from Carnegie Tech, showed up with an assistant and pads on which they scrawled page after page of notes and diagrams. Lee Miller came with flashbulbs and took our pictures. Virgil Thomson seemed satisfied:

> The production grew as naturally as a tree. I kept the tempos firm and the words clear while Ashton choreographed the action, standing as choreographers like to do in center stage, and moving the singers around him, at first with their music scripts in hand, so that movements and music all came to be learned together. And Houseman surveyed us all as if unworried, watched over us like some motherly top sergeant and kept the bookkeeping vague.*

One of the main problems of rehearsing in Harlem, I had been warned, was keeping the company together amid the intolerable poverty and harassment in which most of them were living. With Eva Jessye and Perry, I arrived at a figure of fifteen dollars a week to be paid from the first day of rehearsal. We had a few inevitable dropouts, but we succeeded in holding together, for seven weeks, a company of eighteen principals, a chorus of twenty, and six dancers. This was attributable partly to the unusual rehearsal pay but, even more, I believe, to the excitement they were beginning to feel in their work. Here was a chance to get away from the usual musical-comedy, vaudeville and nightclub routines, the standard spirituals and church music they were accustomed to singing. And the people they worked with were different: for Virgil, with his clipped, meticulous severity, they developed a growing musical and personal respect; they found me formal but sympathetic and fair; Freddy was funny, adorable and quite unlike anyone they had ever known. One after another, as rehearsals progressed, they seemed to get the feeling that they were involved in something unique and memorable.

This sense of excitement grew steadily throughout the final weeks of rehearsal. It spread from the basement of St. Philip's Church through Harlem, downtown, until finally, fanned by our demon press agent, Nathan Zatkin, it reached Times Square.

---

* *Virgil Thomson* by Virgil Thomson (Alfred A. Knopf).

The New York Times made Sunday mention of us in its music and drama columns, and the *Herald Tribune,* figuring Miss Stein was always good for a laugh, sent up a bright young reporter named Joseph Alsop to do a short, funny piece on us. He arrived before noon and stayed through the evening:

> Arias and recitatives like no hymns that St. Philip's protestant Episcopal Sunday School children ever sang are echoing through the old church building. Beneath decorated texts in the dark basement *Four Saints in Three Acts* is slowly taking shape and it begins to look as if the mysterious woman so long laughed at would at last be justified to the world—and by Harlem. . . . They did the Prelude to the first act with a strange, long repetition of the phrase "Once in a while," a long series of variations on "When, then" which managed to be anything but ridiculous and a beautiful lyric passage on the words "The scene is changing from the morning to the morning" which seemed to bring a whole dawn into the Sunday school room.

Soon after the New Year we started run-throughs of the first and second acts with Virgil conducting and a very small black girl with thick glasses thumping away on the piano. Meanwhile, the other elements of the production were gradually coming together. My working arrangement with Virgil Thomson was unspoken and simple: in all musical matters and in those areas where his artistic choices had already been made, I deferred to his judgments and did my best to understand and execute them. For the rest he showed complete faith in me and supported without question the countless decisions I was forced to make day by day and sometimes hour by hour.

I spent half my day supervising rehearsals, the other half dealing with problems that were technical, economic and personal. Florine Stettheimer, for one, could never quite accept the limitations of the theatre and of our budget. She was disappointed that the tiny glass beads she had strung on a wire loop to represent the Cathedral portals on her model could not be translated into huge cut-crystal balls on the stage. She worried about the expression on the face of the lion. She wanted an antique lace frame around the proscenium arch and spurned the machine-made stuff that Kate Lawson managed to supply at a reasonable price. Finally, there was the sky—the dazzling cellophane cyclorama, which measured one foot square on her model and fifteen hundred square feet on the stage. Cellophane was a comparatively new substance which had never been used in the theatre. It took Kate two weeks to find a manufacturer who was willing to mount it on a cotton mesh strong enough to sustain, without tearing, the huge weight of those thousands of square feet of tufted and festooned cyclorama. It would take another three weeks to make and deliver it. This brought us dangerously close to our dress-rehearsal date of February 3rd, but we had no choice.

In mid-January I made one final addition to the dramatis personae of our project. As rehearsals developed and the public interest in *Four Saints* grew, it occurred to me that if the opera was all that we hoped it was, it would be a pity to limit its performance to five showings in a 299-seat house in Hartford, Connecticut. Our original sponsors—The Friends and Enemies of Modern Music—were having trouble enough raising their promised ten thousand dollars. Any further financing would have to come from New York, and I knew enough of the theatre to realize that no regular Broadway producer or angel would touch us. Harry Moses was no regular producer. Having made his pile in ladies' hosiery in Chicago, he had arrived in New York with his wife (an eager, talkative lady with artistic aspirations) and, before long, had become the principal backer and co-producer with Herman Shumlin of Vicki Baum's enormously successful *Grand Hotel*, followed by a production of *The Warrior's Husband* that had made a star of Katharine Hepburn. Since then he had been waiting for something prestigious to strike his fancy. I called on him, showed him the Alsop piece and other press references to our existence, then invited him and his wife to St. Philip's to one of our advanced rehearsals. They were impressed by what they saw and heard and by the artistic and social tone of the enterprise. And they were agreeably surprised to discover that I was not asking them for money but only for their interest in bringing the opera to New York if it proved successful in Hartford.

By mid-January we were deep into the third act. Freddy caught the flu and was away for two days; I took over and staged the vision of the Holy Ghost to Virgil's satisfaction. Then it was my turn to be absent for a day on personal business—theatre business.

Lovers, Happy Lovers (its named changed to *And Be My Love*) had reached Canada soon after the New Year and was announced to open at the Ritz Theatre in New York in the last week in January. Three months earlier it had carried all my theatrical hopes. Now I awaited its coming without excitement or pleasure. It was something out of the past that I would have preferred to bury and forget. I attended its one and only dress rehearsal, and it depressed me. I went to the first night by myself, watched it as though it were someone else's work, hated almost every moment of it, thanked the cast and walked home alone in the rain.

Next morning's notices were less lethal than I had feared. Brooks Atkinson of the *Times,* in a review headed "Three Acts of Philandering," found it "a flawless comedy, though dull." It was already closed when Robert Benchley (Galantière's good friend in whose suite at the Royalton some scenes of the play had been written) penned its epitaph for *The New Yorker:*

> There is nothing particularly wrong with *And Be My Love* except that there is nothing particularly right about it. . . . I can best give you an idea of the type of play it is by telling you that a manservant confides he always knows when his master is beginning a new affair when he orders "soufflé exquis" and that he is terminating one when he orders "crêpes Suzette" for the *diner à deux.*

By then I was beyond hurt in Connecticut, wholly absorbed in the final rehearsals of *Four Saints in Three Acts.*

*   *   *

On the afternoon of Wednesday, February 1, 1934, Virgil and I were driven up to Hartford, to be followed by Freddy and the company two days later. It was near zero when we arrived and it grew colder from day to day. Each evening thousands of starlings, chirping piteously, sought refuge under the eaves of the Wadsworth Athenaeum. But inside all was light and beauty and warmth. Unlike most new buildings, the Avery Memorial wing was complete and ready for its inauguration. Designed under Austin's guidance in a conservative modern style, it rose around a main courtyard of white marble with two cantilevered balconies, each with a gallery behind it. Feeling that a modern form with so much flat surface needed contrast, Chick had installed a baroque Italian fountain topped by a marble female nude twelve to fifteen feet high, gracious and full of curves, in the center of this severe contemporary interior. It was all magically illuminated as we arrived; so were the upper galleries in which the Picasso retrospective—with pictures ranging from before the pink and blue periods to the newest bones, from placid classic giantesses to two small rape scenes hardly larger than postage stamps—was already hung, violent and startling in its brilliant variety against the white walls.

Austin was there to welcome us and proudly took us on a grand tour of the Museum, ending with his new theatre in the basement. Then he drove us to his house for dinner, the last serious meal I was to have in a week. Over brandy, under the seventeenth-century Venetian panels, which were his latest acquisition, he informed us with a boyish smile that the Friends and Enemies were in a financial bind. The ticket sale was going swimmingly: we were already sold out for three of our five performances. Unfortunately most of the tickets had been ordered by out-of-towners and would not be paid for until the people arrived. I pointed out that the cast and technicians expected to be paid before the weekend. Chick said he would try to think of something. Then he drove me back to the theatre where Feder and his men were at work spotting lines and hanging equipment on the empty stage. They were a curious crew: his close friend and counsellor, Teddy Thomas (born

Tomashevsky of the illustrious Yiddish theatre dynasty), and a silent apprentice whose name I never knew—not even when he sliced off the tip of his little finger while cutting gelatins at five in the morning and we had to drive him to the hospital to have it sewn back on while Feder kept abusing him for getting blood on the equipment. Chief of the local helpers was a gargoyle of a man, bald as an egg, with a huge beak of a nose, a former acrobat and escape artist, whom Chick used as an assistant and victim in his magic shows. Since he was also something of a human fly, it was he who was sent up the high ladders to do all the impossible jobs. He never complained, but during one of our interminable night shifts we were startled by a loud, continuous, hollow banging overhead. It was the escape artist, high up on a twenty-foot ladder, bashing his head against the back wall of the theatre to keep himself awake.

I have said that the new wing was complete: this was not strictly true. Since the theatre lacked rigging, ropes, pipe, cable and many of the necessities of a professional stage, several cars and a truck were in constant motion between New York and Hartford that week bringing urgently needed equipment, over two hundred costumes, our so fragile props and the huge mass of our cellophane firmament, which arrived with Kate Lawson on Thursday morning and took all of that day and most of the following night to install. Owing to the lowness of the proscenium and grid it was impossible to achieve the feeling of sky and space suggested in Florine's models. Kate solved this, in part, by sewing hundreds of tapes into the mesh and then using these to create an infinite number of cellophane loops, which gave the impression of a grand opera drape ready to soar into the flies at any moment.

The company arrived with Freddy by bus at noon on Friday. They were greeted by the Negro Chamber of Commerce and billeted in black households all over town. That afternoon we began transferring our rehearsal movements to the stage. We worked until midnight, then sent the company home till noon of the next day. As the singers left, the technicians moved in and began their nightly task of lighting the show.

Abe Feder was the first of the prima donnas in the American lighting field. *Four Saints* was his big chance, and he was determined to make the most of it at no matter what human cost. Lighting in those days, before electronic switchboards and reasonably reliable intercommunication systems existed, was an agonizing process of trial and error, of exasperated howling back and forth between the front and back of the house. And Florine Stettheimer's decor, with its dazzling, diamond-bright background was, in Feder's words, "a creeping bitch"—especially the first act, which she wanted inundated with pure white light. In vain Feder attempted to explain (to Florine, to Virgil, to me, to anyone who would listen) that there was no such thing as white light in the spectrum—that it was obtained by the expert mixing of primary colors projected through various shades of red, blue and yellow gelatin in the two hundred or more projectors with which he had covered the ceiling and sides of Chick's theatre. Florine repeated that she wanted clear white light—as in her model. Feder refused to believe her. For three successive nights he had the escape artist and his crew clambering up and down ladders, changing gelatins, which he then blended with infinite care and skill at diverse intensities. And each morning, when he proudly exhibited his night's work to Florine, she would say quietly that what she wanted was clear white light. Reluctant and unconvinced, he finally gave it to her at dress rehearsal, and she was grateful. He had a more rewarding time with the light blues and greens of the second act picnic and deeper cobalt of the Spanish sky darkening for the appearance of the Holy Ghost and achieving a livid splendor during the procession in the third.

On Sunday afternoon, with Kate Lawson alternately scolding and cajoling, we held a dress parade—act by act. (Florine was pleased on the whole but horrified to discover that the Saints' hands were bare—and dark! White gloves were rushed from New York for the opening.) This was followed by a run-through in costume with props. (Florine was satisfied with the lion but desired more palm trees.) When it was over, I invited the company to meet me in the main court in front of the baroque marble nude. Against this impressive background, at one-thirty in the morning, I told them of the Friends and Enemies' financial straits. They looked at me and said nothing. I said we would be most grateful if they could wait until opening night for their money. Though most of them must have been close to penniless, not one of them demanded payment.

The next morning Alex Smallens and his orchestra of twenty arrived from New York and held their first musical reading in the pit, which could barely hold them. This resulted in one of our worst crises, the only time in thirty-seven years I have seen Virgil Thomson seriously shaken. To save money, he and Maurice had prepared the orchestral score together on the Mediterranean island of Porquerolles the previous summer: Virgil composing in pencil at the rate of ten pages a day and Maurice keeping up with him, going over the notes in ink. Proofreading by eye (no piano being available) proved unreliable: hundreds of errors survived in the score and were copied into the orchestral parts. Smallens was furious as hours and hundreds of dollars in musicians' overtime were spent while Virgil, white and tight-lipped, corrected his errors. But by the next evening we were ready to hold our first full dress rehearsal with orchestra. It ran far into the night with only one major blowup—the classic conflict of conductor and director over performers so placed on the stage that they had difficulty in following the beat. Smallens was a bully and a shouter. His yelling drove Freddy Ashton up the aisle in tears, stopping long enough to shout "I have worked with Sir Thomas Beecham! A genius! And he never spoke to me as you have!" before leaving the theatre. Since it was fifteen below zero outside, he returned almost immediately and the rehearsal continued. When it was over, members of the Saints' chorus on the upper tier of their pyramidal bleachers on either side of the stage complained that their off-stage ears had been blistered by seven hours of continuous exposure to Feder's massed overhead projectors.

On February 7th and 8th the New Haven Railroad added extra parlor cars to its afternoon train for the New York fashionables, the press and members of the international art world coming to Hartford to honor the new wing's opening and to see the Picasso show and the opera. It was known that Mrs. Harrison

Williams, America's perennial best-dressed woman of the year, had ordered a special dress for the occasion: a cocktail dress on the train, it loosened to full-length for the reception and the theatre. I remember that evening vaguely as through a bright, heavy haze: the terrible cold outside as the cars began to arrive and the starlings screaming their heads off and the galleries overhead filled with people in evening dress with champagne glasses in their hands moving among the strong colors of the Picasso canvases.

Backstage everyone except me seemed surprisingly confident and relaxed. Fifteen minutes before curtain time I went out to get a breath of air. The birds were still screeching, and as I stood in the street for a moment, pierced by the icy wind, I became aware of an astonishing thing: silently, as in some German film of the early twenties, there appeared out of the darkness a huge smooth object unlike anything I had ever seen. Black and shiny and shaped like a gigantic raindrop, it came to a stop before the Museum; and from a sliding panel in its side stepped two beautiful ladies, one blonde and one dark, in shimmering evening dresses accompanied by a small, wiry, balding man in a dinner jacket who, I discovered later, was Buckminster Fuller, creator of the Dymaxion car (of which this was the first specimen) escorting Dorothy Hale and Clare Boothe. Leaving their vehicle at the curb, they entered the building and disappeared into the crowd that was beginning to flow down from the galleries into the theatre.

When I got back downstairs the Saints were assembling on the stage, ascending their pyramids and checking their costumes and props. At 8:47 Chick Austin appeared to tell us that everyone was seated and we could begin. We embraced each other. Then the Saints took their opening positions and waited for the sharp drum roll that announced the start of the opera.

Since I spent the entire time of the performance rushing around backstage, checking entrances, light cues, props and effects, I do not have the faintest recollection of how the opera looked or sounded that night. Virgil was pleased and so, apparently—each in his own way—were our distinguished audience and critics:

When the bright red curtain went up or, rather, was pulled apart, there was a gasp of astonishment and delight. This audience all knew something about pictures and could see at once that the Saint kneeling in front and clad in voluminous purple silk was quite as ecstatic as anything El Greco had ever devised in that line, and that the costumes of the two Saint Teresas as well as the effect produced by the cellophane background and the remarkable lighting were all addressed to the painter's eye.

So wrote the art critic of the New York *Sun*. A music critic, in a review headed ECCLESIASTICAL RAG, found the opera replete with "hints of blues songs, Negro spirituals, folk carols and recitatives with an ecclesiastical flavor." The dance critic of *The New York Times* found it "the most interesting experiment that has been made here in many seasons and the most enlightening." An excited gentleman in tails was heard to declare, "It's like Grand Opera only it's got more sense!," while Carl Van Vechten, ever enthusiastic, wrote a letter to the *Times* the next morning giving it as his opinion that "this performance of *Four Saints* is just about as perfect as would seem humanly possible." The United Press informed its millions of readers that the show might anger and annoy them, but like a war or a flood, they would regret having missed it. Stark Young pronounced it "the most important event of the season—important because it is theatre and flies off the ground, most important because it is delightful and joyous and delight is the fundamental of all art, great and small."

But it was Lucius Beebe, columnist for the *Herald Tribune*, who gave the premiere its most vivid sociological coverage:

> By Rolls Royce, by airplane, by Pullman compartment and, for all we know, by specially designed Cartier pogosticks the art enthusiasts of the country descended on Hartford last night in a manner that would have made Mr. Keats's foldbound Assyrians the merest amateurs. . . . The curtain was conveniently late and everyone had a chance to make at least two grand entrees and some of the more enterprising got around as many as five times. But the real show was at

the intermissions. For the first five minutes conversation was
as guarded as that in a Pullman smoker in wartime. But as
soon as Messrs. Kirk Askew and Julien Levy burst into un-
abashed tears because they "didn't know anything so beautiful could be done in America," the hysteria was on and a
blizzard of superlatives was in progress, with little groups
letting down their back hair and crying quietly in corners
for beauty. . . .

After the last curtain there was an uproar that would have
brought the police from the Central Station if Mr. Austin
hadn't warned them in advance. There were curtain calls by
the score. Professor Hitchcock of Wesleyan smashed his opera
hat with gay abandon and called for Mr. Thomson. Mr.
Thomson made a bow. Professor Hitchcock tore open his
collar and shouted for Mr. Austin. Mr. Austin made a bow
to a bedlam and a sea of fluttering handkerchiefs. It was a
good thing for the proprieties that there weren't many more
people to call for.* After that everyone went on to an enormous party at Mr. Austin's—not forgetting to take their programs which contained a portrait of Mr. Thomson by Miss
Stein beginning "Yes ally yes as ally"—and called it a night.

The party, unlike the performance, is entirely clear in my
memory, with Salvador Dali, seated in a love seat in Chick's drawing room beside the wife of one of Hartford's most enlightened
young art lovers, gazing intently at the mother-of-pearl buttons
on the bosom of her dress and inquiring courteously, as I happened to pass by, if they were edible. (*Madame, ces boutons,
sont-ils comestibles?*) In the next room Nicolas Nabokov, exasperated by the triumph of the international epicenes, sat at a
piano thumping out Russian folk songs, in which he was joined
by a male chorus that included the poet Archibald MacLeish and
other red-blooded Americans. The next night we danced till
dawn at a ball given by the Negro Chamber of Commerce, and

---

*Russell Hitchcock's enthusiasm must have been prodigious that evening,
for another reporter described him as "red-bearded, with flaming eyes,
running up and down the aisle screaming bravos and tearing his stiff-
bosomed shirt into shreds with each huzzah."

on Saturday we gave our two final performances to sold-out, cheering houses.

By then several things had happened: the cast had been paid in full, the artistic success of the opera was established and Harry Moses, throwing caution to the winds, had announced our New York opening for Tuesday, February 20 at the 44th Street Theatre, half a block from Times Square.

With that, our struggle against seemingly impossible odds began afresh. We had exactly one week to transfer a production that had been conceived and designed for a miniature theatre to one of the largest musical-comedy houses on Broadway. The human elements gave us little trouble. Virgil and Smallens decided to increase the chorus by four and the orchestra by two. Both sounded better in the new house, while our Saints, accustomed to vast halls and cavernous churches, had no difficulty in filling the fourteen-hundred-seat auditorium with their voices. Freddy was delighted to expand movements that had been cramped for space in the Athenaeum. Once again, it was with the scenic aspects of the production that we had our most serious problems—technical and emotional.

One afternoon in midweek, Lee Shubert, from whom we had leased the theatre and whose interest had been aroused by our first three days' box-office action, walked into the back of the theatre, watched part of a run-through and asked when the scenery was arriving. Informed that this was it, he smiled contemptuously and left. On that vast bare stage, without costumes and under the cruel glare of a worklight, our set pieces and props, which had been so greatly admired in Hartford, must have seemed pitifully flimsy and small. To correct this and to reduce the immense stage opening, Kate Lawson rented a black velour portal with which she framed in the stage to a reasonable width; she also found a new red velvet inner curtain, brighter and twice the size of the first. We extended our third-act wall, doubled the size of our cellophane sunburst and the number of our tarlatan trees. Our greatest difficulty was with the sky, which now reached barely halfway up the back wall of the 44th Street Theatre. A squadron of seamstresses added several hundred square feet of cellophane and mesh left over from our original order and redraped the entire firmament in huge festoons that rose fifty feet into the air. To illuminate this enormous surface Feder emptied New York's electrical supply houses of projectors and cable, which he added to our already lavish equipment.

He came close to not using any of it. Exactly fifty hours before the opening, just as rehearsal was breaking up, the fire marshal entered the theatre, walked up to our highly publicized cellophane cyclorama, took out a penknife, cut off a strip, set a match to it and dropped it just in time to save his hand from being burned. One minute later, while the flames from the glue and the cellophane were still licking the stage floor, he left the building, having condemned every single physical element of our production—our sky, our sunburst, our arch, our grass mats and our tarlatan trees.

For a long time no one spoke. There was nothing to say. Even if we could find other equivalent materials, which seemed unlikely, it would take a week or more to rebuild the production. Our opening was two nights away and sold out. It could not be canceled or postponed without puncturing the rising excitement which the Hartford reports, fanned by Zatkin's whirlwind publicity campaign, had stirred up among New York's fashionable theatregoers. Kate was pale and grim and Feder chewed at his moustache. Then just in time to save Harry Moses (who had already spent close to ten thousand dollars) from slitting his throat, some young fellow in the Shubert maintenance department suggested we try a chemical substance known as "waterglass." Within an hour a bucket of it was in the theatre and several square feet of the cyclorama had been smeared with the viscous and smelly substance. Hurridly dried under fans and projectors, it formed a stiff, grayish, transparent skin. A match was held to it, then a piece of flaming newspaper. Nothing happened. The fire marshal was located backstage in some Broadway theatre and arrived shortly before midnight, grumbling, with an assistant. They, too, applied matches, a candle, finally a blow torch and said they'd be back in the morning.

ACT ONE

All that night, on double and triple time, men on ladders with huge brushes and buckets sloshed gallons of water-glass over our beautiful, draped sky, while others toiled, high up on the grid, under Kate's direction, putting in new lines to carry the huge added weight of our tarnished firmament. By dawn we were done, dry by noon, and formally okayed in time for our final dress rehearsal. (If the cellophane lost a little of its brilliance, it was not noticeable from the front under lights. But during the entire run of *Four Saints*, all day and all night, under the glare of Feder's projectors or in the darkness of the empty theatre, there was the constant faint sound of falling rain as thousands of little globs of crusted water-glass flaked and dripped off the cyclorama onto the stage floor below.) Having grudgingly accepted our cellophane sky, the Fire Department vented its spleen on Florine's starched tarlatan trees, each branch of which had to be dipped, in the marshal's presence, into a strong fireproof liquid. When dried they sagged pathetically, having lost both shape and color. We salved our artistic consciences and endangered our singers' and audiences' lives every night by replacing these fireproofed fronds, just before curtain time, with crisp, bright, fresh tarlatan leaves, which Kate Lawson removed and locked away the moment the curtain had fallen.

WHO SAYS EVERYONE IS IN FLORIDA?
asked Cholly Knickerbocker of his readers the next morning as he described the premiere of *Four Saints* in Hearst's *American*:

> Every row of seats in the 44th Street Theatre held its quota of names from the Social Register and the Intelligentsia.
> From the latter was Neysa McMein, the "never-say-die" originator of parlor games whose escort was Bob Benchley, Alan Campbell seated in Row A with one who looked suspiciously like that "champeen wise-cracker" Dorothy Parker, Blanche Knopf with Douglas Parmentier and ever so many more intelligent souls.
> Among the Social Registerites who laughed, cheered or snorted at *Four Saints* were Cecil Beaton and Michael Herbert who had the fascinating Tilly Losch in tow; Symphorosa

121

Bristed, wearing a neat-looking diamond tiara; the ermine-enveloped Lucia Davidova, Isabel Townsend Pell, Mrs. "Bill" Rockefeller and numerous Ryans.

Also from the fashion-belt I noted the Chlodowig-Hohenlohe-Schillingfursts (Mabel left the next day for Palm Beach), "Mudge" Howard who insisted that she was going in strongly in her future decorative schemes for cellophane; pretty blonde Mrs. Grant Mason and Mrs. Herbert Simpson, who was seated in the rear of the Orchestra—not quite the place for a lady who assumed such an imperial social air.

We opened in a blizzard. Snow had begun to fall in the night and became thicker and heavier through the day. By midafternoon there was more than a foot of it in the streets and traffic came to a stop all over the city. But the press and the fourteen hundred "members of the Social Register and Intelligentsia" who formed our opening night audience were made of sterner stuff. They sensed an event and they were not going to miss it for fifteen inches of snow.*

The curtain went up almost half an hour late. Once again I stood breathless, backstage, waiting for the sharp opening drum roll and for the crimson curtain to rise on the lone purple figure kneeling at the edge of the stage. When it did, it was immediately apparent from the difference in the sounds out front how dissimilar the mood of these Broadway first-nighters was from the knowledgeable intimacy of our audiences at the Athenaeum. They applauded the opening tableau, but the early scenes of the two Teresas in Avila, "half in and half out of doors," were received, as they had not been in Hartford, with ripples of self-conscious and slightly embarrassed laughter. It was only gradually, as the two ladies in their red cardinal's robes went about their saintly business "seated and not standing half and half of it and not half and half of it seated," while the chorus made it clear

---

* Playing it safe, Zatkin had sent tickets to every drama critic, music critic, art critic, book critic, fashion reporter and sportswriter in New York. It worked. According to *Variety*, *Four Saints* got more coverage than any other opening of that or any other recent season.

that "Saint Teresa can know the difference between singing and women" and that

> Saint Teresa could be photographed having
> been dressed like a lady and then they taking
> out her head and changed it to a nun and a
> nun a saint and a saint so

that the magic of the opera really began to work. With the entrance of Saint Ignatius in green moiré silk—

> A scene and withers.
> Scene three and scene two.
> Pear trees cherry blossoms pink blossoms
> and late apples and surrounded by Spain
> and lain

the issue was no longer in doubt. As the curtain fell on the first act, I ran out the stage door through the snow and arrived in the lobby just in time to meet the first wave of emerging fashionables. Five minutes later I raced back to give the cast the news that all was very well.

I went out front once again near the end of the last act. Anxious to see the effect of our procession on a large stage before a full house, I joined the crowd of standees that had accumulated in the rear of the theatre. From there I watched the front of the double line appear far downstage left, chanting as they advanced slowly—

> Letting pin in letting let in let in in
> in in in let in wet in wed in dead

all forty-four of them, moving from left to right across the stage, their black-and-white cloaks and hoods and banners silhouetted against the livid sky, till they filled the entire proscenium and stood there swaying gently in their solemn, syncopated, baroque funeral march:

> With wed led said with led dead said
> with dead led said with said dead led
> wed said dead let dead led said wed

they sang fervently, their eyes raised to heaven; then, almost imperceptibly, their swaying became once more a slow forward motion till they were lost to sight and their voices died away in the darkness of the wings.

The closing scene of the opera was short and bright and melodious. And as the crimson curtain fell quickly on the Chorus' final, abrupt "Which is a fact!" I heard for the first time in my life that most wonderful of all backstage sounds—the brief, terrifying silence followed by the sudden crash of applause from a huge, invisible audience, breaking in great waves against the velvet wall behind which it could be heard beating like an angry, insistent flood. When the curtain finally rose again it was as though a dam had burst. With a triumphant roar, through which I could vaguely distinguish the sharper tones of cheers and bravos, it came rushing at us out of the darkness, sweeping over the bright-lit stage, overwhelming the small, solemnly bowing figures of our astounded Saints.

I have no idea how many curtain calls we took that night. Smallens appeared out of the pit and was dragged on stage, his collar wilted, his tails flying behind him as he waved the orchestra to its feet. It was Virgil's turn after that, amid a new burst of bravos. With formal precision, his patent leather shoes held tightly together, he kissed the hands of the two Saint Teresas, then (since Miss Stein was in Paris and Florine was unwilling to appear) summoned Freddy and me from the wings. Flowers were handed up in the best operatic tradition as bow followed bow. Still, the audience refused to budge, and we went on bowing and smiling as wave after wave of sound swept over us and the sweating stagehands, like demented bell ringers, hauled away at their ropes, sending the huge curtain up and down, up and down till, finally, in sheer exhaustion, they stopped and the audience slowly evacuated the theatre. And when it was all over and the Saints had gone off to their dressing rooms and the crew had cleared the deck on which a single, bare worklight remained burning, I found myself alone in the sudden stillness, lying front and center of that vast, dark, empty stage, with my face against the splintered wooden floor, sobbing like a child.

Four Saints in Three Acts ran for four weeks in the vastness of the 44th Street Theatre in what was at the time (before *Porgy and Bess* and *The Medium*) the longest continuous run ever enjoyed by an American opera. Our gross receipts wavered between twelve and fourteen thousand dollars a week.*
In our fourth week, in what *Variety* described as "a hearty jump considering weather" we went over fifteen thousand. This so encouraged Harry Moses, though he complained incessantly that the venture was ruining him and made weekly attempts to cut our royalties and percentages, that he decided to extend our run. Since the 44th Street was already booked for an incoming musical, we moved our cellophane sky, still dripping water glass, to the Empire Theatre three blocks away, for an additional two weeks. That Sunday evening I conducted Saint Teresa I to her dressing room, the shrine of so many illustrious ladies—from Helen Hayes and Katharine Cornell up the years to Ethel Barrymore and Maude Adams. Mrs. Robinson-Wayne, who, until two months before, had never dressed anywhere but in a church vestry, was unimpressed. Surveying the room with its silken draperies and large window, she said she was afraid it might be a bit drafty.
The Empire was everyone's favorite New York theatre, and I was proud and excited at the idea of occupying it, even for a short time. In that glamorous and perfectly proportioned house, with Virgil Thomson conducting his own work, the Saints looked and sounded better than they ever had before. We played to fair houses the first ten days, then to standing room only for the rest of the run when it became known that this was the public's final

* Our Broadway competition in this worst winter of the Great Depression included *Ah Wilderness, All the King's Men, As Thousands Cheer, Dodsworth, The Green Bay Tree, Mary of Scotland, Men in White, Roberta, Richard of Bordeaux, She Loves Me Not, Tobacco Road, Yellow Jack* and *They Shall Not Die.*

chance to see this astonishing work. Our last night was wildly emotional, with much embracing and shedding of tears.

Lying in my narrow bed on 57th Street the morning after our closing, I felt like a man reluctantly awakening out of a delightful dream. For fifteen enchanted weeks I had been wholly absorbed in the opera and its production, committed without reservation to a creative project in which I was playing an indispensable part with people whom I loved and admired.

Now suddenly it was over. The small world to which I had belonged for four months was breaking up: Freddy Ashton had returned to England two days after our opening; Kate Lawson was back with the Theatre Guild; Feder was ranging Broadway in search of new electrical opportunities. Only Virgil remained through our run at the Empire: then he too sailed away to report to Miss Stein in Paris and to spend the summer composing there.

After the final curtain I watched the Saints clear the dressing rooms of their scant personal belongings before vanishing into the night from which they had emerged to appear in our opera. With their going I suffered a sentimental and physical loss; I had become accustomed to their warm, rich world of color and scent and resonance: its sudden withdrawal made the all-white world to which I was returning seem pale and arid and cold.

The next day I stood around while the show was dismantled, the rented crimson curtain returned to its owners and the rest of the things that had been so much admired—the costumes, lion, portal, tarlatan trees and cellophane sky—packed and sent to storage.* And when it was all done and the trucks had driven off,

* *Four Saints* was resurrected that fall by a six-foot-three female impresario who presented it in Chicago in the great Sullivan Auditorium. In that shabby golden shell, with its huge stage opening, some of the impact and brilliance of the show was lost. But the acoustics were good and there was one element in our Chicago engagement which had been missing in New York—the presence of Miss Stein herself. She was in America lecturing and arrived with Miss Toklas in a specially chartered plane which our impresario had filled with American Beauty roses and a sign reading "A rose is a rose is a rose." I sat silent on her left at the supper that was given in her honor after opening night. She was formidable but agreeable and declared herself pleased with the work.

a deep gloom descended upon me. In four months I had become used to friendship, responsibility and power. Now these were being taken from me. Once again I was alone, and though my tide of fear never again reached its earlier high-water mark, I was aware of its constant, hateful murmur as I found myself beginning to worry, once again, about my future.

III

THE SUCCESS of *Four Saints in Three Acts* had been phenomenal but not decisive. It earned me a reputation in certain circles for organizing ability, taste and a capacity for creative collaboration from which I continued to profit for years to come. But it brought me no immediate professional credit in the commercial world of Broadway. Rather it marked me as a maverick and a highbrow. In the weeks and months that followed I received no offers, no proposals, not even the conversational approaches to a theatrical job. I was not foolish enough to believe that another *Four Saints* would turn up in a hurry; on the other hand it was becoming clear that if I was to find a place for myself as a producer or director in the American theatre it must be in regions that were not normally attractive or accessible to my competitors. As I began to look around, it was only natural that my thoughts should once again turn north toward Harlem.

Through Edward Perry I had come to know the black poet Countee Cullen in whose dramatization of Arna Bontemps' novel *Never Come Sunday* I now became interested for its exciting production possibilities. While we were working on that we discussed other, more ambitious theatrical notions, among them one that James Light had put into my head months before. Both he and Countee were close friends of Rose McLendon, the Negro actress who had created Bess in *Porgy* and the mother in Paul Green's *In Abraham's Bosom*. Sober and in his cups, Jimmy kept telling me how great Rose would be as Medea—a dark, savage princess no longer young, betrayed by her white lover in the alien, hostile land to which she had followed him across the sea. Since no satisfactory text was available (Gilbert Murray's much admired Swinburnian verse being quite unsuitable) we set about preparing a version of Euripides' tragedy that would bear some relation to the style of Miss MacLendon's playing. Once again, that spring, I became a commuter on the IRT, shuttling between 57th Street and the corner of 123rd Street and Seventh Avenue, where Countee's adoptive father was minister of the Salem Methodist Church, one of the largest in Harlem. I brought with me the Greek text (which, thanks to my Clifton education, I was able to translate with the aid of a crib), a number of existing English versions and various other verse and prose ventures in classical adaptation, including those of Yeats, Cocteau and Gide.

We decided to do the personal scenes in prose; once the right tone was found, these were quickly done. The choruses in verse were more difficult and, when Countee had finished them, we sent them off to Virgil in Paris for his approval. He composed the *Medea* choruses in Europe that summer and brought them back with him when he returned to America in the fall.* By that time Chick Austin had designed a handsome Chiricoesque set with Minoan costumes and we were all set to do the *Medea*—with Rose MacLendon, a Negro women's chorus, two mulatto children and the rest of the cast white—as next winter's offering of The Friends and Enemies of Modern Music.

* They have been performed extensively over the years under the title —*Seven Choruses from the Medea of Euripides for Women's Voices and Percussion* (publ. G. Schirmer). They also appear in Countee Cullen's *Medea* (Harper and Row).

But that was still months away. And in the meantime I had received an offer which, when it was first made to me, seemed far too good to be true. Nathan Zatkin, our publicist for *Four Saints,* was a short, forbidding-looking man with curly blue-black hair, a beard that needed shaving three times a day and a small bulbous nose that was perpetually wreathed in smoke from the evil-smelling cigars he held clamped between his nutcracker jaws. Without his abominable personality he might have been another Ben Sonnenberg or even an Edward Bernays. As it was, he worked only occasionally and never long in one place. His private life seemed to be chaotic, and the incessant begging and borrowing with which he exasperated us all was generally attributable to some current personal crisis connected with one or other of the large, handsome, mostly gentile girls who occupied his life.

I met him first through Zita, who had known him at the Civic Repertory where he was doing press work for Eva Le Gallienne. When the time came to publicize *Four Saints* he was the first person I thought of. We could not afford a regular Broadway press agent; besides, I needed the total dedication and the particular combination of erudition and vulgarity that only Zatkin could bring to the task. His accomplishment exceeded my fondest hopes and taught me lessons in theatrical promotion that I have never forgotten.*

With the success of the opera Nathan Zatkin had tasted

* In a varied career Zatkin could boast of at least two other sensational successes. He was responsible for the international publicity received by the skinless hot dogs which their Britannic Majesties consumed as picnic guests of the Roosevelts in 1939. He also scored a near triumph when he was engaged by Warner Brothers to publicize Max Reinhardt's film of *A Midsummer Night's Dream.* In the weeks preceding the opening he spent several days in Washington conferring with Senator Carter Glass (framer of the Federal Reserve Act under Woodrow Wilson), who was a confirmed Baconian. According to Zatkin the Senator agreed to let the American Bacon Society, of which he was president, seek a court injunction against the film on the grounds of misrepresentation, since it was being advertised as written by William Shakespeare whereas it could be proved conclusively that it was the work of Francis Bacon. At the last moment the Senator reneged. But it was a notable idea.

theatrical blood. Publicity was no longer enough for him. He was seized with a raging desire to become a producer. Almost immediately, from a surprising quarter, the opportunity presented itself. He had an acquaintance, also formerly of the Civic Repertory, the granddaughter of one of New York City's most illustrious mayors. Considered for a time one of the more promising ingenues in the American theatre, she had come close to creating the part of Saint Joan for the Theatre Guild when Shaw's play was first done in New York. Now, at twenty-seven, Mary Hone was beautiful, intelligent, well-bred and talented—but no one was asking her to appear on the stage. It was at this point that a friend of the family, a platonic admirer and a man of means, offered to finance her to the tune of fifteen thousand dollars, to be used entirely at her discretion, for her appearance on Broadway in any part her heart desired. In her perplexity she turned for advice to Nathan Zatkin who, in febrile agitation, set about helping her to plan her production, which very soon became *his* production. One of the first things he did was to persuade her that, no matter what play she wanted to do, there was only one man worthy of directing her in it: his friend, the hero of *Four Saints in Three Acts*—John Houseman.

The trouble was—she knew exactly what play she wanted to do. Diffident and wavering in most respects, she revealed a will of iron in her choice of the piece on which she was about to spend her benefactor's money. Suffering, like so many serious young actresses of her day, from an Eleonora Duse obsession, this unfortunate girl decided to undertake, in her late twenties, a role which the Italian tragedienne had made famous in her sixties—that of Ibsen's *Lady from the Sea*. Stark Young, who wrote so perceptively of Duse's greatness, threw a revealing light on her interpretation of Ibsen's heroine:

> She thought Ibsen's play so completely unrealistic that she played Ellida as in a dream—a woman without age or place. To her, Ellida had only the reality of the ideal.

For a young woman of limited experience and modest personality to attempt such a part in the New York commercial theatre was deliberate suicide. We not only let her do it; we encouraged her and abetted her in her preparations. I am not too proud of my part in this conspiracy; I have always felt that in agreeing to direct *The Lady from the Sea* I participated in a con game of which Mary was the willing dupe. Yet it played such a vital part in my theatrical education that I cannot ignore it.

Zatkin had no such qualms. To be known as the producer of a serious play on Broadway he would, without hesitation, have assassinated his nearest and dearest. Besides, as a press agent by training and inclination, he had the capacity to persuade himself of whatever it was necessary for him to feel for the efficient execution of his job. Having once accepted the notion of presenting Mary Hone in *The Lady from the Sea*, he was no more capable of giving it up than a hungry dog is of dropping a half-eaten bone. In the end, he proved the less dishonorable of the two. As publicist for the production he fulfilled his function beyond reproach. As its director, I did not.

In some respects, I did a passable job of putting on *The Lady from the Sea*. Amateur though I was, I had intelligence, taste, a sense of style and a certain superficial competence, which I exercised in the selection of designer and cast. Donald Oenslager, the former, did so well that he stole the show; our actors were the best it was possible to assemble for such a maverick production. My failure lay not so much in the staging, which had a certain fluidity and style, as in my inability to bring any clear or unified concept of Ibsen's play onto the stage. Here, for the first time in my life—alone, incompetent and unprepared—I faced the challenge of translating a script of notorious difficulty into some sort of viable theatrical performance. In my own opinion, as in that of most of the critics, I did not meet it.

It took more than a dozen years of humiliation and suffering for me to assemble enough technical and psychological knowledge to walk into a rehearsal with some degree of assurance and a real, rather than a simulated confidence in my ability to control all the elements of a production. In *The Lady from the Sea* my shame and fear were almost unbearable, my ineptitude so glaring that I could conceal it from nobody—least of all, myself. The chief victim of this insecurity was Mary Hone. I had no experience in shaping a role of such magnitude and no technical or personal resources on which I could draw to sustain this sensitive but emotionally and professionally immature girl in her time of need. We opened on May 1st at the Little Theatre next to Sardi's, to reviews that were generally poor, with most critics divided between their dislike of the play and of my production. Most severe was Brooks Atkinson of the *Times,* who was exasperated by my "pallid direction" of "mincing folk who frankly seem to be lacking in thyroid. . . . Every Jack stammers before every Jill as though he were addressing a work of Dresden china." Stark Young, the only New York critic whose opinion I truly valued on such a production, devoted most of his review to an evocation of Duse's performance but found space for a few kind words about my direction:

> As a whole, the direction was easy, graceful and right. There was no highhorse Stonehenging about the scenes and there was, in general, a freshness of movement and position. Ibsen-directing like Mr. Houseman's, without cudgels and tests, is a promising sign.

After which he heaped what, in my state of sensitivity and guilt, I regarded as coals of fire upon my head:

> Ellida needs from Miss Hone who plays the part with real purity of intention more of a continuous absorption. She should, in her performance, permit herself more of the glamor and release possible to her temperament, technique and physical equipment.

By the time Mr. Young's review appeared in the *New Republic,* our raked platforms and stormy backdrops had already been reduced to ashes and I was moving toward the next painful stage of my theatrical education.

The day of our closing, to get away from *The Lady from the Sea,* I accepted Mina Curtiss' invitation to spend a week with her in the Berkshires. I had met her years before—as Mina Kirstein—

with Henrietta Bingham, but this was the first time I had been to Chapelbrook since her brief happy marriage to Harry Curtiss. There were changes—some they had made together, others she had made since his death. But it was still his house and in the sun and rain of that late spring it was filled with his presence. Before the fire at night—Mina seated on the low cobbler's bench with her dark, handsome head outlined against the flames—we talked of the past and of the strange ways of love, remembering my first sight of Chapelbrook under the snow one Sunday morning when we had driven up from Northampton (before she and Harry were married and she was still teaching at Smith) and the car got stuck in a ditch and we made the last half-mile on foot, through snowdrifts, laughing, with the food and wine held high over our heads—she and Harry and Henrietta and I. We spoke of Henrietta—of the curious glamor she had shed over us all, and of the obsessive romantic fantasy of which she had formed the center during my first two years in America. I could talk of her now, after almost ten years, without confusion or pain, with only a vague echo of emotion—as of someone I had known long ago, in another world, at another time.

We ate delicious food, drank, picked blueberries by the Baptist's Hole and walked in the woods above, and on Sunday there was a lunch party to which Archibald MacLeish came with his wife. They had driven over from their home in Conway nearby, the poet looking lean and handsome in a French sailor's striped blue-and-white jersey with taut white-duck pants and very proud of his hands that were torn and bruised from building a rock dam across the stream on his estate. Mina's brother Lincoln was not there that weekend but George Kirstein, her younger brother, had driven up with a dark, intelligent, fine-featured girl from Smith. When I left, Mina said she would be spending the winter in New York and I said I hoped we would see each other.

New City was hot and agreeable that summer. There were two swimming holes within walking distance of my aunt's house. One was Wally Fleischer's, peopled by his wife, Millia Davenport (who later designed two shows for us at the Mercury), and a dark, slender beauty, his daughter—married at the time to

Donald Friede, the publisher—for whom I had a burning desire but could never find a convenient time or place in which to satisfy it. The other was Maxwell Anderson's on the South Mountain Road. Fed by springs that become the headwaters of the Hackensack River, it was filled with children of various ages, to whom Mab, as Max's new wife, was trying to be an acceptable stepmother while fulfilling her other, multiple and delicate duties as mate, mistress, secretary and inspiration to that large, vain, industrious man, her husband. Up the road lived my friends the Poors. Their stone house in the woods was, once again, a place of release and refuge—my emotional home, that summer, as it had been two years before. Only this time Bessie went beyond sympathy and encouragement: she became my champion, secret agent and broker. Through her intervention and due entirely to her machinations, before the summer was over, I had achieved the impossible: seven months after entering the theatre, with a record of one collective success and one personal failure, I had signed a contract to direct a major production for America's leading producer—the Theatre Guild.

The Guild, in 1934, stood high in prestige and power. With the Depression it had run into financial problems over its new theatre building and there had been some falling off in the numbers of its subscribers. But it remained the country's most active and distinguished theatrical organization—the accredited producer of O'Neill, Shaw, the Lunts and, more recently, Robert Sherwood and Maxwell Anderson. Its reputation was high with the public, less good with theatre people, for whom it occupied an equivocal position between an art theatre and a commercial management. Actors, in particular, felt that promises of a permanent acting company had been betrayed by that small, closed, extremely voluble and violent group of men and women who had guided the destinies of the Guild, from its modest beginnings, downtown, to its present dominant position in the American theatre. This Board or governing body, when I first encountered it, was just entering a period of drastic change. Maurice Wertheim, the banker, was reducing his participation in its affairs; the Lunts were concerned only with their own productions; Helen Westley, the actress, Lee Simonson, the designer, Philip Moeller, the director, had each, for different reasons, seen their authority diminish over the years and find its way into the capable and eager hands of Lawrence Langner and Theresa Helburn, who, between them, gradually assumed the management of the Theatre Guild's artistic and financial affairs.

Maxwell Anderson had had two successes with the Guild: *Elizabeth the Queen* (with the Lunts) and *Mary of Scotland* (with the two Helens—Hayes and Menken). His relations with the Board cannot have been entirely satisfying, for when he offered the Guild his new play, *Valley Forge,* in the summer of 1934, he insisted on a degree of artistic control that they had never given before. This led to hurt feelings, recriminations and long negotiations at the end of which (since they badly needed the play for their subscription season) the Board capitulated to what they sincerely regarded as his ungrateful and imprudent demands.

Max was a soft, kind, possessive, competitive man with a gigantic ego. He had written his first play after hearing a reading by one of his neighbors on the South Mountain Road, and deciding, then and there, that if John Howard Lawson could get a play produced, so could he. *The White Desert* was the result, soon to be followed by *What Price Glory?, Gods of the Lightning* and others. Now he had begun to have the same feeling about production and direction as he had about writing—that he could do it better himself. In this opinion he was encouraged by Mab, one of whose conjugal duties it was to tend and nurture the self-esteem of the great man she had recently married. But theatrical production is neither a subjective nor a one-man task. Faced with the necessity of getting *Valley Forge* onto the boards, Max soon lost confidence in his own ability to stage it. Unwilling to surrender his work to a strong, opinionated director, he began to look around for someone competent, intelligent and sympathetic, through whom he could retain control of his play during rehearsal.

The South Mountain Road, in those days, was one big family:

it did not take Bessie long to convince her neighbor Mab, and, through her, Max, that I was heaven-sent to fill his present need. There were two dinner parties, one at the Poors' and one at the Andersons', during which I felt myself being watched, inspected and probed. Finally I was given a script of *Valley Forge* to take home and read. I read it in bed that night, in my aunt's house at the other end of South Mountain Road, and I never really changed my mind about it—either during rehearsals or in the grim days before the Pittsburgh opening. Although I basically disliked what I felt to be Max's derivative and sterile use of the Elizabethan iambic pentameter, I felt that *Valley Forge* contained some of his best male scenes and some of his most eloquent writing about the dream and the reality of America's vision of freedom. I detested all the episodes involving Washington's first love, Mary Philipse, and did my diplomatic best, before and during rehearsals, to get her thrown out of the play altogether. I failed—and I got the job.

The Theatre Guild, when Max presented my name, yelled bloody murder. They investigated my brief career in the theatre and received reports that were generally, though not unanimously, unfavorable. However, they had no choice. Sometime in August I signed my contract as director and received, for my first payment, a sum far greater than any I had yet earned in the theatre. But my position in this production was, from the first, an impossible one—more untenable than I realized, in my initial excitement, during the busy days of planning and casting. It was not until we reached the grim test of rehearsal that I understood to the full what I had got myself into. To the Guild I was a nuisance, something that had been shoved down their throats by an egomaniacal playwright. To Anderson I was, mainly, a buffer between himself and the Guild's opinionated and domineering board. To the cast I was a mystery; and if there is one thing that upsets actors, it is a mystery—particularly if he is inexperienced, pretentious and ingratiating, with a strong smell of fear about him.

It was during rehearsals of *Valley Forge* that I received my most painful lessons in the human relations of the theatre—that strange process of meeting and parting, wooing and testing, trusting and knifing that forms part of the business of getting a play onto the stage. I tried hard not to repeat my previous mistakes. In *The Lady from the Sea* I had gone into production unprepared, improvising desperately from day to day. I arrived at rehearsals of *Valley Forge* with every move, tempo and reading of the first act worked out—on paper. This preparation gave me self-confidence, and though it was not to the taste of the hardened Broadway professionals who formed our company, some of it worked—particularly in the male ensemble sequences, which began to take on shape and movement in the first week of rehearsal. Where I failed miserably was in all the scenes involving our star, Philip Merivale, who was in no mood to accept direction of any kind, and most certainly not detailed and specific direction from an amateur of my kidney. He was suffering, throughout rehearsals, from a severe attack of hives, which I felt he attributed somehow to my presence. It was not until later that I discovered that much of what I took to be personal hostility was, in fact, the normal professional behavior of this moody, sentimental and frustrated man, who had only recently, to his own surprise, become a successful romantic leading man, specializing in reticent British charm. His idea of a well-staged scene was one in which he remained modestly standing with his back to a fireplace, upstage center, while the rest of the cast went about its business downstage and to either side of him. There was such a scene in Washington's headquarters at Valley Forge in which my repeated and not so subtle attempts to dislodge him, even temporarily, from his impregnable position were bluntly rebuffed. My patent inability to deal with our star confirmed the Guild in its misgivings about me and helped to undermine what authority I might have had with the rest of the company.

It was unfortunate, too, that halfway through rehearsals, I had to leave for four days to supervise the production of *Four Saints in Three Acts* in Chicago. When I got back to New York I found *Valley Forge* falling apart. Max Anderson had been conducting rehearsals in my absence and the Guild board had deliberately chosen the eve of my return for a run-through which, from what

I was told the next day, could not have gone worse. The soldier scenes had been low in energy, George Washington had sulked and the romantic subplot had been exposed in all its absurdity. The Board's automatic reaction was to replace the girl who was playing Mary Philipse. Since she and our star were, by this time, amorously involved, her tears improved neither his hives nor his temper. We continued to rehearse in an atmosphere of animosity and defeat.

Our premiere in Pittsburgh ten days later was hardly triumphal. The production had a raw, unfinished look, which was partly the result of my total inexperience with out-of-town openings. The soldier scenes, which Max had continued to improve and develop, had a certain energy and eloquence; the sentimental interludes and, more particularly, the Philadelphia Society scenes (complete with Major André and the first singing of "Yankee Doodle") seemed shoddily written and ineptly directed—as indeed they were.

That night, immediately after the show, over whiskey and sandwiches in a suite of the hotel where Duse had suffered her fatal illness, Lawrence Langner and Theresa Helburn fired me from *Valley Forge*. I had known before the curtain went up that my replacement was sitting in the theatre, watching the performance. Yet the blow, when it fell, was no less painful for having been long expected. The meeting was brief and deadly. Mab was present, holding Max's hand, her face white and pinched; so was Harold Freedman, Max's agent, looking serious. Merivale had been invited but declined. Langner (in a brown suit) spoke for the Guild and Miss Helburn seconded him. Ignoring me completely, they addressed themselves to Max, who, shocked and deflated by the first public reaction to his play, was in no state to withstand their concerted and calculated attack. Things were bad, they said grimly, but not hopeless. The situation could still be saved—on certain conditions. Till now, they had given Max everything he asked for; against their own better judgment, they had conceded his every request—and see the result! Now, they insisted that they be given a chance to get the production into shape before it reached New York. This meant taking it entirely into their own experienced hands. It was at this point that I asked for the floor. Soberly, in a style not unlike that in which I had addressed the creditors of the Oceanic Grain Corporation, I pointed out to Max what he and everyone else in the room already knew—that he had no choice in the matter. With becoming modesty, after thanking him for the chance he had given me and regretting my failure to give him a successful opening performance of his play, I resigned as director of *Valley Forge*. Max protested vaguely. I insisted. Less than one minute later I was out, and my successor, Herbert Biberman, who had been waiting in his room on the floor below, was called and asked to join the meeting. Soon after his entrance, and after chivalrously wishing him the best of luck, I withdrew.* But the evening was not quite over.

I was walking away, blasted and brokenhearted, down the long hotel corridor, when I heard footsteps padding behind me. As I stood waiting for the elevator, half-blinded with tears, I did not immediately recognize the dark-brown figure that entered the cage and rode down with me toward the lobby where I had to go for my key. It was Lawrence Langner. Standing beside me at the reception desk, he said he realized I must be a bit upset, but things like this happened all the time in the theatre and I mustn't take it too hard because, on the whole, I'd done a good job on a weak play under difficult conditions and he hoped I would remain with the production at Max's side. He then added, while I stared at him openmouthed, that while he admired Herbert Biberman's vitality, he was, personally, not at all sure of his taste. For that reason it was most important, during the crucial days to come, that I should carefully observe all rehearsals and, if I saw anything of which I disapproved, report to him personally. Then, without waiting for a reply, Lawrence Langner

---

* Herbert Biberman, later a film director and one of the "Hollywood Ten," staged several plays for the Guild in the thirties, including an adaptation of Meyerhold's constructivist *Roar China*, in which the stage was filled with the prow and superstructure of a gigantic battleship resting in two feet of water and surrounded by sampans and dozens of New York Chinese extras.

cheerfully wished me good night, reentered the elevator and went back up to the conference with his new director.

This was my first exposure—but by no means my last—to a duplicity so constant and innate that it could not, in fairness, be described as treachery; an egotism so deep and all-embracing that it left its owner genuinely (or, perhaps, deliberately) unaware of the ghastly things he was doing to others. With this went a certain sensitivity and kindness, a tireless and eager brain, a curiosity, a tenacity and a lack of moral principles that made Lawrence Langner one of the leading patent lawyers of the world and placed him, for forty years, at the heart of almost every new and significant movement in the American theatre. He is one of the very few men in my life whom, in spite of a grudging admiration, I have devoutly and consistently hated.

I attended rehearsals of *Valley Forge* for a week, watching the soldier scenes being "deepened" through voluble applications of the "inner technique" and appeals to the "affective memory." The wretched Philadelphia party scene was enlivened but not saved by the addition of four extras and two Negro servitors in white perukes carrying candelabras. Margalo Gillmore had taken over the role of Mary Philipse to no avail, and I was interested and pleased to observe that Merivale was even ruder and more contemptuous toward Biberman than he had been to me. But I was not happy. My relations with Max continued cordial, but they did not wholly survive the strain of our joint ordeal. I remained with *Valley Forge* till it reached Baltimore, where it was rather more coolly received than it had been in Pittsburgh. After that, since there was absolutely nothing for me to do, I left.

Some weeks later, with mixed feelings, I attended the New York opening of *Valley Forge,* which did rather better, critically, than had been expected. Atkinson found it a "grandly motivated drama," commended Maxwell Anderson for having "mind enough to perceive honest heroism in a great character, independence enough to translate it into manly terms" but added that "it is hard to worship a great character in the theatre without slopping over. To tell the truth *Valley Forge* gives a splash or two." The staging was mentioned: "Although the problem of direction has raised considerable hazards, Herbert J. Biberman and John Houseman have acquitted themselves with credit." But the success of the evening was Merivale's; he was widely praised for the "craggy candor" of his George Washington and "the frankness and strength and interior understanding that distinguish all his acting." Stark Young found in the love scenes "an unfortunate reflection on the method and style of the author" but was impressed by

> . . . a good last curtain in which the theme of liberty, through the dramatic and poetic imagination, is suddenly realized, warm and compelling.

Not warm and compelling enough, however, to overcome the allergy that afflicts the American public each time the Father of his Country appears on stage or screen. *Valley Forge* barely outlasted the Theatre Guild's subscription period and closed after less than five weeks—by which time Max was well into his next play, *Winterset,* and I was, once again, in search of work.

* * *

The year 1934 was not ending as well as it had begun. The previous Christmas I had been completely absorbed in a collective enterprise, which, for all its apparent recklessness, had been carefully planned and efficiently executed in an atmosphere of confidence and love. Since then, I had suffered two serious personal defeats, from which I emerged with an almost total loss of faith in my own creative ability. I also became aware that, besides the usual hazards of inexperience, I was facing the dangerous consequences of my own shrewd opportunism, through which I had worked myself into theatrical jobs that I was incapable of executing. By moving too fast, far beyond my capabilities, I had done myself what seemed like irreparable harm.

Yet in the circumstances, what choice did I have? Having entered the theatre after the age of thirty in the confusion of the

Great Depression, from the top, I had no alternative but to try to maintain myself at the top, learning my trade as I went along and hoping I would not break my neck in my repeated and inevitable falls. Even if I had been willing to take a stage manager's or assistant's job, where I might have learned the technical rudiments of my profession, no such job was available to a man who had already directed a play for the Theatre Guild. (Besides, I was even less capable of stage-managing a professional production than I was of directing it.)

If my prospects of making a living on Broadway seemed bleak, they were no less discouraging in the other places where theatre was practiced at the time. I had learned, during my brief stay at Green Mansions, that I did not belong in the collective but exclusive world of the Group Theatre; I was even more remote and alien from the new left-wing organizations that had sprung up with the Depression. The Theatre Union had been in existence for almost a year at the old Civic Repertory Theatre on Fourteenth Street. Having produced three plays, of which the last, *Stevedore,* was a solid success, it already had more liberal-intellectual amateurs on its staff than it needed. Alfred Saxe's *Workers' Lab*—renamed the Theatre of Action—was a youthful proletarian group in which I had friends (Nicholas Ray and Elia Kazan among them) but to which I was quite obviously unsuited. At the other extreme, my associates in Hartford and Sixty-first Street were of little help to me that winter. Virgil Thomson's choruses and Chick Austin's sets and costumes for Countee Cullen's *Medea* had been ready for months, but Rose MacLendon, the Negro actress for whom the piece was intended, had fallen ill and Austin had economic problems at the Athenaeum. The Askew salon continued, each Sunday afternoon, to furnish me with some of the most agreeable hours of my week, but here too I smelled a danger: though the tone of the salon remained personally cordial, I could not help sensing a certain official disappointment, verging on grievance, over the artistic and commercial failure of my last two ventures. It was a warning, whispered, but not to be ignored.

So I waited and hoped. Against all reason I continued to

cherish the conviction that once again, any day now, some golden opportunity would present itself, and that I must be alert and resourceful enough to grasp it when it appeared. When it did, it came, once again, from an unpredictable quarter and by a circuitous route. On the night of December 21, 1934, some weeks after the opening of *Valley Forge*, Jo and Annie Mielziner had invited me to the opening night of Katharine Cornell's *Romeo and Juliet*, for which Jo had designed the sets and costumes. It was one of the events of the Broadway season: *The New York Times* placed it

> . . . on a high plane of modern magnificence—another jewel on the cheek of the theatre's nights.

That glossy and successful evening was marked for me by one astonishing vision: not Miss Cornell's fervent Juliet, nor Edith Evans' admirable Nurse, nor Basil Rathbone's polite, middle-aged Romeo, nor Brian Aherne's Mercutio exuberantly slapping his yellow thighs as he strutted through Jo's bright Italianate scenery—those were all blotted by the excitement of the two brief moments when the furious Tybalt appeared suddenly in that sunlit Verona square: death, in scarlet and black, in the form of a monstrous boy—flat-footed and graceless, yet swift and agile; soft as jelly one moment and uncoiled, the next, in a spring of such furious energy that, once released, it could be checked by no human intervention. What made this figure so obscene and terrible was the pale, shiny child's face under the unnatural growth of dark beard, from which there issued a voice of such clarity and power that it tore like a high wind through the genteel, modulated voices of the well-trained professionals around him. "Peace! I hate the word as I hate Hell!" cried the sick boy, as he shuffled along, driven by some irresistible interior violence to kill and soon himself, inevitably, to die.

Orson Welles's initial impact—if one was sensitive or allergic to it—was overwhelming and unforgettable. Michael MacLiammoir, the Irish actor, has described a similar impression received when he and his partner, Hilton Edwards, were first confronted on the stage of the Gate Theatre in Dublin by a young man looking "larger, taller, softer and broader" than anyone they had ever seen, who bounded on stage with glaring, Chinese eyes and, in a tearing rage, began to enact for them the part of the Duke in *Jew Suss:*

> It was an astonishing performance, wrong from beginning to end, but with all the qualities of fine acting tearing their way through a chaos of inexperience. His diction was practically perfect; his personality, in spite of his fantastic antics, was real and varied; his sense of passion, of evil, of drunkenness, of tyranny, of a sort of demoniac authority was arresting; a preposterous energy pulsating through everything he did.*

Such extreme reactions were personal; in the professional evaluations of a fashionable opening night, dominated by the personality of a glamorous and beloved lady star, Welles's appearance as Tybalt created no special stir. His reviews the next day were not outstanding, and when I went backstage with the Mielziners and stood politely in the background while the proper amenities were exchanged with Miss Cornell and Guthrie McClintic, I looked around vainly for a glimpse of the red and black costume.

I left without seeing him; yet in the days that followed, he was seldom out of my mind. My agitation grew and I did nothing about it—in much the same way as a man nurtures his sense of excited anticipation over a woman the sight of whom has deeply disturbed him and of whom he feels quite certain that there will one day be something between them. He postpones their meeting until the feared and eagerly awaited moment when their confrontation, with its predictable consequences, can no longer be delayed. In the meantime, I found myself eagerly absorbing that already considerable body of personal legend—partly apocryphal but largely authentic—which had already formed about Orson Welles before the age of twenty.

Today, most of those early episodes are worn thin and flat with

* *All for Hecuba,* by Michael MacLiammoir.

1 4 5

repetition: the prodigious son of a Chicago beauty and a society playboy, who made his first acting appearance as the baby in *Madama Butterfly* and a rabbit in a Marshall Field's Christmas show; who at the age of five had confounded theatrical scholars ten times his age; who, at twelve, played Marc Antony, the Soothsayer *and* Cassius in a prize-winning Todd School production of *Julius Caesar,* which he also directed and of which, a few years later, he edited, illustrated, printed and published his own acting version; of his voyage, as a painter, through Ireland in a donkey cart, from which he descended, at the age of sixteen (claiming to be a well-known star of New York's Theatre Guild) to play leading parts in Dublin's Gate Theatre; of his departure, when they would not let him play Othello, and of his solitary voyage through Morocco, where he resided, for a while, as a favored guest of the Glaoui in his mountain fortress; of the total neglect which awaited him on his return to his native land till the afternoon, at a cocktail party in Chicago, when he met Thornton Wilder, who sent him to New York via Alexander Woollcott to Guthrie McClintic, by whom, after one reading, he was engaged to play Mercutio, Octavius Barrett and Marchbanks opposite Katharine Cornell on her national repertory tour. His conduct, on that tour, was a legend in itself—a sequence of brawls, debauches, missed trains and breaches of discipline (including the wearing of his Mercutio beard at a Chamber of Commerce luncheon in San Francisco) which were without precedent in a company known for its outward propriety and decorum.

At the end of the tour, as an outlet for his repressed energies, he had organized a summer festival of his own at Woodstock, Illinois, on the grounds of his former school, to which he invited his onetime Irish employers, Edwards and MacLiammoir, to appear with him in *Trilby* (in which he played a ferocious Svengali), Merejkowski's *Czar Paul* and *Hamlet* (in which he created a prodigiously lecherous Claudius). During this unexpectedly successful season, he used up many pounds of makeup and took to wife a delicately beautiful Chicago debutante, with whom he returned to New York and the Cornell company in the fall. Considered too immature at nineteen to play a metropolitan Mercutio, his fury as Tybalt was not entirely histrionic.

The period of waiting, during which the conditions of my meeting with Orson Welles were ineluctably shaping themselves, was about three weeks. But the event which finally brought us together had been germinating for months. The previous summer, among the guests at Mina Curtiss' Sunday lunch party at Chapelbrook had been Archibald MacLeish. His epic poem *Conquistador* had won him the 1932 Pulitzer Prize for poetry. His following work, *Frescoes for Mr. Rockefeller's City,* had been received with reservations on the Right and with open hostility by writers and critics of the Left. He seemed to have taken these strictures to heart, for he spoke, that Sunday, of the new directions to be taken by American poetry, including his own, and mentioned that he was in his final weeks of work on a play with a contemporary American theme.

I may have reported this to Nathan Zatkin one day as we were raking over the coals of past and future projects. Knowing Nathan, I should not have been surprised, a week later, when I discovered an item, prominently featured in that greenhouse of theatrical fantasies, the Sunday drama section of *The New York Times,* reporting that Archibald MacLeish, the eminent poet, Pulitzer Prize-winner and editor of *Fortune* Magazine, had completed a play in verse on a contemporary theme and had entrusted its production to Nathan Zatkin and John Houseman as the first presentation of their newly formed Phoenix Theatre. I called Zatkin, who professed utter, unconvincing amazement. Two days later I received a sharp little note from the poet, to which I replied with an abject apology and the hope that his legitimate indignation would not prevent him from letting me read the play when it was ready.

In the months that followed, I learned through Mina, who was spending that winter in New York, that he had submitted it to the Theatre Guild, to Jed Harris and finally, to Charles Walker at the Theatre Union—without results. Then one morning, soon after the New Year, came another letter from the poet asking if I still wished to read his play. He invited me to lunch somewhere near the foot of the Chrysler Building, where *Time* and *Fortune* had their offices, and handed me the script, which I read that night. Two Sundays later it was once again announced in the drama section of *The New York Times* that *Panic,* a play in verse on a contemporary subject by that eminent poet and Pulitzer Prize-winner, Archibald MacLeish, would be presented by John Houseman and Nathan Zatkin as the opening production of their newly formed Phoenix Theatre. This time, there was no protest from the poet.

I had nothing to lose and, by my own mysterious calculations, a lot to gain by rushing in where every other New York management, Right and Left, feared to tread. The fact that MacLeish's play was so patently uncommercial and presented such obvious and apparently insurmountable production problems gave me a kind of perverse protection and made it essential that I produce it immediately. Unable to function within the patterns of the existent commercial, social or art-theatre setups, it had become necessary for me to create the image of a man who would undertake what no one else would venture. *Panic* was the perfect vehicle for such a demonstration.

Besides, I had found in *Panic* a personal empathy that excited me. Without identifying myself with the doomed tycoon McGafferty, I, too, had felt the thrill of the "creeping ruin"—

Closing the veins as cold does—killing secretly
Freezing the heart—ruin following ruin . . .

Reevaluating the play today, thirty-five years later, in a changed context, with a full awareness of its historical and social fallacies and of its prosodic and dramatic limitations, I still see merit in *Panic.* I find it stronger in texture, more direct and effectual in its dramatic action than the same author's later and more successful *J.B. Panic,* for all its tricks and poses and its literary attempt to impose upon the economic phenomenon of the Crash the fatality of a Greek tragedy, carries the unmistakable mark of deep personal shock—the despairing fear a man feels at the sudden, inexplicable collapse of a world of which he, himself, has been a secure and confident part. Besides, at the time, *Panic* was the only anticapitalist play I had come across that was written from above; the only one that afforded a vision of the Crash seen through the eyes of a man high up, in the instant before he jumps to his shameful death.

Taking off with the speed of desperation, somewhere, somehow, between us, Zatkin and I managed to raise five hundred dollars, out of which we presented the poet with a token advance, incorporated ourselves as the Phoenix Theatre and had a telephone installed in the squalid one-room office that we rented by the month on the second floor of a Burlesque house on Forty-second Street. This became the headquarters of the Phoenix, and it was from there that an eager, harassed and unpaid secretary began to mail out the innumerable and astonishing releases that poured from Zatkin's fertile brain till, within a fortnight of our first announcement, *Panic* seemed well on its way to becoming one of the main theatrical events of that spring.

After that we came to a sudden stop—for two good reasons. We had no money and we had no leading man. The latter was the more serious. To announce *Panic* without a McGafferty was like preparing to put on *Lear* without the king. And like Lear, McGafferty was an almost impossible role to cast in the American theatre—a formidable J. P. Morganesque figure "in his late fifties, the leading industrialist and financier of his time," who was expected to convey an almost legendary greatness through speech after speech of extremely tricky, rhetorical and frequently repetitive verse.

We went through the usual producers' motions. We indulged in the usual fantasies—the Lunts, Edward G. Robinson, the two Barrymores—till it came to our attention that Paul Muni, then at the height of his movie fame and bursting with a desire to do "something fine," was in town. His wife consented to receive the script, or rather an advance printed copy of the play. We never heard from her again. It was at this point that I paid a secret visit one evening backstage at the Martin Beck Theatre, where *Romeo and Juliet* was playing. I appeared around ten o'clock—

by which time I knew that Tybalt was dead. While the doorman, with my fifty cents clutched in his hand, slowly climbed the stairs to announce me, I remember looking past the painted flats and the shirt-sleeved stagehands to the hot brightness of the stage where Miss Cornell was receiving the fatal news of her imminent marriage to Paris. On the third floor corridor leading to Welles's dressing room, I could hear the voices from the stage; they continued to rise faintly from below as I entered the cramped and cluttered cubicle where he sat, naked to the waist, before his mirror under the glaring bulbs, waiting for his long-delayed curtain call. His black-and-scarlet Tybalt costume, stiff and heavy with sweat, lay over the back of a chair. The beard was off, and under the viscous, mottled slime of greasepaint and the multiple lines and shadings round the eyes and the false nose, it was still impossible to distinguish the real face from that of the "King of the Cats." But the hands were extraordinary; in life as on the stage, they were pale, huge and beautifully formed, with enormous white palms and incredibly long, tapering fingers that seemed to have a life of their own. There were sheets of paper scattered among the greasepaint, the bottles and the beard, all covered with large, well-formed writing, doodled figures and gruesome faces (a play he was writing about the Devil, he explained, smiling) to which he returned when I left to wait for him in a bar across the street.

It was always a shock to see Welles without the makeup and the false noses behind which he chose to mask himself. When he walked into the bar, with his hair combed, in a sober, dark suit, I did not know him for a moment; then, as he moved toward me, I recognized the shuffling, flat-footed gait, which I had found so frightening in Tybalt and which was really his own. I could see his features now, finally: the pale pudding face with the violent black eyes, the button nose with the wen to one side of it and the deep runnel meeting the well-shaped mouth over the astonishingly small teeth. Against the darkness of the wooden table I was conscious once more of the remarkable hands and the voice that made people turn at the neighboring tables—startled not so much by its loudness as by its surprising vibration.

We had one old-fashioned and then another while I told him of our project and gave him a copy of the play and my telephone number. Afterwards I walked across town with him toward Grand Central Station, then watched him vanish, with astonishing speed, into the tunnel leading to the Westchester commuter trains. After he had gone, I was left not so much with the impression of his force and brilliance as with a sense of extreme youth and charm and of a courtesy that came very close to tenderness.

Orson called at twelve the next day to say he wanted to play McGafferty. He could get leave from the Cornell company or, if necessary, he would give his two weeks' notice. When did rehearsals begin?

Twenty-four hours later I saw MacLeish's eyes narrow in exasperation as a tall nineteen-year-old boy in gray pants and a loose tweed jacket, followed by a delicious child with blond, reddish hair and ivory skin, entered our bare, one-room office over the Burlesque house to read for the role of the aging tycoon, McGafferty. I gave him the hardest part first: the last despairing phase when McGafferty, harried and weakened with fear, becomes convinced, through the suicide of his last trusted associate, that his own end has come:

> What did he see do you think?
> What did he see on the ground glass of
>   the door—the
> Light behind it—see or think he saw there?
> Something not to run from: not to meet.
> Something inescapable enough to
> Jerk the gun hand . . .

Sitting stiffly in that small grimy office (with only two wooden chairs, so that Zatkin and I sat on the floor with our backs against the wall), hearing that voice for the first time in its full and astonishing range, MacLeish stared incredulously. It was an instrument of pathos and terror, of infinite delicacy and brutally devastating power:

> You think they're shadows!
> You think this creeping ruin is a shadow!

You think it's chance the banks go one by one
Closing the veins as cold does—killing secretly—
The Country dying of it—towns dead—land dead—
Hunger limping every road—you think it's
Chance that does it? You think! So did I!
I do not think so now. I think they wish it.
We cannot see them but they're there: they loom
Behind the seen side like the wind in curtains . . .

And hour and a half later, the poet had heard his play—including the choruses—read as he would never hear it again. After the young couple had left (there was a matinee of *Romeo*), while the walls were still echoing with the sweet thunder of that fabulous recital, Zatkin asked the glowing poet if he had any idea where we could borrow two thousand dollars. The next morning a bank draft was delivered, by hand, from the office of Robert Lovett, of Brown Bros., Harriman & Co., for twenty-five hundred dollars. This, with another thousand that we borrowed later from MacLeish himself, constituted our entire financing for a production that had nothing modest or experimental about it.

The script of *Panic* called for twenty-five speaking parts, to which we added a chorus of twenty-three. These fifty-odd persons were to appear on a stage which, according to the author, showed "a bank president's office, raised by several steps and enclosed, on the sides, by open square columns, at the back by a double door" and "a street before an electric news bulletin of the Times Square type"—the whole to be "impersonal, bare, huge, on a scale to dwarf the shapes of men and women." To achieve this titanic effect, we managed to rent, for ten days, the most desirable musical-comedy stage in New York—that of the Imperial Theatre. To create our decor I conned one of Broadway's leading designers, Jo Mielziner, into working for nothing. The set was plain but enormous and called for a raised, sharply raked platform separated from the forestage by a trench or pit, forty feet long and two feet wide, running some fifteen feet upstage and parallel to the footlights, which we hacked out of the expensive linoleum-covered stage flooring and filled with electric projectors whose beams, shooting straight into the air and blending with another bank of lights pouring down from behind the proscenium arch, formed an opaque wall or curtain of light between the upper and lower parts of the stage. (Used again in the Mercury *Julius Caesar*, we came to refer to them as "Nuremberg lights" after Hitler's use of similar lighting tricks in some of his great Nazi night ceremonies.) *

To regulate traffic among the men and women on the forestage I persuaded Martha Graham to join us. Virgil Thomson agreed to supply music for the sum of one hundred dollars—later reduced to fifty when he decided that the only sounds needed were a real telegraph key tapping out real Morse Code and a metronome. With a special dispensation from Actors' Equity that allowed us three weeks' rehearsal in exchange for a guarantee of one week's salary at Equity minimum (forty dollars in those days) and including the cost of a whirlwind promotion and subscription campaign and one hundred dollars apiece for Zatkin and myself, the total estimated cost of *Panic* came to around $4,500 for a production that was planned and announced for no more than three performances.

This number was fixed following a careful and realistic appraisal of our chances. In three performances before diversified audiences in a large theatre, we hoped to draw whatever spectators we could reasonably expect to attract to as special a piece as *Panic*. By restricting our run we were able to cut our production cost virtually in half; also, by limiting our call on the actors' time, we were able, in the words of one reviewer, "to beguile a large company of excellent and willing actors into donating their services to an unusual artistic cause."

For our first reading on the bare stage of the Imperial Theatre we had, in fact, assembled a huge and, for that time, quite surprising cast. In the principal parts, besides Welles as McGafferty, we had George Glass and Richard Whorf as his principal henchmen and my ex-wife Zita Johann (back from Hollywood for

---

* "The effect would not have been as successful" according to Jo Mielziner "if the air of the old building *Panic* played in had not been so full of dust that all we had to do was light it up and magic happened."

a while) as his loyal mistress, Ione. From the Group Theatre, during one of their periodic layoffs, came Russell Collins, Tony Kraber, William Challee and Walter Coy. Harold Johnsrud was the Blind Man. (He was sometimes accompanied to rehearsal by his wife—a dark, beautiful, serious, girl-writer by the name of Mary McCarthy.) Among the Bankers, the Unemployed and the Men and Women of the street were Rose McLendon, Joanna Roos, Paula Trueman, Osceola Archer, Karl Swenson, Abner Biberman, John O'Shaughnessy, Vincent Sherman, Wesley Addy, and Bernard Zanville—later Dane Clark of the movies.

After that first general reading, until the final run-throughs began, we rehearsed at different times and places: the street scenes under Martha Graham, the personal scenes under the direction of James Light. I had intended to stage the play myself, but, overcome by the responsibilities of producing and promoting this monster-on-a-shoestring (and having, besides, lost what little self-confidence I had in the fjords of Norway and the snows of Valley Forge), I withdrew, before the start of rehearsals, in favor of James Light, whose talent I had admired since the days of the old Provincetown. Except on the days when they were sawing up the floor or moving in scenery and lighting equipment, the stage of the Imperial was occupied mostly by Miss Graham, her chorus, her metronome and her incredible energy. Actors who worked with her during those exhausting three weeks still talk with awe of the disciplined fervor and the rigid perfectionism with which she drove them—with charley horses and screaming tendons—through the slow, angular ballet that grew before our eyes out of the moods and rhythms of MacLeish's unrelenting three-beat lines:

> "Foreclosures in . . .
> closed . . .
> Foreclosing . . .
> Factories closing doors . . .
> Billions in balances frozen . . .
> Doors closing foreclosed . . .

ACT ONE

A WOMAN

Closed as doors close with
Death in a Woman's house when the
Wind closes them.

A MAN

Thousands
Silent at closed doors.

*(Their eyes turned upward, conscious of
the electric sign spelling out doom, somewhere overhead, invisible to the audience.)*

AN OLD MAN

Slowly the thing comes.
There are many signs; there are furnaces
Dead now that were burning.
Thirty years in a town—
Never dark: there are foundries—
Fires drawn: trestles
Silent. The swifts nest in
Stacks that for generations
Flowed smoke. The patience of
Hawks is over the cities:
They circle in clean light where the
Smoke last year frightened them.

This use of the chorus, "the attempt to use the crowd as an actor which results in a chorus speaking, not with the single voice of a Greek chorus, but with the many voices of the American street," constituted the most challenging element of the production. I have never been quite sure whether the formal, controlled tension with which Martha Graham filled that forestage helped to carry, or diverted attention from, the sense and feeling of the poet's lines. Stark Young wrote that the best thing in *Panic* was Martha Graham's arrangements of the crowd groups and that "a considerable amount of firmness appeared in the pattern that these people in the street sought to establish for their numerous and gradually less exhilarating scenes." A critic of the Left, on the other hand, accustomed to the more realistic motions of "agitprop," felt that "in the mass-scenes, Martha Graham does her best *not* to convey swift-moving street action. Although the poet successfully carries across the footlights a nervous, staccato, urban rhythm, the dancer slows down the figures and masses of the chorus into a Grecian frieze."

The office scenes, which revolved around the doomed figure of McGafferty, were rehearsed mostly underground in the lounge of the Imperial and on the stage after the battered chorus had been sent home. I had heard hair-raising stories of Welles's behavior in rehearsal with Guthrie McClintic and the Cornell company. With us, from first to last, his conduct was perfect. Toward James Light, who regarded him with continually growing amazement and admiration, he was respectful and courteous; he remained understanding and gentle when Jimmy started to crack up in the final, harrowing days of rehearsal. With his fellow actors he was considerate and, perhaps for the only time in his life, punctual. With Zita, who was nervous and disturbed over her difficulties with the rigid, unfamiliar verse in a role that she found affected and unmotivated, he was helpful and patient. And to his own part of the sexagenarian McGafferty, he brought us, as a free gift, the strength, the keen intelligence, the arrogance and the prodigious energy of his nineteen and a half years.

It was a gift for which I was truly grateful, for, almost from the first day of rehearsal, it had become evident where the principal dangers of *Panic* lay: McGafferty, as MacLeish had written him, was not so much a man as the symbol of a condemned class—a stiff, inflexible figure with little emotional growth, whom neither his enemies nor his entourage of partners, lieutenants, lawyer and mistress could ever quite warm into theatrical life. Add to this my gradual realization that, by the spring of 1935, *Panic* was already out of tune with its time. The climate had changed since the bank closings. The days of window jumpers, apple vendors and bonus marchers were over; blind fear and passive acceptance were things of the past. By 1935 the rage to live was returning to the American people; as they started to thrash their angry and untidy way back to plenty, there was one thing they were united in abhorring: the contemplation of their own immediate and shameful past.

(The present was perturbing enough, at home and abroad: on the day of our first dress rehearsal of *Panic* the Saar territory formally changed hands after a plebiscite in which over ninety percent of the population had chosen to return to the Germany of the Third Reich under Adolf Hitler, the Belgian currency tottered and France added a year to its compulsory army service. At home, violent dust storms were reported in the Southwest and unemployment reached a new figure of fifteen million, while Mae West's earnings in the third year of the Great Depression were evaluated at $480,833.)

Meantime, over the Burlesque house, in addition to the endless stream of releases with which the ineffable Zatkin continued to deluge not only the drama but also the feature, book and business sections of the national press, our harried volunteers had been mailing out thousands of subscription blanks and opening-night announcements which now, slowly, began to yield sufficient cash, in checks hastily banked, to keep up with our rising cost of production.

For our three performances of *Panic* we had tried to mobilize three quite distinct kinds of audience. Our third and last night was already disposed of—sold for one thousand dollars to *New Theatre,* a left-wing magazine intended to aid in "the mass development of the American theatre to its highest artistic and social level—a theatre dedicated to the struggle against war, fascism and censorship" which, in general, closely followed the cultural line of the American Communist Party. *New Theatre* and *New Masses* firmly and deliberately supported *Panic,* pressed the sale of tickets and, as an added attraction, offered a symposium on the stage after the show, featuring Archibald MacLeish in debate with three leading intellectuals of the American Left.

Our first performance was a "subscribers' preview," open to members only. Such was New York's continuing theatrical faith that, in spite of the Depression, the Phoenix, a totally unknown organization, received between four and five hundred paid responses, most of them for two or more seats. It was these hurriedly mustered subscribers, together with relatives and friends of the cast, who witnessed the first public performance of *Panic*. They were respectful, impressed by the magnitude of our effort, mildly admiring and sincerely grateful but, also, worn and confused. No such generous feelings animated the audience that attended our second performance—the official first night of *Panic* on March 15, 1935. At the then astronomical price of $5.50 a seat, we had succeeded in half-filling the theatre with as grimly elegant and forbidding an opening-night audience as it was possible to imagine. They applauded Jo's set when the curtain rose. After that, for any number of reasons (including the lack of an intermission and their bitterness at being reminded, by one of their own, of things they were trying so hard to forget), they were unanimous in detesting what they saw and heard. Their attitude was expressed by Lucius Beebe and a gentleman friend who, at the end of the performance, rose in their fifth-row orchestra seats and added their hisses to the perfunctory applause of the exhausted and exasperated first-nighters around them.

Much of the atmosphere of resentful gloom was reflected in the press the following morning. Only Brooks Atkinson of *The New York Times* gave the poet and his producers a good mark for effort; he congratulated the youthful Phoenix for reviving "an impulse that our middle-aged theatre has long been lacking" and praised the poet for "the terse beauty of his bare, lean verse, which is modern in choice of words and vigor of sound." He had kind words for Orson Welles's "excellent performance," for Zita Johann, Richard Whorf and the "crisp and forceful thrust" of James Light's direction. After which, Mr. Atkinson confessed his perplexity at Mr. MacLeish's basic theme "that the collapse of industry is no rational disaster but a visitation of fate, the furies and the Gods." He also expressed reservations as to the theatrical quality of Mr. MacLeish's verse, which he found "overpacked with assertion" and concluded with the verdict that the poet had "not brought fire down to the earth at our feet." *Variety,* the organ of show business, described *Panic* as

Simple and Grecian in its forthrightness, it is still ultra-con-
temporaneous—a highly effective and forceful dramatic interpretation of the big-banking, busto-crusto days of March 1933.

The weeklies and monthlies, when they appeared, long after
we had closed, were thoughtful and mixed; they ranged from
highly technical discussions of MacLeish's verse theories to reviews, both Left and Right, written with a frankly political bias.
John Gassner, covering a group of current plays that also included *The Petrified Forest* and *Three Men on a Horse*, complained:

> Gifted with a poetic expression unapproachable by anyone
> writing in the theatre here or abroad, MacLeish's failure is
> due to dramaturgic ineffectiveness caused by the fragmentary
> and uncertain character of his social critique.

The same argument was repeated in the symposium that followed the *New Theatre* benefit of March 16th—the night on
which *Panic*, for the first and only time, played to a packed house
before an audience swept by one of those ground swells of excitement that were characteristic of the period. It was a Depression
phenomenon through which, for a short time and for large
numbers of predominantly young people, the theatre became far
more than entertainment or even artistic release. It seemed to
offer them an escape from the anxiety and squalor of their own
lives and a direct participation in that "joyous fervor" that
accompanies the creation of a brave new world. It was the kind
of theatrical excitement of which Harold Clurman was writing
when he described the first performance of *Waiting for Lefty*.

> . . . audiences and actors had become one. The actors no
> longer performed: they were carried along by an exultancy
> of communication that seemed to sweep the audience toward
> the stage. Line after line brought applause, whistles, bravos
> and heartfelt shouts of kinship.*

* *The Fervent Years* by Harold Clurman.

Panic was no *Waiting for Lefty;* in style, emotional content and dramatic tone no two works could have been further apart. Yet some echoes of that same excitement (if not of the warmth and the joy) filled the Imperial Theatre on that Saturday night, for what was by far the best of our three performances. Not all this excitement was theatrical; some of it was frankly political and much of it had been quite deliberately induced and encouraged by the operators of the Party's cultural apparatus to whom this performance of *Panic* represented a means to an end: the intellectual kidnapping of that eminent bourgeois poet, Pulitzer Prize-winner and *Fortune* editor—Archibald MacLeish. MacLeish had not always enjoyed the favors of the Left, in whose press he had often been attacked for being "antiradical," even "fascistic." *New Theatre,* in announcing our benefit, found it necessary to assure its readers:

> MacLeish is well aware that America is no longer the Wasteland of Capitalism but the new-found land of America's toiling masses.

The Party's plan was clear, if a trifle ingenuous: to capture alive America's most fashionable poet and put him to work, eager and eloquent, on the side of the Revolution. To accomplish this, the heads of the Party's cultural apparatus assembled their strongest and subtlest forces on the stage of the Imperial Theatre for a ceremony which seemed to fall somewhere between an exorcism and a conversion, a kidnapping and an auto-da-fé.

John Howard Lawson, swarthy and forceful in his agitated, limping motion from one side of the stage to the other, led off the debate; Burnshaw, the pedant of the Party, followed with a prepared and tedious academic paper. But these were merely the banderillero and the picador of the occasion; the main attraction, the matador, who rose at last and moved slowly down to the footlights, was the head of cultural activities for the American Communist Party—V. J. Jerome. His face was pale, his eyes sorrowful, his voice gentle and cultivated with a faint trace of a Whitechapel cockney accent. He began quietly enough: "Last night, in this theatre, I saw *Panic* at its premiere performance. As

I sat in the audience I heard hissing from the front rows." He paused and waved a white hand in the direction of Eugene Meyer (head of the Federal Reserve Bank) who happened to be sitting in the third row center with his wife and Ada MacLeish. "Tickets were five dollars and fifty cents: that will help you to appreciate who the majority of those first-nighters were." There was laughter at that, but he quickly continued, "I am not here to discuss the ethics of the hiss, though its aesthetics cannot altogether be separated from its politics. One thing I did feel, however—that the hiss of the bourgeoisie is the applause of the proletariat!"

When the clapping and the laughter had subsided and after an unflattering reference to "that court singer of British imperialism, Rudyard Kipling"—the speaker got down to the serious business of the evening: "MacLeish has taken for his subject matter a certain moment in the economic crisis of American capitalism and has dealt with it in a manner that is new to him and something of a shock to those who have hitherto been his followers." He glanced at Eugene Meyer before continuing: "MacLeish's play has as its theme the doom of capitalism, a doom that proceeds out of the very being of capitalism, organically, by an inexorable dictate. In this sense *Panic* is an anticapitalist play and represents a significant transition in the career of Archibald MacLeish as a writer."

There was desultory applause, but he checked it. "*Panic* was conceived as a tragedy. In this lies its significance. Its protagonist is McGafferty. He must fall, but he goes down in grandeur. The political villain of the piece is seen advancing to his doom with the poetry of high resolve. He will not wait for his overthrow. He will make his exit graciously, with the demise of a noble loser." He paused, looked at MacLeish, shook his head slowly. "But in reality that is not how McGafferty will fall! The stage in which capitalism enters its decline ushers in the epoch of its revolutionary overthrow. The one implies the other. Was it not Lenin who said, 'The Bourgeoisie does not fall. The Proletariat drops it!'"

There was loud applause at that. The speaker waited, raised his hand for silence, then continued more quietly, a thin smile playing about his lips as he referred to the "significant" fact (mentioned by MacLeish in his preface to the play) that "while the bankers are endowed with lines of *five* accents, the proletariat received only minced *three*-accented lines!" He smiled knowingly at Archie, as one cultivated man at another. "I should say in justice to MacLeish that this differentiation was probably not intended as a belittlement of the workers; it is due, as he himself tells us, to the fact that the unemployed constitute the element of chorus and, as such, traditionally, I dare say, do not need full extension of speech." The smile lingered for a moment, then vanished. The tone rose. "But his error lies precisely in this conception of the unemployed as *chorus*—not as *Dramatis Personae!* Hence the fatalism that pervades the play; hence the pallor and the shadowiness of the workers and their leader! When the playwright fuses into his blood the red corpuscles of faith in the revolutionary power of the proletariat—then and not till then will his unemployed workers be given flesh and blood and muscle; will his chorus emerge from the background and assume the position of the protagonist!" There was some applause but he did not stop for it. With great intensity, his eye fixed on the poet on the stage beside him, he drove on to his finale.

"Archibald MacLeish has given evidence, I believe, of his sincere desire to proceed along that road. I think the play we have seen this evening justifies us in expecting to see him advance from his present point of splendid, lonely poet to sing the epic of the proletariat advancing through day-to-day struggle to power, to be one of the poets that the American working class has drawn into its ranks—to work as poet, singing the epic of the New Conquistador!"

With that, V. J. Jerome sat down amid loud and prolonged applause, which faded down, then broke out again, swollen by cheering as the poet rose to his feet and moved slowly to the front of the stage—a slim, boyish, elegant figure, seriously and modestly acknowledging their bravos. This was the high point of the evening, the climax to which everything else had been a prelude.

So they continued clapping and cheering for a time, while Mac-Leish stood there, facing them and waiting. Then, gradually, the sounds died away and the house was silent—waiting for the poet to give his answer.

What did they expect? Did they seriously believe they had him trapped? Backed into a corner from which the only exit lay in a public conversion to Marxism? Did they really expect to see him hit the sawdust trail? Or did they hope that in the agitation of the moment, out of embarrassment or vanity, he would let slip some irretrievable condemnation of his former associates or some rash, irrevocable hope for the triumph of the Proletariat? If so, they did not know their man.

The poet's voice, as he began to speak, was soft but clear, full of sincerity and severe charm. He opened with expressions of gratitude; he thanked his collaborators—his actors, his director, his choreographer, his producers and, last but not least (with a slow, emotional look around the jammed and silent theatre) his audience. Contrasting the arid, jaded gang of the previous night with the eager, intelligent and vital crowd he saw before him, he let them share his hope for a new theatre in America.

"The American theatre is dead! And the American theatre is now alive!" he announced dramatically. "For the first time since I knew anything about such matters, there exists in this country a theatre in which dishonesty is not demanded, in which hokum and sex are not compulsory ingredients. There is offered, in other words, a theatre for art—a theatre for the people!"

There was solid applause after that. When it had subsided the poet turned to his fellow panelists on the stage and thanked them briefly for their constructive consideration of his work. After that, he repeated his thanks to all those who had helped make the occasion possible, including the editors and subscribers of *New Theatre*. It was during this final expression of gratitude that he uttered his most radical sentiments of the evening.

"Social injustice is no novelty in the world. What is new is the recognition of social injustice; the recognition, specifically, that it *is* injustice and that it *is* hateful!"

He sat down amid scattered applause. It was about midnight

and everybody was tired and the theatre emptied quickly as people went for their subways and taxis.

On the second day after the closing of *Panic* I received a letter postmarked Conway, Mass.:

> Dear Jack:
>
> It's hard to say it—easy to write it. My gratitude to you and to Jimmy and to Zatkin. I don't think you will ever regret what you have done however you may feel about it now. You have created one of the most beautiful productions of the modern theatre—a production incredibly more beautiful than the verse which occasioned it—and you have thrown that verse and that production uncompromisingly into the teeth of the commercial critics. If you have gotten back affected boredom instead of anger the compliment is all the greater. I wish to God I could feel you were as completely happy about it all as I am. . . .
>
> Can you have the chair sent back to 129 E. 10? The carpenter has the two missing casters. They might drop a clotch over it to keep it as clean as possible. I'll be down Wednesday and we can clean everything up then and forget all the stuff that has worried you so much. Poor Jack.
>
> Wasn't that Saturday night audience superb? What more could any of us ask? With all my thanks for more than all I can say,
>
> Affectionately,
> Archie

The letter was delivered on the afternoon of the day which Zatkin and I had spent checking our accounts and ascertaining that, after paying to have the light trench filled, the damage to the stage floor of the Imperial Theatre repaired and the scenery removed and burned, the final net loss on *Panic* would amount to about thirty-five hundred dollars.

On Wednesday, by appointment, we visited the poet high up in the Chrysler Building, showed him our figures and explained that we saw no possible way of repaying the money we had borrowed from him and from Mr. Lovett. He behaved admirably and undertook to explain the situation to his friend. On my way to Mina Curtiss' apartment I bought an evening paper. It was full of stories of real panic in the streets—the Harlem riots. Though the outbreak was over, with one dead and many injured, tension remained high, and Governor Lehman had been asked to send military assistance. The Mayor had opened an investigation during which the District Attorney blamed it all on the Reds: "Let the Communists know they cannot come into this country and upset our laws!" Meantime more than five hundred police, in cars and on foot, continued to patrol the Harlem area in which we had rehearsed *Four Saints* the year before and the streets through which the massed bands of the Monarch Elks were to march one year later to celebrate the grand opening of the Negro *Macbeth*.

But for the moment my preoccupation, now that the crises of *Panic* were past, was once again with the immediate and pressing problem of what I should do next with my life. At long last, after so many false starts and frustrations, I had begun to find in the theatre a possible realization of those hopes and ambitions that had previously existed only in my most fantastic dreams. This passage from fantasy to reality remained a slow and precarious one: it was made easier for me that winter and in the months to come by the presence of Mina Curtiss and by the certainty that her intelligence, her instinctive understanding and her warmth were available to me without embarrassment or reservation whenever I urgently needed them.

Of that spring's false hopes the first came when I received a call one night over Lewis Galantière's phone to present myself at George Gershwin's apartment the next morning. He received me in his music room, among the French paintings—the Modiglianis, the Soutines—and his own. He had seen *Four Saints* and liked its production; he had heard that I worked well with Negroes in the theatre. Now he was looking for someone to stage the opera he and his brother Ira had created out of Du Bose Heyward's *Porgy*.

I spent two mornings listening raptly to Gershwin's playing

and singing; I asked questions and made a few guarded suggestions. When I left, he bound me to secrecy. A few weeks later I read the Theatre Guild's announcement that Rouben Mamoulian, who had successfully staged *Porgy* as a play six years before, had arrived from California to prepare for the production of *Porgy and Bess* in the fall. I was disappointed but not surprised. My hopes had not been too high and I enjoyed my few days of private fame.

Meantime, I tried to keep myself occupied. I staged Gustav Holst's one-act Falstaff opera, *At the Boar's Head,* for a choral society in the East Seventies; also a fragment of an opera by Avery Claflin based on *The Scarlet Letter* as part of a series of musical evenings organized by Virgil Thomson for Hartford's Friends and Enemies of Modern Music, at which classical and contemporary chamber music was played in sets designed and executed by Eugene Berman, Tchelitchew and Alexander Calder.*

That spring I worked with Nathanael West, who had already written *Miss Lonelyhearts,* on a new kind of revue he had thought up—based on traditional American musical and dramatic material. All the notions were his; I helped him to organize and present them in the hope of directing the show if it was ever produced. He was a charming, sensitive man and within a month we had prepared a forty-page outline that contained much of the Americana that was so successfully exploited by others in the decades that followed. No manager showed the slightest interest, and West departed for Hollywood, where he wrote *The Days of the Locust* before he was killed with his wife in a motor accident on Ventura Boulevard.

But my best times, that spring and early summer, were those I spent with Orson Welles. In the frenzy of rehearsing and opening *Panic* we had had little chance to talk together. It was not until

* One of these was followed by what came to be known as "The Paper Ball," held in the marble courtyard of the Athenaeum and decorated for the occasion by Tchelitchew with festoons, draperies, streamers, and even costumes made of newspaper dyed in pale acid colors—"tous, mon cher, trempés dans du pipi!"

after we closed, and he had come out from behind his sexagenarian's wig and putty nose, that we began to meet and to make plans for the future. He and Virginia had given up their Bronxville apartment and moved into a curious one-room residence on Riverside Drive. I went there one day to collect Orson for lunch. He said he had been working all night, and when I arrived he was still in his bath—a monstrous, medieval iron cistern which, when it was covered at night with a board and mattress, served them as a marriage bed. Orson was lying there, inert and covered with water, through which his huge, dead-white body appeared swollen to gigantic proportions. When he got up, full of apologies, with a great splashing and cascading of waters, I discovered that his bulk owed nothing to refraction—that he was, in reality, just as enormous outside as inside the tub, which, after he had risen from it and had started to dry himself, was seen to hold no more than a few inches of liquid lapping about his huge, pale feet.

Since neither of us had a residence suited to conversation, we spent hours drinking coffee in odd places, until Nathan Zatkin one day presented us with the key to a large suite in the Sardi Building on 44th Street, the abandoned headquarters of the Mendelssohn Society of America. A bronze bust of the composer, an enormous oak table and four straight chairs were the only furnishings of what became the temporary headquarters of the catatonic Phoenix Theatre. Here Orson and I spent hours, talking, dreaming, laughing and vaguely developing schemes for making bricks without straw. "Planning" is the wrong word for what we did together—then or later. Of the manifold projects we cooked up in the four and a half years of our association—the ones that succeeded and the ones that failed, the ones that were begun and abandoned and the ones that never got started at all—each was an improvisation, an inspiration or an escape: our response to an emotional impulse rather than the considered execution of a plan.

Now, toward the end of April, 1935, sitting in our bare office on West 44th Street, we were seized with a sudden, compulsive urge to produce a play together. It did not matter too much what it was, nor that it was too late in the season, nor that we had no way of financing it. Orson's dominant drive, at the moment, was a desire to expose the anemic elegance of Guthrie McClintic's *Romeo and Juliet* through an Elizabethan production of such energy and violence as New York had never seen. For this demonstration, we hesitated between Marlowe's *Tragical History of Doctor Faustus* and John Ford's *'Tis Pity She's a Whore,* which we finally selected.

Welles spent a weekend in and on his bathtub devising a handsome and extremely complex Italian street scene (complete with balconies and interiors), in which the stage became a theatrical crossroads where the physical and emotional crises of the tragedy converged. After that, he began to produce costume sketches in great number. The rest of our time was taken up with the sociable business of casting. During the weeks of our occupancy, the premises of the Mendelssohn Society of America had become a sort of lighting place and refuge for young actors of our acquaintance on their weary and discouring rounds of Broadway's theatrical offices. Now, in addition to serving them tea or coffee, brought in at their own expense from the drugstores on Times Square, we set them to reading Elizabethan verse, for their own benefit and ours. These exercises—readings, dialogues and staged scenes—continued day after day behind the locked doors of our office and in Whitford Kane's basement on Fourteenth Street, till we had the play admirably cast and more than half-rehearsed. Miriam Batista was our Annabella, Alexander Scourby the incestuous brother who brings her heart to court on the point of his dagger. For Poggio, the tragic buffoon who is stabbed in error and who dies in the dark, mistaking the lifeblood oozing from his pierced belly for the incontinence of fear, Orson chose a boyhood friend from Wisconsin by the name of Hiram Sherman, of whose talent he was so fanatically convinced that he would not rest till he had proved it to the world.

As a frame for our production we found the perfect theatre—the run-down, six-hundred-seat Bijou on 45th Street, at the north end of Shubert Alley, which had lain dark for many months and was available on reasonable terms. So, by the middle of May, a few days before the end of the theatrical season, we were all ready to go—cast, designed, housed—and even, possibly, financed. Our angel, this time, was no benevolent banker but an aging lady of great wealth who was in the habit, before retiring, of washing and ironing whatever bills (from one dollar 'to a hundred) she found in her pocketbook at the end of the day. She was the "protectress" of one of the most outrageous of Orson's many singular friends, Francis Carpenter, who had given us his solemn assurance that she was good for the ten thousand dollars we needed for our production, provided we left all financial dealings with the lady entirely to him. (She was terribly nervous, he explained—and for good reason. Firmly convinced of the innocence of Bruno Hauptmann, the convicted kidnapper of the Lindbergh baby, she had vowed, if he was executed, never again to sleep in a bed. For two years now she had lain every night, fully dressed, in fitful slumber, on one of the many sofas in her Fifth Avenue mansion.) In exchange for his intervention, Francis, who claimed to have appeared on the stage with Maude Adams and Minnie Maddern Fiske, was awarded the part of a venal courtier, which he read for us with prodigious obscenity.

When we were less than a week from our announced rehearsal date and still no money had appeared, we began to press him. Francis was mildly offended. Three days later we spoke to him again in desperation: we told him not to reappear without a check. The next morning he was back, all smiles, and told us that we had been wrong to doubt him. The ten thousand dollars were in the bank and at our disposal—with one provision. Since neither he nor his patroness could bear the thought of such a beautiful production playing in an unworthy setting, her ten thousand dollars were to be used *not* for production but for the redecoration of the Bijou Theatre, beginning with sandblasting of its facade!

If Orson had not started to laugh at that moment, I doubt if Francis Carpenter would have left the premises of the Mendelssohn Society alive. His hilarity was infectious. Actors who dropped in to inquire about the start of rehearsals found us, an hour later, still howling, roaring, crowing and slapping ourselves in wild and uncontrollable hysteria. That afternoon, after an extravagant lunch, we announced that we were abandoning our production for lack of funds. A few days later, we vacated the office, and Orson and Virginia went west to see a man about a summer theatre somewhere in Wisconsin. We parted friends—without promises or commitments, and with no particular reason to believe we would ever be associated again. Yet our time together had not been wasted.

To me, those weeks were a revelation. I was almost thirty-three years old. Welles was twenty. But in my working relationship with this astonishing boy whose theatrical experience was so much greater and richer than mine, it was I who was the pupil, he the teacher. In certain fields I was his senior, possessed of painfully acquired knowledge that was wider and more comprehensive than his; but what amazed and awed me in Orson was his astounding and, apparently, innate dramatic instinct. Listening to him, day after day, with rising fascination, I had the sense of hearing a man initiated, at birth, into the most secret rites of a mystery—the theatre—of which he felt himself, at all times, the rightful and undisputed master. I watched him, with growing wonder, take as mannered and decadent a work as John Ford's tragedy, bend it to his will and recreate it, on the stage of his imagination, in the vivid, dramatic light of his own theatrical emotion. 'Tis Pity She's a Whore (which neither of us ever again considered as a possible project) served its function—that of a dry run for the productions that followed. Through it we learned each other's language and laid the foundation and set the form and tone of our future collaboration.

I missed Orson when he left. Then, as the spell lifted, I resumed my life of plots and maneuvers, of watching and waiting for my next chance. In this, my last fallow summer before the raging activity of the years ahead, I divided my time between my attic room on 57th Street and my aunt's little house on the South Mountain Road, where I was assured of huge and delicious meals over the weekend. Halfway between New York and New City, and a frequent resting place for my throbbing Model A, was Sneden's Landing, where Pare Lorentz had just moved into a new house higher up the hill. Pare, besides being America's liveliest movie critic, was becoming increasingly concerned with the changing state of the nation under the New Deal. After a series of magazine articles, he had turned to documentary films as a way to tell his story: that summer he was working on the first of his films. *The Plough That Broke the Plains,* in which he dealt dramatically and poetically with the calamity of soil erosion in Texas and Oklahoma—on those same burning plains over which I had traveled during my first Southwestern summer, seven years before. Pare was a man of exasperating eloquence who was outraged if you broke off a conversation before four in the morning; in the years during which we were friends and occasionally worked together, he taught me a lot about America and the painful but exciting realities of its growth.

Another of my companions that summer was Albert Bein, a former boy-hobo who had lost one leg under the wheels of a freight train from which a brakeman had thrown him. His play *Li'l Ol' Boy* directed by Joseph Loscy, had been an admired failure on Broadway. Now he had another, *Heavenly Express,* which made me think of my nights in the freight yards in Kansas City, on which we worked together intermittently for some months. I loved it, but it never seemed quite right and I never got to produce or direct it.*

So passed another anxious, idle summer in the green, steaming heat of the Hudson Valley. Twice I drove with Lincoln Kirstein into the Berkshires and once Mina came down and spent three days with me in New City. Defying the copperheads with which the South Mountain Road abounded that summer, other ladies paid platonic visits—Marya Mannes, Stella Adler and Elizabeth Hawes with her two camel-haired Afghans. Lewis Galantière came once but found the atmosphere too rustic for his taste. Walking down the center of the South Mountain Road at hours set aside *"pour la promenade,"* in his light flannel trousers, straw hat and jacket, he surprisingly resembled photographs of Marcel Proust.

---

* It still was not right when it was produced on Broadway four years later with Robert Lewis as director and John Garfield in the leading role.

By the middle of August the last of my savings were gone and I was nervous and anxious to get back to town to work I did not have. The little house in New City, which had been my refuge, two years before, against the devastating winds of national and personal catastrophe, no longer served my needs. The time for a storm cellar was over. Things were on the move all around me and, outsider though I was, I must move with them or perish. When my opportunity came, it was, once again, from an entirely unexpected quarter—from the Government of a country in which I had been, for more than five years, an illegal resident.

IV

BY 1935, halfway through the energetic confusions of Roosevelt's first term, the outline of the New Deal had begun to appear. One significant symptom was the change-over from relief—from a national acceptance of "defeated, discouraged, hopeless men and women, cringing and fawning as they came to ask for public aid"—to the revolutionary idea of work-relief. To twenty million Americans dependent on public charity (amid cries of socialism, communism and worse), work was to be supplied by the Federal Government within their own skills and trades. This mutation took place during the dog days, with only moderate attention on my part; it was not till September that the Works Progress Administration, newly formed under Harry Hopkins, received an allocation of five billion dollars of Federal funds, to be spent at the rate of four hundred and twenty million a month. Of this, a small fraction (less than one percent) was to be devoted to the arts—including the theatre.

The Federal Theatre of the Works Progress Administration, which, within two years, was to be described by a leading critic as "the chief producer of works of art in the American theatre" and which came to play such a vital part in so many of our lives, was not primarily a cultural activity. It was a relief measure conceived in a time of national misery and despair. The only artistic policy it ever had was the assumption that thousands of indigent theatre people were eager to work and that millions of Americans would enjoy the results of this work if it could be offered at a price they could afford to pay. Within a year of its formation, the Federal Theatre had more than fifteen thousand men and women on its payroll at an average wage of approximately twenty dollars a week. During the four years of its existence its productions played to more than thirty million people in more than two hundred theatres as well as portable stages, school auditoriums and public parks the country over.*

To guide and administer this, the most controversial of all his work projects, Harry Hopkins had chosen a national director who was not drawn from the commercial hierarchy of Broadway but from among the dreamers and experimenters—the eggheads of American theatre. Hallie Flanagan, like Hopkins a graduate of Grinnell in the Middle West and head, since 1925, of Vassar's famed Experimental Theatre, was a wild little woman who believed and publicly stated her conviction that "the theatre is more than a private enterprise; it is also a public interest which, properly fostered, might come to be a social and an educative force"; a fanatic, armed with millions of taxpayers' money, who, on assuming office, had heretically announced that "while our immediate aim is to put to work thousands of theatre people, our more far-reaching purpose is to organize and support theatrical enterprises so excellent in quality and low in cost, and so vital to the communities involved that they will be able to continue after Federal support is withdrawn." To those who were fortunate enough to be a part of the Federal Theatre from the beginning, it was a unique and thrilling experience. Added to the satisfac-

---

* Hallie Flanagan in her book *Arena* has left us a dramatic history of the Federal Theatre from its birth in the depth of the Depression to its political assassination in Washington four years later.

tion of accomplishing an urgent and essential social task in a time of national crisis, we enjoyed the excitement that is generated on those rare and blessed occasions when the theatre is suddenly swept into the historical mainstream of its time.

My own connection with the project began quite suddenly one evening in Rosamond Gilder's apartment on Gramercy Park. As associate editor, with Edith Isaacs, of the *Theatre Arts Monthly,* she had come to form part of the inner circle of Miss Flanagan's aides and advisers. She told me my name had come up in discussions over the formation of the New York WPA Negro Theatre. She asked if I would be interested: I told her I would. Two weeks later my friend Rose MacLendon, the Negro actress, called and asked me to meet her in Hallie Flanagan's office. She was late as usual and I spent half an hour alone with Mrs. Flanagan—a small, forthright, enthusiastic lady with strong teeth, whose matted reddish hair lay like a wig on her skull and who seemed to take her vast responsibilities with amazing self-confidence and sang-froid. When Rose arrived, there was a general meeting, with Philip Barber, Hallie's assistant, and Elmer Rice, newly appointed head of New York's Federal Theatre project.* By the end of it I had been offered and had accepted the post of joint head of the Negro Theatre Project in association with Rose MacLendon, with instructions to fill out papers and begin work the following morning. In the confusion of transferring three and a half million men and women to the Federal payroll before Christmas, it was not noticed that I was not only an alien but also illegally residing in the United States under a false name. Or maybe nobody cared. My application went through as urgent, non-relief, executive personnel at a salary of fifty dollars a week. It was not until many months later that I understood the true circumstances of my nomination to a job which I took on eagerly, with only a confused awareness of its hazards and implications. I was not stupid enough to underestimate the difficulties that lay ahead, but for anyone who was as frightened of life as I was,

---

* Elmer Rice was the only successful theatre man to throw in his lot, actively, with the Federal Theatre, from which he resigned five months later on an issue of censorship.

there was an irresistible attraction and even a perverse sense of safety in my commitment to such a manifestly impossible task.

I had known Harlem in the mid-twenties as a late-night playground; I had found it again, eight years later, as the scene of my first and happiest theatre experience. Both times, in different ways, I had been made sharply aware of the corrosive misery that filled its streets and houses. The so-called Harlem Riots of March, 1935, shocked and frightened New Yorkers but surprised no one who knew conditions in that unhappy, restricted corner of Manhattan. It was the sudden boiling over of a long-fermenting mess of corruption, exploitation and official indifference. Harlem had a church on every other corner; it also had the highest crime rate in the city. Vice, gambling and bootlegging in its various forms were Tammany preserves of long standing; rents were double or more what they were in any equivalent white area of the city, with no leases given, no control or inspections enforced and an organized landlords' blacklist against protesting or "troublesome" tenants. Local businesses and stores (many of them survivals from the days when Harlem was a New York suburb) refused, almost without exception, to employ Negro help. Unemployment had long been endemic in Harlem; with the Depression, it became critical. Under the spur of despair, passive resignation turned into active resentment—stirrings of revolt in which the Left found fruitful ground for its expanding activity. The first Negro unemployed demonstrations had been met with police brutality; soon after, the Harlem edition of the *Daily Worker* began to call itself *The Liberator* and the Communist Party's vice-presidential candidate in the two next national elections was a Negro. Yet the Party's influence remained limited and superficial, for Harlem followed the typical minority pattern: united in misery, it remained fragmented in every other respect. Father Divine was in his heyday. The churches, with their multiple denominations, continued to perform an important and soothing function in the life of the community, though many of their preachers were considered old-fashioned, in some cases mercenary, and generally suspected of

"Uncle Tom" attitudes. Roused by Mussolini's threat to Ethiopia, small groups gathered on street corners to listen to advocates of "Back to Africa" and to participate in various small Negro nationalist movements—echoes of Garvey and forerunners of Black Nationalists and Muslims. "Segregation" and "integration" were still academic words, in use among the intelligentsia, but devoid of any wide emotional affect.* Economic discrimination, on the other hand, was general and acutely felt; it was the main and immediate cause of the rage and fear that filled Harlem's littered and neglected streets during the worst of the Depression. *"Don't buy where you can't work!"* had become a battle cry long before the riots. Still, nothing was done. Rents and unemployment continued to rise; so did the anger in the streets. The riots were inevitable—a spontaneous explosion of hysterical despair rather than part of any organized campaign of protest. Now, six months later, the New Deal's continuing increase in Federal relief and the promise of local works projects on a large scale had taken some of the fever out of the Harlem crisis without curing its underlying causes. Discrimination and rent gouging continued; so did the bitterness and the disunity.

The Negro Theatre Project of the Works Progress Administration was announced in mid-September and immediately became Harlem's leading topic of agitated dispute. It was known that between seven and eight hundred actors, technicians, service personnel and theatre staff were about to be hired: this would make the project the city's largest employer of Negro workers in one unit, with activities that promised to be far more attractive than leaf raking, street cleaning, construction or office work. For years show business had occupied a special place in Negro city life as one of the few open roads to self-expression and fame: here was a chance to enter it—at Government expense. No wonder that from the first day, and increasingly as rumors began to fly, the question was asked in curiosity, suspicion and anger: now

* The word "black" was taboo. "Negro" was in official and general use though there was some ideological disagreement as to whether it should be spelled with a small or a capital N.

that Harlem was finally to have its own project—who was going to run it? And not only "who?" but "of what color?"

There were three theatrical factions in Harlem at this time. The first centered around the former Lafayette stock company, which had enjoyed a long and successful career before talking pictures in that same theatre building in which the WPA was now about to house its project. Ex-members of the Lafayette Players and their friends felt that the Government's effort to revive Harlem theatrical life should be entrusted to veterans who had run their own show once before without a white man—and who needed one now?

They were opposed by a second, larger and more influential group. Among the intelligentsia—the teachers, social workers and race-relations experts—there was a general feeling of condescension toward Negroes in show business, who were felt to be lacking in the experience, the education and the vision required to administer a major Negro project in a white man's world. This group recommended the appointment of a white man "of stature," flanked by Negro advisers, whom they were eager to supply. Between these two stood a third small but powerful group of successful Negro performers, respected union members whose talent had won them full acceptance in the white world. Many of these were now torn between a desire to lead their people into the theatrical promised land and a reluctance to be sucked back into the Harlem broil from which they had only recently emancipated themselves. They, too, for all their strong racial feeling, were generally of the opinion that without a white man at its head—with connections in Government circles and some reputation on Broadway—the Negro unit would receive scant recognition or respect in Washington or New York.

There was one other element which, finally, came to exert a determining influence in the choice of a project head for the Negro Theatre. This was the Communist Party, which, having few acceptable candidates of its own, threw its support behind those Negro "names" who had shown a willingness to collaborate (for artistic or other reasons) with United Front organizations. One such name was that of my friend Rose McLendon. Rose was not well—ravaged already by the cancer that carried her off six months later. Besides, she was a performer, not an administrator or a director. When the job of heading the Negro Theatre Project was offered her by general consent, she demurred, then finally accepted on one condition: that a suitable white associate be found who would work with her, on a basis of complete equality, as her artistic and executive partner. Asked if she had any suggestions to make, she gave my name as that of someone she knew and trusted.

Our collaboration was never put to the test. In the early days of the project she made one or two formal appearances before she fell finally and hopelessly ill. My visits to her bedside after we got under way gave her a feeling of participation, but soon she was too ill even for that and resigned. By then the project was so far advanced that no one was willing to risk the delays and confusions that would have resulted from a change of leadership. Besides, by that time, things seemed to be going surprisingly well for the Negro Theatre of the WPA.

Our first month had been devoted to one single activity—getting people off relief and onto the project. This transfer took place in a temporary building on lower Madison Avenue, in a vast area of bare concrete floor with makeshift partitions amid hurriedly assembled secondhand desks and benches. Here, day after day, the hallways, elevators, stairways and improvised waiting rooms were jammed with hundreds of men and women, many with children, who arrived and stood around in herds, sent by their local relief agencies to be interviewed, processed and transferred to WPA jobs for which they were more or less qualified.

For admission to the Negro unit the rush was such that guards had to be summoned to control the flow of milling applicants, many of whom arrived downtown in a state of bewildered and angry hysteria. Besides the established relief cases, hundreds of new applicants had suddenly appeared, excited by rumors of jobs and opportunities in a work area where skills and credentials were almost impossible to verify. Anyone with an authentic relief status was hired, sight unseen; as the days passed and the rolls began to fill up, our task was to make sure that men and women with legitimate theatrical backgrounds got on the project even if their relief status (through pride or bureaucratic confusion) was not entirely satisfactory.

In making these vital and sometimes distressing decisions about people with whose background and circumstances I was totally unfamiliar, I had to rely on the advice of two Negro aides. One was Edward Perry, my stage manager from *Four Saints;* the other, who became my counselor, protector, instructor, deputy and intimate friend, was Carlton Moss. One of the Negro "new generation," a graduate of Morgan College in Baltimore, he had directed a community project for the New York Public Library and worked as a drama counselor for the CWA and a writer in radio. When he came to work for the WPA at the age of twenty-five, he was already a bitterly skeptical man. But behind his smiling pose of protective sarcasm lay a deep and sympathetic understanding of the inner workings of the Negro world. For ten months he was my Machiavelli—briefing me before every meeting, sitting by my side and whispering to me or slipping me scribbled notes along the table each time he saw me getting ready to make a fool of myself or to surrender some essential point of which I had failed to grasp the importance.

These meetings were held in various places—in vestries, board rooms and the back rooms of shady bars. And each was entirely different. Around the polished table of the Urban League, sober, conservative well-spoken men and women were interested mostly in employment, culture and decorum and were concerned lest the Negro Theatre's offerings be too exclusively concerned with squalor, violence, bawdry or sex. Here I brought my English accent into play and marshaled my artistic record of *Four Saints,* Ibsen and *Valley Forge* for further reassurance.

The Party, on the other hand, represented by the perennial vice-presidential candidate, James Ford, and his white advisers, wanted no "handkerchief-heading" on the project: they wanted plays of social protest and a voice in the assignment of executive jobs. I did my best to reassure them, citing my production of *Panic* as evidence of my liberal position.*

"We believe we will find on the relief rolls people with the energy, ability and talent to achieve any program set up," Mrs. Flanagan had declared. But for added safety, to ensure the artistic and professional standards of the Arts Projects, a special dispensation was granted by WPA which permitted each unit to hire up to ten percent of its creative and executive personnel from outside the relief lists, at relief wages of between twenty and thirty dollars a week. In our case, that meant actors, directors, technicians from the professional theatre and experienced administrators—mostly from Civil Service. Of these the most earnest and ambitious was a West Indian by the name of Harry Edwards, a former champion long-distance runner, who saw in the project a useful springboard for his own rise to power in the world of Negro affairs. Two of our minor executives, both white, and both appointed at the specific behest of the Communist Party, lasted less than two months in their jobs. Following some mysterious internecine dispute, the Party demanded their dismissal on charges of "white chauvinism." Since they had done nothing wrong on the job, I refused to fire them, and this led to bad feeling between me and the Party's Harlem representatives which lasted for several months, until both men, under intolerable pressure, requested and obtained transfers to other projects.

Another non-relief, non-Negro member of the project was a plump, pink-cheeked, bouncing Jewish virgin named Augusta Weissberger. We desperately needed a secretary; she was moderately competent; there was no one else available and she was willing to work in Harlem. But most of my non-relief appointments—black and white—were on the creative side. These included a number of the country's best Negro actors, whom pride and an obstinate sense of status had kept off the relief rolls.

* Five years later, when Orson Welles and I produced Richard Wright's *Native Son*, there were two separate sets of protesting pickets in front of the theatre on opening night—the Communist Party's and the Urban League's.

Their names appear with honor on the cast lists of that year's Lafayette productions. Negro writers included Countee Cullen and Zorah Hurston, a young female novelist from Florida. Clarence Yates was our best-known dancer and choreographer; Perry Watkins, who designed our first show, was that rare thing—a Negro member of the Scene Designers' Union. Among our musicians, we had the great Eubie Blake, Joe Jordan, and Leonard de Paur, who, years later, founded and led one of the country's most distinguished male ensembles—the Infantry Chorus. Langston Hughes was a frequent visitor, but he already formed part of the Writers' Project and saw no reason to change.

The rest of our artistic staff came from among my own friends and associates. They included Manny Essman and Nat Karson, the designers, Virgil Thomson, who had the title of musical supervisor, and Abe Feder as technical director and lighting expert with his inseparable assistant, Teddy Thomas. They came, certainly not for the thirty dollars a week, nor primarily out of friendship for me, but because they saw in the project a wide-open field for those creative activities which they were denied within the narrow limits of the commercial theatre; also, perhaps, out of a vague, undefined feeling that, as cooperating members of the Negro Theatre unit, they were helping to start something new and significant in the cultural life of their country.

Late in October 1935, about the time Mussolini was invading Ethiopia, the Negro Theatre Project, with its more than seven hundred and fifty men and women and its battered desks, chairs and filing cabinets, began its move from lower Madison Avenue to Harlem. Soon after that, while the Japanese were invading the Chinese mainland, we started to take down the rotting boards which had long covered the doors and windows of the old Lafayette Theatre on Seventh Avenue between 132nd and 133rd streets. Built around the turn of the century when Harlem was a theatrical tributary of Broadway, the Lafayette was a sordid, icy cavern when we moved in—with peeling plaster, a thick accumulation of grime, burst bulbs, rotting carpets and broken seats in the hairy recesses of which lurked rats, lice and other horrors.

Within a month the auditorium had been restored to some semblance of respectability and warmth. On stage, behind the lowered, flaking asbestos safety curtain, equally miraculous changes were being wrought by a stage crew that was the equal in zeal and skill to the best of Broadway. Consistently refused admission to the Stagehands' Union on grounds of color, these carpenters and electricians had been forced to make their living for years outside the nonexistent Negro theatre. Now they were back in their chosen profession: the miles of new rope and cable that Feder had requisitioned, the scores of up-to-date electrical units hanging overhead and the six portable dimmer boards with their dozens of multicolored switches and levers were a source of excitement and pride that made theirs the most consistently enthusiastic department of the project.

Of our seven hundred and fifty workers, between four and five hundred were officially classified as actors, singers or dancers. Of these approximately one third had never acted, danced or been on a stage or a concert platform in their lives. Half of the rest had, at one time or another, danced in a chorus, sung with a group or appeared as extras in films. This left us with around a hundred and fifty professional performers, including African drummers, veteran stock actors, Broadway stars and locally celebrated elecutionists like Venezuela Jones. To devise productions in which we could properly employ even a fraction of such variegated talents—this became my main challenge as the project got under way.

None of the tried and obvious ways would work. In the current temper of the Harlem community, the old "stock" pattern of performing recent Broadway hits with Negro casts was undesirable, if not downright offensive. Equally unsuitable, for different reasons, was the revival of such celebrated Negro successes as *The Emperor Jones, In Abraham's Bosom, All God's Chillun* or even *Porgy,* which Harlem audiences had applauded downtown but would resent on the stage of their own community theatre. This same inhibition seemed to apply to the revues and musicals that had long been the Negro performers' main source of theatrical fame and employment; under ideological censure from both

Left and Right, they were regarded as "handkerchief-head" and so, for our purposes, anathema.

In the solution of this problem, Virgil Thomson, with whom I was sharing the first of the five Manhattan apartments we inhabited together over the next two and a half years, was of inestimable aid to me.* He reminded me that our casting of *Four Saints* had been done on purely artistic and theatrical grounds. Our black singers had been chosen because their voices, diction and movements were perfectly suited to the execution of a work that had nothing Negro about it. Their performance had justified our choice and this encouraged me in the position I now took—that our only hope of functioning in a vital and constructive way lay in dividing the performing personnel of the Negro Theatre into two separate, though still interrelated, halves. One would be devoted to the performance of plays written, directed and performed by and for Negroes, in Negro locales and, preferably, on contemporary Negro subjects. The other would devote itself to the performance of classical works of which our actors would be the interpreters, without concession or reference to color. The choice as to which group they joined was to be made by the project members themselves, with the clear understanding that they could, if they chose, shift their allegiance from production to production. This would give diversity to our shows, increase our use of manpower and stimulate public interest in our activities. It would also arouse a feeling of emulation that would, I hoped, act as a sharp and constant spur to our morale.

For this fine scheme to work, there was one essential condition—that the quality of these "classical" productions be exceptionally high. It would be fatal to undertake the risky and difficult business of producing Shakespeare in Harlem until I had found a director of whose creative imagination and power I was

---

* He was the perfect companion—neat, even-tempered, intelligent, lively, wise and agreeable in the morning. Our hours were well adjusted: I was away all day, leaving the place empty for him to compose in and receive his friends. Almost every evening he went out, leaving me free to entertain young women who did not have places of their own.

completely confident. With this in mind I went down one evening to the basement apartment on West Fourteenth Street into
which Orson and Virginia Welles had just moved. Orson had
spent a feckless summer in Wisconsin—his impresario having gone
broke even before he opened. On his return to New York, in
order to keep himself and Virginia alive, he had been forced into
what soon became a meteoric career in radio, where his magnificent voice was put to such base uses that fall as *The Shadow,* the
voice of chocolate pudding, and *The Great McCoy,* besides his
weekly impersonations on the March of Time of such diverse
characters as Haile Selassie, Hindenburg, Sir Basil Zaharoff and
the Emperor Hirohito.

I told him of my plans for the Negro Theatre and formally
invited him to join us. I suggestd that our dream of staging a
whirling Elizabethan drama might now be realized under unusual but attractive conditions—with Uncle Sam as our angel.
Orson said yes immediately, then called me at two in the morning to announce that Virginia had just had an inspiration: our
first production would be *Macbeth,* laid in the island of Haiti in
the early nineteenth century, with the witches as Voodoo priest-
esses! Within a week he had constructed out of Plasticene, on a
sheet of laundry board, a scale model of what later appeared on
the stage of the Lafayette as the basic unit of *Macbeth.* At the
same time he and Nat Karson, with Virginia as their legman,
began to amass research on Directoire modes, Napoleonic uniforms and tropical vegetation.

As soon as it was known that we were considering doing *Macbeth,* it became a matter of general controversy in Harlem. The
community was fascinated but wary: some thought this Shakespearean venture an unnecessary risk, others saw it in a white
man's scheme deliberately hatched to degrade the Negro and
bring the Theatre Project into disrepute. Our first auditions
tended to confirm these misgivings. I had announced that we
would hear anyone who wished to try out for the classical wing of
the project. For the best part of a week, they followed each other
onto the platform of a large recreation hall belonging to the
Ancient Order of Monarch Elks: old and young, male and

female, singers, dancers, semiliterates and intellectuals—some in deadly earnest, some giggling in self-conscious embarrassment; still others who came suspiciously, regarding the whole thing as an elaborate joke. By the end of the week more than three hundred had been auditioned and classified under mysterious symbols that signified rejects, dancers, soldiers, witches, walk-ons and principals. Within another week, with Edward Perry as associate supervisor, *Macbeth* was in rehearsal. Orson had asked me to stay away for the first few weeks. Overwhelmed by the problems of getting the theatre open, I was only too glad to oblige.

For obvious reasons it was desirable to open the Lafayette with an "indigenous" and, preferably, a realistic contemporary Negro work. And here, immediately, I had encountered our first predictable hazard—the absence of performable Negro scripts. Precedents were scarce: *Stevedore,* notwithstanding its use of the Negro as victim and hero, was, essentially, a white play; Hall Johnson's *Run Little Chillun,* for all its boundless energy, was less a play than a choral and declamatory tour de force. Of the many scripts submitted to us, two were possible, though far from good: *Turpentine* by Peter Morrell and Gus Smith—a powerful actor of the Left—was a stereotyped play of protest laid in a turpentine-workers' camp in South Carolina; Frank Wilson's *Walk Together Chillun!,* which he was eager to direct himself, was an awkward hodgepodge of theatrical clichés, complete with church scene, dance-hall sequence, comedy routines and a preachment that could offend absolutely no one. Wilson was one of America's best-known black actors, the creator of Porgy, a church member and a man whose confused and voluble sincerity had won him the patronizing approval of most organized sections of the community. I chose his play for tactical reasons, fully aware of its weaknesses but equally aware of its advantages for our opening show. My assignment, as head of the project, was not, primarily, the production of masterpieces. I had been instructed to find suitable theatrical activity for the hundreds of needy men and women on our payroll and to find it quickly. *Walk Together Chillun!* seemed to meet this requirement.

For all their many divisions, every member of the project seemed to agree on one thing: that the Negro Theatre must be the first New York unit to open its doors to the public. With this objective very much in mind, we put *Walk Together Chillun!* into rehearsal early in December, first in a church, then on the reconditioned stage of the Lafayette. And, in spite of our difficulties with the play (half the second act was removed in the fifth week of rehearsal) and the problems normally attendant upon the opening of a dark theatre, it soon became evident, following the cancellation of the Living Newspaper's first show, *Ethiopia,* that we would, in fact, be the first major project to present a WPA Federal Theatre production in New York City.

Walk Together Chillun! opened with a suitable official flurry on the night of February 5, 1936. Its reception was cordial but not enthusiastic. Harlem was relieved that the Project's opening show was neither a disaster nor an "Uncle Tom" piece and proud that the first Federal Theatre play in New York should be a Negro production. People who remembered the old Lafayette were impressed by the condition of the house, the size of the pit band led by Joe Jordan and the lavishness of the new technical set-up—the lighting particularly. Downtown was generally uninterested. Brooks Atkinson's reaction in *The New York Times* was condescending but kind:

> After displaying patience enough to make Job envious, The New York Federal Theatre raised the curtain on its first legitimate production, *Walk Together Chillun!* According to Broadway standards, it is artless and sometimes unintelligible, but its actors attack their parts as vigorously as though a Broadway manager was footing the bill . . .
>
> Setting his play in an unnamed city in the North, Mr. Wilson shows how an infusion of Negroes from Georgia makes trouble and precipitates a race riot which stirs up the whole town. When the Negroes are in trouble their sectional differences lose importance. When the whites are aroused, they draw

no distinctions. *Walk Together Chillun!* concludes with an impassioned plea for racial solidarity.

. . . Although *Walk Together Chillun!* is a patchwork play by Broadway standards, there is obviously more to it than any white man is likely to understand. Mr. Wilson is talking to his comrades. He is not appealing for Times Square applause.

This, our opening production, ran for less than a month to moderate attendance. Our second—also from the "contemporary" wing of the project—was *Conjur Man Dies* by Rudolph Fisher, a well-known Harlem physician and novelist. It was less earnest than its predecessor and a lot more fun. Directed by Joseph Losey, it was a comedy-mystery in three acts with fourteen scenes, whose theme song was "I'll Be Glad When You're Dead, You Rascal You!" It opened on March 11th (three days before the first of the WPA's Living Newspapers, eight days before *Murder in the Cathedral*) and it was a smash. Unlike Wilson's ingenuous preachment, this was big-city entertainment—fast-moving, topical, crammed with inside allusions and bitter minority jokes (e.g., the detective, Dooley Wilson, stands beside the police doctor in the morgue as he looks through his microscope at a suspicious blood smear. "It's not moving," says the doctor. "It must be colored blood," says Dooley* to roars of laughter.) An earnest white man's perplexity was reflected in *The New York Times* review:

HARLEM MUMBO-JUMBO

To a paleface, fresh from Broadway, the new play seemed like a verbose and amateur charade, none too clearly written and soggily acted. But the Layfayette Theatre was bulging with family parties last night who roared at the obese comedian and howled over the West Indian accent of a smart Harlem landlady. This column doesn't know everything after all.

* Five years later Dooley Wilson was starring with Ethel Waters and Katherine Dunham in Broadway's *Cabin in the Sky;* two years after that, as Sam in *Casablanca* with Ingrid Bergman and Humphrey Bogart, he was launching one of the year's biggest song hits, "As Time Goes By."

From every practical point of view, even from that of those who disapproved of it, *Conjur Man Dies* was good programming, an asset to the project and a welcome escape from the many stresses and anxieties that continued to harass us. Its success allowed me to turn all my attention to our next opening—the first production of our classical wing, which was generally referred to, by this time, as the *Voodoo Macbeth*.

My functions on the project, so far, had been essentially administrative and diplomatic. Though I had personally supervised both our contemporary shows and, in the case of *Walk Together Chillun!*, actively intervened as a director when I thought it necessary, I had not identified myself creatively with either of them. The gauge of my success, so far, had been the efficacy and harmony with which the project was conducted, rather than the theatrical or artistic quality of its productions. Now, suddenly, with *Macbeth*, all this was changed. For besides its potential value to the project in opening up new fields for black performers, I could not help regarding this production as a direct, personal challenge and the first serious test of my theatrical collaboration with Orson Welles, on which I was setting such high hopes and on which I was preparing to risk not only my own future but that of the Negro project as well.

I had acceded to Orson's request that I stay away from early rehearsals of *Macbeth*. When I finally visited the Elks' Hall, what I heard and saw delighted but in no way astonished me. I had never seriously doubted the company's ability to speak Elizabethan blank verse when they encountered it under the right conditions and, though he had never staged a play except at school, I had complete faith in Welles's ability to direct them. We had chosen the cast together: Jack Carter, the creator of Crown in the original *Porgy*, was the Thane, with Edna Thomas as his murderous lady. For the Macduffs we had Maurice Ellis and Marie Young; J. Louis Johnson was the Porter, Canada Lee was Banquo and Eric Burroughs (a graduate of London's RADA) played Hecate, a composite figure of evil which Welles had assembled out of fragments of witches' lines and to whose sinister equipment he presently added a twelve-foot bullwhip. Our supernatural department was very strong at the Lafayette. In addition to the witches and sundry apparitions called for by the Bard, we had a troupe of African drummers commanded by Asadata Dafora Horton (later minister of culture of the Republic of Sierra Leone). Except for their leader, who had a flawless Oxford accent, they spoke little English: the star of the troupe, Abdul, an authentic witch doctor, seemed to know no language at all except magic. Their first act, after they had been cast in *Macbeth*, was to file a formal requisition for five live black goats. These were brought into the theatre by night and sacrificed, hugger-mugger, according to approved tribal ritual, before being stretched into resonant drum skins.

This supernatural atmosphere added to the excitement that was beginning to form around our production of *Macbeth*. By the end of February it had become the most debated subject in Harlem—one on which the entire future of the Negro Theatre Project was felt to depend. Partly, this had to do with the nature of the show—the first full-scale, professional Negro Shakespearean production in theatrical history. Partly it was the effect of sheer mass. For *Macbeth* had grown steadily with the months until it had become an undertaking of such magnitude that the whole project was beginning to sag under its weight. Backstage at the Lafayette, to make room for the huge slabs of scenery and acres of painted backdrops that continued to arrive from the shops, *Conjur Man Dies* was gradually being edged down toward the footlights, to the fury of its director and cast. And, in the basement, the glow of hundreds of Karson's gorgeous uniforms, stiff with gold braid, the sheen of satin ball gowns and the gnarled and hairy horror of the witches' hides could not fail to arouse the envious resentment of members of the project's contemporary wing, who were confined to the realistic drabness of street clothes and denim. Soon, ugly rumors began to fly: someone had been told downtown by an authoritative source that *Macbeth* would never open; so much of the project's money had been spent by me on my boyfriend's folly that all future productions of the Negro unit had been canceled. And a stale but dangerous whispering campaign was revived: that what was being so secretly prepared was, in reality, a vast burlesque intended to ridicule the Negro in the eyes of the white world. As a result, Orson was attacked one night, as he was leaving rehearsal, by four alcoholic zealots determined to prevent this insult to their race.

Partly, too, there was the agitation generated by the show itself. Since the first day of rehearsal, from behind the locked doors of the Elks' Hall, waves of excitement had been radiating in ever-widening circles through the Harlem streets. These were created in part by Orson, whose demonic energy was transmitted first to his leading actors, then to his exhausted and bewildered but enthusiastic company and finally, through them, to the whole puzzled community. When the *Macbeth* troupe came out of hiding and began to rehearse, often all through the night, on the stage of the Lafayette, this sense of anxious anticipation continued to grow—especially after drummers, dancers and sound effects had been added and could be heard, like distant thunder, seeping through the walls of the theatre into Seventh Avenue and the surrounding streets.

Including his regular midtown radio jobs, to which he commuted by taxi (sometimes two or three times a day), Orson was now working about twenty hours out of the twenty-four. When he was not drilling the company in mass scenes of battle, revelry or witchcraft, or rehearsing individually with the Macbeths and Macduffs, he was working with Virgil on music, Karson on costumes, Feder on lights or Asadata on voodoo.

It was during the preparation of *Macbeth* that Orson revealed his surprising capacity for collaboration. For all the mass of his own ego, he was able to apprehend other people's weakness and strength and to make creative use of them: he had a shrewd instinctive sense of when to bully or charm, when to be kind or savage—and he was seldom mistaken. With Feder, who was a garrulous masochist, Orson was abusive, sarcastic and loud. At light rehearsals he would set him impossible tasks, then howl at him, shamefully and continuously, before the exhausted company, who were so delighted to hear someone else (a white man, especially) catching hell, that they persevered with their own stage maneuvers long after their normal span of patience had run out. As a result Orson completed his light rehearsals, preserved the morale of his troupe and retained Feder's professional devotion—if not his love. With Virgil Thomson it was less easy. For here Orson was dealing with a temperament, an intelligence and an attitude of a kind he had seldom encountered. Virgil was wary of the boy genius:

> You brought Orson to the flat where we were living on Fifty-ninth Street. We argued late one night and as an older man I tried to beat him down because I felt he was full of bluff and because his verbalization of what he wanted to do in the theatre was not entirely convincing. I argued hard and not always fairly against Orson and you told me later to stop it because he was a very, very good man in the theatre. You were the one that believed in him . . .

Then as they began to work together, things got easier.

> Orson was nearly always likable. He was never hateful or brutal with me, though I was a little terrified of his firmness. He was extremely professional and he knew exactly what he wanted. He knew it so well and so thoroughly that I, as an older musician with a certain amount of pride, would not write him original music. I would not humiliate myself to write so precisely on his demand. On the other hand, I respected his demands dramatically. So, as your employee, I gave him sound effects and ready-made music—trumpet call, battle scenes and percussive scores where he wanted them—and, of course, the waltzes for the party scene.
>
> Orson and I never quarreled—as you and he did; but we never really agreed. We used to take each other out to elaborate dinners; and it was I who taught him to drink white wine, and not whiskey, at rehearsals . . .

Another quite different set of problems arose during our collaboration with Asadata Dafora Horton and his troupe of African drummers. With the exception of Abdul, the witch doctor, who several times during rehearsals fell into deep and agitated trances from which not even his fellow witches could rouse him, our Gold Coast contingent was thoroughly professional, adaptable and eager to please—except in the matter of spells. One day, after Orson, Virgil and I had been auditioning their voodoo numbers, we complained to Asadata that his chants did not sound evil enough. Virgil, as usual, got right down to the point.

"Are those really voodoo?"

"Oh, yes. Yes, indeed, Sirs. That is absolutely real, authentic voodoo."

"They don't sound wicked enough."

"Sirs, I . . ."

"Sometimes for the theatre you have to exaggerate."

"I am sorry, Sirs. You can't be any more wicked than that!"

I stayed behind with Virgil and the drummers. As fellow musicians they argued for most of the afternoon. Finally Asadata admitted what those chants of his really were: they were strong spells intended to *ward off* the beriberi—not to induce it. He dared not give us the real thing, he explained. It might have worked.

Later, when we insisted, they did somewhat darken the tone of their incantations. For that reason I was unnerved when, one night, in the first witch scene, through the moaning and banging of drums, I quite distinctly heard, amid the incomprehensible sounds of Abdul's unknown tongue, the words "Meesta Welles" and "Meesta Houseman" several times repeated. I never told Orson, for he was ridiculously superstitious. Besides, he was haunted throughout rehearsals by the old English theatrical tradition that of all the plays in the canon, *Macbeth* is the most ill-fated and accident prone. (It was, in fact, the only play I ever did with him in which he neither sprained nor broke a limb nor otherwise incapacitated himself before or after its opening.)

The *Macbeth* troupe, including understudies, stage managers, cripples, children and dependents, finally numbered one hundred and thirty-seven. Orson led them with an authority that was extraordinary in a boy just out of his teens. He had the strength; but he also had the infinite and loving patience which, in my experience, distinguishes the great from the competent director. And he displayed a capacity for total concentration without which our whole perilous venture could never have been brought off. For this *Macbeth* troupe of ours was an amazing mishmash of amateurs and professionals, church members and radicals, sophisticates and wild ones, adherents of Father Divine and bushmen from Darkest Africa. It was one thing to handle them administratively and paternalistically as I did (firm but understanding, not always truthful but generally fair) and quite another to lead them creatively through unknown country during months of rehearsal in an atmosphere of gathering enervation and doubt. Orson kept them going by the sheer force of his personality. His energy was at all times greater than theirs; he was even more mercurial and less predictable than they were—driving and indolent, glum and gay, tender and violent, inflexibly severe and hopelessly indulgent. I once estimated that a quarter of his growing radio earnings, during *Macbeth,* went in loans and handouts to the company; another quarter was spent on the purchase of props and other necessities (including a severed head) held up by bureaucratic red tape; a third quarter went for meals and cabs; the rest was spent on the entertainment of Jack Carter.

Jack Carter was the most furious man I have ever kown. Six foot four, elegant and malevolent in his bespoke shoes and his custom-made English suits, he had bright blue eyes and a skin so light that he could pass as white anywhere in the world, if he'd wanted to. He didn't. The son of one of the famed beauties from the original Floradora Sextet, born in a French chateau, unaware of his own Negro blood and brought up in the lap of European luxury, he had never heard of a race problem until he returned to America in his teens. What he then discovered made an outlaw of him; he became a pimp, a killer and finally an actor. As Crown in *Porgy* he scored a big personal success, which was soon threatened by bouts of misbehavior. His favorite diversion on tour was to register in a town's leading hotel, then invite his black friends, male and female, up to his room and fight till the blood flowed when they were denied admission. He had not worked much in recent years, but made a living somehow through his underworld connections in Harlem. His life was a nagging tor-ment, not knowing whom he despised and hated most—his mother's people for submitting to humiliation or his father's for inflicting it.

When it became known that Jack had been cast for the part of Macbeth, in which he would be directed by a twenty-year-old white man, eyebrows were raised all over Harlem and people waited with mixed emotions for the outcome of their first en-counter. If they hoped for mayhem, they were disappointed. From the moment at the first reading when Orson threw his arms around Jack, his eyes brimming with tears of gratitude and ad-miration, a close and passionate friendship had sprung up be-tween these two giants who, together, measured close to thirteen feet. For four months they were seldom apart, driven by a need for each other's presence which caused Jack to appear at every *Macbeth* rehearsal, whether he had been called or not, and which sent them, when work was ended, at four or five in the morning, roaring together through the late-night spots and brothels of Harlem till it was time to rehearse again.

I never really knew how much of all this was director's strategy calculated to nurse a difficult leading man through opening night or how much it reflected a true and urgent affinity between these two troubled and dangerous men. (I used to wonder, some-times, seeing Orson returning from these nocturnal forays, if they did not perhaps evoke some echo of those other long, wild nights which he had spent as a boy, with his father, in the red-light districts of the Mediterranean, Hong Kong and Singapore.) This curious intimacy proved of inestimable value to the project. In the state of anxiety and exhaustion which the company had reached by the beginning of April, Jack Carter's loyalty was a major factor in sustaining its morale. Not only was he above reproach in his own behavior, but he constituted himself Orson's champion with the company—scornful of its fatigue, quick to detect signs of revolt and to crush movements of disaffection.

This zeal sometimes got us into trouble. One night, not long before opening, around four in the morning, a minor mutiny broke out on stage. In sheer exhaustion, weighed down by the heavy uniforms in which they had been working for almost ten hours, the company exploded suddenly into open anger and refused to go on. First Eddy Perry, then I, then Orson—sweating and gray with fatigue—pleaded with them, explaining that, for technical reasons, certain stage movements must be fixed that night or not at all. They shook their heads and started to scatter. At that moment a tall figure, superb in full Napoleonic regalia, vaulted onto the parapet of Glamis Castle and began to harangue the rebellious troops. Jack was in a towering rage; he looked and sounded magnificent, full of the unrestrained fury which Orson had been trying to infuse into the last act of *Macbeth*. He told them he was tired too, for he had a bigger part than they did; they might have worked for nine hours but he had been rehearsing for thirteen—and, anyway, what was a little fatigue when the whole future of the Negro Theatre was at stake? Here was the chance they had never been given before; the opportunity for which they had never even dared to hope. If these men (Orson and I, Harry Hopkins and the President of the United States) were willing to risk their reputations on such a project—to work on it as Welles had done, night and day, month after month, on their behalf, when he could easily have been earning a fortune in radio, as they goddamn well knew—there was only one thing that they, as self-respecting Negro actors and human beings could do: follow him, unquestioningly, to the ends of the earth and stop screwing up his wonderful production with their fucking stupid complaints. If they were tired, let them rest after opening! Because if the opening was a bust and the production failed through their fault—they'd have the rest of their goddamn lives to rest in!

The company listened in silence. When he finished they began to pick up their props and to drift back into their positions; the mutiny was over; they were ready to rehearse till dawn or longer. It was then that the demon that drove him made it necessary for Jack Carter to add one more sentence to his oration.

"So get back to work!" he yelled. "You no-acting sons of bitches!"

In the brawl that followed, some scenery was smashed and a

court lady was slightly injured when she was pushed off the stage. And no more work was done that night.

Finally, not an hour too soon, the end of rehearsals drew near for Orson Welles and his *Macbeth* company. April 14th (which also happened to be the first day of the national baseball season) was announced as our opening date: it promised the Harlem community an emotional release such as they had not known since the riots of 1935. Little else was talked about above 125th Street. The news that Haile Selassie's troops were in headlong flight before Mussolini's mechanized army and airforce made no stir at all in a week that was entirely monopolized by the activities of the Lafayette Theatre. Nor did the downtown press neglect us. A reporter named Bosley Crowther was sent north by *The New York Times* to report on this latest version of "the Bard's most slaughterous drama."

> Midnight was the time. It seems that twenty-four hours makes too short a day for the WPA's Negro Theatre and, with its house pretty well filled up by workmen during the day and the performances of *Conjur Man Dies* during the evening, the only time left for the final rehearsals of *Macbeth* has been from midnight on till dawn. Sounds fantastic, but it's true . . .
>
> This scout, upon arrival, discovered a goodsized crowd of Negroes milling around the back of the theatre. These were the Shakespearian thespians waiting to begin rehearsal. Not to them, however, but to John Houseman and Orson Welles, supervisor and director, respectively, of the Negro *Macbeth*, it was that this scout went for information. Why, he wanted to know, had they mustered the audacity to take the Bard for a ride? What sort of Thane of Cawdor would find himself in Haiti? Whither would Malcolm and Donalbain flee—to Jamaica or possibly Nassau?
>
> Both Mr. Houseman and Mr. Welles were pleased to talk, brightly and intelligently, about their unusual creation. But they were also quite serious about it. "We were very anxious to do one of Shakespeare's dramas in the Negro Theatre," said Orson Welles, "and *Macbeth* seemed, in all respects, the most adaptable. The stormy career of Christophe, who became 'The Negro King of Haiti' and ended by killing himself when his

cruelty led to a revolt, forms a striking parallel to the history of Macbeth. The costumes and settings of the production are therefore in the period of Haiti's grimmest turbulence. Place names have been altered with particular care to retain the rhythm to Shakespeare's lines. Malcolm and Donalbain don't flee to England but to 'the Coast. . . .' "

As to the company itself, they seemed as alert and enthusiastic as the day—or night—they started. The New Deal, not only in the theatre, but in Shakespeare, was meat and drink for them. And any actor who will rehearse from midnight until dawn, the rosy-fingered, must be interested in something more than a pay check. At least that's the way it looked to this scout.

Some of this excitement was spontaneous; some of it was induced and stimulated. Three days before opening, Harlem woke up to find *Macbeth* stenciled in luminous paint on every street corner from 125th to 140th—from Lexington to Broadway. The Tree of Hope, a gnarled relic that survived with difficulty on Seventh Avenue in front of the Lafayette Theatre and which was credited with magic properties of some sort, was festooned with garlands and bright-colored ribbons for luck. By April 10th every seat in the theatre (except those reserved for U.S. Government officials and the press) had been sold, sometimes twice over, as ticket scalpers became active in Harlem's fancier bars. A free preview, given two days before opening, drew three thousand more would-be spectators than the theatre could hold—necessitating the calling of a police emergency squad to disperse the crowd. From the downtown WPA press department came word that every first-string critic in town would attend. (One of them, tactfully, requested that he and his wife should be seated, if possible, "not next to Negroes.")

On opening night, just before dusk, the massed bands of the Monarch Lodge of the Benevolent and Protective Order of Elks, in uniforms of light blue, scarlet and gold, began to march in two detachments through the streets of Harlem behind two huge, crimson banners that read:

MACBETH

by

William Shakespeare

By six-thirty they had converged before the theatre where they continued to play eighty-five strong, standing around the Tree of Hope, while ten thousand people milled around them and dozens of police, including two on horses, tried in vain to keep a way clear into the Lafayette. As reported in *The New York Times:* "All northbound automobile traffic was stopped for more than an hour, while from trucks in the street, floodlights flared a circle of light into the lobby and cameramen took photographs of the arrival of celebrities." Later, someone wrote of "the flash of jewels, silk hats and ermine," but I was too nervous to notice and too anxious to get the curtain up before eight o'clock.

It rose, finally, following the customary overture, on a jungle set "luxuriant, savage and ominous with shadows," where the trees met in a great overhead arch of twisted trunks that suggested a gigantic, living skeleton. Within five minutes, amid the thunder of drums and the orgiastic howls and squeals of our voodoo celebrants, we knew that victory was ours.

> The Witches' scenes from *Macbeth* have always worried the life out of the polite, tragic stage; the grimaces of the hags and the garish make-believe of the flaming cauldron have bred more disenchantment than anything else that Shakespeare wrote. But ship the witches into the rank and fever-stricken jungle echoes, stuff a gleaming naked witch doctor into the cauldron, hold up Negro masks in the baleful light—and there you have a witches' scene that is logical and stunning and a triumph of the theatre art.*

The next scene to stop the show was that of the Macbeths' royal reception immediately following the murder of Banquo: dozens of shimmering couples in their court finery swirling with wild abandon to the crashing rhythms of our Thomson-orchestrated

* Brooks Atkinson in *The New York Times,* April 15, 1936, under the headline MACBETH OR HARLEM BOY GOES WRONG.

nineteenth-century waltzes—then, suddenly, a wild, high, inhuman sound that froze them all in their tracks, followed by Macbeth's terrible cry as the spirit of Banquo, in the shape of a huge luminous death mask, suddenly appeared on the battlements to taunt him in the hour of his triumph.

For Birnam Wood, Central Park and half of Rockland County had been stripped of their burgeoning boughs, till the floor of the stage became a moving forest above which Macbeth, cornered at last on the highest platform of his castle, first shot down the "cream-faced loon" who brought him the news of Macduff's approach, then kicked him, for an eighteen-foot drop, into the courtyard below. It was here that the defiant hero vainly emptied his pistol into the body of the tall, dark, bearded man whose wife and children he had murdered and of whom he discovered, too late, as they closed for their final duel, that he had been "from the womb untimely ripped." A moment later, as Macbeth's head came sailing down from the battlements, a double cry rose from the stage—of jubilation from Macduff's army over the tyrant's death, and of triumph from the assembled members of the Negro Theatre Project's classical wing at the successful outcome of their long and agonizing ordeal.

> At the conclusion of the performance there were salvos of applause and countless curtain calls as bouquets of flowers were handed over the footlights to the leading players.

Here again, the clapping and cheering that filled the theatre for fifteen minutes had a double meaning: it was the natural enthusiasm of a delighted audience; it was also Harlem's explosion of relief at the project's final vindication after months of anxiety and doubt.

The notices the next morning were a joy to read: "As an experiment in Afro-American showmanship, *Macbeth* merited the excitement that fairly rocked the Lafayette Theatre last night," concluded *The New York Times*. Others wrote of "an Emperor Jones gone beautifully mad," of "the dark, sensual rhythms, the giant tropic fronds" and of "a tragedy of black ambition in a green jungle shot with such lights from heaven and hell as no other stage has seen." Arthur Pollock of the Brooklyn *Daily Eagle* commented on the "childlike austerity" of the performance: "With all their gusto, they play Shakespeare as though they were apt children who have just discovered and adore the old man."

There were reservations, of course. Atkinson, after rhapsodizing over our "fury and phantom splendor," questioned our company's grasp of poetic tragedy: "They speak the lines conscientiously, but they have left the poetry out of them." There were others, with preconceived notions of "poetic delivery" and "vocal passion," who complained of the very thing that Welles had gone to such pains to accomplish with his Negro cast: the elimination of the glib English Bensonian declamatory tradition of Shakespearean performance and a return to a simpler, more direct and rapid delivery of the dramatic verse.

Because the Negro *Macbeth*, before and after it opened, was a news event as well as a show, the most revealing reactions are to be found in reporters' rather than in critics' accounts. Martha Gellhorn, describing her visit to Harlem, saw at once that

> . . . these Negroes had taken Shakespeare to themselves and that *Macbeth* would remain in this audience's mind from now on, as a play about people living in a Haitian jungle, believing in voodoo, frightened and driven and opulent people, with shiny chocolate skins, who moved about the stage superbly, wearing costumes that belonged to them and suddenly belonged to the play. Macduff, in the battle scenes, wore a pair of epaulets a foot wide made of heavy red cord, complemented by a pair of satin-striped red and white breeches. Macbeth wore superb military costumes of canary yellow and emerald green and shining boots. Women came on and off the stage in salmon pink and purple. The impression was of a hot richness that I have almost never seen in the theatre or anywhere else.
>
> The lines were spoken without Negro accent, but in those beautiful voices made for singing; and the gestures were lavish, but not amateur or overdone. The audience sat and watched and listened as if this were a murder mystery by Edgar Wallace, only much more exciting.

Roi Otley, a militant Negro journalist, was less concerned with these picturesque aspects than with the racial significance of the production:

> The Negro has become weary of carrying the White Man's blackface burden in the theatre. In *Macbeth* he has been given the opportunity to discard the bandana and burnt-cork casting to play a universal character . . .
>
> From the point of view of the Community, Harlem witnessed a production in which the Negro was not lampooned or made the brunt of laughter. We attended the *Macbeth* showing, happy in the thought we wouldn't again be reminded, with all its vicious implications, that we were niggers.

Like all WPA productions, *Macbeth* was judged by standards that were not purely theatrical. Percy Hammond, dean of New York drama critics, representing the city's leading Republican journal, the *Herald Tribune,* wrote what was not so much of a review as an attack on the New Deal:

> The Negro Theatre, an offshoot of the Federal Government and one of Uncle Sam's experimental philanthropies, gave us, last night, an exhibition of deluxe boondoggling.

He went on to ridicule the whole idea of a popular theatre supported by government funds, citing the size of our cast, the brightness of our costumes and the loudness of our music as evidences of criminal extravagance and presumptuous folly. As an example of political polemic it was savage but eloquent; as a theatrical notice it was irrelevant and malignant. It did not surprise us, nor were we unduly disturbed. But there were some that were.

Early in the afternoon of April 15th, the day of the *Macbeth* reviews, Orson and I were formally visited in my office by Asadata Dafora Horton and his corps of African drummers, including Abdul, the authentic witch doctor. They looked serious. Asadata was their spokesman. They were perplexed, he said, and desired guidance. He then produced a sheaf of clippings from which he detached the *Herald Tribune* review. He had read it to his men, he declared, and it was their opinion, and his, that the piece was an evil one. I agreed that it was.

"The work of an enemy?"

"The work of an enemy."

"He is a bad man?"

"A bad man."

Asadata nodded. His face was grim as he turned to his troupe, to Abdul in particular, and repeated what I had said. The men nodded, then silently withdrew. Excited by waves of praise and a line a block long at the box office, we quickly forgot both them and Percy Hammond. We stayed for that night's performance, which was better played and no less enthusiastically received than the first. We thanked the company, had a brief, violent personal row on the sidewalk over the *Times* notice in which my name had been coupled with Orson's as director, then went home to get some sleep.

It was reported to us by our disturbed house manager when we arrived at the theatre around noon of the next day that the basement had been filled, during the night, with unusual drumming and with chants more weird and horrible than anything that had been heard upon the stage. Orson and I looked at each other for an instant, then quickly away again, for in the afternoon paper which we had picked up on our way uptown was a brief item announcing the sudden illness of the well-known critic Percy Hammond. He died some days later—of pneumonia, it was said.

Macbeth played for ten weeks at the Lafayette with never an empty seat, then downtown at the Adelphi on Fifty-fourth Street (in competition with *Tobacco Road, Three Men on a Horse, Mulatto, Dead End, Bury the Dead, On Your Toes* and *New Faces of 1936*) for an additional run of two months. This move was celebrated with a six-column Hirschfeld cartoon on the front page of the *Times* Sunday drama section and brought great renown to the Negro Theatre Project, but it had one unfortunate consequence: we lost our Macbeth.

Between Jack Carter and Edna Thomas—that amazingly

handsome royal couple—there flowed an old and strong emotion, protective and tender on Edna's part, filled with ambivalence on Jack's. Orson had worked to enrich their scenes with these almost incestuous overtones and to create the feeling of an alliance in crime between a middle-aged wife-mother and a passionate husband-son. Perhaps none of this came across the footlights; if it did, it was smothered in the thunder of voodoo drums until it erupted suddenly one night on the stage of the Adelphi. For five months Jack, against all predictions, had been the mainstay of *Macbeth*. Now he began to crack. I have always believed that playing before white audiences may have had something to do with the drinking on which Jack started soon after we opened downtown; once that began, his feeling of guilt toward Orson and Edna (the two people on the project of whom he was really fond) did the rest. He knew that it upset Edna to see him drunk; he felt he was embarrassing her in their scenes together and hurting both their performances. One night as they were leaving the stage together, she started to cry. Jack went back to his dressing room for the long intermission, removed and carefully hung up his bright uniform, washed, got into his street clothes and his bespoke shoes and left the theatre—and the project.

Illness and mortality being alarmingly high among Negro performers, we had carefully protected ourselves with understudies. Macbeth was doubly covered—by Maurice Ellis (Macduff) as Jack's probable successor in the role, and by our chief stage manager, Tommy Anderson (formerly of *Four Saints*), who knew every word of every part as an added cover in case of emergency. When he called the second act and found Jack's room empty, Anderson telephoned first to Orson, then to me, failed to find either of us, tore a uniform off the nearest soldier and went on as Macbeth. No announcement was made and the audience, that night, had the strange experience of seeing the first half of Shakespeare's tragedy performed by a very pale, six-foot-four hero in a glittering, bright yellow costume and the second by a dark, wiry, moustachioed, five-foot-seven Macbeth in the dark-red uniform of one of Macduff's barefoot soldiers.

After running through the long, hot New York summer, *Macbeth* was sent on a triumphal national tour of WPA theatres —to Bridgeport, Hartford, Chicago, Indianapolis, Detroit, Cleveland and, surprisingly, Dallas, Texas. In Indianapolis Maurice Ellis, who was playing Macbeth, fell ill. Orson had been waiting for just this chance: he flew out and played the role in blackface for the rest of the week.

* * *

Soon after the opening of *Macbeth,* it became necessary for the Negro Theatre's contemporary wing to put its next production into rehearsal. And here the usual problem arose—the scarcity of suitable scripts, aggravated by a widening split between the "social-conscious" members of the project and the others. For a few days I thought I had found a solution in a new play by Zorah Hurston, our most talented writer on the project, who had come up with a Negro *Lysistrata* updated and located in a Florida fishing community, where the men's wives refused them intercourse until they won their fight with the canning company for a living wage. It scandalized both Left and Right by its saltiness, which was considered injurious to the serious Negro image they both, in their different ways, desired to create. So I had to give that one up. There was another piece I liked, Carlton Moss's adaptation to Harlem middle-class life of George Kelly's *The Show Off,* with the name part to be played by Dooley Wilson. I had put that into work the previous month, but it was nowhere near ready to open. So finally, we had to fall back on *Turpentine,* which Gus Smith, his white collaborator and his partisans on the project had been rehearsing for months.

Turpentine opened on June 25th. A routine play of protest, full of leftist clichés, but adequately performed and produced, it ran through the summer with left-wing support. *New Theatre* Magazine conceded that "as a realistic drama *Turpentine* creaks and, in its last few moments, collapses like a punctured tire," but recommended it to its readers for other reasons:

Although crude by comparison with the others, *Turpentine*
deserves welcome as one of a group of plays including *Black
Pit, Stevedore* and *Let Freedom Ring* which is familiarizing
metropolitan audiences with American life.

The local *Amsterdam News* reported that though plain working people and their problems were movingly dramatized on the
stage of the Lafayette, the downtown public would not be interested, "since in this production the Negro is not exotic." But our
most emphatic review appeared in the *Naval Stores Review and
Journal* of Norfolk, Virginia, which described *Turpentine* as "a
malicious libel on the naval stores industry of the South" and
added that "a censorship of WPA plays cannot come too soon."
Two years later, when the Arts Projects were in their death
throes, this attack was dug up by Senator Russell of Georgia
before the Appropriations Committee of the U.S. Senate as evidence of subversive influences in the Federal Theatre.

Turpentine was my last production for the Negro Theatre. For
weeks, now, I had been approaching the moment of personal decision—one which would drastically affect the whole course of my
life in the theatre. For while the triumph of *Macbeth* and the
classical wing had been complete and satisfying, it had created
new and urgent problems—for the project and for myself.

In the months since we had started work on *Macbeth*, I had
come to think of my association with Welles as a continuing and
possibly a permanent one. Already, I was totally committed to
that unreasoning faith in his theatrical genius that was an essential condition of our partnership. Then and later, friends and
intimates, especially women, used to reproach me for what they
considered my submission to Orson and for devoting so much of
my time and energy to promoting his achievements rather than
my own. It was difficult to explain to them (since I was not
entirely clear about it myself) that if I did subordinate myself,
consciously and willingly, to a man twelve years younger than
myself, it was for a compelling and quite selfish reason: it was the
price I was willing to pay for my participation in acts of theatri-

cal creation that were far more stimulating and satisfying than any I felt capable of conceiving or creating by myself.

Macbeth had been such a creation. I knew there were others to come. Yet I was also aware that Welles's position on the Negro Theatre and his attitude toward it were quite unlike mine. I had invited him to Harlem for one single production. Having achieved enormous success with his *Voodoo Macbeth,* I knew that he had no intention of undertaking another long grind which, at best, could only bring him a repetition of his earlier triumph and that he was already dreaming of other worlds to conquer. My own situation was different. Though I had shared (rather more than Orson liked) in the victory of *Macbeth,* my main achievement, as far as the Federal Theatre was concerned, lay in my successful organization and administration of this most vital and flourishing unit.

Now I had to make my choice between two alternatives: one was to let Orson go on his dazzling way while I stayed on as the respected head of Harlem's Negro Theatre unit, fostering and encouraging the "indigenous" projects as best I could while I tried to follow up our first classical achievement with what must inevitably be diminishing returns. My second course was to get out while the going was good: to leave on a note of triumph, abandon my position of power with the Negro Theatre (turning it over to those to whom it rightly belonged) and risk my whole future on a partnership with a twenty-year-old boy, in whose talent I had unquestioning faith but with whom I must increasingly play the combined and tricky roles of producer, censor, adviser, impresario, father, older brother, and bosom friend!

If I chose the latter (and it was inevitable that I should) I had not a moment to lose. I must immediately supply those new theatrical opportunities of which he dreamed and find fresh scope for Orson's terrible energy and boundless ambition, before someone else did and before he became wholly absorbed in the commercial success-mill which was beginning to grind for him.

As I tried to plan our future partnership, during that summer of 1936, I found myself facing what, thirty years later, remain the essential theatrical challenges of our time. I considered the possibility of grandiose single productions, privately financed, but soon gave that up as hopeless, considering the sort of play we intended to do. I thought vaguely of reviving the tiny moribund Phoenix, with its potential subscription audience, as the basis for a new kind of Theatre Guild. I even talked with Orson about renting a theatre and assembling a repertory company of our own—but without conviction, remembering the money problems of *Panic* and the frustrations of our sojourn in the offices of the Mendelssohn Society. Finally, as time began to press and Orson's offers became more numerous and seductive, I had an idea. I called Hallie Flanagan and requested a meeting with her at a moment when my overwhelming success as producer and administrator of the Negro unit made it difficult for her to refuse any reasonable proposal I might put before her.

I told her of my feeling about the project: that it was now viable and ready to be placed entirely in Negro hands. I also told her that Orson Welles and I wished to devote ourselves to forming and running a new Federal unit, to be known as the Classical Theatre. I suggested Maxine Elliott's Theatre at Thirty-ninth and Broadway which I knew the WPA had just rented from the Shuberts.

The answer came within a few days. If I agreed to stay long enough to set up my succession in Harlem, I was authorized to start organizing a classical theatre immediately. And I could have the Maxine Elliott. (Privately I was told to waste no time, for the freewheeling days of the Arts Projects were nearing their end and drastic reductions seemed certain in the months to come.) Through the end of June and the first part of July, half my days were once again spent on the IRT, shuttling by express subway between 125th and 42nd Street, rushing from the Lafayette to the Maxine Elliott and back again.

It had been my hope to withhold the news of my departure for a time, but it was all over Harlem within a day of my second interview with Mrs. Flanagan. This meant that the change of management had to be made more precipitately than I would have wished. I felt strongly, partly out of personal vanity, I suppose, that the future leadership of the Negro Theatre should be drawn from among men I had trained inside the unit, which was still far too young to be subjected to the strain of new concepts and personalities. To take my place I recommended a triumvirate—in the middle, as administrator and bureaucrat, Harry Edwards, a man unloved but dignified, honorable and efficient. On either side of him, with equal powers, I suggested two producers: to his left, Gus Smith—actor, director, and co-author of *Turpentine,* who had proved himself a man of energy and strength but of little cultivation or taste; to his right, Carlton Moss, shy of responsibility and reluctant to lead, but skillful, progressive, educated and sensitive to every changing breeze of Harlem opinion. He was already well advanced with his production of *The Show Off*—the first successful presentation of the Negro Theatre after my departure.

Of the new leaders, Carlton (in spite of the advantage he would gain by my exit) was the only one who was truly sorry to see me go. He protested against what he called my betrayal—to me personally and, officially, to Mrs. Flanagan. For the project's sake, he would have preferred to waive his own promotion—and this out of a special kind of racial pride. For almost a year now the Negro Project had been the first, the biggest and the most acclaimed of all the Federal Theatre units; Carlton hated the idea of the Lafayette, of which he had become inordinately proud, becoming "just another WPA theatre." For my own part, at the last moment, I was filled with that sense of loss and sorrow and guilt that I have felt with each of the many departures and desertions of which my life is the sum.

Our final farewells from the project were long and emotional, full of protestations of love. Orson's parting scenes were particularly passionate. He and his company had been through hell together and come out victorious: he had given them a vision of theatrical magic which none of them would forget and few of them would ever glimpse again.

Viewed in the perspective of years, my accomplishments with the Negro Theatre seem far from impressive. Theatrically, their final effects were almost nil: Negro playwriting was not appreciably encouraged by our efforts, and Negro actors (with a few notable exceptions) were held, for another twenty years, within the galling bounds of stereotyped roles. The theatre technicians whom Feder had trained (being excluded from every professional union theatre in America except as cleaners or janitors) went back into other trades. No Negro company came into existence for thirty years after the dissolution of the Federal Theatre and no Negro audience clamored for a continuation of the entertainment they had apparently enjoyed under the auspices of the WPA.

The short view was rather more favorable. My ten months on the project had been among the busiest, happiest and proudest of my life; they also represented the period during which I had come nearest to being God. I had enjoyed my power and out of chaos I had created a comparatively well-ordered and smooth-running universe. Through the rear window of the cab that was carrying me, with Augusta Weissberger and several large files, to our new domain in the basement of Maxine Elliott's Theatre, I looked back at the worn and dirty face of the Lafayette and saw what I had wrought. And behold, it was good.

V

MAXINE ELLIOTT's Theatre had been built at the turn of the century by J. P. Morgan for his favorite actress. *Romance* had opened there with Doris Keane; Ethel Barrymore had appeared on its stage in *The Constant Wife,* Jane Cowl in *Twelfth Night* and Jeanne Eagels in *Rain* for six hundred and forty-eight performances. More recently, *The Children's Hour* had run there for two full seasons. After years of abuse and neglect, with its yellowing marble and discolored brocades, it retained traces of its former splendor and seemed particularly glamorous after the moldering squalor of the Lafayette.

Leading to the ladies' toilet in the basement was a large powder room with a worn Aubusson carpet and walls of faded rose-pink velvet. Here, amid remnants of the original furnishings —an ormolu bureau, a cerise tailor's dummy, and two tall mirrors—Augusta Weissberger had set up my office. Feder and his aides did their paperwork at the foot of the opposite staircase, in the white-tiled area surrounding the men's room. Backstage, between rehearsals and radio shows, Orson occupied the star dressing room, which had a bath and a small sitting room with a bed.

My first activity, after moving in, was to assemble a staff and a company of actors to the full limits of our appropriation. Hundreds came to be interviewd, most of them rejects or fugitives from older and lesser WPA Theatre projects—vaudeville and circus, tent shows and units in dissolution. It was a bizarre collection of aging character actors, comics and eccentrics that delighted Orson's heart. We also took on a number of middle-aged, garrulous ladies with bright-colored hair whom no one else wanted and several young females, among them a strangely beautiful waif from Brooklyn with olive skin and a Cretan profile named Paula Lawrence.

The special character and the obvious limitations of this hastily collected troupe may have helped to influence us in the choice of our first play, but mainly, I believe, it came from a determination not to do what was expected of us after the success of *Macbeth*. Soon after our arrival downtown Orson and I sat in the powder room one afternoon lamenting our inhibiting title of "classical theatre." We tried various alternatives: "repertory" was inaccurate, "people's theatre" pretentious. While we were talking, a requisition was put before me which I signed as managing producer of WPA Project #891. Orson was looking over my shoulder and, in that instant, we had our name. Soon after that, Project #891 announced its first two productions: *The Italian Straw Hat* by Eugène Labiche, with Marlowe's *Tragical History of Doctor Faustus* to follow. Among the ideas we rejected but filed for future use were a modern-dress *Julius Caesar*, Ben Jonson's *The Silent Woman*, Dekker's domestic comedy *The Shoemaker's Holiday* and *The Duchess of Malfi*.

To justify our first choice we explained to the authorities that nineteenth-century situation farce (*"le vaudeville"*) was a classical theatrical form "taught in schools" and that Labiche was its recognized master. Having made our point, we changed the name of the piece to *Horse Eats Hat* and began to plan its production. At Virgil Thomson's suggestion we entrusted the adaptation to his friend Edwin Denby, a poet-critic and dancer recently returned from Europe, where he had made a name for himself in advanced theatrical circles. Aided, driven and abetted by Welles, he inflated and expanded Labiche's text to astonishing proportions; he also devised a prologue, known as the "horse ballet," in which he himself appeared as the rear half of the offending hack.

> The plot is that of a horse that eats a hat and the owner of the horse, a bridegroom on the way to his wedding, must find the hat's owner a similar hat immediately because she, the hat's owner, cannot go home to her husband without it. . . .

This is the only cold-blooded attempt anyone seems to have made at the time to tell the plot of *Horse Eats Hat*. It was written by a man who never saw it.

Scenery and costumes, like those for Macbeth, were flamboyantly designed by Nat Karson. The score was by Paul Bowles, aided in his orchestrations by Virgil Thomson. An enormous amount of music was needed and we had large musical forces available: thirty-three men in the pit and a grand piano in each of the lower boxes, plus pianola, lady trumpeter and gypsy orchestra. In the time available it was not possible for Paul to write all the music required. He did compose, for the occasion, two long pieces of continuity, three overtures, the horse ballet and several songs, including the "Father-in-Law's Lament." For the rest—the dances, the marches, the chamber music, the piano solos and some added songs—we used existent compositions by Bowles or pieces from public domain. Authentic period rolls for our mechanical piano were obtained from an establishment in the Bronx.

Our cast of many dozen was drawn from among our recent recruits, to whom we added as many non-relief actors as we could get onto the project under the ten percent special talent ruling. Orson Welles played the bride's ferocious father, Virginia Welles the shy bride, Hiram Sherman her libidinous cousin and Joseph Cotten, the harried bridegroom. Paula Lawrence was the unfaithful wife whose Leghorn straw hat the horse chewed up while she lay behind a bush in the Bois de Boulogne with a dashing hussar. Arlene Francis played Tillie, the glamorous modiste, in whose seven-doored shop the hat had been bought. Other characters included the world's grandest countess (Sarah Burton), its most corrupt valet and an aging cuckold with the gout. There were also wedding guests, party guests, a bevy of Tillie's girls and two regiments of Zouaves.

Of all the shows Orson and I produced together, *Horse Eats Hat* is the one in which I was the least involved. Sitting in my pink underground lair, deluged with paperwork for the new project, negotiating with WPA administrators and representatives of the Workers' Alliance and City Projects Council, I listened enviously to the wild and wonderful sounds of rehearsal on the stage above. For besides the hazards of starting and running a new government project with more than two hundred employees, I had problems of my own to occupy me that summer.

During the fall of 1935—about the time I was setting up the Negro Theatre—I had two meetings with Leslie Howard, who was passing through New York on his way from England to Hollywood. I had met him briefly, four years before, when Gilbert Miller had first bought *Lovers, Happy Lovers* as a possible vehicle for Howard to star in. This time I was brought to him by Helen Deutsch, whom I had known as the Group Theatre's press agent up at Green Mansions and Clifford Odets' girl. In her mid-twenties, she had suddenly become the most successful theatrical press agent in America. The Theatre Guild, the Playwrights' Theatre, The Group, Guthrie McClintic and Gilbert Miller were among her clients; now Leslie Howard had engaged her to handle publicity for the *Hamlet* which, after several false starts, he was preparing to produce and play on Broadway. When I met him he had already gone quite far in the planning of his production; he had chosen Stewart Chaney to design the sets and costumes and Schuyler Watts, a glib and passionate young man fresh out of Yale, to arrange and edit the text. Now he was looking for someone to collaborate with him on the production and direction of the play.

My conferences with Leslie Howard were agreeable and moderately productive. I had long admired the skill and delicacy that had made him one of the most admired romantic leading men of his time. His voice was thin but under perfect control, his stage presence remarkably organized and effective. I saw no reason, if he remained true to his own personal qualities, why he should not be a fascinating and moving Hamlet. Before he left for California to appear in the film of *The Petrified Forest* (which he had created on Broadway), I had, without telling Orson, signed a contract to co-direct his *Hamlet* the following spring. Then, within a month of his arrival in Hollywood, he accepted an offer to co-star in *Romeo and Juliet* with Norma Shearer, and our *Hamlet* date had to be moved forward to another season. By that time I was full of my own excitements with the Negro Theatre Project and welcomed the postponement. But I was delighted, soon after the opening of *Walk Together Chillun!*, with *Macbeth* already in rehearsal, when Howard invited me to fly out and visit him in California to discuss plans for a late summer tryout and a Labor Day opening of *Hamlet* in New York. Since the mention of any theatrical activity except his own provoked in Orson an automatic reaction of ridicule or rage, I did not tell him where I was going. I stayed with the Howards in Beverly Hills and spent my days at MGM on the set of *Romeo and Juliet* talking to Leslie between set-ups. I remember seeing Norma Shearer on a large stone balcony and Howard moving toward her through acres of artificial orchard across the false grass, while a carefully measured rain of apple blossoms fell on him from the branches as he passed.

I flew back to New York on the third day, convinced that there would be no *Hamlet* production till late in the fall. Two months later, after the opening of our *Macbeth,* Leslie and Ruth Howard passed through New York on their way to England, where he was to spend the summer on his estate, "preparing" himself for *Hamlet.* We discussed casting, and I came up with a list of actors (including Estelle Winwood, Orson Welles, Whitford Kane and Julie Haydon) who seemed to complement his own virtues and limitations. Leslie listened attentively, then boarded his ship for England, inviting me to join him there at some time during the summer. I accepted, knowing that I would not go.

My commercial visa, issued to me in the name of Jacques Haussmann as a naturalized British citizen under the Anglo-American Treaty of Commerce and Navigation, had become invalid five years before with the dissolution of the Oceanic Grain Corporation.

Having been born in Rumania, I was, according to U.S. immigration rules, a Rumanian; and since the Rumanian quota was minimal and perpetually filled, there seemed to be no way in which I could ever inhabit the United States as a legal and working resident. As an indigent playwright and freelance director this had not bothered me. But now, for over a year, I had been conducting a large, official and partly political operation for the U.S. Government in direct violation of the country's laws and in an exposed position from which it would have taken no more than one single anonymous postcard addressed to the Department of Justice to have me dismissed and summarily deported, without hope of return.

Project #891 had been formed and *Horse Eats Hat* was already in rehearsal when I learned, through cautious inquiries, that now, finally, after four years of international depression, the Rumanian quota was unfilled. Canada was the nearest foreign territory, and a series of urgent and eulogious letters from the heads of the WPA to the U.S. Department of Labor and the consulate in Toronto had won me the firm assurance, by late July, that I was qualified for readmittance to the U.S. as a permanent resident.

I left for Toronto in my trusted Model A on the first Sunday of August, 1936, telling everyone I would be back the following Wednesday at the latest. I drove all night and, after the sun came up, I had to slap my face every few minutes to keep awake in the rising heat. At nine-thirty I crossed into Canada over the International Bridge at Buffalo, high above the Niagara River. Behind me through the rear-view mirror, I saw the gate close between me and the country in which I had lived for eleven years—in which I had been successful and bankrupt, married and divorced and in which everything I possessed and held precious was waiting, in a state of suspended animation, for my return.

The U.S. consulate in Toronto was closed for lunch when I arrived. I took a room at the Royal York, bathed and shaved and returned to the consulate at two o'clock. By three my papers had been examined and pronounced in order. I was just beginning to regret having taken a room and planning to be halfway back to New York by nightfall, when the blow fell—so soft and sudden that it took me some time to understand what was happening to me. I could have my visa, the vice-consul assured me, just as soon as I obtained a quota number. This, he explained, was not in his province, but in that of the U.S consulate in Bucharest, Rumania. How long would that take, I asked. He was vague. It depended on the mails, he said, which were none too reliable these days. I showed him my contract with Leslie Howard; I pointed to Hallie Flanagan's letter addressed to the Department of Labor in Washington, D.C.:

> Our Federal Theatre Project, as you know, has had a very large success in New York, especially with the outstanding performances of our colored groups of which Mr. Haussmann has been the Managing Producer. I would point out to you how urgently we need his presence in New York, with the very large expenditures that have been made by us on the units of which Mr. Haussmann is in charge.

The vice-consul was not impressed. He said that if I was willing to pay the cost, a cable could be sent to Bucharest. In that case we might receive an answer within two days. But he warned me not to expect too much. With the utmost luck, he said, I might obtain a quota number by September 1st; on the other hand, there might be a delay of several months. I paid the money and the cable was sent.

The next forty-eight hours were among the worst of my life. Sleep was out of the question. I lay fully dressed on my bed in the Royal York Hotel, listening to the trains below, too frightened to move, while the whole carefully planned and precariously balanced structure of my career shivered and swayed around me. I was filled with self-pity; I had been right to be afraid all my life. Just when it seemed that I had finally achieved acceptance I was, once again, to be harshly and coldly rejected. I wrote to my mother in Paris. Then I went downstairs and collected newspapers and magazines from the hotel lobby. Back on my bed I learned that the Eleventh Olympiad had opened in Berlin, with Hitler as host to a worldwide gathering. Hope for peace had been voiced during the opening ceremonies and Jesse Owens had won the hundred-meter dash in record time. The American Federation of Labor was threatening to suspend ten unions with a membership of over a million unless they quit John Lewis' newly formed CIO, while, in Greece, Premier Metaxas' crushing of the general strike was seen as a prelude to dictatorship. The civil war was spreading in Spain, and from Washington it was reported that U.S. business gains in 1935 had been the most sustained and balanced since 1929.

Early in the morning I went out, found two continuously grinding movie houses and spent the rest of the day there. Between programs I ate and paid a visit to the vice-consul, who rather curtly told me not to come back till the afternoon of the following day because the cable, assuming it came, would not be decoded till then. I saw three more films before midnight, then returned to my hotel room with a pile of detective stories. Around noon of the next day I bathed, shaved and combed my hair with propritiatory care. There was a decoded cable waiting for me at the consulate with a Rumanian quota number, good on September 1st—more than three weeks away. As I made an appointment for 9:30 of that distant morning, the vice-consul wished me a happy holiday. He suggested the Laurentian Mountains as a region of great natural beauty and bracing air.

Back at the Royal York, I wrote to Hallie Flanagan to explain my absence and, later that evening, called Welles at home. Virginia answered and said not to worry; the way Orson was directing *Horse Eats Hat* they'd all be in jail anyway. That night I slept like a baby and early the next morning, having conceived a lasting horror for the city of Toronto, I started east, driving at water level beside the St. Lawrence, roughly along the route I had taken by boat, with my father and mother, twenty years before. In Montreal there was a money order waiting for me at the desk of the Ritz-Carlton Hotel with a letter from Augusta Weissberger, reporting that all was well on the project. That afternoon I drove east again to Trois Rivières, then north by slow stages into the Laurentians, where only French was spoken and the Catholic churches had bright aluminum-painted roofs. I spent four days in a family hotel in St. Jovite, from which I wrote several dozen postcards to friends and a long, soul-searching letter to Mina Curtiss. On the fifth day I grew restless and turned south and east again. And hour out of Trois Rivières, on the river road, I passed a speeding black foreign convertible which seemed curiously familiar. At the Ritz-Carlton mail desk in Montreal there was a letter from Augusta with the latest news of the project and a cable from Leslie Howard that confirmed his arrival in New York on September 14th; there was also an unstamped note, left that morning, in a small, crabbed writing I had almost forgotten. That evening I went back to Trois Rivières, where Henrietta Bingham, to whom Mina, on an ironic impulse, had telephoned my whereabouts, was waiting to drive me to her brother's fishing-camp in the mountains where she was spending the end of summer.

So this voyage which had begun as a nightmare ended in a strange holiday reunion beside a dark mountain lake high in the Laurentian hills. It was more than nine years since we had lost our virginity together in a hotel room overlooking the sea: we talked of the curious turn my own life had taken since then; she spoke of hers as an Ambassador's daughter in London. Certain things had not changed at all: the color of her eyes and skin, the warmth of her voice, the way she wore a tailored suit and her hands held the wheel of her car. But there was one major difference—I was no longer in love with her.

Early on the morning of September 2, 1936, I was back in New York (still an alien but now legally resident) in my rose-colored powder room at Maxine Elliott's Theatre. A letter from Leslie

Howard awaited me in which he listed the all-English company
he was bringing over with him. The only name I knew was that
of Lady Forbes-Robertson, the former Gertrude Elliott, sister of
the lady for whom the theatre we were occupying had been
built. She was to play the Queen.

My reaction to this communication and to the selection of a
cast in complete disregard of my opinions and advice took much
of the pleasure and excitement out of my work on Howard's
Hamlet. Other displeasures were to follow during production,
but this, my first gloom, soon melted in my joy at being back
among friends and by the gleeful, frenetic tempo of the proceedings on-stage where *Horse Eats Hat* was entering on its final
weeks of rehearsal. To the endlessly repeated refrain of the
Wedding Song:

> This is Myrtle's Wedding Day
> Oh, hurray, hurray, hurray!
> Myrtle's doing it today;
> Oh, hurray, hurray, hurray!

sung to the tune of *"Les fraises et les framboises,"* were added
girls' screams, cries of jealous rage and outraged virtue, the
thump of falling scenery, Orson's bellowing, Feder's answering
howls and the ooom-pah-pah of the pit band rehearsing under
Virgil's supervision. All these were reassuring and homelike sounds.

One week later we held our first dress rehearsal, which was no
less calamitous than *Macbeth's* but less frightening, since we were
presenting a farce in which it was difficult to differentiate the
catastrophes which were deliberately planned from the accidental disasters, some of which were so splendid that we absorbed
them into the show. Feder came in for more than his usual share
of abuse, since, as technical director, he was responsible not only
for the illumination but for all the special effects, breakaways,
magic devices and acrobatic equipment that Orson called for.

A few days later we began a series of previews for theatre-
loving, fund-raising parties of the Left, who found our Parisian
extravaganza perplexing and vaguely reprehensible—not at all

what they had expected from the producers of *Panic* and *Macbeth*. They laughed but they were uneasy, and as the evening advanced and the antics of the corrupt bourgeoisie became ever more frantic, their uneasiness grew. As madness followed madness through two crowded acts—with actors by the score hurtling across the stage from left to right and from right to left in endless, circular pursuit, in carriages and cars, cycles, tricycles and roller skates, walking, trotting and galloping, like a herd of hysterical elephants, leaving ruin in their wake, scattering the rubber plants in Myrtle Mugglethorpe's suburban home, dispersing the gorgeous, squealing models in Tillie's modish millinery establishment, terrorizing the Countess' elegant guests as they turkey-trotted to the strains of a red coated tzigane ensemble—they continued to laugh, but they were not altogether happy.

It was in the Countess' salon that the wildest scene of the evening took place. It had for its finale one of the most extravagant accumulations of farcical horror ever assembled behind the proscenium arch of a respectable American theatre—not excluding *Hellzapoppin*. In fact, it frightened me so that I usually retired to the basement or left the theatre just before it happened; I can still see Joe Cotten, wearing his bright yellow leather gloves, with the coveted straw hat grasped firmly between his teeth, caught between the Countess' indignant guests and the vengeful pursuit of the wedding party, leaping from sofa to table to piano top to chandelier which, at that instant, started to rise like a great golden bird, carrying him upward in a wild, forty-foot flight till he vanished into the fly-loft, while a three-tiered fountain flung a giant jet upward at the seat of his pants and Cotten himself, clinging to the rising chandelier with one hand and grasping a siphon in the other, squirted streams of soda water over the madly whirling crowd below. As he rose, scenery moved erratically up and down; props, seized with a sudden life of their own, were seen to fly off suddenly in various directions and a huge "Paris-by-night" backdrop came crashing down onto the stage floor, narrowly missing a platoon of stagehands—one of them in red flannel underwear—who had chosen this moment to carry a thirty-two foot ladder slowly, horizontally and imperturbably across the stage.*

So relentless was our determination to entertain our audience that, even during intermission, we gave them no respite. Before they had a chance to rise from their seats, after the chaotic climax of the first act, their attention was caught by a clear brazen blast from the right mezzanine box, where a lady trumpeter in a white satin hussar's uniform, complete with cape and shako trimmed with gold, rendered a loud and brilliant solo of Paul Bowles's variations on the *Carnaval de Venise*, with *Hiawatha* as an encore. Hardly had her well-merited applause begun to diminish when, in the upper stage box opposite, a mechanical piano broke furiously into "Rosy O'Grady." The noise must have disturbed the sleep of a drunken guest, a member of the Countess' ill-fated party, who now appeared, lost and leering, from behind the pianola, seemed to feel himself trapped up there and started to climb out over the edge of the box into the auditorium. Unsteadily, with many slips and falls, he got first one leg and then the other over the side of the box; then, with a great cry, he slipped and fell and remained hanging, head down, with one foot caught in the railing, swinging like an erratic pendulum over the heads of the audience while the mechanical piano switched to Liszt's Hungarian Rhapsody No. 2. The young acrobat's name was Bil Baird; later in the run, growing careless with success, he slipped, fell and broke his leg in several places. It was still in a cast when he and a young woman named Cora, whom he met on the project and later married, began to construct the puppets of the Seven Deadly Sins which were used with such striking effect in our production of *Doctor Faustus*.

Horse Eats Hat opened officially on September 26, 1936, to "mixed" notices. Reviewers were shocked and, in some cases, offended by the extravagant frivolity of the production. The Hearst press used it as a stick with which to beat the New Deal:

* Two of our older male actors died during the run of *Horse Eats Hat* —but not in the line of duty. One was struck by a truck in the Bronx; the other was found hanged in the closet of the theatrical hotel where he had lived for a number of years with his wife, who had recently died.

"Does U.S. Sanction Vulgar Play?" asked a front-page headline in the New York *American*. And the answer was emphatically "Yes":

> Dozens of young men and women are compelled by stress of circumstances to participate in this offensive play, that represents a new low in the tide of drama.

Chapman in the *News* wrote testily of "a stage that is in a continual state of explosive disintegration." *The New York Times* reported that "half the audience was pretty indignant and the other half quite amused."

> Probably it is bad, certainly it is not good in the usually accepted sense of the theatre, but it *is* the only one of its kind.

The weeklies and magazines were no less divided. *Cue* reported that *Horse Eats Hat* was perilously close to being a work of art—"a demented piece of surrealism that leaves art, life, the audience and sometimes the actors behind it." *Stage* Magazine found it perfectly directed and acted and full of pretty girls. Stark Young had praise for "diverse corking moments" but complained that "the impression of the whole is not so much vigorous as unnecessary. I could not get over a sense of waste." On the Left, *New Theatre* was mildly favorable but regretted that the element of social satire had not received added emphasis: "The play flourishes on buffoonery alone. It lacks the incisive portraiture of a caricaturist like William Gropper." Senator Dirksen (Rep., Illinois) described the work, officially, in the *Congressional Record,* as "salacious tripe."

We played for nearly three months to good houses—many of them repeaters. For while audiences continued to be divided and perplexed, there were groups of sophisticated New Yorkers—fancy folk of diverse intellectual shades—who found in *Horse Eats Hat* a source of unending, zany delight and who came to see it (at a fifty-five-cent top) as often as ten, fifteen and, in one case, twenty-one times in a row.

After the launching of *Horse Eats Hat* there was a lull in the operation of Project #891. Orson had signed a Broadway contract to play the juvenile lead in Sidney Kingsley's antiwar play, *Ten Million Ghosts*. On his departure for rehearsals, the part of Mugglethorpe, the father of the bride, was taken over by his understudy, a diminutive actor, almost a midget. When *Ten Million Ghosts* closed after one performance and Orson returned to 39th Street he could not resist the bald dome, the putty and the greasepaint. It became an added attraction for our faithful aficionados that on certain nights Myrtle, the bride, had a gigantic, and on others a miniscule but equally indignant, daddy.

Horse Eats Hat was still in previews when Leslie Howard was finally ready to begin rehearsals. Here another surprise awaited me when it became evident, at the first reading, that our star's vaunted summer preparations for *Hamlet* had not included a serious study of the name part. This, I discovered, was consistent with his nature and with the phenomenon of his stardom. Leslie Howard impressed me, during the months that I worked with him, as the most completely fatalistic man I had ever met. He was secretly and sincerely convinced, I believe, that his sudden, miraculous success was due to some mysterious accident—some error in the celestial filing system—to which his own efforts had contributed little and which would one day be discovered and corrected. This seeemed to explain the curious combination of humility and arrogance, indolence and obstinacy that marked his personal and professional behavior. In the role of Hamlet these inconsistencies were not without their dramatic value. In the presence of his father's ghost, the conflict between suspicion and devotion was fascinating to watch; the Ophelia scenes were, at once, kind and cruel; the baiting of Polonius had a careless, chilling venom and the calm after the grave scene, before the final duel, was ominously equivocal.

It had been agreed that Howard and I would share the work and the credit of direction; he was so busy learning his lines that the staging—within the limits of Chaney's handsome unit set—became almost entirely mine. Rehearsals were courteously but firmly conducted under the devoted eye of Eddie McHugh, stage manager to Arthur Hopkins and the Barrymores for two decades.

Jacques Haussmann.
(Braila, Rumania, 1906)

May Davies Haussmann—"a
beautiful Mama in a beautiful
hat that actually had three
storeys." (Paris, 1909)

Georges Haussmann and family on a wartime mission to the United States for the French Government. (Niagara Falls, 1916)

John Houseman and members of the winning De Gex house team. (Clifton Junior School, 1915)

Otto Siepmann, head of the Modern Language Department at Clifton College, who transformed the teaching of French and German in the British Isles.

John Houseman. (London, 1922)

John Houseman with Zita Johann before their marriage. (Hollywood, 1929)

Zita Johann and Clark Gable in their joint Broadway debut.
(September, 1928)

"St. Virgil," painted by Florine Stettheimer during her conception of *Four Saints in Three Acts.*

A. E. (Chick) Austin, curator of the Wadsworth Athenaeum and founder of The Friends and Enemies of Modern Music.

Frederick Ashton, photographed by Lee Miller during rehearsals of *Four Saints in Three Acts*. (New York, 1934)

A Saints' Picnic. Compère and Commère in stage box, left, with St. Teresa II, St. Chavez and St. Ignatius. Extreme right, in her tarlatan tent, St. Teresa I.

Before the Cathedral at Avila. St. Teresa I at left with St. Settlement by her side. One of the chorus "pyramids" with apprentice-angels before it and, in the archway, guarded by a lion, St. Teresa II decorating an Easter egg.

Jo Mielziner's set design for *Panic*.

THE TWO MURDERERS

WITCHES

Nat Karson's costume designs for the Voodoo *Macbeth*.

THE PRIEST

Macbeth's Castle: the Court Ball following the murder of Banquo.

Jack Carter as the Thane and Edna Thomas as Lady Macbeth.

Opening night at the Lafayette. (April 14, 1937)

Hamlet (Act I, Scene 3): Leslie Howard on the battlements, with Joseph Holland (Horatio) and Edward Ballantyne, who also played Marcellus with John Barrymore.

Horse Eats Hat: Sidney Smith as the Hussar, Paula Lawrence as the Wife, Edwin Denby inside the Horse and Joseph Cotten as the desperate Bridegroom.

Horse Eats Hat: The Wedding Party on its way to the Comtesse's reception.

Orson Welles's design for his own costume as Doctor Faustus.

Orson Welles as Doctor Faustus.

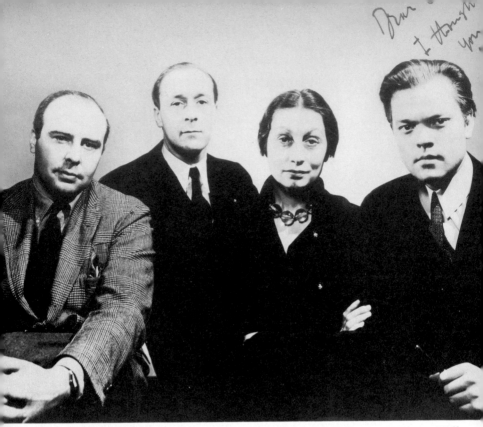

John Houseman, Pavel Tchelitchew, Aline McMahon and Orson Welles before the first reading of *The Duchess of Malfi*.

Mina Curtiss and her brother Lincoln Kirstein.

As one of his assistants, in charge of light cues, I engaged a small, smiling child with a boyish haircut named Jean Rosenthal, recently out of Yale, whom I had discovered working under Feder in the basement of the Maxine Elliott. Of the company (including eight of the most gorgeous court ladies in history), the lesser members had been cast by me in New York; the principal parts, with the exception of Horatio and Osric, were held by English actors whom I had not met and whose work I had never seen. Some of them gave me agreeable surprises. Pamela Stanley was a joy to work with—one of the best Ophelias I have ever seen. She would have been even better if Howard, in his scenes with her, had managed to conceal the fact that he did not find her physically desirable. But it was with the royal couple that I had my real problems. Wilfred Walter was a massive stock leading man with a large voice; his Claudius was domineering but hollow. He presented no emotional threat to the Prince, his stepson, and Leslie Howard seemed either unwilling or incapable of creating one of his own. As a result, a large piece was missing from the heart of the play. With the Queen it was even worse: from the first day it was evident that she was a catastrophe.

Gertrude Elliott was in her middle sixties when Howard invited her to appear with him in *Hamlet,* in which she had first played Ophelia with her celebrated husband, Sir Johnston Forbes-Robertson, thirty-seven years before. Not only was she of an age to be Leslie Howard's grandmother; she had a theatrical tone (full of echoes of Sir Johnston's golden voice as I had heard it in the "big school" at Clifton in my teens) which bore not the slightest relation to the subtle and intimate style of Leslie's playing. The closet scene, in which Hamlet pursued this frail sexagenarian with accusations of criminal lust, was such an embarrassment that, after we had staged it, Leslie refused to go near it again for days. At the end of each day, after the second week, I would ask him what he was going to do about Miss Elliott, and Leslie would sigh and shake his head and smile, as though to say that it was not for him, a former Hungarian bank clerk, to fire Lady Forbes-Robertson from a Shakespearean production.

She was still with us when we arrived in Boston. At our first dress rehearsal she and Leslie played the closet scene amid appalled silence. At two in the morning I took Ruth Howard aside and begged her to intercede with her husband: the most I could achieve was permission to go to New York and retain somebody—anybody—who was familiar with the part, as a possible replacement. I found Mary Servoss, who had played the Queen with Raymond Massey in the Bel Geddes *Hamlet* six years before and asked her to get up on her lines. Back in Boston the next afternoon I called a rehearsal of the closet scene; Leslie did not appear and Lady Forbes-Robertson and I walked stiffly and politely through the business. She was with us still at the Friday and Saturday dress rehearsals. We were due to open on Tuesday. Then, suddenly, a little before noon on Sunday, I was asked to summon Miss Servoss to Boston immediately. Miss Elliott had vanished. Mary went in that night after one walk-through with the company; the next day Leslie rehearsed with her for two hours and again, briefly, the day after that. Then we opened, and he never rehearsed with her again.

(It was not till days later that I discovered what happened to poor Lady Forbes-Robertson. Among Leslie's many romantic involvements with his leading ladies, there had been a particularly tender one, during the London production of *Berkeley Square,* with Jean Forbes-Robertson, considered the most brilliant young actress on the British stage. Now, learning that she was on her way to America, he had appealed to her by radiophone, in mid-Atlantic, in the name of their former affection, to help him and her mother out of their hideous impasse. The day she landed she had come up to Boston, witnessed one rehearsal and, on grounds of health, taken her mother back to New York with her.)

The dress rehearsals and the out-of-town opening of *Hamlet* took place in the immensity of the old Boston Opera House. As Stewart Chaney's massive eleventh-century sets began to go up and his rich costumes to be loudly admired at dress parade, it became clear that here, too, we were in trouble. The show would be impressive and beautiful and we would all receive bouquets for a notable production—which we did. But these very qualities of grandeur made it the worst possible background against which to present Leslie Howard's delicate and tender prince. In the end, to counteract the archaic splendor of the setting, we were forced to play most of the personal scenes far downstage, on steps or narrow platforms. The evening's most memorable moment, visually, was that of Hamlet standing in the prow of the ship that was to carry him to England. It was a lovely sight, but the soliloquy which he delivered on high was largely inaudible.

This same preoccupation with period rose to plague us in another department. For our music I had turned, as usual, to Virgil Thomson, who had just finished recording *The Plow That Broke the Plains* with Pare Lorentz. The score he now composed for us—for ketteldrums, open trumpets and bagpipes—was a model of theatre music, which I used again in Stratford twenty years later. But it was this *Hamlet* collaboration that almost put an end to our friendship and threatened to break up an artistic association that has, finally, endured for close to forty years.

The play scene in *Hamlet* is a notorious trap; few theatrical areas are so cluttered with the bones of bright and pretentious ideas. Agnes De Mille (engaged by Howard in Hollywood where she had choreographed the dances for the film of *Romeo and Juliet*) was determined to make a "mime" of it, while Virgil insisted that it must be performed as *"melodrame,"* with the speeches chanted to a formal musical accompaniment. As a result, rehearsals were a misery—with Leslie off in his hotel room trying to learn his lines and I, like Solomon, trying to arbitrate the insoluble conflict between composer and choreographer. (Virgil suspected me of favoring Agnes' dancers, because I was making love with the Player Queen; Agnes assumed, from the start, that I was against her.) The outcome was a compromise and a mess—aggravated by one quite unpredictable calamity. Seeing Chaney's eleventh-century Danish sets, props and costumes, Virgil decided that his instrumentation, on stage, should be no less authentic than the decor. Recorders were easily procured, so were the small drums and tiny cymbals which formed part of our strolling players' musical paraphernalia. Our trouble was with the "serpent"—a splendid, curling, medieval instrument covered with antique leather, of which Dr. Bilstin, president of the Ancient Instrument Society of America, was understandably proud, and which (since the copper tubing, within, had rotted with the centuries and could not be replaced without damaging the original leather sheath) he had learned to play by humming into it, in the manner of a kazoo. As a result, each time Virgil's *"melodrame"* called for a sustained note to support Joseph Anthony's and his fellow mummers' none too secure voices, the serpent, in the hands of Dr. Bilstin (dressed as a mountebank from the dark ages), would begin to buzz, reach for the note and after two or three seconds of wavering exploration, occasionally hit it. At the final preview, to which a number of eminent Bostonians had been invited, several dozen persons in the auditorium (Ruth Howard was suspected of leading them) rolled their programs into little horns through which they began, first to imitate and, finally, to compete with the serpent. That night the dramatic effect of the play scene was not fully achieved; next day both "mime" and *"melodrame"* were dissolved and Agnes and Virgil left, in separate rages, for London and Paris.

Our Boston reviews were satisfactory and our business was terrific. But two things disturbed me more deeply than the misfortune of the serpent. One was the realization that, in the presence of an audience in a large auditorium, Leslie had begun to lose those qualities which alone made his Hamlet worth doing. Egged on by his entourage and backstage visitors from New York, he began to "broaden" and "enlarge," to project and posture. And, gradually, what might have been a subtle, sinuous and intelligent performance began to look like ineptitude and bombast. My other, more immediate concern was that John Gielgud had just opened triumphantly in New York with a performance of Hamlet that it had taken him ten years to mature. For Leslie to appear against him would inevitably give the impression of a contest—a contest in which Howard, who only just knew his lines, could only be the loser.

I asked Leslie to give me half an hour alone in his dressing room. I was as direct with him as it was possible to be. I urged him to switch, before it was too late, from a New York opening to a national tour. The huge business he was doing in Boston clearly indicated how profitable such a venture would be. Late in the spring, with his investment recouped, fortified by the prestige of a triumphal national tour and Gielgud forgotten, he could enter New York with a virtual assurance of success. This was one of the times when I saw Leslie's fatalism most clearly at work. He listened attentively (as he always did where money was concerned), agreed with every point I made, thanked me for my frankness—and opened three weeks later in New York at the Imperial Theatre, where the stage still bore the scars of our *Panic* trench.

"*Hamlet* with the Hamlet left out"; "Comparisons are not inevitable, they are impossible"; "It is quite unnecessary to discuss the performance with any idea this is an interpretation of Hamlet"—these were among the savage wisecracks that appeared in the press the next morning. The most temperate review was Brooks Atkinson's, which described it as "a thoughtful and beautiful production" with "nothing tepid or nebulous about its staging." He commended Leslie Howard for "his integrity of spirit and personal courage" and listed

> the resources that are happily familiar to Mr. Howard's multitudinous admirers—a gracious figure, a beguiling personal beauty, a winning manner, a pleasing voice, an alert intelligence. These being the resources, Mr. Howard's Hamlet is the logical sum of them. But it is necessary to add that most of the qualities that make Hamlet a commanding figure lie outside Mr. Howard's compass . . . He is lucent but tame on a wild and whirling occasion.

Leslie was resigned, by now, to an unfavorable press, but the lack of business stirred him to drastic action. Undaunted by his New York defeat, he packed up his huge handsome *Hamlet*, opened it in Chicago on Christmas Eve and toured it for four months, with cut-down scenery and a shrunken harem of court ladies, from one end of the continent to the other. No stand was too remote, no move too arduous. By the end of the tour he had recouped every cent of his ninety-thousand-dollar loss and salvaged his national reputation. And as his anxiety diminished, his performance improved: by the time he reached the West Coast he was once again playing Hamlet as we had rehearsed it in the beginning—in the only way in which he was capable of playing it.

I had no percentage of the gross receipts, unfortunately. After Boston and my scene in the dressing room, I left the production and returned to the Maxine Elliott and Project #891. Orson had chosen to regard my *Hamlet* activity as I had regarded his appearance as the juvenile lead of *Ten Million Ghosts*—as a sort of absurd and shameful interlude of which the least said the better. It was more than two years before I undertook any new theatrical work of my own. For, by now, I was completely committed to my partnership with Welles and happier within the creative excitement of that collaboration than I could be, by myself, on the outside. I returned to 39th Street early in November, in time for the closing performance of *Horse Eats Hat* and the casting of *Doctor Faustus.* It was pleasant, after the big-time frustrations of *Hamlet,* to find myself once again in my faded-rose basement, with Augusta Weissberger chirping at me from behind her typewriter and the normal bureaucratic agitations of the WPA enveloping me once again in their reassuring confusion.

The holidays, both Christmas and New Year's, were spent in the darkness of Maxine Elliott's Theatre in an atmosphere that was sulphurous and grim with the presence of demons. Struck, carted off and demolished were our bright Parisian sets—Myrtle's happy home, Tillie's gay many-doored establishment, the Countess' Second Empire salon and the flowering park where the horse had nibbled the hat. Their places were taken by acres of funereal velour, dun and drear in the hard glare of the worklights which illuminated rehearsals by night and the labors of the construction crews and straining electricians by day. Downstage, spanning the orchestra pit, a tapering apron was built to Orson's specifications: it stuck prow-like into the auditorium and necessitated the removal of two dozen seats from the center of the orchestra floor.* Into its surface and into that of the entire stage, traps were cut—with a deafening hacking of axes, screeching of saws and banging of hammers—holes of all shapes and sizes, some too small even for midgets, others vast, yawning pits, mouths to the nether regions, capable of holding whole regiments of fiends and lakes of flame. With all the WPA's manpower, these traps took weeks to dig and install, not to mention the reinforcements that had to be built to support the weakened stage. Since Orson insisted on rehearsing in the theatre, he and his actors could be seen, nightly, threading their way between deadly chasms and mountains of lumber as they moved from one stage position to another. Surprisingly, except for one sprained ankle (Welles's) and one exhausted electrician who fell off a thirty-foot ladder at four in the morning, no one was injured.

Doctor Faustus has a special place in the history of my collaboration with Orson Welles. Macbeth had been created in circumstances that were unique and fantastic; Horse Eats Hat, though it was my idea to begin with, had turned into Orson's personal joke. Faustus was the first of nine shows he and I produced together during the next two years in the course of a partnership in which our mutual functions were only vaguely defined and of which it is difficult, after so many years and so much recrimination, to describe the creative workings with any degree of honesty or accuracy. Looking back, it seems that my two main functions (beginning on the WPA projects, uptown and downtown, and later, through the first triumphal year of the Mercury Theatre) were, first, to supply Orson, beyond the limits of prudence and reason, with the human and material elements he required for his creative work; second, to shield him not only from outside interference but, even more, from the intense pressures of his own complicated and destructive nature.

* I believe ours was the first such breach of the proscenium line in a Broadway playhouse. We repeated it (as far as the double balcony would allow) when we took over the Mercury Theatre and tried it again, to our cost, with Five Kings in Boston and Philadelphia. Today the "thrust stage" is a commonplace of theatrical architecture.

What direct creative aid I was able to give him on our productions was exerted mainly during the early stages of conception and preparation and, then again, during the final crises of dress rehearsals and previews. Throughout Orson's main periods of rehearsal, during which he jealously guarded his intimacies with his actors, I did not appear unless he specifically invited me. I had my own secret and intuitive ways of following his progress but, mostly, I was forced and willing to take it on faith. Run-throughs were unheard of. Welles, like most imaginative directors, had a pathological reluctance to submit work in progress to the cruel test of another man's viewing—especially mine, whose taste he trusted and whose premature judgments he therefore doubly feared. Our relationship became particularly strained on productions, like *Faustus*, in which Orson himself was playing a leading role. At such times I became not merely the hated figure of authority, to be defied and outwitted as I refused further delays and escapes, but the first hostile witness to the ghastly struggle between narcissism and self-loathing that characterized Orson's approach to a part.

Once this barrier had been cleared, I was welcome again. Indeed, during the latter stages of production, there were times when Orson refused to rehearse unless I was in the theatre. As the nights dragged on and our long agony was stretched to the breaking point, it became my main responsibility to preserve him from exhaustion and confusion, to disentangle the essentials of the production as he had originally conceived it from that obsessive preoccupation with insignificant detail in which he was inclined to seek refuge when fatigue or self-doubt had begun to wear him down.

These conflicts existed to an unusual degree in *Doctor Faustus*. Of all the shows we did together, *Faustus* looked the simplest and was the most complicated; it was also the most brilliantly executed. In its acting style, its sound patterns, its scenic conception, its costumes (which Orson designed), its props and its magic tricks, it gave unified and vivid expression to Welles's very special theatrical talent.

Marlowe's *Tragical History of Doctor Faustus* (in the form in which it has come down to us) is a curious stage piece in which are to be found, side by side, some of the most noble verse, bombastic rhetoric and earthbound slapstick in English dramatic literature. Orson, with his vast energy and his timeless theatrical instinct, succeeded, as director and actor, in fusing these conflicting elements into a dramatic whole of surprising power. In all his theatrical work (from his schoolboy *Julius Caesar* to the nights, during the Second World War, when he sawed Marlene Dietrich in half at the Hollywood Stage Door Canteen) Orson was always, at heart, a magician. His production of Marlowe's tragedy was designed and executed as a magic show, employing as its basic technique one of the oldest and most effective of stage-magicians' deceptions—the trick professionally known as "black magic." Used for vanishing acts and miraculous appearances, it exploits the absorbent properties of black velvet so that, under certain lighting conditions, not only do black surfaces become totally invisible against each other, but all normal sense of space, depth and perspective becomes lost and confused in the eye of the spectator. Orson, with Feder's assistance, extended and elaborated this device. By using almost no front light and crisscrossing the stage with parallel light curtains and clusters of units carefully focused from the sides and from overhead, he was able to achieve mystifications that would have impressed the great Thurston.

Not the least ingenious and maddening of his inventions was a series of collapsible, forty-foot black velvet cylinders, each carrying in its head one or more 1,000-watt spotlights pointed vertically downward. Hung high up against the grid, these circular curtains were so rigged on large curtain rings along lines of strong, smooth cord, that they could rise or fall, concertina-wise, at high speeds in complete silence. With these cylinders Orson was able to conjure Marlowe's characters out of limbo and, then, equally miraculously, to snuff them out by means that remained quite inexplicable to the audience.

Far away, from depths of darkness, Faustus is disclosed, surrounded by his diabolical books while Mephistophilis is first

233

> seen as two gigantic horrible eyes which Faustus conjures into
> a human head

wrote one perplexed reviewer.

There were other equally magical effects, culminating in Faustus's reception by the Pope in Rome. Here a procession of scarlet and purple princes of the Church and their servants, carrying golden platters piled with roasts and sweetmeats, paraded across the stage to ceremonial music on their way to the banquet hall. Suddenly, under the Pope's nose, a suckling pig was seen to rise from its golden dish, fly straight up to a height of twelve feet, execute a few steps of an obscene dance, then melt into thin air. A haunch of beef followed, then two fat chickens and a gaudy pudding. In consternation, the procession faltered. At that moment, to the accompaniment of subterranean thunder, three Cardinals' hats flew off like giant saucers. When the Pope's own miter rose from his head and a flash box exploded under his skirt amid cries of terror and fiendish laughter, the procession broke up, leaving Faustus alone on a stage that was suddenly and completely bare.

This mystification was accomplished with the aid of eight dancers, dressed from head to foot in black velvet, moving alongside the procession, just far enough upstage to be out of the blaze of the light curtain and thus completely invisible to the audience against the darkness of black velvet. In their black-gloved hands, they held like fishing poles thin, black, flexible steel rods whose ends were affixed to the meats, the pudding and the episcopal headgear that were marked for flight. On cue the boys in black swung those loaded rods up over their heads and brought them down behind them, where their own black costumes formed a screen for them till they were able to leave the stage unobserved in the confusion of the dissolving parade.

Still another form of magic was achieved through trap doors which permitted characters to enter and exit as though they were rising or sinking through the solid black ` floor of the stage. Among their users was that sinister puppet troupe, the Seven Deadly Sins, who appeared, one by one, through small holes in the apron—obscene, diminutive specimens of evil that flapped and wriggled and squeaked their lewd temptations at the doomed doctor's feet. These, together with the explosions, subterranean rumblings and jagged sheets of lycopodium flame that swept the stage with bursts of hellish brightness, were the gaudy theatrical devices with which Welles adorned his revival. But underneath, at the center of the production, there was deep personal identification which, across a gulf of three and a half centuries, led him to the heart of the work and to its vivid recreation on a contemporary American stage.

The truth is that the legend of the man who sells his soul to the devil in exchange for knowledge and power and who must finally pay for his brief triumph with the agonies of eternal damnation was uncomfortably close to the shape of Welles's own personal myth. Orson really believed in the Devil. (The first time I met him he was writing a play about the Fiend and illustrating it with drawings that were, in fact, grotesque caricatures of himself.) This was not a whimsey but a very real obsession. At twenty-one Orson was sure he was doomed. In his most creative, manic moments, in his wildest transports of love or on the topmost peak of his precocious victories, he was rarely free from a sense of sin and a fear of retribution so intense and immediate that it drove him through long nights of panic to seek refuge in debauchery or work. Quite literally, Orson dared not sleep. No sooner were his eyes closed than, out of the darkness, troupes of demons—the symbols of his sins—surrounded and claimed him, body and soul, in retribution for crimes of which he could not remember the nature, but of which he never for a moment doubted that he was guilty. Neither running nor hiding could save him from their clutches. And when they had seized him with their bleeding claws, they would drag him off into some infernal darkness, there to inflict upon him, through all eternity, those unspeakable torments which he felt he so richly deserved.

Some of this anguish found its way nightly onto the stage of Maxine Elliott's Theatre. Amid the rank fumes and darting flames, there were moments when Faustus seemed to be expressing, through Marlowe's words, some of Orson's personal agony and private terror. This sense of conviction was heightened by Welles's inspired casting of the fiend Mephistophilis, played by the Negro actor Jack Carter, whom Orson had insisted on bringing back onto the project in spite (or perhaps because) of his drunken walk-out from *Macbeth*. Years later, in *The New York Times*, Carter's appearance with Welles was cited as an early and successful example of integrated casting. It was that and far more. Their presence on the stage together was unforgettable: both were around six foot four, both men of abnormal strength capable of sudden, furious violence. Yet their scenes together were played with restraint, verging on tenderness, in which temptation and damnation were treated as acts of love. Welles was brightly garbed, bearded, medieval, ravenous, sweating and human; Carter was in black—a cold, ascetic monk, his face and gleaming bald head moon-white and ageless against the surrounding night. As Orson directed him, he had the beauty, the pride and the sadness of a fallen angel. He watched Faustus sign his deed in blood and, later, officiated at his destruction and listened to his last gasping plea for respite:

> Ah Faustus,
> Now has thou but one bare hour to live
> And then thou must be damned perpetually!

with the contemptuous and elegant calm of a Lucifer who is, himself, more deeply and irrevocably damned than his cringing human victim.

There was one final hazard in the staging of *Faustus:* the clown scenes. Orson treated them frankly for what they were— the standard slapstick routines of the company's funnymen, recorded at performance by some sixteenth-century stage manager. Among the low comics who kicked, tripped, goosed and groped each other on that jutting forestage were actors who followed us out of *Horse Eats Hat* through *Faustus* and *The Cradle Will Rock* into *Julius Caesar, The Shoemaker's Holiday* and beyond. Joseph Cotten was one; Hiram Sherman another. Of the older men, there was George Duthie, whom we promoted from cuckold to Pope,* and a very ancient, bald vaudevillian by the name of Harry McKee, whose theatrical devotion was ended by death that spring but of whose last stage appearance in *Faustus* Stark Young wrote that he was the best clown he had ever seen in an Elizabethan revival.

There is only one woman's part in *Doctor Faustus*. Paula Lawrence was transformed from the Parisian adulteress of *Horse Eats Hat* into a silent Helen of Troy which she played, far upstage, in a gray mask and pale gray velvet gown "looking like Diane de Poitiers on a tapestry in a silver moonlight, the long open bodice, the high breast, the coif, the stiff folds."

Faustus was to open early in January. New Year's Eve and the first nights of 1937 were spent in technical rehearsals. Despite their satanic complication, I remember those unending electrical sessions with pleasure as a time when we were all very close together—in our work and in our lives. Around two in the morning the stage crew (except the electricians and flymen needed to work the black velvet "cones") went home and Orson, his face still swollen with makeup, was ready to start lighting. The company had been dismissed by then, except for our stage managers, a few insanely devoted volunteers (usually including Jack Carter) and a handful of girl friends and wives (led by Virginia Welles) who remained to the end, taking turns dozing and "standing in" for actors—moving back and forth, up and down on the bare, perforated stage while Orson, Feder and I yelled at them and at each other, and electricians on tall, shaky ladders focused lamps overhead and the men on the switchboard tried to get the feel of those sequences of delicately overlapping light cues upon which the movement of the show was so wholly dependent. Around four in the morning hamburgers, milkshakes and brandy were brought in from Times Square. Between seven and eight we quit, partly because we couldn't see any more but also because Welles usually had a radio call at nine.

That was my winter with a Viennese girl with gray eyes who

* Eleven months later, as the soothsayer in *Caesar*, his was the first voice to be heard from the stage of the Mercury Theatre.

was born in the same hour of the same day of the same year as Orson, and whom it seemed to me, for a time, that I loved. Since she insisted on spending every night at the theatre, we had taken a room in a small hotel on 39th Street, to which we returned in the late winter dawn, made love, had breakfast and slept together for an hour or two before I reappeared in the powder room of the Maxine Elliott, ready to deal with the list of the day's emergencies which Augusta Weissberger had waiting for me:

Item: It has been reported to Phil Barber that the baggy-pants routine in the second clown scene is in bad taste, if not actually indecent. Please investigate and, if necessary, speak to Welles.

Item: The Workers' Alliance has complained to Actors' Equity about the excessive rehearsal hours on Project #891. Equity, in turn, has called Mrs. Flanagan.

Item: Mr. Murphy at the bank says a check of yours is going to bounce for lack of funds. I have guaranteed the deficiency till Friday.

Item: The Fire Department is disturbed over the open flames in the final scene. They have talked to the Shuberts who are threatening to cancel the lease of the theatre. Please deal with this.

On the evening of our first dress rehearsal Orson arrived a few minutes before seven from the studio where he had been broadcasting *The Shadow*. A huge meal was laid out in his dressing room, which he ate with one hand while he was building up his putty nose with the other. We were due to start at eight. The curtain went up after nine and never came down. Hallie Flanagan dropped in during the evening with Kate Lawson (who now was technical director of the New York Federal Theatre project). She noted in her journal that the Maxine Elliott had become "a pit of hell . . . total darkness punctuated by stabs of light, trap doors opening and closing to reveal bewildered stagehands and actors going up, down and around in circles; explosions; properties disappearing in a clap of thunder and, on stage, Orson muttering the mighty lines and interspersing them with fierce adjurations to the invisible but omnipresent Feder."

Welles's dress rehearsals and previews were nearly always catastrophic—especially if he was performing. I think he enjoyed these near disasters: they gave him a pleasing sense, later, of having brought order out of chaos and of having, singlehanded, plucked victory from defeat. It is true that his productions were, on the whole, more complicated and delicate than other men's; being magic shows, they required minute adjustments and perfect coordination before they could function effectively. It is also true that, suffering more than the usual actor's fears, Orson welcomed and exploited these technical hazards as a means of delaying the hideous moment when he must finally come out on the stage and deliver a performance. I remember that our second dress rehearsal of *Faustus* was held up for almost an hour while Orson raged at me behind the lowered curtain. Thoughtlessly, at the Askews' one Sunday afternoon, I had told Tchelitchew he could attend a rehearsal of *Faustus*. Arriving unannounced with a Russian princess and Charles Henri Ford, he was spied through the peephole by Orson, who flatly refused to begin the run-through until they had left the theatre. Vainly I argued that Pavlik was a friend, an admirer and a theatre man who, in his years with Diaghilev, had lived through far wilder crises than ours. Orson, having found an excuse to postpone his opening scene, sat grim and obstinate, while around us, as we quarreled, I could feel the company and crew, nervous from lack of sleep, becoming dangerously restive. When I finally went out front, full of apologies, to inform our visitors, in French, that they must leave, I could hear Orson's voice from behind the curtain howling triumphantly of Russian pederasts and international whores.

By the third preview the show had begun to work, though Welles's own performance did not finally emerge until opening night. Though the *Daily News* and the Hearst press continued to involve us in their dispute with the New Deal, a majority of the daily press approved of us—especially the *Times:*

Everyone interested in the imaginative power of the theatre will want to see how ably Orson Welles and John Houseman have cleared away all the imposing impedimenta that makes most classics forbidding and how skillfully they have left *Doctor Faustus,* grim and terrible, on the stage . . . They have gone a long way toward revolutionizing the staging of Elizabethan plays and a good many people will now pay their taxes in a more charitable frame of mind.

The weeklies and monthlies were favorable on all sides— Liberal, Left and Catholic. Even *Commonweal,* "tired of propaganda from the stage," congratulated the Federal Theatre on "securing the services of two young men who are precisely the type of artist the American theatre is so badly in need of." Edith Isaacs, in the *Theatre Arts Monthly,* cited our success as "proof that the professional theatre has thrown away an audience eager for its gifts and responsive to the least of them." But our most detailed and perceptive appraisal came, as usual, from Stark Young, who attended a crowded performance some days after the opening and was astonished to find Marlowe's tragedy, "with all the radiance of its ambition and the spell of its audacity," coming "straight over the footlights to an audience whose attention is such as I have not seen elsewhere in the theatre this year." He admired Paul Bowles's music "that can often float you into the scenes' Elysium" and Feder's lighting through which "the settings appear to be some chiaroscuro of the cosmic—a concentration in space—the agent between the creator and the creation." And though he complained that Orson's appearance was unnecessarily "mussed and grimy," he was one of the first to give him his full due as a performer:

Only a variety of emotional pressures on the part of the actor who plays the leading role can register for the audience the stages of Faustus' struggle and his progression toward the climax of his deep damnation. Marlowe's poetry is spoken far above the average by Mr. Orson Welles, who has a beautiful even voice, perfectly placed, and has, too, a remarkable sense of timing. He possesses also both naturally and by study a notable gift for projection, no mean asset for Marlowe's lines.

Not only were the audiences at the Maxine Elliott consistently attentive: they were also surprisingly numerous. *The Tragical History of Doctor Faustus* ran from January 8th to May 9th to a total of eighty thousand paying customers including thirty-six hundred standees.

One night, about halfway through the run, Harry Hopkins appeared unannounced and bought a seat far in the rear of the theatre before he was recognized by the agitated and obsequious house staff. At the close of the performance, after Faustus had sunk howling into a lake of flame, I led the head of the New Deal's Works Progress Administration between gaping stage traps, through sulphurous fumes, backstage, to where Welles lay—huge and half-conscious on a broken sofa—gasping and sweating from his descent into hell. After the usual backstage amenities Hopkins asked us one official question. Were we having a good time on the Federal Theatre? We told him we were.

VI

I T WAS customary, after each of our successful openings, for Orson and me to drift apart for a time, relieved at being suddenly free of one another after so many days and nights of shared anguish and enforced intimacy. With the triumph of *Doctor Faustus* our estrangement lasted longer than usual. This gave me a chance to catch up on my sleep and to try to pick up the pieces that remained of my personal life after almost two years of Federal Theatre.

Of my world of the early thirties little was left. The couples were separated, the girls married. Lee Miller was an Egyptian princess residing in Cairo and Paris, Anna Friede the wife of a labor leader in Detroit, Henrietta was back in Kentucky breeding race horses, Mina Curtiss in Northampton, teaching. The Mielziners were divorced and Phil Wylie had moved to Florida. Virgil Thomson, with whom I was once again sharing an apartment, was working day and night on the music for Pare Lorentz's second film, *The River*. The Viennese girl was gone: she had left suddenly for Paris to model a collection, then moved on to

Rome, from which she sent me gay, tender letters and a snapshot of herself in the seat of an Alfa-Romeo roadster whose owner she presently married. No one replaced her. For the rest of that year and the next the only passions I seemed capable of experiencing were those that related to my work. The physical and sentimental adventures with which I continued to fill my nights and weekends provided only mild satisfactions compared to the sustained excitements and violent consummations of my life in the theatre.

Now for a few weeks there was a lull. My days were still spent in the powder room dealing with the increasingly difficult administrative problems of Project #891. And several times a week, for all or part of the evening, I was drawn back to *Faustus,* which never ceased to amaze and delight me with its dangerous beauty. (During the five months of its run I never heard the clanging of fire engines in the streets at night without feeling sure that our lakes of lycopodium flame had finally set the Maxine Elliott alight.) Sometimes I would go backstage to Orson's dressing room and we would talk vaguely about our next production. Ben Jonson's *The Silent Woman* was mentioned as a possibility—but without enthusiasm. Neither *Julius Caesar* nor *The Duchess of Malfi* could be cast from within Project #891. So we let the weeks slide by, waiting for our next enthusiasm to declare itself.

In part, this inertia reflected the deep collective unease with which the Federal Theatre was becoming infected in this, the second year of its existence. Flushed with our early successes, hailed by the critics as "the chief producers of works of art in the American theatre," we had lived and worked, for eighteen months, under the growing illusion that we formed part of a permanent theatrical organization—pioneers in the development of a nationally supported popular Art Theatre. Now we were harshly reminded, from outside and inside the project, that the institution to which we belonged was, in fact, nothing but a temporary emergency relief agency, born of poverty and fear in a time of national calamity. The irony of our situation lay in this—that as the economic panic receded and the misery and the human need began to diminish, so did the creative potential of our work. By the end of 1936, though the unemployed still numbered over twelve million, it was clear that the national economy was finally turning that long-awaited corner. This was bad news for the project. For with each new sign of recovery, the Government came under increasing pressure to cut back on the vast, costly machinery of work relief: in any such reduction, it was evident that the Arts Projects would be the first to suffer.

With the new year our problems seemed to come to a head. Demands for cuts in the WPA were heard more frequently and insistently in Congress and in the conservative press. And the counterattacks from the Left were growing in violence:

FDR JUGGLES WPA

screamed a City Projects Council handbill dated January 1937.

> Under the verbal sleight-of-hand of President Roosevelt, relief appropriations are rapidly becoming a game of "now-you-see-it-now-you-don't!" This is a shameful deception of the unemployed and relief worker! It is a surrender to the Chamber of Commerce, Hearst and the whole reactionary Wall Street crowd whose "STARVE AMERICA" program FDR once promised to fight tooth and nail!

Ever since its belated formation as a "classical theatre," Project #891 had been the most purely theatrical, the least social-minded or politically involved of the New York Federal Theatre's five major theatrical units. Now, in the high wind that was beginning to blow all around us, this isolation was swept away. Caught between repeated, demoralizing rumors of reduction and liquidation and the rising tide of desperate, organized resistance among project workers who felt their very lives threatened by the impending cuts, it was becoming daily more difficult, in spite of our past successes, to preserve the morale and muster the energy for creative work on a project in whose future we ourselves were ceasing to have faith.

Our torpor lasted for almost two months—till the beginning of March. Then, overnight, in one of those sudden, total reversals that formed one of the few consistent patterns of our erratic collaboration, we temporarily abandoned all thought of classical repertory. Instead, with our energy and affection miraculously restored, Orson and I launched Project #891 on a huge new production that bore absolutely no relation to anything either of us had done before and which was guaranteed, in the circumstances, to land us both in the most serious possible trouble.

The Cradle Will Rock, which its author, Marc Blitzstein, described as "a play with music" (while others, at various times, called it an opera, a labor opera, a social cartoon, a marching song and a propagandistic tour de force), had been written at white heat one year earlier—in the spring of 1936. I had known Marc slightly in the early thirties, soon after his return from Europe, where he had gone from a substantial, middle-class Philadelphia home and the Curtis Institute of Music to study composition, first with Schoenberg and then, in Paris, with the celebrated Nadia Boulanger. A musical sketch of his—*Triple Sec*—had been admired in the last of the Theatre Guild's *Garrick Gaieties* but, generally, he was considered a sophisticated composer of "serious," "modern" music.

Blitzstein's father was a banker and a socialist of the old school, of whom his son once wrote that he was "as modern in social thinking as he was conservative in musical taste." Marc's own political conversion and its creative expression came late, after the advent of the New Deal. In the summer of 1934 he was swimming in the Mediterranean with his wife, the daughter of the former Viennese operetta star Lina Abarbannell. One afternoon, as they lay drying in the sun on a beach at Majorca, he said to her, "I don't think I want to stay here any more. I want to be working in my own country. There are things going on there I want to be part of." "I've already packed," Eva said.

The next year, at Provincetown, Marc wrote a dramatic sketch around the song "The Nickel Under the Foot" which, later, formed the basis of the streetwalker's scene in *The Cradle Will Rock.* He showed it to Bertolt Brecht, who was in New York and who approved but said it was not enough. "To literal prostitution you must add figurative prostitution—the sell-out of one's talent and dignity to the powers that be." Nine months later, soon after Eva's death, Blitzstein wrote *The Cradle Will Rock* in five weeks—partly in a friend's house in Connecticut, partly in his sister's home at Ventnor, New Jersey—and dedicated it to Brecht.

Among the directors and producers who heard Marc audition his work during 1936 were Herman Shumlin, Martin Gabel, Harold Clurman for the Group, Charles Freedman for the Theatre Union and members of the Actors' Repertory Company, a left-wing group which had successfully produced Irwin Shaw's *Bury the Dead* the previous spring and who now announced *The Cradle Will Rock* for the season of 1936–37. I was not present when Welles and Blitzstein met backstage, one night, during the run of *Horse Eats Hat,* to discuss the possibility of Orson's directing Marc's play with music. Apparently, it was love at first sight. Marc was entranced by Orson's brilliance and power; Orson was excited by the challenge of this, his first contact with musical theatre. I remember listening jealously, with an ill-concealed sense of rejection, to Orson's enthusiastic comments about the piece (which I had not heard) and to his ideas for casting and staging it, which he elaborated for my annoyance. *Hamlet* had opened and closed and *Faustus* was deep in rehearsal when the Actors' Repertory Company abandoned *The Cradle* for lack of funds.* Orson never spoke to me of his disappointment, but I gathered that he and Marc had parted with a mutual promise that if ever a producer was found for such a costly and difficult work, Welles would direct it.

So things stood in March 1937 when, in the midst of our doldrums and as part of the complicated game of one-upmanship that Orson and I were constantly playing together, I suggested one night in his dressing room that if I were ever invited to hear Marc's work, I might conceivably find it suitable for production at the Maxine Elliott by Project #891. I did. And soon after

---

* It was a bad winter for theatrical troupes. That same month the Group Theatre disbanded for the year. "We shall go on," declared Harold Clurman on the eve of his departure to join Clifford Odets in Hollywood.

that Hallie Flanagan was invited one Sunday evening to a well-planned dinner at the apartment on East 55th Street which Virgil Thomson and I were occupying that spring. Afterwards—

> Marc Blitzstein sat down at the piano and played, sang and acted with the hard, hypnotic drive which came to be familiar to audiences, his new opera. It took no wizardry to see that this was not just a play set to music, nor music illustrated by actors, but music and play equaling something new and better than either. This was in its percussive as well as its verbal beat Steeltown U.S.A.—America 1937.*

The next day *The Cradle Will Rock* was officially announced as the next production of Project #891. There was some feeling, later, in New York and Washington that Hallie had been irresponsible in allowing so controversial a piece to be produced at such a precarious time. I believe she knew exactly what she was doing. She had no way of guessing (none of us had) that a double accident of timing would project us all onto the front pages of the nation's press; but she did sense which way the political winds were blowing and realized, better than her more timid colleagues, that in the storm into which the Arts Projects were headed, there was no safety in prudence and no virtue in caution. For my own part it was not entirely out of caprice or competitiveness that I had embarked on *The Cradle Will Rock*. The truth is that I was finding in Marc's opera a welcome release from the mounting tensions which were closing in on us that winter and spring.

Work on *The Cradle* started calmly enough. We had singers and dancers on the project, but Will Geer was brought in from the outside to play Mr. Mister, the lord of Steeltown, and Howard da Silva to be the proletarian hero—Larry Foreman. And to make up our chorus of thirty-two we borrowed or traded singers from other units. Rehearsals (which lasted for almost three months) were mostly musical at first and were conducted by Marc with help from Teddy Thomas, whom I promoted to

---

* *Arena* by Hallie Flanagan.

associate producer. Lehman Engel, our conductor, came over daily from the Music Unit where he was working to sit in on rehearsals. Orson, between radio shows, spent hours learning the music and working with his designer on the sets, which, he informed me, were to be extremely elaborate and expensive.

Marc had created *The Cradle Will Rock* in haste, out of a burning conviction which he never quite recaptured in his subsequent work. As a result, it is free of those conflicts—between his wanting to be a serious composer, an artist with a social message and a Broadway winner—that confused so many of his other pieces. Its prime inspiration, admittedly, was *The Threepenny Opera* by Brecht and Weill, to which Marc added "whatever was indicated and at hand. There were recitatives, arias, revue patters, tap dances, suites, chorales, silly symphony, continuous incidental commentary music, lullaby music—all pitchforked into it without a great deal of initiative from me." There were also patches of Gilbert and Sullivan and echoes of the Agitprop experiments of the early thirties.

Like *Waiting for Lefty, The Cradle Will Rock* was both angry and sentimental. Like Odets (but more satirically), Marc used vignettes and flashbacks to develop his theme of corruption, then returned to the present with a direct appeal to the audience's emotions for his final climax. *Waiting for Lefty* was written for, and has always been played on, a bare stage. For America's first proletarian musical, Orson had devised an extravagant scenic scheme that called for a triple row of three-dimensional velour portals between which narrow, glass-bottomed, fluorescent platforms, loaded with scenery and props, slid smoothly past each other as the scene shifted back and forth from the night court to a street corner, a church, a drugstore, a hotel lobby, a faculty room, a doctor's office and the front lawn of the finest house in Steeltown U.S.A.

The style of the piece as it began to take form at rehearsals (before costumes and scenery came between the performers and their material) fell somewhere between realism, vaudeville and oratory: the singing ranged from *Sprechstimme* to arias, patter and blues. A few of our older, staider performers were vaguely uneasy in their satirical roles, but no more than they had been with the magic of *Faustus* or the bawdry of *Horse Eats Hat*. For the rest, the piece had the fascination that goes with the creation of something new and unusual in the theatre. And almost from the first day, there were strange, prophetic stirrings in the air—a turbulence that grew with the weeks as the harsh realities of the national crisis met the rising theatrical excitement that was being generated on our bare, worklit stage. As opening night approached, those winds reached tornado force. How they finally blew *The Cradle* right out of our theatre onto another stage nineteen blocks uptown has become part of American theatrical history.

It is not easy, with a world war, a cold war, Korea, Vietnam and some twenty years of inflation in between, to re-create the world we lived in during the mid-thirties. Nineteen thirty-seven was, in some ways, the most confused and disturbed of those difficult years—a time of transition between the end of the Great Depression and the beginning of the slowly gathering industrial boom that accompanied our preparations for World War II. It was the year in which the President of the United States, in his second inaugural address, referred to "those tens of millions of our citizens . . . who at this very moment are still denied the greater part of what the very lowest standards of today call the necessities of life." It was also the year in which labor violence vied for space with international news on the front pages of the nation's press.

The week we opened *Doctor Faustus*, sit-down strikes closed seven major automobile plants in the Midwest; deputies were mobilized for the ejection of sit-down strikers in Flint, Michigan, and the auto union voted a general strike against all plants of General Motors, whose president, Alfred Sloane, Jr., had just announced his refusal to deal with "labor dictators" or to consider their "demands for Union recognition and a thirty-hour week." The day *The Cradle Will Rock* went into rehearsal there were riots in Akron and Pontiac and strikes halted work in the Chrysler and Hudson auto plants. That same week the CIO under John L. Lewis started a drive to unionize the steel industry.

By May the main battleground had shifted from autos to steel; five mills of Republic Steel were struck and picketed. At Canton and Massillon, strikers prevented night-shift workers from reaching plants. "They started in holiday mood and waved baseball bats, billiard cues and makeshift clubs." On May 29th in South Chicago, a thousand steel workers marching on a mill of the Republic Steel Corporation were beaten back by police after a sharp fight. Twenty strikers and six policemen were injured, "one of them struck on the head by the pole of an American flag carried at the head of a marching mob." Two days later ten were killed and eighty-four hurt as strikers again battled police in Chicago. The crowd used guns and rocks; the police employed clubs, tear gas and bullets. (Two months later it was brought out by the La Follette inquiry into police brutality that seven of the dead strikers had been shot in the back.)

During the first week of June, as we were starting our technical rehearsals, five thousand CIO sympathizers invaded the business section of Lansing, Michigan, forced the closing of factories and stores and blocked all traffic in protest against the arrest of pickets. Later that same week Johnstown, Ohio, was placed under martial law (CITY SWEPT BY STRIKES—RIOTING THROUGHOUT NIGHT —THOUSANDS JOIN IN BATTLE ON EIGHT MILE FRONT) and Representative Clare Hoffman wired instructions to his son back home: "Have hundred reliable citizens who are willing to go to Monroe to aid in defending city from invasion promised by CIO. Leave names, addresses, lists of arms, tents and cots at office. Have Carl locate 200 rounds of 12-gauge number one choked, 100 rounds 30:30 automatic."

These national disturbances were echoed in the small, special world of the Arts Projects of the WPA—with one significant difference: in the spreading industrial struggle both sides had their eye on the future; they were maneuvering (and fighting, if need be) for positions that they regarded as vital for the years to come, in preparation for expanding production, with huge future benefits at stake. On WPA there was no such hope. Both sides realized that they were engaged in a losing battle: they knew that at the first signs of a restored national economy, the administration would be under irresistible pressure to reduce and, eventually, to dissolve all work-relief projects, especially those relating to such superfluous activities as the arts. By the summer of 1937 the pressure was at its peak. It was known that the appropriation under which the WPA had been formed was due to expire on June 30th and that its renewal would involve drastic reductions and, quite possibly, liquidation of the Arts Projects.

Rumors of cuts and pink slips filled the air. These were denied by administrators who still hoped against hope to preserve at least a part of the work-relief structure they had so devotedly and conscientiously erected and by those who, like Hallie, sincerely believed that the Federal Theatre, through its good work, had earned the right to live on as a form of national theatre. But they brought panic to those who, on WPA (some for the first time in their lives), held steady jobs and enjoyed a sense of belonging, and who now faced the prospect of being thrown back into the despair of unemployment and local relief. YOU WON'T DIE TODAY, said the handbills. BUT HOW LONG CAN YOU LIVE WITHOUT YOUR JOB? Fanning the fear and the anger were the extremists on both sides. On the one hand, there were those, in and out of Congress, who had never ceased to feel that relief workers were bums, encouraged by a "socialist" administration to believe that the world owed them a living, and who regarded the Arts Projects as a particularly dangerous form of Trojan horse, loaded with screwballs and Reds. On the other, there were those for whom the projects and their human problems had, from the first, formed useful beachheads for political action—those who now saw in the relief reductions a weapon of agitation and propaganda of which they were determined to make the widest possible use.

F.D.R. JUGGLES W.P.A.

JOBS—OR WHAT IS OUR FUTURE?

At a time when private industry has no jobs to offer us, we the young people of the W.P.A. are having our jobs taken away from us. We are being virtually thrown onto the streets to starve. UNEMPLOYED! HOMELESS! HUNGRY! WHAT ARE WE GOING TO DO?

asked the mimeographed handbills of the day. And the answer was given:

Join in the City Project Council-Workers' Alliance struggle for more security, adequate appropriations, sick-leave, vacations with pay, and a 20% increase in salaries.

At the bottom is a perforated strip:

I want more information about the Young Communist League:

Name:

Address:

Mail to: Y.C.L., c/o W.P.A.,
Federal Theatre Branch
161 West 28th Street, New York

(All replies will be treated in confidence)

To the same period belongs a smudged, crude, pale-green poster:

TO THE PEOPLE OF NEW YORK!

To you—manual or White Collar Project Worker!
To you—Brother New Yorker out of a Job!
To you—Emergency Relief Bureau Staff Employee!
To you—Organized Trade Union Member, Negro or White!

ON TO CITY HALL!

Let the City Fathers Know that New York's
Unemployed and Relief Workers face a CRISIS.

252

MAYOR LAGUARDIA!

In Washington you said "WPA must be continued and expanded."

In New Orleans you said "Relief in New York is too low."

But how about back home, Mr. Mayor?

Stop the 40,000 lay-offs on W.P.A. and provide City-Wide projects to take care of the dismissed and unemployed!

SATURDAY APRIL 4th

!! MARCH !!

(From Battery Place 11 A.M.)

ON TO CITY HALL!

March to make the Mayor

ACT NOT TALK!

It was in this tense but appropriate atmosphere that we concluded our rehearsals of *The Cradle Will Rock*. On May 27th most members of the project had taken a day off when the Federation of Architects, Engineers, Chemists and Technicians, the WPA branches of the Teachers' Union and Newspaper Guild, the Artists' Union, the City Projects Council and the Workers' Alliance called a one-day, city-wide strike of all WPA work in protest against threatened cuts. Seven thousand joined the stoppage. Some days later, after a performance by the Dance Unit of works by Tamiris and Charles Weidman at the Nora Bayes Theatre, audience and cast joined in an all-night sit-down while outside "44th Street was filled with marchers." This was the first major sit-down on the project. Asked to comment, the following day, at a convention of the American Theatre Council, Hallie Flanagan replied that the Federal Theatre workers had struck "for what was once described as life, liberty and the pursuit of happiness . . . If we object to that method, I feel that some word should come from this gathering as to a better one." *The New York Times* reported that no one in the audience had any suggestions.

253

Then, within a fortnight, came the announcement everyone had been dreading: a cut of thirty percent in the New York Theatre Project, involving the immediate dismissal of seventeen hundred workers. In protest, a number of sit-downs were called: in Harlem, at the Lafayette, three hundred members of the Negro Unit sat down at the close of a performance and four hundred members of the audience sat with them through the night while other sympathizers formed a picket line outside. That same night at the Federal Theatre of Music, where the first of a series of Brahms concerts was being presented, ticket holders rose and urged others in the theatre to remain all night in their seats. Three hundred and fifty responded.

Such action was not for us. Project #891 had a challenge of its own which I was determined to meet—to get Marc Blitzstein's play with music onto the stage of Maxine Elliott's Theatre against a variety of odds. These included all the hazards that normally went with the opening of Orson's productions. By the end of May our three great portals were in place and our illuminated glass-bottomed floats were cruising across the stage, pursued by panting players, trailing yards of black, writhing cable in their wake. Dress rehearsals were as painful as usual: actors accustomed to an open stage and four months of piano accompaniment were startled to find themselves confronted by gliding platforms and a twenty-eight piece orchestra between themselves and the auditorium. Transitions had to be repeated interminably; there were the customary scenes of recrimination and reconciliation. But our real perils were not theatrical. What Hallie had taken, in mid-February, for a dynamic piece of Americana had turned, by early June (with the WPA in turmoil and steel strikers on the front page) into a time bomb that threatened to bring the entire project tumbling about her head. Already, some weeks earlier, following reports in Washington that the opera was "dangerous," a special envoy had arrived in New York, watched a run-through with Mrs. Flanagan and "pronounced it magnificent." Now, ten days before our opening, with more than eighteen thousand tickets sold, a new set of rumors began to fly. Unfamiliar faces were glimpsed around the theatre;

inside dopesters assured us that the curtain would never rise on *The Cradle Will Rock*. We ignored them and continued rehearsing and selling tickets. Our first public preview was scheduled for June 16th, with our official premiere announced for two weeks after that. On June 12th the blow fell—in the insidious form of a routine memorandum received by all national directors prohibiting "because of impending cuts and reorganization, any new play, musical performance or art gallery to open before July 1st."

As producers, Orson and I were not noted for our punctuality. Our *Macbeth* opening had been postponed five times, *Horse Eats Hat* twice, *Doctor Faustus* three times. Normally, we would almost certainly have postponed the opening of *The Cradle*. But now, suddenly, we became demons of dependability, scrupulous to honor our public and artistic commitment. Hallie asked me how I felt about the delay. I told her that we refused to accept it. She called Washington and tried to get an exception to the ruling: she cited the quality of our show, its vast cost in materials and man hours, the size of our advance sale and the adverse publicity an enforced postponement was bound to provoke at such a time. When she failed, Orson and Archibald MacLeish, to whom we had turned for help, flew to Washington and visited the WPA administrators just as they were preparing to meet a Congressional committee on appropriations for the coming year. Hopkins was not available. In a sharp scene with David Niles, they were told that the show was postponed—not canceled. Welles said he did not believe this, and that if *The Cradle* failed to open as advertised under Government auspices, he and I would launch it privately. "In that case we would no longer be interested in it as a property," said Mr. Niles. The interview was brief and Orson was back in time for that night's dress rehearsal —the one before the last.

Early next morning we started telephoning; we called everyone we could think of—Right and Left, professionals and outsiders—and invited them to that night's final run-through which, we intimated, might be their last chance to see *The Cradle Will Rock*. There was no specific rule forbidding invited guests at rehearsals: several hundreds made their way past the guards at the doors, mostly theatre people, musicians and enthusiasts of the far Left. Among our audience that night, Marc was happy to identify such celebrities as Arthur Hopkins, George Kaufman, Moss Hart and V. J. Jerome. For my own part I remember little of the evening except that I felt it was not going too well. The glass wagons slid in and out—not too precisely; the actors, concerned with finding their places and lights, still lacked the fervor and energy of our earlier run-throughs; Lehman Engel, our conductor, was still struggling to establish a balance between their untrained voices and the twenty-eight not so subtly orchestrated instruments in our shallow pit. But near the end of the evening the piece came suddenly alive: I can still see Howard da Silva as Larry Foreman, with his dirty-blond toupee, his fist clenched and his jaw jutting out around his flashing teeth as he sang, with the chorus behind him, right over the blaring band into the faces of the cheering audience:

> That's thunder, that's lightning,
> And it's going to surround you!
> No wonder those stormbirds
> Seem to circle around you . . .
> Well, you can't climb down, and you can't sit still;
> That's a storm that's going to last until
> The final wind blows . . . and when the wind blows . . .
> The Cradle Will Rock!

(Music, bugles, drums and fifes)

CURTAIN

The audience which left the Maxine Elliott that night, filing out past the guards in the doorways and the Workers' Alliance handbill distributors on the sidewalk, was the only one that ever saw and heard Marc's work performed as he wrote it. After they had left, the lights were turned out and the doors of the theatre were locked. For us, they were never reopened.

The next day, June 15th, a dozen uniformed WPA guards took over the building in force. Project members arriving to sign in found their theatre sealed and dark. The Cossacks, as they came to be known, guarded the front of the house and the box office; they hovered in the alley outside the dressing rooms with orders to see that no Government property was used or removed. This included scenery, equipment, props and costumes: Howard da Silva, who attempted to retrieve his toupee (purchased with Federal funds) had it snatched from his head at the stage door and confiscated. But there was one place in the building from which the Cossacks were excluded—the pink powder room in the basement, which now became headquarters in the fight to save *The Cradle*. Here Orson, Marc, Lehman Engel, Feder, Teddy Thomas, George Zorn and I lived for the next thirty-six hours, sustained by Augusta Weissberger with coffee and sandwiches and by food and drink brought in by well-wishers from the outside, for we were afraid to leave the theatre lest the Cossacks prevent us from returning. Our telephones had not been cut off and we made the most of them.

Our strategy was as simple as it was unrealistic. WPA might have problems of its own, but these did not concern us: as artists and theatre men we felt obligated to honor our commitments. The authorities had notified the organizations which had bought our previews that these must be postponed or canceled. We called them back and urged them to show up in full force. They needed no urging, for they were all part of that new left-wing audience that had sprung up with the Depression—the crowds that filled the houses on *New Theatre* nights and made *Lefty* and *Bury the Dead* and *Stevedore* the thrilling theatrical events they became. The Federal Theatre, with its half-dollar top, had further expanded this audience. Fifty percent of our public came from organized theatre parties, mostly of the Left—prejudiced and semieducated but young and generous and eager to participate in the excitement which the stage alone seemed to offer them in those uncertain times. These were the audiences whose members had "sat in" with the WPA workers earlier in the month. We were determined to keep faith with them and the authorities were determined that we should not.

For by this time, after the trip to Washington and the arrival of the Cossacks, peace was no longer possible between us and the Works Progress Administration. Since we refused to appreciate their official dilemma (which was real and grievous), we must be silenced and disciplined as an example. We, on our part, convinced that Washington had no intention of letting us produce the piece (on July 2nd or at any other time), saw no point in passively conniving at its murder. Besides, I think we realized that our own days with the project were numbered: we had served it well and had, in the process, made reputations such as we could not possibly have achieved elsewhere. Having nothing further to gain, we might as well make our departure as explosive and dramatic as possible.

Throughout the day of June 15th we continued blithely announcing to the press—and to anyone else who called to inquire—that we would give our first public preview of *The Cradle Will Rock* on the following night, as announced, in this or some other theatre. At some time during the afternoon, MacLeish made a final, vain attempt to reach Harry Hopkins at the White House. Toward dusk Mina Curtiss, who liked crises and had driven down from the Berkshires, made her way past the guards in her black Bergdorf Goodman dress, bearing cherries, roast beef and a bottle of brandy. Later in the evening Helen Deutsch appeared and asked us bluntly but helpfully what we intended to do on the morrow. We said we would give the show. She asked us where and how. And we couldn't answer.

We had been so busy proclaiming our integrity that we had not given much thought to the problems of our performance. These were serious. The Administration, through the Cossacks, controlled our scenery, costumes and lights—not to mention our stage and our auditorium. That left the human element. We now discovered that we didn't control that either. Our orchestra, all craft union men, members of one of the most potent and cohesive organizations in the country (whose leaders never approved of *The Cradle,* which they regarded as straight CIO propaganda or worse), had been notified of their union's decision: if we moved to another theatre not only must the men be paid for full new rehearsal sessions at full Broadway salaries, but in view of the "operatic" nature of the work we must also increase the size of the orchestra. This was clearly impossible. Of our actors and singers less than half were Equity members; but they were the important ones, sufficient to make the performance impossible if they were refused permission to appear. We queried Equity and were promised an answer for the following day. Anxiously we awaited the Council's verdict, knowing that no matter how deeply and passionately involved our actors might be in the fate of *The Cradle*, they would not knowingly defy their own union's ruling.

The dawn of June 16th found us still in the powder room. The Downtown School of Music, main buyers of that night's theatre party, called early to know if there was any change in the situation. We assured them that the show would go on. Time? Eight-thirty. Place? To be determined later. In midsummer, with more than half of New York's theatres dark, this seemed the least of our problems. George Zorn, our house manager, in whom I had absolute confidence, was sent out to find a theatre broker and returned an hour later with a small, seedy man in a black felt hat—a specialist in distressed theatres. He had a long list of available houses.

Five hours later, their number had shrunk to zero. Every half-hour or so he would look up from the phone we had put at his disposal at Augusta's desk under the lavender mannequin and announce that we had a theatre. And each time, a few minutes later, it would turn out not to be so. Mostly, this failure was due to lack of time, an inability to reach the owner in midsummer or a reluctance on his part to reopen a dark house for such a brief and uncertain engagement. Once, early in the afternoon, we closed a deal for a house only to discover, as we were about to take possession, that its management was deep in a dispute with the Stagehands' Union and that we would have to cross a picket line to get in. After that the man in the black hat was ordered from the powder room in disgrace. He stayed on, unnoticed, making futile calls and, occasionally, trying to attract our attention. But by then we had other, more awful problems to occupy us.

Actors' Equity had reached its decision at two o'clock. Around three the company, assembled on stage between the glass-bottomed platforms, received from its deputy the Council's reasonable but catastrophic verdict. Actors who had been rehearsing a play for four months and who had been receiving pay during that time from one management (the Federal Theatre) could not perform that same play for another management (Houseman and Welles) without the permission of the first—which was, of course, not forthcoming. In consequence, Equity members in the cast of *The Cradle Will Rock* were enjoined from appearing in that piece on any stage or for any management other than their current employers—the Federal Theatre of the WPA. Our cast (Equity, non-Equity and chorus) heard the ruling in silence. One or two signed out and went home but the rest stayed around, waiting to see what would happen.

For fully an hour after this bomb burst in the basement of the Maxine Elliott Theatre, all activity ceased. The man in the black hat spoke once but no one heard him. We were defeated. We had nowhere to turn. We could give a show without scenery and without an orchestra—but not without actors. Marc's despair at this point was ghastly to behold. He who had come within a day of seeing his work presented by the director, the conductor and the performers of his choice, amid elegant settings, in a Broadway theatre, with a cast of sixty and an orchestra of twenty-eight, had seen these gifts snatched from him one by one, until, now, he was back where he had started a year ago. And the unkindest cut of all came with the realization that the final, fatal blows had been dealt him by those very unions in whose defense the piece had been written.*

Around five, members of the press summoned by Helen Deutsch began to arrive, including Lewis Nichols of the *Times*

---

* Like most recent converts, Marc was surprisingly naive about the realities of union strife. It seems not to have occurred to him that by plugging the CIO he was risking the displeasure of its rival, the still powerful AFL, and that the spectacle of Larry Foreman clenching the fingers of his raised right fist was no more pleasing to an old-time craft-union official than it was to a member of the reactionary Liberty League.

and Jack Gould of the *Tribune*. They had heard about Equity's ruling and wondered what our next step would be. They were invited to wait in the powder room while we held a meeting in the Ladies' toilet next door. Meantime, Jean Rosenthal, with a ten-dollar bill in her hand, had been sent out to rent a piano, before the stores closed, on the chance that we might need it. When we emerged, the man in the black hat tried to speak to us, but we thrust him aside. Jean was on the phone to say that she had located a piano (an upright) for five dollars a day and what should she do with it? I told her to hire a truck, load the piano onto it, then call for further instructions. After that we turned to face the press—Orson radiating confidence, I looking worried and Marc, recovered from his state of shock, looking pale but determined and eager for martyrdom. We told them that *The Cradle Will Rock* would be presented that night, as announced, even if Marc had to perform it alone on a piano and sing all the parts. When they inquired where this tour de force would take place we suggested they stay around and find out. Then we went up to talk to the actors who were still waiting, sitting and lying around in the darkened auditorium under the disapproving glare of the Cossacks. I told them of our decision and explained the fine legal point we had evolved in the Ladies' toilet: that while they were forbidden by their union to appear *on* the stage, there seemed to be no interdiction against their playing their parts from any other position in the theatre. "There is nothing to prevent you from entering whatever theatre we find, then getting up from your seats, as U.S. citizens, and speaking or singing your piece when your cue comes," we told them.

Their reaction was mixed. The stalwarts, Will Geer, Howard da Silva and the rest of the non-relief ten percenters, were enthusiastic. Others—especially our older members and the predominantly Negro chorus—were understandably reluctant to risk the loss of the small weekly income that alone kept them and their dependents from total indigence through a quixotic gesture for a cause which they did not really understand or altogether approve. On these (on the chorus especially) we were careful to exert no pressure or moral suasion. Each had his own personal problems and each must do what seemed sensible or right, regardless of collective or personal loyalty. Amid applause and tears we returned to the powder room, where Archibald Mac-Leish in a white linen suit had now appeared. The press, in growing numbers, was being entertained by Helen Deutsch; the man in the black hat was still in his corner, looking glum and intimidated, and Jean Rosenthal was on the phone again. She reported success: after standing on the corner of Broadway and 37th Street, in the heart of the garment district, for forty minutes, propositioning New Jersey trucks headed home across the river, she had found one, hired it by the hour with its driver and loader and hoisted the piano aboard. Now, what should she do? "Keep riding around," I said, "and call in every fifteen minutes for orders."

It was now after six; the press was getting restless and we seemed no nearer to finding a theatre than we had been at noon. We tried ballrooms, night clubs and Turnvereins; Mina Curtiss offered the living room of her apartment, but that was useless for it was clear by now that no matter what form the performance of *The Cradle* would take that night, it would be given before a considerable audience.

Already, two hours before curtain time, officials of the Downtown School of Music, who had bought the preview and refused to cancel it, were standing before the locked doors of the Maxine Elliott Theatre on which a handwritten sign had been tacked: NO SHOW TONIGHT. Around seven Orson and I came out through the stage door and gave our personal assurance that the show would go on—"Somewhere! Somehow!" By now, sensing excitement, a considerable crowd had assembled on 39th Street; they formed little indignant knots, between which members of the City Projects Council circulated, distributing handbills:

YOUR FRIENDS HAVE BEEN DISMISSED!
YOU MAY BE NEXT!

June 30th marks the End of all W.P.A. Projects.
42,000 W.P.A. Workers are being dismissed in

preparation for the dismantling of W.P.A.
The City Projects Council is your organization!
Join NOW! Save Your Job!
Fight for an American Standard of Living in
the W.P.A.!

At seven-twenty, as the swelling crowd began to get restless, several of our actors appeared on the sidewalk and offered a brief preview of the show to come. With their shadows lengthening in the early summer twilight, Hiram Sherman sang "I Wanna Go ter Honolulu" and Will Geer (veteran of many a union picnic and hootenanny) enacted one of Mr. Mister's more repulsive scenes.

Meanwhile, inside the theatre, the gloom deepened. In the pink powder room a hopeless silence had fallen, broken only by the uneven whir of a single fan that barely stirred the stale air of the overcrowded basement. It was now seven-forty—an hour from curtain time; our piano, with Jean Rosenthal on top of it, had been circling the block for almost two hours and the driver was theatening to quit. Clearly, this was the end. After all our big talk, for lack of a theatre, *The Cradle* would not be performed— on this or any other night.

It was then that the miracle occurred. The man in the black felt hat, the down-at-heel theatrical real estate agent, rose from his corner and moved toward the stair. In the doorway he paused, turned and spoke. It was an exit speech, uttered in a weak, despondent tone. No one, later, could remember exactly what he said, but the gist of it seemed to be that since there was nothing more he could do, he might as well go home. Only he still couldn't understand what was wrong with the Venice Theatre. With a sigh he turned and started up the stairs. He was already halfway up when he was seized, turned, dragged down, shaken and howled at. What was he talking about? What Venice Theatre? He then explained in a flat, aggrieved voice that for three hours he had been offering us a theatre that was open, empty, available, reasonable, unpicketed and in every way suitable to our requirements—but that none had listened to him.

Within one minute, five twenty-dollar bills had been thrust into his hand: the Venice Theatre was ours and Feder, Teddy Thomas and Marc were in a cab headed north. Two minutes later Jean Rosenthal, reporting for orders for the sixth time, was told to route her truck at full speed up Seventh Avenue to the block between 58th and 59th. She got there first and her men from New Jersey dumped the piano on the sidewalk and drove off. Four firemen from the hook and ladder station next door were carrying it into the theatre for her when Feder arrived (with a spotlight he had picked up en route) and broke open the stage door for them. Back on 39th Street, the moment we had word of their safe arrival, announcements were made—inside and outside the theatre. From the Maxine Elliott to the Venice is a distance of twenty-one city blocks. To cover possible delays in transit, our curtain time was changed to 9 P.M.; and since our adopted theatre was more than twice as large as our own, everyone was urged to invite one or more friends. There was cheering as the voyage began—by bus, subway, taxi and (it being a fine June evening) on foot.

In this unique migration, the largest single element was the preview audience from the Downtown Music School benefit, numbering six or seven hundred. Rumors and phone calls must have sent another thousand scurrying uptown, singly and in groups, not counting the press and a number of WPA official observers—friendly and unfriendly. Finally there were our own people—members of the staff, company and chorus. Not all of them arrived. It was one thing to make resolutions of solidarity, another for them to appear in open defiance of the authority on which they depended for a living. Now, as the move north began, a few stayed behind in the theatre, signed out and went quietly to their homes. Others who remained in doubt were willing to risk the voyage; they entered the Venice Theatre and took their seats, not knowing whether they would take part in the performance as spectators or performers. Howard da Silva made a final attempt to recapture his Government toupee, failed, rushed home to get his own, could not find it, and still managed to be one of the first to arrive on 58th Street. Lehman Engel, our conductor, was among the last to evacuate the Maxine Elliott. Two of the Cossacks, sweating gently in the early summer heat, must have been surprised to see him leaving the building in a large overcoat, but failed to search him. If they had, they would have found, clasped against his stomach, the piano and vocal score of *The Cradle Will Rock*.

By seven-fifty the Maxine Elliott was dark. Only a few guards and workmen remained to patrol its emptiness. Orson and I left with Archie MacLeish in someone's white Nash roadster with never a look back at the building in which we had prepared three shows together and opened two. Driving up Broadway through the light summer traffic, MacLeish seemed troubled; he was afraid we were going too far in our insubordination, yet he was reluctant to abandon us. Besides, there was a strong smell of history in the air which he was unwilling to miss.

The Venice Theatre, the scene of our first venture in independent management, was variously known, before it was finally torn down, as the Century, the Jolson, the Venice, the New Century and the New York Video Tape Center. In the forties it knew temporary prosperity as the home of *Kiss Me Kate* and *Up in Central Park*. But in the summer of 1937, it was run-down and dark save for occasional weekend performances by a local Italian stock company. This explained the stained and fading Neapolitian backdrop which Feder and his cohorts found hanging "in one" when they forced their way, with their spotlight and piano, past a sleepy, protesting watchman, onto the stage. The piano, a battered upright, was placed in front of the drop, and Feder immediately set about "lighting" it. One minute later, with a sharp flash of bright-blue flame, a whole bank of dimmers on the rusted switchboard blew out and Feder, his right arm bleeding and burned, was taken by Teddy Thomas to a doctor on 58th Street for emergency treatment. Marc's hand was blackened but unhurt; by the time we arrived he was sitting at the piano, trying it out and demanding that its front be pulled out ("so that the guts showed") for greater volume in such a vast house.

By this time, the audience had begun to arrive from downtown and was milling around the front of the house with Cokes, hot dogs and preview tickets* in their hands. As soon as the house crew appeared (obligatory under union rules), puzzled and disgruntled, the sleazy front curtain was lowered, the house lights turned on and the doors opened. There were no ticket takers that night, no ushers and no programs. By eight-thirty the main floor was more than half-filled except for the front two rows, which we had hopefully reserved for the cast. Upstairs, his arm in a sling, Feder was howling at his single electrician as the follow spot was hurriedly installed on the balcony rail. While they were testing its focus, the light beam fell accidentally on a large Italian flag draped over the edge of the upper right stage box. Instantly the crowd began to protest (Mussolini's activities first in Ethiopia and then in Spain had not endeared him to the Left) till, amid loud booing, someone climbed up and hauled it down. This gave the crowd a release: they laughed and applauded. Orson and I were backstage by that time but there were rents in the drapes through which we could peer out at the rapidly filling house. By eight-fifty there was not an empty seat; standees were beginning to accumulate at the back of the theatre and along the walls of the side aisles. Marc, seated stiffly at his piano, ready for his great moment, could hear the excited buzzing behind the thin curtain. At nine-five, they began to clap. We decided it was time to begin. We shook hands with Marc. Then, like partners in a vaudeville act, Orson and I made our entrance together from the wings onto the stage.

As supervisor of Project #891 I spoke first—sincerely but disingenuously. I made it clear that ours was a gesture of artistic, not political, defiance. I traced the history of *The Cradle Will Rock* and the circumstances leading up to this night's crisis. I expressed the gratitude we all felt to Mrs. Flanagan† and the Federal

---

* One way in which we raised money on this and subsequent nights was to collect these preview tickets at the door and cash them in the next day at the Maxine Elliott box office.

† Hallie, herself, was torn between her loyalty to Harry Hopkins, her pride in what we were doing and her duties as head of the Federal Theatre.

Theatre for allowing us to undertake a new American work
which no private management had been willing or able to
produce and which we had been preparing for months, with
dedication and love, till it had reached that stage of readiness
when it must be shared with an audience. Now, suddenly, for no
good reason, we were being denied permission to open. As artists
and theatre men, we had no choice but to defy this arbitrary and
unjust order. That is why we were here tonight, in this unfamiliar place—keeping our word to ourselves and to our public in
the only way that was left open to us. (Since we still did not
know exactly what this way would be, I left this part vague.)
Then I introduced our director—Orson Welles. Looking tall and
boyish, Orson thanked them in a deep voice for making the long
voyage uptown; he told them of his feeling for Marc's work and
of the performance they would have witnessed if our theatre had
not been taken over by the Cossacks of the WPA (boos and
laughter). While he set the scene and described the characters of
Steeltown, I had a chance to look around at what, till then, had
been nothing but a dark, frightening blur before my eyes: the
huge house packed to the roof, the aisles crowded and, in among
this mass, down toward the front, a few familiar faces: Lehman
Engel in the second row, without his overcoat, the score propped
up against the arm of the seat beside him and, in the boxes, calm,
fierce and confident, Geer, da Silva, Blanche Collins and the
other stalwarts. "We have the honor to present—with the composer at the piano—*The Cradle Will Rock!*" Orson concluded.

Amid applause we withdrew as gracefully as we could into the
wings, then raced through the fire door into the front of the
house just in time to see the curtain rise and Marc, in his shirtsleeves, with his suspenders showing, sitting pale and tense at his
eviscerated piano before a washed-out view of the Bay of Naples
with Vesuvius smoking in the distance. Feder caught him in the
spotlight. "And there I was alone on a bare stage—myself pro-

---

Later, in her book, she rationalized: "Probably it is worth a case of censorship to launch a group of our most brilliant directors and actors with a
play for which the cast had been provided as well as an audience and a
springboard for publicity."

duced by John Houseman, directed by Orson Welles, lit by Feder and conducted by Lehman Engel. I started, ready to do the whole show myself."*

The Cradle Will Rock started cold, without an overture. A short vamp that sounded harsh and tinny on Jean Rosenthal's rented, untuned upright, and Marc's voice, clipped, precise and high-pitched: "A Street corner—Steeltown, U.S.A." Then, the Moll's opening lyrics:

> I'm checking home now, call it a night.
> Going up to my room, turn on the light—
> Jesus, turn off the light!

It was a few seconds before we realized that to Marc's strained tenor another voice—a faint, wavering soprano—had been added. It was not clear at first where it came from, as the two voices continued together for a few lines—

> I ain't in Steeltown long;
> I work two days a week;
> The other five my efforts ain't required.

Then, hearing the words taken out of his mouth, Marc paused, and at that moment the spotlight moved off the stage, past the proscenium arch into the house, and came to rest on the lower left box where a thin girl in a green dress with dyed red hair was standing, glassy-eyed, stiff with fear, only half audible at first in the huge theatre but gathering strength with every note:

> For two days out of seven
> Two dollar bills I'm given . . .

It was almost impossible, at this distance in time, to convey the throat-catching, sickeningly exciting quality of that moment or to describe the emotions of gratitude and love with which we saw and heard that slim green figure. Years later, Hiram Sherman

---

* Marc Blitzstein: "As He Remembered It," reprinted posthumously in *The New York Times* from the Spoken Arts recording—"Marc Blitzstein Presents."

wrote to me: "If Olive Stanton had not risen on cue in the box, I doubt if the rest of us would have had the courage to stand up and carry on. But once that thin, incredibly clear voice came out, we all fell in line." On technical grounds alone, it must have taken almost superhuman courage for an inexperienced performer (whom we had cast in the part only because we had already exceeded our non-relief quota) to stand up before two thousand people, in an ill-placed and terribly exposed location, and start a show with a difficult song to the accompaniment of a piano that was more than fifty feet away. Add to this that she was a relief worker, wholly dependent on her weekly WPA check, and that she held no political views whatsoever.

> So I'm just searchin' along the street
> For on those days it's nice to eat.
> Jesus, Jesus, who said let's eat?

That was the end of her song. A flash-bulb went off. The audience began to clap—not sure what they were applauding—the girl, the song, Marc or the occasion. And, immediately, with no musical transition—

"Enter Gent."

said Marc at the piano and was prepared to speak the next line, but again it was taken out of his mouth, as a young man with a long nose rose from a seat somewhere in the front section of the orchestra and addressed the girl in green in the stage box.

GENT
Hello, baby!

MOLL
Hello, big boy!

GENT
Busy, baby?

MOLL
Not so very.

So a scene which, three nights before, had been acted in atmospheric blue light, around a prop lamppost, downstage right, was now played in the middle of a half-lit auditorium by two frightened relief workers thirty yards apart.

From then on, it was a breeze. Nothing surprised the audience or Marc or any of us after that, as scenes and numbers followed each other in fantastic sequence from one part of the house to another. Blitzstein played half a dozen roles that night, to cover for those who "had not wished to take their lives, or rather, their living wage, into their hands." Other replacements were made spontaneously, on the spot: Hiram Sherman, word perfect, took over for the Reverend Salvation, whose unctuous part he had never rehearsed, and later repeated this achievement, from an upper box, in the role of Professor Scoot, an "academic prostitute." Scenes were played, at first, wherever the actors happened to be sitting, so that the audience found itself "turning, as at a tennis match" from one character to another, and from one part of the house to the other. Then, as the act progressed and their confidence grew, the actors began to move around, selecting their own locations, improvising their actions, while instinctively communicating with each other from a distance. No one later remembered all that happened. But I do recall that Mr. Mister and Mrs. Mister sang and danced "I Wanna Go ter Honolulu" in the same center aisle in which Mr. Mister and his stooges later played their big bribery scene. Mrs. Mister did both her scenes upstairs in a balcony loge (directly above the Moll), from which she wafted down imaginary "donations" to the Reverend Salvation, who stood on the orchestra floor at the head of the aisle with his back to the stage facing the audience, as did Ella Hammer later for her "Joe Worker" number. The chorus were clustered in the third and fourth rows, surrounding Lehman Engel, where they presently provided another of that evening's memorable moments.

Just before leaving 39th Street I had made a last round of the theatre, thanked the members of the chorus for their loyalty and urged them not to take any unnecessary chances. It was all the

more startling, therefore, in Scene Three, to hear the Reverend
Salvation's booming pieties:

> Righteousness conquers! Iniquity perishes!
> Peace is a wonderful thing!

answered by an "Amen" reverently intoned by two-dozen rich
Negro voices. On their own, without consulting anyone, they had
traveled uptown and found their places behind their conductor.
Now, as their first cue came up, without rising, taking their beat
from Lehman Engel, they sang like angels. Melting into the half-
darkness of the crowd, they were not individually distinguish-
able, and this gave their responses a particularly moving quality.
A moment later they were on their feet savagely clamoring:

> CHORUS
> WAR! WAR! Kill all the dirty Huns!
> And those Austrungarians!
> WAR! War! We're entering the War!
> The Lusitania's an unpaid debt.
> Remember Troy! Remember Lafayette!
> Remember the Alamo! Remember our womanhood!
> Remember those innocent unborn babies!

To which the Reverend Salvation suavely responded—

> REV. SALVATION
> Of course, it's peace we're for—
> This is war to end all war!

And the Chorus sang—

> CHORUS
> (*reverently*)
> Amen. . . .

Another surprise came when Marc suddenly became aware
that, instrumentally, he was no longer performing alone. Of the
twenty-eight members of Musicians' Local 802, not one was to be

seen that night at the Venice—but one was clearly heard. Some-where, high up in the balcony, Rudy, the accordionist, sat hidden among the audience with his instrument open on his knees, playing along with his composer in passages where he felt it would help.

The Cradle, at the Maxine Elliott, was to have been performed without an intermission.* This night, at the Venice, we impro-vised an act break after Scene Six. Scene Five shows the planting of a bomb by company thugs, the death of the young Polish couple and the druggist's son. This is followed immediately by a scene in the hotel lobby where Yasha and Dauber, the kept artists, in a comic vaudeville routine, first insist that "There's something so damned low about the rich!," then serenade their patroness, Mrs. Mister, before leaving with her for the weekend to Beethoven's *Egmont* motif played on her limousine horns out-side. The curtain fell to laughter and applause as the houselights came up full. Then somebody, probably George Zorn, began calling out that there would be a fifteen-minute intermission and please not to smoke in the theatre.

The "inflammatory" scenes of *The Cradle Will Rock* occur cumulatively, toward the end. During the intermission the crowd milling around the jammed lobby and spilling out into Seventh Avenue was agitated and happy but not overexcited. They kept meeting friends and inquiring how they got there and telling each other how splendid it all was. It took a long time to get them back inside—which was just as well, for Marc was limp with exhaustion. We were backstage with him when MacLeish appeared, his fears now entirely dispelled, and said he would like to say a few words before Act Two. Orson conducted him before the curtain in his crumpled white suit, looked down on the hundreds who were still making their way back to their seats and announced: "When you have all sat down, the one man still standing will be the poet—Archibald MacLeish."

It was a warm speech—a revised and augmented version of the

* Which is how Leonard Bernstein played it in his concert performance at City Center in November 1947.

one he had delivered on the last night of *Panic* two years before. He praised the creative forces in the Federal Theatre, with particular reference to Project #891 and its directors. He lauded Marc Blitzstein. But above all he hailed the "new" audience that he saw before him as opposed to the "supine" audience of the commercial theatre. In his introduction to the published version of *The Cradle*, the following winter, he wrote of that evening—

> There was no audience. There was instead a room full of men and women as eager in the play as any actor. As actors rose in one part and another of the auditorium the faces of these men and women made new and changing circles around them. They were well-wishing faces: human faces such as man may sometimes see among partisans of the same cause or friends who hope for good things for one another.

The second act went like a house afire. It opens with The Moll's "Nickel Under the Foot" blues, followed by the long-retarded entrance of the labor hero, Larry Foreman, and the first hearing of the title song. Mr. Mister is seen again in his doctor's office, increasingly scared and malignant, corrupting the medical profession as he has the Church, the University and the Press. After that comes the angriest number in the show—"Joe Worker":

> One big question inside me cries
> How many frame-ups, how many shake-downs,
> Lock-outs, sell-outs,
> How many toiling, ailing, dying, piled-up bodies
> Brother, does it take to make you wise?

And then, finally, the showdown: Larry Foreman confronting Mr. Mister and his Liberty Committee in the crowded night court. Only this night they were all on their feet, singing and shouting from all over the theatre as they built to the final, triumphal release—

> That's STEEL marching out in front! but one day there's
> gonna be
> Wheat . . . and sidewalks . . .

Cows . . . and music . . .
Shops . . . houses . . .
Poems . . . bridges . . . drugstores . . .

MR. MISTER
(the surrender to fear)
My God! What do they want with me?

LARRY
Don't worry, that's not for you . . .
That's thunder, that's lightning,
And it's going to surround you!
No wonder those stormbirds
Seem to circle around you . . .

He sang it without his toupee, his scalp gleaming under the strong spotlight:

When you can't climb down, and you can't
sit still;
That's a storm that's going to last until
The final wind blows . . . and when the wind
blows . . .
The Cradle Will Rock!

There were no "bugles, drums and fifes" that night—only Marc's pounding of an untuned piano before a wrinkled backdrop of the Bay of Naples. As the curtain fell and the actors started to go back to their seats, there was a second's silence—then all hell broke loose. It was past midnight before we could clear the theatre. We had rented it till eleven and had to pay twenty dollars extra, but it was worth it.

Afterwards we went to Helen Deutsch's apartment to wait for the morning papers. We got our notices—not in the drama section but in headlines on the front pages where *The Cradle* became known as the "runaway opera." And after we had gloated over them, we spent the rest of the night trying to decide what to do next.

Early next morning I spoke first to Hallie Flanagan and then to Washington. I offered to let bygones be bygones if they would permit us to perform *The Cradle* that night in our own theatre. They refused as we knew they would. That set us free to take the next steps. We had checked Marc's contract with the Federal Theatre: it was a lease of his play without exclusivity. Over coffee I made a deal with him, then started telephoning around for money (we needed three thousand dollars). This proved to be no problem. Mina Curtiss was our principal backer; others were Herman Shumlin, two friends of Marc's, and Helen Deutsch, in whose name a bond of $1,400 was posted that afternoon with the Actors' Equity Association. Meantime, we held a meeting with our cast and told them that Welles and I proposed to present the show, exactly as performed, for two weeks "commercially" at the Venice—two weeks being the maximum time allowed for leave from Works Projects without loss of relief status. Flushed with success, they agreed enthusiastically—including two who had defected the previous night. We immediately set them to filling out their WPA forms and, in many cases, their applications for Equity membership. (The initiation fees of $59 apiece were considered part of production expense; so was the cost of Marc Blitzstein's joining not only Equity but also the Musicians' Union and the Dramatists' Guild.)

The Cradle Will Rock opened its "commercial" run on June 18. We had no advance sale, no opening-night drama reviews, lots of publicity but no money to advertise. Performing at low prices in a huge theatre and paying full Equity salaries, we managed to break even for the run. Part of our audience came from organizations which had contracted for theatre parties and had been shut out of the Maxine Elliott. Others came through curiosity, good word of mouth or Party loyalty. And each saw a slightly different show.

The afternoon we opened, a dress rehearsal was held, in which we tried to reproduce exactly what had been done at that improvised performance two nights before. Already much had been forgotten or was remembered differently by the various actors involved, so that other members of the company and even spectators had to be consulted. Orson, not to be denied as a director, made certain modifications of his own. Indeed, such was the nature of the show that it continued to change throughout our fortnight run at the Venice, where we played to houses that grew in enthusiasm and number from performance to performance.* In our second week we received help from an unexpected source: Tom Girdler, head of Republic and spokesman for Little Steel, made the headlines with a vow that he would "never sign a written contract with an irresponsible, racketeering, violent, communistic body like the CIO." The next night we had thirty standees and, two days later, we found it necessary to warn customers through the press that our last night was sold out, but "a few tickets are still available for the special matinee tomorrow." There was the usual emotional clamor for extension but the cast's leave from Project #891 was limited to two weeks. On July 1st, two days after our originally scheduled premiere at the Maxine Elliott, we reimbursed our angels and led our company back, without casualties, out of private enterprise into the Federal Theatre Project of the WPA.

The Cradle Will Rock had made front-page news but it was not covered by the drama critics of the New York press. It was six months before Blitzstein got to see his reviews, which appeared, finally, early in December when Orson and I again presented *The Cradle Will Rock* for a special Sunday night performance

---

* During our run at the Venice we gave one additional Sunday performance—in an amusement park in Bethlehem, Pennsylvania, for the local branch of the Steelworkers' Union. It was a poor turn-out—less than two hundred including stool pigeons and informers, but they seemed grateful to us for coming. In a letter to Mina I reported that Marc's sophisticated satire had "left them cold and bewildered but they were moved by the second half and knew all about the corrupt police and press and found Mr. Mister clearly recognizable as Mr. Grace. . . ." In their embarrassed apology for the poor turn-out they gave a more convincing picture of a company-dominated town than Marc with all his satire and drama. The town has one paper which won't print Union releases and has prohibitive rates for Union ads like the ad for this event. As soon as the Company heard of it they immediately set up a rival picnic of their own, to which sixty-five hundred tickets were sold in one day *by foremen on the job* with the clear implication that it was a small price to pay for keeping their jobs.

on the stage of our new Mercury Theatre. They were worth waiting for.

Written with extraordinary versatility and played with enormous gusto, it is the best thing militant labor has put into the theatre yet.

An exciting and savagely humorous social cartoon with music that hits hard and sardonically and must be put down as one of the most interesting dramatic events of the season.

reported the *Times* and the *Tribune* respectively. According to John Mason Brown in the *Post:*

The Cradle Will Rock is the most evciting propagandistic tour de force our stage has seen since *Waiting for Lefty* burst like a bombshell upon this town.

The sincerity of the actors sweeps across the footlights carrying everything before it. There is no room for humbug in this kind of unaided acting. To reach our hearts it must come from the hearts of its creators. It is this very quality of burning earnestness which the players at the Mercury provide. . .

The cast—the same as at the Venice—was widely praised:

They conjure Steeltown out of the air and set it raw and terrible before your eyes.

Dull would be the soul who would pass by the living theatre here presented. It makes one proud, makes one swell, believing in the reality of talent and impetuosity, chances taken and the assertion of vividness. Great talent goes into this piece.*

Marc, in his double capacity of composer and performer, received special notice:

If Mr. Blitzstein looks like a mild little man as he sits before his piano, his work generates current like a dynamo . . . He can write anything from tribal chant to tin pan alley balladry, and when he settles down to serious business at its conclusion,

* Stark Young in the *New Republic.*

his music-box roars with rage and his actors frighten the aged roof of the miniature Mercury Theatre.*

Not all of our reviews were favorable. One complained that our actors were not singers and that the music of the piece received "only a noisy hearing from voices that were generally strained" and even "harshly disagreeable." Another warned theatregoers unhappily seated down front that they were "entitled to ear muffs and shower curtains." Edith Isaacs, our friend and goad, conceded that "the whole thing came off" and that "it introduced a new theatre form," but felt that the writing was "neither very wise nor very witty." Political emotions colored judgments, as usual: the Left which had hailed us in July now redoubled its praises. The organized Right detested us. And the Catholic *Commonweal*, which had consistently supported Orson and me in all our ventures to date, reported to its readers that *The Cradle* "had nothing fresh in material" and was written "clumsily and without wit."

> That these proletarian exhibits have neither charm nor beauty nor basic honesty doesn't seem to worry their admirers, so I suppose they will have to go through their attack of radical measles before they are immune.

One columnist who attended both the July and the December performance noted, without comment, that Mr. Blitzstein "unlike on his previous appearance," was now wearing a jacket.

Three days after *The Cradle Will Rock* ended its runaway engagement at the Venice Theatre, the Works Progress Administration in Washington, made an announcement to the press:

W.P.A. PERMANENTLY

ABANDONS LABOR OPERA

> After postponing, amid much hue and cry, *The Cradle Will Rock*, the Federal Government has finally made up its mind about Mr. Blitzstein's storm-tossed opera. It has decided to

* Brooks Atkinson, *The New York Times,* December 6, 1937.

278

have nothing more to do with it, the formal order to that effect having been received yesterday by Mrs. Hallie Flanagan, National Theatre Director.

So now we knew where we stood. We also knew that our days on the project were numbered. In New York alone, that month, fifteen hundred pink dismissal slips had been distributed to theatre workers amid renewed demonstrations and sit-ins. The Federal Theatre Magazine had already been liquidated; now in mid-July it was announced that leases would not be renewed on two of the Federal Theatre's five New York playhouses. The honeymoon of the New Deal and the Theatre was over.

Project #891 was in a special state of disgrace and uncertainty. We had nothing in rehearsal and no plans for the future. Our two hundred and thirty-eight workers continued to report daily at the Maxine Elliott, signed their time sheets and went home while they waited to be fired or transferred to other units. On their way in and out of the theatre they would look in on the basement where I continued to sit with Augusta Weissberger, using the Government's stationery and telephones, waiting for my own pink slip to arrive. Orson had already resigned. When he appeared, between radio shows, to dictate letters to Augusta or to have a check cashed, we had little to say to each other. Our immediate emotional response to the success of *The Cradle Will Rock* was the usual need, on both our parts, to prove that each of us could exist without the other.

We both got our chance—almost immediately. Orson's, predictably, was the more spectacular. It came from Arthur Hopkins, no longer the most successful but still the most esteemed producer in the American theatre. It had been Hopkins' dream, early in the twenties, to found a great American classical acting company with the Barrymores at its center. Lionel's controversial *Macbeth,* John's *Richard III* followed by his celebrated *Hamlet* (all with sets and costumes by Robert Edmond Jones) had encouraged him in this hope, which had foundered finally on the rocks of the Barrymore temperament. Now, fifteen years later, though he was no longer young and not in the best of health,

Hopkins saw a chance to revive his dream around the figure of the fabulous twenty-one-year-old Orson Welles. He proposed *King Lear* as a starter and Orson, flattered and excited, accepted. They had several luncheon meetings at which visions were exchanged, after which Orson went to work with Pavel Tchelitchew on a production scheme which he assumed Hopkins would approve. By the first week of August announcements of the Welles-Hopkins *Lear* had begun to appear in the theatrical columns, where I read them with a distaste that was all the more acute since my own situation was beginning to seem far from brilliant.

For twenty months, first in Harlem and then on 39th Street, I had been so wholly absorbed in collaboration—not only with Welles but with all the human elements that went to form the unique organism of the Federal Theatre—that the thought of working alone again was repulsive and terrifying to me. For two years the Federal Theatre had been my life. Within its peculiar structure I had found myself wielding authority and power such as I was unlikely to find again elsewhere; as its leading producer I had been responsible for a series of creative achievements which had been quite remarkable for their variety and success. Now all this was being taken from me.

That was my state of mind when the phone rang one afternoon in the powder room of Maxine Elliott's theatre. It was Hallie Flanagan calling from the headquarters of the Federal Theatre on Eighth Avenue, wanting to know if I could come over and see her the next morning. It was the first time we had spoken since the *Cradle* disturbances and I assumed that the purpose of her summons was my formal dismissal from the project. I was right. My severance (under a new rule that permitted only American citizens to work on WPA) would take place on August 15th. Hallie thanked me for my great contributions to the project and expressed the hope that Orson and I would continue our fine work elsewhere. For her own part, she must stay on and fight a losing battle to retain even a fraction of the gains achieved by the Federal Theatre under her direction. Meantime, she explained, she was still head of Vassar's Experimental Theatre and Drama Production Department, which she had founded. She asked me if I would consider taking the job for a year. I thanked her, said I would have to think about it, but agreed, since a decision must be made quite soon, to meet President MacCracken and the head of Vassar's English Department, the formidable Susan Smith.

Driving back from Poughkeepsie down the Hudson Valley on an August evening, I stopped off at Sneden's Landing, where Orson and Virginia were spending the summer in a small house I had found for them in the woods. When I told Virginia, who was two months pregnant, that I was about to become an associate professor of English at Vassar College for Girls she laughed so hard that she had to be sent off to bed. Orson was too preoccupied with his sketches and models for *King Lear* to hear what I was saying. But, later that week, after I had accepted Hallie's offer, I found him sitting glumly in the powder room, glaring at a letter that had just been delivered by hand. In it Arthur Hopkins released him from his commitment and reluctantly abandoned all plans for *King Lear*. The reason he gave was a newspaper interview in which the Wonder Boy, without once referring to Mr. Hopkins, had expatiated on his own ideas for the production of *King Lear* and on his personal conception of the old king's progressive stages of madness. It was like prematurely uncorking a vintage wine, Hopkins wrote; it was no longer worth drinking. Was this the whole or the true reason for his change of heart? Or did he run into difficulties finding backing in mid-depression for an expensive production of a difficult classic with an unknown star? Orson never found out. But three days later, when I passed by Sneden's Landing on my way to New City for the weekend, all his models and sketches for *Lear* had disappeared. And after supper, as he was walking me out to my car between the trees, Orson said suddenly, "Why the hell don't we start a theatre of our own?" I said, "Why don't we?" and I did not go home that night or the next day or the day after that.

ACT TWO

VII

To START a repertory theatre in New York City today would take a million dollars, months of high-minded discussion, a major real estate operation, City, State and Federal involvement and the benevolent participation of two or more gigantic foundations. The Mercury Theatre was conceived one summer evening after supper; its birth was formally announced ten days later and it opened on Broadway within ten weeks in a playhouse bearing its own name with a program of four productions, a company of thirty-four and a capital of ten thousand, five hundred dollars.

We had no difficulty formulating a program, for we had announced our favorite plays the previous winter on the Federal Theatre and our tastes had not changed. We came upon our name on the cover of a two-year-old magazine in the corner of an empty fireplace at Sneden's Landing; we were registered and incorporated four days later in Albany as the Mercury Theatre, Inc., with me as president, Orson Welles as vice-president, Augusta Weissberger as secretary and a paid-up capital of one hundred dollars. It was mid-August and if we wanted our theatre for the 1937–38 season we had not a moment to lose.

Our first step, once we had a name, was to find a home. Neither Orson nor I could conceive of running a company without a theatre and in the state of the real estate market at the time we were confident of finding one. Our search led us downtown to Second Avenue, where we looked at huge, desolate playhouses left over from the boom days of the Yiddish Theatre. We looked at the Irving Place Theatre, once the home of New York's German repertory, now sunk to burlesque and foreign films; it remained a handsome, dignified house, but too large and expensive for us to run. We got excited for a few days over an abandoned medical amphitheatre in the East Forties. Then one morning, George Zorn called and suggested we meet him at the Comedy Theatre on Forty-first Street and Broadway. One look—and we knew we had found our home.

The Comedy, an intimate, rococo, two-balcony theatre with six hundred and eighty-seven seats and a good stage, was for many years one of Manhattan's most elegant smaller playhouses. Producers from Granville Barker to Cecil B. De Mille and the Washington Square Players had occupied it, and among the stars it had sheltered were John Barrymore, Holbrook Blinn and Katharine Cornell in her first Broadway appearance. It had also been used for small musicals, which accounted for the narrow orchestra pit and a booth for follow spots high up in the rear of the second balcony.

Jean Rosenthal was hastily summoned from the basement of the Maxine Elliott two blocks away. While we made our way by flashlight through cobwebs and scuttling rats, exploring the twilit, long-abandoned desolation of our new home, Zorn hurried off to make inquiries about its availability. He returned in half an hour with a confused report that the house was currently controlled by an Italian known as the "Commendatore" who ran a bar on Eighth Avenue and fronted for a gangster in Chicago. More important—it was available at the reasonable rental of $187.50 a week, on a three-year lease, so long as it was clearly understood that the owner would not spend one cent to restore or maintain it. Furthermore he didn't care what we did with it so long as the Fire Department stayed off his back. There was only one thing wrong with the deal: the first three months' rent had to be paid in advance.

So now we were incorporated; we had a theatre available and a program to announce. But we had not one cent of backing and not the faintest notion of where to look for it. Clearly the time had come for a manifesto.

I made an appointment with Brooks Atkinson of *The New York Times* whose Olympian benediction was desirable, if not essential, for such a project.* We met in the *Times* commissary, where I outlined our plans for an independent, low-priced repertory season on Broadway; he approved and offered to publish our declaration of principles in the Sunday drama section, where it appeared on the front page on August 29, 1937, under the headline:

PLAN FOR A NEW THEATRE

At the height of our success, *Time,* describing our origin, wrote that "the Mercury was at first just an idea bounded North and South by hope, East and West by nerve." Actually our venture was less rash than it seemed. The WPA had given us an opportunity to feel our power and to try our wings. It had done more than that: through our achievements with the Negro Theatre and Project #891, we had acquired not only a national reputation but also a more direct and varied experience than anyone in the country in the conduct of this kind of theatre, in this particular climate and for this particular audience. We founded the Mercury with the sublime confidence of our youth and our reck-

---

* Though it did not hold the monopolistic position it does today, *The New York Times,* through its drama critic, exercised a dominant influence in the theatre of the thirties and forties. Brooks Atkinson, who occupied that position for over thirty years, took his responsibility seriously and did his best to support what he considered new and valuable theatrical activities on and off Broadway. His judgments were often emotional but over all his influence was salutary and protective of what was best and most vital in the American theatre.

less temperaments—and with a substantial accumulation of theatrical knowledge and skill. This was reflected in our "manifesto" in which I tried to avoid the tone of vague, verbose grandeur generally associated with the announcements of embryo, indigent artistic groups. In my third and final draft, completed an hour before deadline, I tried to convey an impression of self-confidence and continuity based on our successful operations of the past two years.

> When its doors open early in November, the Mercury Theatre will expect to play to the same audience that during the last two seasons stood to see *Doctor Faustus, Murder in the Cathedral* and the Negro *Macbeth.*
>
> It was surprising that they came in such numbers, but that was not the only surprising thing about this audience. It was fresh. It was eager. To anyone who saw it night after night as we did, it was apparent that this was not the regular Broadway crowd taking in the hits of the moment. Even less was it the special audience one had learned to associate with "classical revivals." (A million people do not make a special audience.) One had the feeling, every night, that here were people on a voyage of discovery in the theatre . . . people who either had never been to the theatre at all or who, for one reason or another, had ignored it for many seasons.
>
> By filling out the questionnaires we placed in their programs during the run of *Doctor Faustus* some forty thousand of them made their theatrical confessions to us. A large number professed themselves disappointed in the regular run of Broadway plays but stated that the theatre had once again assumed importance for them with the productions of the Federal Theatre. We asked for specific suggestions: the overwhelming majority of their requests was for "more classical plays," "classical plays excitingly produced," and "great plays of the past produced in a modern way."
>
> This is the audience the Mercury Theatre will try to satisfy.

With no money, no theatre, no company and no organization of any sort, it was essential that our initial release be specific and credible.

We shall produce four or five plays each season. Most of these will be plays of the past—preferably those which seem to have emotional or factual bearing on contemporary life. While a socially unconscious theatre would be intolerable, there will be no substitution of social consciousness for drama. . . . We prefer not to fix our program rigidly too far ahead. New plays and new ideas may turn up any day. But we do know that our first production will be Shakespeare's *Julius Caesar.* As in *Faustus,* by the use of apron, lighting, sound devices, music, etc., we hope to give this production much of the speed and violence it must have had on the Elizabethan stage. The Roman Senators when they murder the Dictator will not be clad (any more than were the Elizabethan actors) in traditional nineteenth-century stage togas.

Next we hope, with George Bernard Shaw's consent, to produce what we consider his most important play, *Heartbreak House.* Also William Gillette's *Too Much Johnson,* Webster's *Duchess of Malfi*—one of the great horror plays of all time—and Ben Jonson's farce *The Silent Woman.* We expect to run our first play between four and six weeks. After that, without clinging to the European system of revolving repertory with its disturbing nightly changes of bill, the Mercury Theatre expects to maintain a repertory of its current season's productions. However at no time will more than two different plays be seen in one week.

We expect to occupy a theatre of medium size on the edge of the Broadway district. With a top price of two dollars, there will be four hundred good seats at fifty cents, seventy-five cents and one dollar available at every performance.

Our manifesto may have raised a few eyebrows on Broadway but, in the places where it mattered, our mad plan to start a classical repertory theatre in the heart of Manhattan's commercial theatre district was taken seriously. *The New York Times* hailed it as "an opportunity to revise a good many shibboleths about the American theatre." A leading Catholic weekly likened our recent work to that of England's Old Vic: "It is just such a theatre that New York needs today. It is the duty of all who love the theatre to rally back of them."

Within a few hours of its appearance the phone had begun to
ring in the hole in the wall I had rented from Richard Maney,
the press agent, on the mezzanine of the Empire Theatre building. There were congratulations, expressions of hope and re-
quests for employment—from members of our Projects up and
downtown; from friends on Broadway and in radio; from actors
and technicians we had never met but who were excited by the
repertory idea; from audience groups inquiring about theatre
parties for November, December and January. Seated with Augusta Weissberger in the airless cubbyhole which a sheet of
yellow foolscap paper, glued to the outside of the door, identified
as the office of the MERCURY THEATRE, INC., I received visits, answered phone calls and worried about money. Accustomed to the
manna of the U.S. Government with its regular payrolls and
inexhaustible requisition forms, I had never learned the essential
theatrical skill of money raising. I called several well-known
Broadway angels and one rich acquaintance on the Produce
Exchange and was politely refused. Meantime, not knowing how
I was going to pay the phone bill, I continued to make vast plans
for our future. Paralyzed with embarrassment and fear, I sat day
after day radiating confidence and waiting, as I had so often
done before, for a miracle to happen.

One afternoon during my second week of waiting the phone
rang and a cultivated voice introduced itself as that of George
Hexter, whom I remembered vaguely from the Federal Theatre,
where he had held a supervisory position in the fiscal department. He said he had long admired our work and was delighted
to hear of our new program. If we were not fully financed would
we consider him as one of our investors? As calmly as I could I
asked him what kind of sum he had in mind. Around five
thousand, he replied. I set a meeting in our lawyer's office for the
next morning, at which he turned up, to my amazement, with a
certified check for forty-five hundred dollars. Ten minutes later,
having converted the Mercury from a dream into a reality,
George Hexter vanished as silently as he had appeared, and I did
not see him again until the opening of *Julius Caesar*.

Within a week I had landed our second angel—William Rapp,

editor of *True Story* magazine, whom I had first met in William Harris' office during *Three and One*. A man of great warmth and enthusiasm, he gave us a thousand dollars and brought in a retired builder by the name of Myron Falk, who put in three thousand five hundred dollars in the name of his daughter Mildred. He was a gentle, shrewd, sincere, white-haired gentleman with inflamed eyelids who plagued us with sound advice and did his best to help us, later, when we were in trouble. Our first gentile investor was Gifford Cochran, heir to a New England carpet-manufacturing fortune, who came in for a thousand, followed by a similar sum from Bill Sweets, a radio director who liked Orson's work, and five hundred from Charles Schnee, a law student at Harvard, who had a passion for the theatre. And that was it. Except for one final crash contribution of twenty-five hundred dollars received on the night of our third dress rehearsal, the total capitalization of the Mercury Theatre was ten thousand five hundred dollars.

Treasury regulations were less stringent in those days. Legally, there was nothing to prevent us from using our investors' money as it came in. And I did. Two-thirds of George Hexter's investment was spent on the day we received it: it went in advance rent on the threatre, back salaries, secondhand furniture and additional telephones for our rapidly multiplying staff. We had got into the habit on the WPA of having a lot of people around, so we started the Mercury with more personnel than most established, big-scale Broadway producers. From the first day we regarded ourselves as an institution: as such it was necessary to have publicity and promotion departments long before we had a production.

(One person who worried about this premature expansion was Augusta Weissberger, who alone knew the real state of our finances. This occasionally placed her in an awkward situation. Soon after our move to the Empire she protested the pitiful WPA wage we were continuing to pay her for fourteen hours a day's work. When we ignored her she demanded a showdown, confronted Welles and myself and once again presented her very modest demand. We accused her of presumption, treachery and blackmail. Pale as a sheet, she stuck to her guns. Finally, tired of the game, we agreed to her request. Instead of gloating, she burst into tears. "But you can't afford it!" she sobbed.)

Among my first visitors, following our manifesto, had been Nathan Zatkin. He arrived full of ideas, ready to take over as publicity director of the new organization. It became my painful duty to inform him that Orson was allergic to him and that the position was already filled by a quiet, devoted, pleasant and competent young man named Henry Senber. Promotion was handled by Sylvia Regan, formerly of the Theatre Union, an expert in left-wing audience development and theatre-party sales. She brought in a myopic assistant and then an office girl to answer the telephone. Her name was Judy Holliday; she was fifteen, received five dollars a week and wept each time I used a four-letter word.*

Already on the payroll at exiguous salaries were George Zorn (moonlighting from WPA) as company manager and Jean Rosenthal, replacing Abe Feder (who had other fish to fry) as our technical director. I paid myself fifty dollars a week and raised it to a hundred when we went into production; Welles as director and principal actor received two hundred from the day he began rehearsals.

The Comedy Theatre, when we moved into it, was in even worse shape than we had supposed. The stage house, particularly, was a dilapidated, sordid and dangerous shell, caked with rust and corrosive grime. Jeannie spent a week crawling around its dangerous darkness. Then she presented me with a formidable list of absolute and immediate necessities, which included major repairs to the grid, new rigging and power lines and a new stage floor to replace the rotting planks through which huge, fearless rodents could be seen emerging on their hunting excursions. I told her to go ahead and to hire whatever help she felt she needed to make the theatre usable within a month.

Meanwhile, in Orson's basement on West Fourteenth Street, in

---

* I did not know at the time that she and three of her friends—Adolph Green, Betty Comden and Alvin Hammer—were already performing satirical sketches in obscure Village joints under the name of The Revuers.

the one-room apartment on East 61st Street into which I had recently moved, in borrowed offices and between desks in our cramped cubbyhole in the Empire Theatre building, Orson and I were interviewing dozens of actors each day. They came, attracted by the chance of good classical roles, by the excitement of belonging to a theatrical organization of the sort serious actors had long dreamed of and by the reputation we had acquired over the past two years. As we auditioned and talked with them, we were thinking primarily of *Julius Caesar*, but also of an acting company and a repertory season.

It was the first time we were entirely free to select our cast: like Antony and Young Octavius, we sat with our lists in front of us, weighing each name and arguing over each choice: Orson took in Martin Gabel, with whom he had worked in radio, John Hoysradt, who had been his companion on the Cornell tour, and the veteran Irish actor Whitford Kane. My candidates were Joseph Holland, who had played Horatio for me in Leslie Howard's *Hamlet*, George Coulouris, who, since I first met him in Stockbridge, had become a successful Broadway actor, Norman Lloyd, whom I had admired in the WPA's Living Newspaper, and Grover Burgess, a fugitive from the Group Theatre. From Project #891 we brought in Joseph Cotten, Hiram Sherman and George Duthie. To each of them we offered contracts at the Equity minimum (forty dollars a week for senior members and twenty-five for juniors) plus a dubious sliding scale based on an improbable weekly gross. Not one turned us down. We exacted no monastic vows or long-term commitments; we signed no run-of-the-play contracts. They were free to quit at any time on two weeks' notice. During our first Mercury season not one of them left us or talked of leaving.

In mid-September Orson announced that he needed to go into a retreat before the start of the season. I drove him north the next morning, through woods that were turning red and gold, into the White Mountains. We arrived late in the afternoon at a huge, half-empty New Hampshire resort hotel that looked suspiciously like the one from which my father, my mother and I had been turned away twenty years before. Here I left him to his meditations. On my way back I stopped off at Chapelbrook for a weekend with Mina, then drove across into New York State to Poughkeepsie for my first formal appearance as head of the Drama Production Department of Vassar College. When I got back to Forty-first Street, I was told by Sylvia Regan that a quarter of a million handbills announcing:

JULIUS CAESAR

!! DEATH OF A DICTATOR !!

with an opening date of November 11th, had been scattered all over town by volunteers who were bound by oath not to throw them in trash cans or empty lots, but to distribute them conscientiously in schools, colleges, cafeterias, drugstores and bookshops all over the five boroughs. She also reported sales of theatre parties well into the new year and told me that she was adding two more assistants to her department—an eager young couple named Goodman, specialists in the sale of student tickets. With their arrival the average age of our subscription department went down to below twenty and the Empire cubbyhole became so intolerably crowded and noisy that I moved over to the theatre into the only space available—the former projection booth at the rear of the upper balcony. On one side of a beaverboard partition sat Augusta, with her typewriter and her filing cabinets. On the other, squeezed between a day bed, a table, two chairs and three telephones, I conducted the affairs of the Mercury and, through the gaping hole that had once held a follow spot, followed the frantic activity below.

From the day she joined us Jean Rosenthal was not so much our technical director and lighting expert as our partner. We demanded daily miracles and she gave them to us. She also gave us love. Throughout her long and brilliant career one of her invaluable assets was her ability to enlist the loyalty and enthusiastic cooperation of the technicians with whom she worked. Through personal suasion, a sense of theatrical excitement and the prospect of continuous employment, she managed to sign up, as our department heads, three of the best stagehands in New

York City. Under Joe Patterson's direction walls were pierced and stage boxes breached to accommodate our light towers and augmented power lines. Amid the blue flames of blowtorches and the screeching of power drills, a large iron platform was hung high overhead, stage right, strong enough to hold the eight dimmer boards needed for the elaborate light effects we were in the habit of using. Under Harry Rose, our head carpenter, the rotting stage floor and grid were checked and repaired, decaying hemp removed from the fly floor and replaced by twelve sets of new, beautiful, pale-yellow lines. Over what had been the orchestra pit a wooden apron was constructed, similar to the one we had built for *Faustus* but wider and shallower because of the sharp angle of the double balcony. This meant sacrificing eighteen of our best orchestra seats—a loss which George Zorn bitterly protested. As house manager, he was outraged that I should be spending so much money on the stage and so little on the front of the house, which was in even worse shape. I told him that if our shows were good enough nobody would notice the state of the auditorium.

Eventually bootleg painters and plasterers were brought in at night to patch up our crumbling walls and proscenium; by day, looking down through my peephole, I could see the shapes of women writhing in the aisles as they stitched away at the torn red carpeting and the frayed seats I was not about to replace. In the basement plumbers tinkered skeptically with our clogged, disgraceful toilets and banged away at a furnace that was crusted with thick, dark-brown rust but seemed to function. Remembering our landlord's warning, there was nothing we could do but pray that it would continue to work through the worst of the winter. The few dollars we had for decoration were spent on the small outer lobby and box office, for which we chose pearl-gray walls and a secondhand crystal chandelier. When the painters were done, Gifford Cochran, our gentile investor, spent days with gold leaf and camel-hair brush, restoring the Edwardian green-and-gold woodwork of our façade. One day while he was at work a truck drove up carrying a large electric sign. For two hours all other activities stopped while the entire organization

helped to unload it and hoist it into place. We cheered when the
current was turned on and the letters

M
E
R
C
U
R
Y

flashed pale in the sunlight. That night they could be seen shining
encouragingly all the way from Sixth Avenue to Broadway.

When Orson returned from his ten-day retreat in New Hampshire, he brought with him a completely reedited text of *Julius
Caesar,* including music and light cues, and a suitcase full of
notes, sketches and a Plasticine model of his production. We had
four weeks in which to adapt them to the Mercury stage. At Jean
Rosenthal's suggestion we engaged a young scenic designer, a
fellow graduate from Yale. He was a dynamic pollywog of a man
with a crew cut and a strong accent, named Samuel Leve—known
also as "the Rabbi" because he taught "schul" each Sabbath at a
Talmud Tora uptown. He absorbed Orson's ideas and sketches,
spent a day marching around the stage with him while Jean and
I watched sight lines from the balcony; then, under her technical
direction, set about converting them into working drawings and
blueprints.

Later, when they saw *Julius Caesar,* many people were under
the impression that they were watching a play performed upon a
bare stage, and praised the Mercury for its return to theatrical
simplicity. I have described the complications of Orson's "simplicity" in *Faustus.* In *Caesar* he called for a series of huge, subtly
graded platforms that covered the entire stage floor. First came
the main downstage playing area—fourteen feet deep including
the apron—which rose in a gentle rake to meet a set of shallow
steps running the full width of the stage. These led to an eight-
foot plateau, the mid-stage playing area, then rose again through

another set of steps to a final narrow crest, six and a half feet above stage level, before falling back down in a steep, fanning ramp that ended close to the rear wall of the theatre. This gave the stage an appearance of enormous depth and a great variety of playing areas—from the intimacy of the downstage scenes acted within a few feet of the audience, to the dominating mid- and up-stage positions on the first and second elevated plateaus. Steps and platforms were honeycombed with traps out of which powerful projectors were angled upward and forward to form a double light curtain (the "Nuremberg lights") through whose beams all actors making upstage entrances had to pass and were suddenly and dramatically illuminated before descending to the playing areas below. It was a brilliant concept, but when the first estimates for lumber, construction and additional lighting equipment were added up they came to twice what we had budgeted or could afford. Moved by my distress, Orson made two concessions: four thirty-foot flagpoles were sacrificed and, at Jeannie's suggestion, he agreed to do without padding on the platforms. As a result they made a hollow, drumming sound which disturbed us during rehearsal until we discovered that they added an ominous and highly dramatic element to our mob scenes.

There was also the small matter of paint. What could be simpler and more economical than a few platforms and bare brick walls daubed with standard barn-red? Precisely because they *were* bare, it meant that hundreds of gallons of paint must be sloshed and sprayed from ladders and scaffolds over an acreage of more than five thousand square feet, including dressing-room stairs, stage door, steam pipes and fire extinguishers.* The first fifteen hundred feet were done at night by bootleg house painters. Then the union stepped in and ruled, not without justice, that

---

* One of our few altercations with the Fire Department was on this subject. "Smokey" Martin, the redoubtable fire fighter assigned to our theatre, insisted that all twelve of our gleaming extinguishers be placed in full view —two of them against the back wall of the stage. We pointed out that since the stage was wide open this was impossible. "Smokey" insisted. But he did permit us to paint them barn-red and there they hung, making interesting shadows throughout the performance.

the walls, having become scenery, must be painted by accredited scene painters. Jean prevailed on her friend Horace Armistead (later designer of the Menotti operas and head of the design department at Boston University) to paint the remaining thirty-five hundred feet. He completed them with an assistant over a period of ten days at the reasonable price of two hundred and twenty dollars.

An even more ingenious solution was found to the problem of our platforms. Jean unearthed a builder who was willing to construct them outside the New York metropolitan area in an abandoned movie studio at Ford Lee, New Jersey, then used as a warehouse by Wee and Leventhal, Broadway's most active shoestring producers and scavengers, who were in the habit of carting away Broadway productions on the night of their closing and storing them against a rainy day. It was from such salvaged lumber and fragments of old sets that our *Julius Caesar* platforms were built at a cost of under three hundred dollars. They were solid enough but, as a result, no two sets of steps were exactly the same height or depth. When the Rabbi pointed this out to Orson, he replied that he preferred steps to be uneven. When Leve continued tremulously that one of these steps might be as high as twenty inches, Orson said, "That's fine! We can use it to sit on!"

Costumes, fortunately, presented no problem. Our production came to be known, later, as the "modern-dress *Caesar*" and we were commended for our shrewdness in avoiding the expense of period costumes and armor. The decision to use modern dress was not an economic one and it was not conceived as a stunt. It was an essential element in Orson's conception of *Julius Caesar* as a political melodrama with clear contemporary parallels. All over the Western world sophisticated democratic structures were breaking down. First in Italy, then in Germany, dictatorships had taken over; the issues of political violence and the moral duty of the individual in the face of tyranny had become urgent and inescapable. To emphasize the similarity between the last days of the Roman republic and the political climate of Europe in the mid-thirties, our Roman aristocrats wore military uniforms with black belts that suggested but did not exactly reproduce the current fashion of the Fascist ruling class; our crowd wore the dark, nondescript street clothes of the big-city proletariat.

Welles, in his final cut version, had eliminated all formal battle scenes and, with them, all need for armor and weaponry. The only arms seen on our stage were the daggers of the assassins and short, bayonet-length blades for the final suicides. This was our greatest single economic break. Uniforms were easily procured on a rental-purchase basis from the Brooks Costume Company. They were old army tunics and overcoats, dyed a uniform dark green. For the rest, the actors wore their own street clothes, supplemented by dark coats and hats picked up in secondhand clothing stores on Orchard Street and the Bowery—all except Orson, who, as the aristocratic Brutus, wore a double-breasted, custom-made black pin-stripe suit with a dark tie "not unlike that which young Bob La Follette might have worn for an afternoon wedding in Madison, Wisconsin."*

Rehearsals began in the first week of October with a company of twenty-one, to which were presently added twelve, then finally sixteen, extras for the mob scenes. The first reading, which was held on our still unfinished stage in the presence of the entire Mercury staff, ran for less than an hour and a half and was electrifying in its clarity and power. Our emotional casting seemed to work: Joe Holland, with his marble brow and big voice, was a pale, truculent dictator—"a mortal confusing himself with divinity and heading toward a fall." Martin Gabel, who looked neither lean nor hungry, was a violent, angry and, finally, heartbreaking Cassius; Coulouris, no longer in his first youth, was a political, persuasive Antony opposed to Orson's high-minded, aristocratic liberal-intellectual Brutus. Chubby Sherman was a smiling, cynical ward-heeler of a Casca; Norman Lloyd a pitiful astonished rabbit as Cinna the Poet. The ladies—Portia and Calpurnia—as so often happened in Welles's classical productions, were decorative, adequate and hardly memorable.

* Stark Young. *The New Republic,* November 1937.

Our stage management at the Mercury was effective but unorthodox: no professional could have functioned for more than a day in the capricious, overheated atmosphere that Orson created backstage. All technical matters, including sound and light, were handled by Jean Rosenthal and her flock of female assistants; the rest was in the hands of a sensitive, overstrung young man with red hair who was with us for eighteen months until he suffered a nervous breakdown and left the theatre forever. His aides, that first season, were Richard Wilson (Welles's patient and devoted slave for the next eleven years) and a chinless shrimp of a boy with a big voice who called himself Vakhtangov or William Alland, neither of which was his real name.* Both of them, besides their assistant stage managers' duties, doubled and trebled as dressers, waiters, male nurses, messenger-boys and actors—playing Flavius and Marullus and members of the mob.

(The manner of Alland's joining the Mercury was typical of the climate in which we lived. The previous spring, while he was directing Aaron Copland's *Second Hurricane* for the children of the Henry Street Settlement, Orson had told me of a boy who called himself Vakhtangov, who hung around day and night, working lights, holding book, sweeping, prompting, moving pianos, talking too much and making himself generally indispensable. In exchange for these services, at some time in the middle of the night, he had extracted a promise of employment in the theatre. Orson was not one to remember such a commitment. He had quite forgotten Vakhtangov's existence when a frail, ragged figure rose out of the sidewalk one evening as we were hurrying back to the theatre, discussing our latest crisis after dining hugely at Del Pezzo's beneath autographed photographs of Caruso, Scotti and Geraldine Farrar. Running backward ahead of us, this apparition began to harangue Orson in an agitated and almost incomprehensible voice. Once he tripped and fell. I told him to call me the next morning. But he picked himself up and con-

* As William Alland, he played the important role of the Reporter in *Citizen Kane*, flew more than forty bombing missions in the Pacific and, after the War, became a successful producer of horror and science-fiction films.

tinued to scuffle backwards all the way to the theatre, alternately pleading and threatening, urging Orson to remember his oath, offering to act, light, valet, pimp, clean the toilets, steal—anything at all, so long as he was allowed to fulfill his destiny, which his dead mother's ghost had told him lay with the Mercury Theatre. Amused, then finally exasperated, Orson brushed past him through the stage door and hurried across the unfinished stage into the dressing room which he used as his office. We were about to start work when the door flew open and Vakhtangov stood before us, wild-eyed and deathly pale, slammed the door shut behind him, locked it, slipped the key into his bosom and announced that he would never surrender it until he had been heard. Then at the top of his voice he launched into a word-perfect recitation of the entire funeral oration, which so surprised us that we hired him on the spot.)

In the second week of rehearsal Orson began blocking his crowd scenes. Two days later he demanded the stage—platforms and all. Jeannie said that even if they were ready it would cost a fortune in crew bills to bring them into the theatre ahead of schedule. Orson didn't care. I did. We were virtually bankrupt already and this would be the final straw. Where were these platforms? Orson asked. Across the river. So for the next ten days the entire company (forty strong by this time) made its way each morning by West Side subway to 125th Street, crossed the Hudson on the Dyckman Street ferry, then took a Palisades Park bus to where our platforms stood among mounds of moldering lumber in Fort Lee, New Jersey. Here, without a trace of heat, the mob scenes of *Julius Caesar* were rehearsed day after day amid the whir of saws, the banging of hammers and the perils of an unfinished set. To his mildly protesting troupe Orson explained that all this was for their own protection: by the time the platforms reached the theatre they would be so familiar with the steps, ramps, risers and sudden drops that they would feel totally secure.

They needed every bit of this security, as it turned out. For when they arrived at the theatre for the first of their all-night sessions, they discovered that the platforms had been pierced by four large stage traps—gaping holes located in strategic positions, each wide enough for the passage of a human body and each supplied with a narrow, almost perpendicular set of wooden steps leading down to the basement below. These open traps provoked some grumbling among the actors, who regarded them as added and unnecessary physical risks—especially when they learned that they were expected to negotiate them in pitch-blackness. When they spoke to Orson about them, he was amazed and indignant. Were they not actors? And were not traps among the oldest and most consecrated devices of the stage? They must stop being amateurish and craven; they must get used to the presence of these traps and learn to use them like professionals!

At our first dress rehearsal, when the lights dimmed up on the assassination scene, all the conspirators were present except one —the honorable Brutus. Orson had been seen starting up the ramp with the others but now he was nowhere to be found. A hurried search of his dressing room (to which he sometimes retired for a quick nip) and of the mezzanine (to which he occasionally climbed to survey his staging) failed to locate him. Rehearsal stopped and the perplexed company waited for his return.

He was found five minutes later, still unconcious in the dark at the foot of the stairs after falling cleanly through an open trap and dropping fifteen feet before striking the basement floor with his chin. He was shaken but uninjured except for a slight sprain of his ankle, which got twisted as he was being helped to his feet. The next morning two of our manholes were plugged up. The others remained open and the company gradually got used to them, as Welles had predicted they would.

Throughout the run of *Julius Caesar* the problem of entrances and exits remained a tricky one on that completely open stage. All the dressing rooms except Orson's were located stage left in a three-story cell block served by a narrow cement staircase set in the wall, from which stage left entrances had to be made. All other entrances meant going on down into the darkened basement and coming up on the other side or through one of the traps. After some initial confusion the company became quite expert at getting into position and timing their entrances while keeping out of sight of the audience. Unfortunately they were not the only ones to use the stage. Since our stage door opened directly onto the acting area and we had a permissive doorman, it was not unusual for people to wander in off the street during performances. On the second night of *Julius Caesar* one critic noted the presence of a New York City fireman in uniform in the background of the assassination scene.* Orson himself, arriving late from Longchamps or Bleeck's, more than once made his entrance into the Forum directly from Forty-first Street. And one Wednesday afternoon, a conscientious delivery boy, carrying a pressed suit on a hanger, made his way across the crowded stage to Orson's dressing room, where he delivered one garment, collected another and departed the way he had come without disturbing the matinee audience or the funeral oration. Other regular visitors were the rats—the size of small dogs—with whom we still shared the theatre and who found in Orson's Elizabethan stage traps a quick and convenient route from the basement to the street. Undeterred by the presence of forty actors, the glare of two hundred projectors and the thunder of Marc Blitzstein's martial music, they trotted about the stage—singly, in troupes, or pursued by impotent cats.

By November 1st, I had spent all our investors' money and we were beginning to go into debt. After two months of euphoric activity, the realities of Broadway were beginning to reassert themselves. Our advance business was encouraging: student and theatre party sales were substantial and more than half our cheap seats were already sold for the first seven weeks of our season. But this was not nearly enough. For the major part of our receipts, we had to rely on the sale of our high-priced tickets. I urged our box-office staff, Georgie Zorn and his cousin, Harry Kaufmann, to try to wring some sort of an advance buy from the ticket agencies which controlled the carriage trade. They got nowhere. Some agents were benevolent but cautious; others refused to let us put

---

* "To me his presence was appropriate. After all, Rome did burn and this is a play and a performance that has caught the crackle." Heywood Broun, November 12, 1937.

our posters in their windows on the grounds that we were "amateur stuff" and not a Broadway show operating at Broadway prices.

I was sitting alone in the projection booth the evening before the first dress rehearsal, considering our situation and listening to Brutus' page singing Marc's lovely setting of "Orpheus with His Lute" on the stage below, when Jean Rosenthal and George Zorn appeared with sober faces and presented me with the estimated cost of our dress rehearsals and previews, amounting to more than two thousand dollars. These were not expenses that could be swept under the rug: the unions required payment at week's end in cash—which we did not have. What about the money from our advance sales? Spent, said Georgie. Our deposits from the theatre parties? Gone.

After they left I lay on my day bed for a while; then I called Mina at Chapelbrook. She had not offered to invest in the Mercury, and I had not pressed her. Now I asked her to lend me the thousand dollars she had got back from *The Cradle Will Rock*. She said she would drive into Ashfield in the morning and mail the check. After that, in desperation, I called Archie MacLeish. I told him of our crisis. Would any of his rich friends care to help us? He was at dinner, and he said he'd think about it. He called back at noon the next day to say that he had talked to Clare Luce: maybe she and Henry would do something, and I should go to the Waldorf Towers between five and six and talk to her myself.

I had met her twice before—once at some summer theatre up the Hudson on the opening night of her disastrous first play, and again on the night when she had appeared in Buckminster Fuller's Dymaxion car at the Hartford premiere of *Four Saints*. Like any beautiful and successful woman, she presented two quite different images to the world: in the one she appeared as a ruthless climber who had exploited her sex and her wits to claw her way to her present position of wealth and power. Others, especially my friend Pare Lorentz, had given me a picture of a warm, generous and loyal friend. In the hour I spent with her—a mendicant in desperate need of a few dollars talking to the wife of the nation's most successful publisher, herself the author of the biggest hit on Broadway*—I was overcome by her charm but, even more, by her instinctive, feminine capacity to bring out in me, even in those circumstances, a sense of my own male attraction, intelligence and power. She encouraged me to talk, listening to every word I said with an eager and fascinated absorption. She had seen all our shows; she knew of our hopes for the Mercury; she wanted to know more about Orson. Just before I left, after my second scotch and soda, Henry Luce came in, and she mentioned the object of my visit. Late that night, halfway through dress rehearsal, the phone rang in the box office, and Harry Kaufmann came down the aisle, found me in the darkness and whispered that a 'Mrs. Clare was asking for me. She apologized for calling at such an hour, but she knew we were worried about money and thought I'd be able to watch the rehearsal more objectively knowing that she and her husband were coming in for twenty-five hundred dollars and that the check would be sent over in the morning.

I had not discussed the details of our situation with Orson. I did not need to. We were both fully aware of the danger we were in and the nature of the risk we were running. On the broad wings of the Federal eagle, we had risen to success and fame beyond our wildest dreams; we had become dazzled with the vision of ourselves as America's youngest, cleverest, most creative and audacious producers to whom none of the ordinary rules of the theatre applied. Now, suddenly, we were facing reality. With the imminent opening of *Julius Caesar,* our moment of truth had arrived. Had we soared too near the sun, and were we about to get our comeuppance? Or were we about to realize our shining vision of founding a great new theatre of our own, comparable to the fabled theatres of the past? Were we about to show a skeptical world that we could achieve the impossible—run a classical repertory company, without subsidy, on Broadway? Or were we about to break our necks?

* *The Women,* by Clare Booth, at the Barrymore Theatre for 657 performances.

Orson Welles was a prodigious, if somewhat erratic, worker. This time he was fanatical in his preparation. Between the personal scenes, which he continued to rehearse long after they seemed to be ready, the crowd scenes which he drilled and repeated endlessly, the setting of lights and the balancing of Marc's musical background, he was spending between sixteen and twenty hours a day in the theatre and making scenes if I wasn't by his side for most of that time. (Since I also had to administer the Mercury by day and put in my ten hours a week with the girls at Vassar, I reached such a stage of exhaustion by the time we opened that it took me weeks to recover.)

Technical rehearsals were going smoothly for the most part; they were long and slow but less painful than usual. After the hysteria of our all-night sessions with Feder, Jeannie's quiet, deliberate politeness, which she seemed to maintain no matter what strain was put upon her, made our lighting sessions an almost agreeable experience. The light plot was complicated and grew daily more elaborate as secondary cues and transitions were added. But the basic electrical setup, carefully conceived and imaginatively installed, was superior to anything we had known in our previous theatres, and Jean's communication with Welles was more direct than any Feder had ever achieved. Having watched rehearsals for weeks, she was familiar with the action on the stage and had carefully prepared herself for whatever effects might be required of her. There is always an element of improvisation in theatrical lighting: one of the loveliest effects in *Julius Caesar*—known as the "orchard lights" because they were used to illuminate the moonlit scene in which Brutus is visited by the conspirators in his orchard at night—was achieved by pure accident when it was found that a worklight, left burning in the flies, threw strange, broken shadows through the grid and hanging ropes onto the blood-red floor of the stage below.

Marc's music gave us no trouble. His flexible score for trumpet, horn, percussion and Hammond organ was strong, effective and easily cued. With this limited combination (the Musicians' Union's minimum requirement for the theatre) he managed to achieve amazingly varied effects—from the distant bugles of a sleeping camp to the blaring brass and deep, massive, rhythmic beat which instantly evoked the pounding march of Hitler's storm troopers that we were hearing with increasing frequency over the radio and in the newsreels. Added to this was the ominous rumble of the electric organ on certain base stops which set the whole theatre trembling and the deep booming of a huge, old-fashioned thunder drum which had been especially constructed, years before, for the American production of *Chu Chin Chow*.

These technical elements of the production took up hours of our time, but it was on the human performances that Welles concentrated his main effort during that last week, dividing his time between the crowd scenes and the personal confrontations—particularly the relationship of Brutus and Cassius, which, in his version, formed the emotional spine of the tragedy.

It would have been hard to find a man less suited, physically, to the role of Cassius, as Shakespeare describes him, than Martin Gabel. Squat, broad, thick-necked with a furrowed brow and massive jaw, his gravid voice had made him, in his early twenties, one of the country's most successful and sexy radio actors. A man of deep sensitivity distorted by insatiable ambition and a furious energy, he was a reckless gambler and a compulsive operator in many fields. All of this fermenting under the outward arrogance of a Jewish boy from New Jersey on his first dangerous venture into the classical theatre, made him the perfect antagonist for Orson's high-minded and meditative Brutus. In their first moment together, waiting for Caesar to return from the Games, there was something recognizable and terrifying in the way he intruded upon Brutus, violating his privacy with his corrosive, vengeful discontent, tearing his way through that serene self-righteousness to plant the seed of murder in his ear. And in their last scene together, in the tent before Philippi, when the final, inevitable conflict between these two irreconcilable men breaks through the frail structure of their enforced association, it was surprising to find that one's sympathy was evenly divided—between the bitter, humiliated partner caught with his hand in the till but still craving respect and affection, and the self-defeating but still noble, sincere and righteous Brutus.

In his fascination with the Brutus-Cassius relationship, Welles had cut out not only the battle scenes (which no one missed) but also much of the Antony and almost all the Octavius material from the second half of the play. As a result, George Coulouris was a highly effective but one-dimensional Marc Antony. In his big scene in the Forum he had to follow a stricken but restrained and dignified Brutus, exasperatingly scrupulous and sincere in his determination not to use the execution of the dictator for his own personal or political advantage. Antony's oration, as Coulouris delivered it, was the exact opposite: it was a cynical political harangue, a skillfully organized and brilliantly delivered demagogic tour de force, a catalyst whose emotional effect on the Roman mob was deliberate and premeditated.*

To achieve these fluctuating mass reactions of pity, indignation and unbridled fury with a crowd of two dozen boys in secondhand overcoats and dark felt hats, Orson spent days and nights of detailed and patient work. One of them recalls how Welles spent hour after hour with them, orchestrating their individual and collective reactions:

> He recorded the speeches of Antony and Brutus on disks and had us speak back specific lines in reaction to the main speeches. It wasn't just a matter of babbling words. We had definite lines to say and definite moments at which to speak.
> When Antony spoke the first words of the eulogy over Caesar's body, one of us said "Aw, shut up!" and others of the mob came in quickly with "Let him talk!" and so on. It was by no means a matter of walking on and off the stage and making noises.

* In the film of *Julius Caesar* which I made fifteen years later with Joseph Mankiewicz, the casting of Marlon Brando as Antony completely reversed the structure of the play. Now it was Marc Antony they were rooting for and the twelve hundred cheering bit players and extras massed on M.G.M.'s Stage 25 were merely reflecting the empathy of future audiences.

Later these ad libs were replaced by appropriate exclamations collected from other Elizabethan plays, notably *Coriolanus*.

There was no realistic scenery in the production and therefore no "pulpit"—just a ten-foot rostrum covered with black velour that was wheeled up the ramp in the dark (under cover of the electric organ and the thunder drum) on which first Brutus, then Antony, seemed to float in space above the mass of the crowd, gathered around Caesar's open coffin between the speakers and the audience. Their reactions during their climactic scenes were not merely verbal: Orson kept them in continuous, fluid movement which, on our hollow, unpadded platforms, gave out a constantly changing and highly dramatic sound which he exploited to the full. Yet it was one of those mob scenes that gave us so much trouble that, for a time, it seemed about to wreck the entire show.

Every director—especially the creative ones—gets stuck sooner or later. There are always certain scenes which, for one reason or another, do not move forward with the rest of the work. This was particularly true of Welles. In every production we did together there were one or more moments which came to embarrass or bore him—either because he had become disillusioned with the performers or because he realized that his own original conception of the scene had failed and he was uncertain which way to turn. In *Julius Caesar* the lynching of Cinna the Poet had become such a block.

In reading the play it seems no more than a brief, tragi-comic episode in which a dreamy, rather silly, poet pays with his life for having the same name as a member of the conspiracy: just another evidence of Shakespeare's distaste for the mob's capricious violence. Orson, in his editing of the play, had given the scene a far greater significance: he saw in it the dramatic consummation of the passions aroused by Antony's inflammatory oration. At the first reading it had seemed to do just that. Then, after a few days, it ceased to progress. Perhaps he was asking too much of the moment and got disappointed and angry when it didn't happen immediately; perhaps he was reacting unfavorably to the challenge presented by the personality of Norman Lloyd, whom I had brought into the company over some resistance by Orson. Whatever the reason—after several false starts, he simply stopped rehearsing the scene. This was not the first time such a block had occurred. In such cases it was my function, as his partner and producer, to cajole, harass 'or shame Orson into going back into the scene and reworking it, sometimes even reconceiving it entirely, until it satisfied us both or I conceded that it was hopeless. With the Cinna scene I got nowhere. When I insisted that it be worked on, he turned it over to Marc Blitzstein, who rehearsed it for several days with a metronome: the rising menace was to be achieved through a crescendo in volume and an accelerating tempo with each move and speech related to a percussive beat. That didn't work either. Lloyd, as the dreamy, oblivious victim was unable or unwilling to adjust his highly personal style of playing to these arbitrarily imposed, external rhythms. By this time the scene looked like a parody of Martha Graham's street movements in *Panic* and, for the first time since the start of the production, the company was beginning to get restless and querulous. So, once again, the scene was abandoned. For our first three dress rehearsals it was missing from the show, which was hurt by its absence.

By that time another crisis had hit us. From the start of rehearsals Orson had been telling me of an astounding sound track that was being prepared for him by his radio friends over at the Columbia Broadcasting System, where sound men and engineers were assembling a sequence of big-city sound effects the like of which had never been heard inside a theatre. Warming to the task, they had recorded a series of traffic backgrounds on which they had superimposed the most powerful police sirens and airraid warnings they could find. These were repeated and rerecorded at various speeds and levels, forward and backward, till finally there were more than a hundred sirens going on the disk at one time. As usual, where electronics are concerned, this all took longer than expected. On the Friday before opening—in time for our second dress rehearsal—the disk was finally ready.

We went over to the CBS building on Madison Avenue and heard it in Studio One on the finest high-fidelity equipment in the business. It sounded terrific. But when we tried to play it back in the theatre, we discovered that our rented quipment was quite incapable of reproducing it. Over the weekend Jeannie managed to find, rent and install a new turntable and six expensive speakers which we hung above and under the stage and on the sides and rear of the house. They were in place when we opened our doors for the first preview—a house that was sold out to theatre parties in the balconies while the orchestra floor was occupied by invited friends and the three hundred Phoenix subscribers who, having waited two and a half years since *Panic* for the second part of their subscription, deserved a better show.

Our first preview of *Julius Caesar* was a disaster. Some of the personal moments worked, but enough music and light cues went wrong to throw the entire cast into a turmoil. Infected by the general insecurity, the crowd scenes fell apart, and the absence of the Cinna scene left a gaping hole in the structure of the play. But all these were negligible flaws compared to the total catastrophe of our sound. Over our still inadequate system the fabulous big-city montage sounded like a subway train in travail. At first the audience was puzzled and irritated as the moaning and crackling of the loud-speakers interfered with their hearing of the actors' words. Then they began to giggle and, finally, to laugh out loud. Some walked out. At the end there was perfunctory applause, and we took no curtain calls.

All through the following day a flock of CBS engineers was tinkering and testing. That night we tried again with results that were only slightly less grim. Halfway through the show Orson ordered all electric equipment cut off. From then on we relied for our sound on Marc's music supplemented by the *Chu Chin Chow* thunder drum and the pounding feet of the forty members of our cast.

Otherwise, our second preview (still without Cinna) had gone rather better than the first. The company, having recovered from its initial panic, recaptured some of the magic it had shown in rehearsal. The end of the play, as it focused in on Brutus and

Cassius and, finally, on Brutus alone, had a tragic and heart-breaking quality which, following the violence and turmoil of the earlier scenes, left our predominantly leftist audience, after one hundred-five minutes of uninterrupted attention, exhausted and stirred—but still not fully involved. We had two more previews before our opening—a matinee and an evening performance. Orson gave the company forty-five minutes for supper. Then he called them back and rehearsed the crowd scenes until morning, repeating the mob's violently changing reactions to Brutus and Antony and going on from there, time after time, into the deceptively quiet opening of the Cinna scene: the slender, red-haired figure in the dark suit, starched collar and neutral tie, emerging from the basement into a ring of light, whistling a little carefree air on his wistful way to death—

> I have no will to wander out of doors
> Yet something leads me on.

Then, suddenly, the crowd was upon him—singly at first, then in twos and threes, scuffling out of the surrounding darkness till they formed a ring around the bemused poet, moving in on him, pressing him with questions, not listening to his answers—"I am Cinna . . . Cinna the poet"—till, with a savage cry of "Tear him!" they swallowed him up in their idiotic, murderous frenzy.

They did it a dozen times till Lloyd and the exhausted mob were on the edge of madness. Orson used some of Blitzstein's rhythmic patterns, some of his own original staging and some of the things Norman Lloyd had patiently and obstinately worked out for himself. Forty-two hours before opening he and Orson suddenly stopped fighting each other: at two in the morning, on their seventh try, the scene began to work, getting tauter and more dangerous as the night wore on. At four-thirty we stopped and it was announced that the Cinna the Poet scene would be in the show for the matinee.

I slept in the theatre that night on my day bed in the projection room. At eight, Jeannie and her crew were back, dismantling the speakers and hanging additional projectors high up on the downstage towers. The switchboard opened at ten. Half an hour later I heard Judy Holliday's small voice announcing that a Mr. Brown was on the wire and that it seemed to be important.

John Mason Brown, to whom I had hardly spoken since that distant time when we were both wooing Henrietta Bingham on lower Fifth Avenue twelve years before, had become drama critic of the New York *Post,* where he had established a reputation as one of the liveliest and best-informed of the men on the aisle. He was on the phone, now, with a troublesome request. Would I mind if he came to the matinee preview of *Julius Caesar?* Called out of town on an emergency, this would be his only chance to see the show and to review it himself rather than turn it over to his second-stringer. Torn between my annoyance at having the show judged prematurely and my reluctance to refuse an important and friendly critic, I had only one choice—to say yes. I told him we were still working on the show. He said he understood and wished us luck. After some hesitation I told Orson; we decided not to tell anyone else.

The audience was already in its seats and the cast assembled in the darkened basement, in position for its first appearance on the streets of Rome, when George Coulouris announced in a voice loud enough to be heard by the entire front half of the orchestra that while he hated to be a Cassandra, it was his considered opinion that the Mercury would be folding on Saturday night. Since he was voicing an apprehension shared by a number of our cast, it may have been this sudden stab of fear that made such a difference to that afternoon's performance. Or, more likely, the show was primed and ready and in the presence of the right audience it burst into flame. Suddenly everything was right: individual performances, transitions, silences, progressions and climaxes—they all seemed to come together in a devastating whole.

At the end of the performance, John Mason Brown came up the aisle to where I was standing, stunned and happy, at the back of the theatre, listening to the audience as it filed out into the fading daylight. He took my hand and held it and made an unusual and unethical request. He asked to be taken backstage.

Orson, sitting before his makeup table in his green military great-coat, looked up in consternation as one of the country's leading drama critics burst into the dressing room and started to tell us such things about the production as we had not hoped to hear even in our most megalomaniacal dreams. They appeared in print two days later in the New York *Post*, where *Julius Caesar* was described as "by all odds the most exciting, the most imaginative, the most topical, the most awesome and the most absorbing of the season's new productions. The touch of genius is upon it."

> The astonishing all-impressive virtue of Mr. Welles' production is that, magnificent as it is as theatre, it is far larger than its medium. Something deathless and dangerous in the world sweeps past you down the darkened aisles at the Mercury and takes possession of the proud, gaunt stage. It is something fearful and turbulent which distends the drama to include the life of nations as well as of men. . . . To an extent no other director in our day and country has equaled, Mr. Welles proves in his production that Shakespeare was indeed not of an age but for all time.

Of all the critics who later came to enthuse over *Julius Caesar,* Brown, in the first rush of his excitement, seemed to convey most vividly the look and sound of the production:

> It is placed upon a bare stage, the brick walls of which are crimson and naked. That is all. And that is all that is needed. In its streamlined simplicity this set achieves the glorious, unimpeded freedom of an Elizabethan stage. It is a setting spacious enough for both the winds and victims of demagoguery to sweep across it like a hurricane . . .
> In groupings that are of that fluid, stressful, virtuoso sort one usually has to journey to Russia to see, Mr. Welles proves himself a brilliant innovator in his deployment of his principals and the movements of his crowds . . . he keeps drumming the meaning of his play into our minds by the scuffling of his mobs when they prowl in the shadows, or by the herd-like thunder of their feet when they run as one threatening body. It is a memorable device. Like the setting in which it is

used, it is pure theatre; vibrant, unashamed and enormously effective.

Word of our first critical triumph spread like wildfire around the exhausted company. As a result, the evening's performance was not as taut as that of our miraculous matinee—but it worked and there were cheers at the end. The following afternoon, having savored the ghastly reviews received by Tallulah Bankhead as Cleopatra the night before, we had a final line reading in the rear of the auditorium while our platforms were being repainted. And that night we opened.

There was a party at Tony's after the show to which I did not go. I sat alone at Bleeck's and waited for Hank Senber to go in and snatch the first proofs of Richard Watts's review off the *Herald Tribune* press. It was a rave. At the *Times* it was more difficult; but if he liked the press agent, Sam Zolotow (sitting at the drama desk late into the night in search of news) could be persuaded to intercept and read the highlights of Atkinson's New England prose in a Bronx accent as it was carried, paragraph by paragraph, from the typewriter to the composing room below. Even the way he read it, it sounded sublime.

The *Daily News,* the *Mirror* and the *American* hit the stands around midnight. All three were good. But by then I was blasé. I tried to call Orson at Tony's but he had already left. So I stayed in the booth and woke Mina in Massachusetts and several friends around the city to read them the reviews. I noticed when I got back to my drink that there was a tall, sunburned, towheaded girl at the next table with a letter made up of a number of yellow foolscap pages taped together to form a seven-foot strip. When I asked her if she would care for a drink she rolled it up and put it away in her bag. She said it was from her boyfriend in Arizona. I showed her our notices and they made not the slightest impression upon her. When Bleeck's closed, she came home with me to Sixty-first Street and we made love without a word. When I woke up in the morning, she was gone and when I got back to the theatre there was a line in front of the single window of our small box office. That night we were sold out before cur-

tain time and there were standees at the Saturday matinee and
evening performances.

BARD BOFFOLA

reported *Variety*—and with such reviews it was not surprising.

> Something to stand up and cheer about! A production so
> exciting and imaginative, so completely fascinating in all its
> phases, there is nothing to do but let ourselves go and applaud
> it unreservedly. Here, splendidly acted and thrillingly pro-
> duced is what must certainly be the great *Julius Caesar* of
> our time.[1]

> Greatly conceived and brilliantly executed, it is the most
> vivid production of Shakespeare seen in New York in this
> generation.[2]

> It is something against which your literary instincts may
> want to rebel but which will smash them down and force
> hurrahs from your aching chest as though a whole football
> team had landed on it. . . . Shakespeare himself would have
> honored and relished it.[3]

> It would have been a fascinating experiment even if it had
> failed. That it succeeds so admirably is enough to blow the
> hinges off the dictionary.[4]

In almost every review much was made of the topical quality
of the production: "the tragedy of the Globe Theatre across the
Thames has become the melodramatic tragedy of modern times
just a few doors east of Broadway."

> From the vague night of dark recesses the characters emerge
> into the light to say their say and do their deeds and that is
> enough not merely to hold an audience tense but to send them

[1] Richard Watts in the *Herald Tribune*.
[2] *The Nation*.
[3] Gilbert Gabriel in the *American*.
[4] John Anderson in the New York *Journal*.

away carrying in their minds both the meaning and the feel of conspiracy in a tottering world.[5]

The grim march of military feet through the ominous shadows of the stage is the doom song heard around the world today.[6]

It is a tragedy that comes nearer the fatal currency of our time and place than any other I have seen.[7]

Memories of recent violence undoubtedly colored the critics' views of the mob scenes that culminated in the lynching of Cinna the Poet, evoking such phrases as:

A scene which for pure power and sinister meaning has never been surpassed in the American theatre. . . . An unforgettable and sinister thing. . . . Never has the restless and brutal terrorism of mob action been more finally pictured on the stage.

This same sense of political relevance was evident in their appraisal of the actors' performances:

Joseph Holland's Caesar is an imperious dictator who could be found frowning at you in this week's newsreels.[8]

George Coulouris is an admirable Antony. So fresh is his characterization, so intelligent his performance that even "Friends, Romans, countrymen" sounds on his tongue as if it were a rabble-rousing harangue he is uttering for the first time.[9]

Hiram Sherman's Casca in a snap-brim black felt hat and raglan coat is a show-piece of street-corner contemporaneousness.[10]

[5] Joseph Wood Krutch in *The Nation*.
[6] Brooks Atkinson in *The New York Times*.
[7] Archibald MacLeish in *The Nation*.
[8] John Mason Brown in the New York *Post*.
[9] John Mason Brown in the New York *Post*.
[10] *The New York Times*.

This was particularly true of Welles's Brutus. There was praise for his "high-minded, clear-souled nobility," for his "beautifully modulated" voice, for his "uncommon gift for speaking great words simply" and for his "admirable study of the somber tones of reverie and calm introspection—all kindness, reluctance and remorse." But never, I believe, in the history of Shakespeare's play, has Brutus' tragedy been so consistently equated with the fallacy of the liberal position in a violent world:

> Brutus as Mr. Welles understands him is the prototype of a bewildered liberal, a great man with all the faults and virtues of liberalism.[11]

> Brutus becomes a familiar figure in American ideology and practice, a believer in moral law and individual liberty, who values free institutions above all other ends. He represents the tragic liberal, the man of character and principle in a world threatened by fascist destruction.[12]

> There seems to be an arbitrary premonition of the unhappy fate of the liberal in a world torn by strife between the extremes of Left and Right. It can hardly be said that Shakespeare sneers at Brutus, but the logic of events is punishing to the man who insists on fighting fire with a bucket-brigade.[13]

There was another side to our notices that had nothing to do with world politics. "Move over and make room for the Mercury!" wrote Brooks Atkinson in his review in *The New York Times* and on the following Sunday he continued:

> The Mercury Theatre which John Houseman and Orson Welles have founded with *Julius Caesar* has taken the town by the ears. Of all the young enterprises that are stirring here and there, this is the most dynamic and the most likely to have an enduring influence on the theatre . . . It has pitched headlong into the thick of the theatre without any-

[11] Stark Young.
[12] Archibald MacLeish.
[13] Heywood Broun.

thing more imposing than a racy enthusiasm for the stage and no apparent ambition to make a fortune. To judge by their first production the Mercury will be a theatre where enthusiasm for acting and boldness are to be seriously indulged by young actors with a merit of their own.

Mr. Welles and Mr. Houseman are both young and experienced which is a combination that is almost unnatural. . . . By moving over to make place for the Mercury, it is obvious that we also move ahead.

"The Mercury has put new fire into the art of the stage"; "a real theatre event"; "the beginning of a new trend in the theatre"; "a splendid beginning for what promises to be the most exciting adventure in the modern American theatre"—these were among the heady greetings we received in the days following the opening of *Julius Caesar*.

On the Monday following our opening George Zorn appeared in my office. He wished to talk to me alone: Welles was a lunatic but I was a reasonable fellow and I must listen to him. His tone was avuncular. Was I aware that *Julius Caesar* was the hottest ticket in town? With most of our cheap seats gone until January 1st and an orchestra floor of under three hundred seats priced at the absurd figure of two dollars plus tax (two-fifty on weekends) we were in a situation that was calculated to drive any professional box-office man out of his mind with frustration and rage. To see half the tickets for the biggest hit of the season sold at an average price of a little over a dollar, while having to turn down dozens of sales of orchestra seats each day to brokers clamoring to pay five times that much under the table—this was idiotic to the point of criminality.

I asked what he would suggest. He told me: run *Julius Caesar* and cancel all other productions; burn all tickets already printed and not sold; between now and the end of December sell only to brokers; after that eliminate fifty-cent seats entirely and sell the second balcony for one dollar, the mezzanine for two and the orchestra for the standard Broadway price of three dollars plus tax. As he spoke I could see his eyes gleaming with the vision of fawning brokers, their pockets stuffed with the green stuff and "ice" on the side for us all. What about our theatre parties and student sales? To hell with them! Repertory? Screw repertory!

He supported his plea with figures. To recondition the theatre and open *Julius Caesar* we had spent almost twice our entire capital. On the present basis, with every seat sold, our profit would amount to a bare one thousand five hundred dollars a week. Thus it would take us three months to get back to solvency, not counting the expense of the second show. On George's suggested system we could treble that weekly figure: by June 1st we would have a hundred thousand or more in the bank with which to present repertory and make art to our heart's content in the future.

Every word he said was true. It was also true that by going into a straight run of our current hit we would be breaking every promise made to our public and to the press. "Oh yeah?" said George. "And where would your 'public' be if you'd got lousy reviews?"

I talked to Welles and I did some research of my own. Sylvia Regan's minions were outraged and said they would quit if we changed our policy. From the press, personally and through Hank Senber, I got the impression that they would be chagrined but not infuriated if we exploited a situation to which they themselves had contributed.* As to the company, I had a feeling that they were divided. They had been assembled with a promise of repertory and though a number of them might have been happy to do less work and enjoy their success, there was a core of strong feeling, most passionately expressed by Hiram Sherman, that if we did not stick to our manifesto we would be betraying both them and the future of the Mercury. Our stockholders, whom I consulted for the first and last time in our history, were of two minds: on principle, they hated to see us abandon the repertory idea which had originally attracted them to us; prac-

---

* "Those who have seen this *Julius Caesar* are now anxious to see *Shoemakers' Holiday* which is promised for December. But in all fairness to the Mercury Theatre, we could not find fault if they should decide to play the present production on and on and on and on" wrote Sidney Whipple in the New York *World Telegram*.

tically, they would have been delighted, for our own security, to see us end the season with an operating fund of one hundred thousand dollars.

Neither Welles nor I was primarily interested in principles or in money. We thought of the Mercury as an instrument of artistic expression and a ladder to fame and power. We had gambled and won: intoxicated with success, we were moving much too fast, with our own special kind of reckless, whirling motion, to stop for any reason—good or bad. To Orson, the prospect of coming to the theatre nightly for seven months to play the part of Brutus was absolutely abhorrent, just as it was impossible for me to think of myself sitting in my projection booth day after day with no other activity than to administer the stable and lucrative routine of a successful Broadway run.

So we had supper at 21, and over our second bottle of champagne we prepared an announcement which was given to the press the next morning: the Mercury Theatre was about to go into rehearsal not with one production but with two.

*   *   *

So began the halcyon days of the Mercury: rehearsing by day, playing nightly to packed and enthusiastic houses, with enough cash coming in from the lines that wound daily around the small pearl-gray lobby under the crystal chandelier to take care of current payrolls and accumulated bills and debts. George Zorn remained glum for a week or two, then he grew resigned to the fact that he was working for a pair of madmen and made the best of it. In fact, this air of dedicated insanity came to permeate the entire organization: from the stage to the boiler room morale was miraculously high during those first few months of our operation.

Our actors had everything to make them happy: they had received great collective and individual reviews; their future was assured for months to come; they were already at work on a second show. And on a purely material plane, under the sliding scale, which I had instituted as an insurance against disaster, they were making far more each week than their basic contract figure.

Jean Rosenthal's stage crew was proud and happy: what with working *Caesar* and building the new show, they, too, were making well over scale. Sylvia and her eager promotion department, once they were convinced I was not going to betray them, lived in a dream world of contentment: they had a schedule through February and they were filling orders as fast as they could answer their phones. Hank Senber was the darling of the press: his days were not long enough to meet the demand for Orson Welles and Mercury stories and interviews. Even the box office was happy: while their personal profits were not all that could be expected from a smash hit, it was a continuing delight to be dealing all day with a line of humble customers and eager brokers.

This high state of morale extended to the meanest members of the Mercury personnel. Our house staff was touching in its devotion. Joe, the engineer, could barely speak English but he kept our furnace going and our toilets flowing throughout the winter. His salary was fifteen dollars a week, which we literally had to force into his hands each Friday evening. Embarrassed and mortified when he had to present his bills for supplies and coal, he went so far as to steal hot air for us through a subterranean pipe which he somehow connected to the heating system of the bank across the street. Our cleaning woman, an Irish lady, worked for us at forty cents an hour instead of the eighty cents she got from her employers in the neighboring office buildings. Our doorman was a retired burlesque bouncer: he was crude but helpful and never complained of the meager tips he received from our predominantly proletarian audience. And, for what may well have been the first time in Broadway theatrical history, the cop on our beat refused the weekly tribute normally exacted for keeping the street clear of traffic at theatre time.

This same dedication was evident among the flock of volunteers (mostly girls) which descended upon us after Thanksgiving. Some were from progressive institutions like Bennington which encouraged professional apprenticeship among their advanced students; others were graduates or fugitives from the drama departments of Yale and Carnegie Tech. They were eager, almost all intelligent, most of them well to do; some were plain and sensibly dressed, a few glamorous as fashion models—and all theatre-crazy. We exploited them without scruple. They did everything from bringing in coffee, running errands, distributing leaflets, pressing and repairing costumes, holding book, cuing actors and, in some cases, performing essential technical services under Jean Rosenthal.* They also had one special, rather curious but absolutely essential duty to perform.

The Mercury Theatre did not have the underground splendors we had known at the Maxine Elliott. Our Gents' and Ladies' toilets, both located in the basement, were not fully insulated from the auditorium. Several times, at previews, a loud flushing was heard during one of our most tense and pregnant silences. In consequence the staff was rigorously forbidden to use the johns during performance. But since *Julius Caesar* ran for an hour and forty-nine minutes without intermission, there was a small, constant stream of anguished customers tiptoeing down to the basement to relieve themselves. We tried locking the toilets, but this provoked such protests that we quickly opened them up again as the law required. We finally solved the problem by having a well-spoken girl posted at the foot of each staircase who would explain the situation as charmingly as she could, then escort and admit the customers to the johns only during scenes so noisy that their flushing was lost in the roar of human voices or in the deep vibrating chords of the Hammond organ and thunder drum.

We did have one mutiny that winter—among the sixteen young men who constituted the crowd in *Julius Caesar*. I had selected them with care out of the three or four hundred who

---

* Those who stayed included Barbara Deming (of Bennington) who stage-managed *The Cradle Will Rock* for us and later became a film critic and an activist in the peace movements of the sixties; Amy Jacobs (from Carnegie Tech), a rich girl who later became a backer of Broadway plays; Ethel Frank (of Vassar) who became a successful radio writer and producer and who remembers buying and bringing in a typical Orson Welles meal consisting of two steaks with baked potatoes, salad, an entire pineapple and a bottle of scotch at a cost of $14.95 for which she was never repaid.

presented themselves at our first public call. From that arbitrary and capricious choice came an energetic, quick-witted gang—cantankerous and independent but passionately dedicated, not so much to Orson and me, as to the kind of theatre they believed the Mercury to be. Their working conditions were appalling. They shared the black hole below stage with the rats; they were on call for as many as sixteen hours at a stretch and, except after midnight or when Orson felt it necessary to buy their cooperation with a treat of ice cream or sandwiches, no food was provided for them. And for all this they received the munificent sum of one dollar a day.*

Two weeks after the opening of *Julius Caesar* the extras requested a conference. Through their spokesman, Jack Berry, they reaffirmed their devotion and their pride in the Mercury but wanted me to know that they could not keep alive on what we paid them. I asked them to wait a few weeks. They repeated that they were hungry. I said I would think it over. When they left I felt I had the situation well in hand. Then a moment later, Zorn came running upstairs and told me they had left the theatre in a body and were on their way over to Actors' Equity.

The intervention of Equity was the last thing I wanted in our unorthodox affairs. I dispatched one messenger, then another to intercept them and coax them back to the theatre. Once there, I reproached them for their treachery and lack of faith. That made them laugh, for in that moment they knew that they had won. I asked what they considered a living wage. Fifteen dollars a week. I said okay—even if it broke us. That made them laugh again, and the mutiny was over.

---

* Bil Baird, the puppeteer, cites this example of our operation:

HOUSEMAN: Hey, Bil! That life mask for Caesar's corpse. It stinks! I'm sending it back!

BAIRD: What's wrong with it?

HOUSEMAN: It's beautiful. But it's two inches thick. How the hell can a boy lie for twenty minutes with that weight of plaster on his face?

BAIRD: Boy? I thought you were using a dummy.

HOUSEMAN: It has to be a boy! We can't afford a dummy!

By late November we were deep in rehearsal—with two shows. In our manifesto we had made much of our intention to present new plays on the Mercury stage on Sunday nights. By announcing *The Cradle Will Rock* as the first offering of this so-called Worklight Theatre we hoped to kill two birds with one stone—to get our experimental series started with an established success and to reaffirm our property rights on Blitzstein's play with music for which Marc was receiving other offers. It was not a difficult piece to put on; our cast of Venice stalwarts was available and enthusiastic—particularly those who still languished on WPA, yearning for a return to their adventurous days on Project #891. Marc Blitzstein conducted rehearsals; he also continued to thomp his eviscerated piano, narrate and play a number of lesser parts.

Since the Mercury Theatre had a small orchestra floor and steep, semicircular balconies, it would have been impossible, even if we had wanted to, to reproduce the positions that had been improvised all over the Venice Theatre. We therefore devised what came to be known as the "oratorio version" of *The Cradle Will Rock*. Using the *Caesar* set, chairs were placed in two rows on the first raised platform, from which the cast descended without effort to join Marc on the apron for their individual scenes, which they performed "in one," in the manner of a vaudeville act, then returned to their seats. The chorus (reduced to twelve) was seated on the second platform, above and a few feet behind the cast.

We opened *The Cradle* on the night of December 5th for a *New Theatre* Benefit audience and the press, which now gave us the critical coverage we had never received at the Venice.* For the second time in a month, our notices surpassed our fondest hopes. Only this time, I was not around to rejoice. Very early the next morning, having read some of the notices the previous night and some by electric light before dawn, I drove up the river to Poughkeepsie on business that had nothing to do with the Mercury.

* See previous chapter.

It is difficult to understand by what miracle of schizophrenic energy I was able to perform the two full-time functions I had undertaken in the winter of 1937–38: to preside at the birth of the Mercury Theatre and guide its destiny during the first mad months of its existence while discharging my duties as associate professor of English and head of the Drama Production Department at Vassar College for Girls.

By getting up at five in the morning two days a week, fast driving and a lot of telephoning I was just able to fulfill my contractual obligations which, in addition to eight hours of teaching each week, called for three productions, of which the first was scheduled for December 10th, five days after the opening of *The Cradle Will Rock*.

There were between twenty and thirty girls in drama production. Less than a third of them were interested in theatre. I conducted my classes informally, with limited preparation, counting on my accumulated theatrical knowledge and the glamor of my recent successes to hold their interest. If I brought them anything, it was the sense of big-time, professional theatre which clung to me as I came roaring onto the campus twice a week and slid to a screeching stop in front of the experimental theatre building—a whiff of show business to which I added visits by such theatrical figures as Marc Blitzstein, Jean Rosenthal, Orson Welles and Virgil Thomson. Whatever deficiencies there may have been in my academic instruction I hoped to make up to them with my production.

Vassar's Drama Production Department had become quite famous under Hallie Flanagan in the late twenties and early thirties for its experimental performances of works by Strindberg, the Italian futurist Marinetti, Auden and Isherwood, Paul Green, Shakespeare, Afinogenov, Lope de Vega and T. S. Eliot, whose dramatic debut had taken place there with *Sweeney Agonistes*. As a suitable successor to these theatrical adventures I chose Jean Cocteau's version of the Oedipus legend—*The Infernal Machine*. It was more difficult than I had expected; during the last two weeks of rehearsal I forbade all girls involved in the production to attend any other classes whatsoever. The sets and costumes, the raked open stage with varicolored floor coverings and the vaguely Cretan line of the clothes, were simple and beautiful; they were designed by a girl from the art department, a pupil of Agnes Rindge, who later became a successful architect. But the real fascination of the production lay in the performance of Jocasta.

My one serious reservation about doing the play had been the problem of finding a nineteen-year-old student capable of playing a sophisticated, beautiful, sex-hungry woman of middle age who would not appear ridiculous as the wife-mother of the thirty-year-old faculty member who was generally regarded as the only possible Oedipus on campus. I found her in my own department —with a ripe figure, a broad, sensual, beautiful face and a rich voice. It was ideal casting—except that this wonderful girl had a horrifying, choking stammer, so grievous that, in class, she would have to write her questions or answers on strips of paper which she passed up to the teacher. She assured me, and so did her friends, that this was a purely nervous impediment and that she had acted before with no difficulty. (Having been a stammerer myself I was disposed to believe her.) I had no choice. I covered her with another girl who could never have played the part and began rehearsal. For a month I ignored the stammer: I let her gurgle and hiccup her way through scenes without comment. Then, very gradually, as she made the transformation from herself to Jocasta, it began to diminish. At the first dress rehearsal, as soon as she got under lights and into her costume (a voluptuous, silken garment with a deep décolleté) it completely vanished and she gave a performance that was surprising and disturbing in a girl of nineteen for its naked, palpable passion.

In February I put on that infallible Elizabethan piece *The Knight of the Burning Pestle:* the part of the simple-minded apprentice was played by Eleanor Ruggles, who may have derived some benefit from the course, since she later became a successful theatrical biographer.* For my third production I did

* *Prince of Players: Edwin Booth,* by Eleanor Ruggles, W. W. Norton, New York, 1953.

a curious bill of three short plays of American family life, directed by the students themselves: O'Neill's *Before Seven,* Wilder's *The Happy Journey to Camden and Trenton* and, through some inexplicable perversity, *I Have Seen Myself Before,* by a former colleague on the Federal Theatre, Virgil Geddes (who had recently picketed the Theatre Guild for not performing his works). It concerned one George Emery Blum, an unemployed mortician of the depression era who, in order to entertain a rich acquaintance who has promised him a job, sacrifices the family's pet chicken and tearfully serves it for dinner. The rich man, impressed by the sacrifice, goes home and murders his wife's lap dog, thus restoring the domestic happiness which had been threatened by her excessive preoccupation with her pet. Both faculty and student body were visibly shaken by this little piece of Americana, but the night watchman, who saw it from the back of the house, pronounced it the first sensible play he had seen in his ten years of attending D. P. productions.

By mid-December *The Infernal Machine* had gone off, the girls had left for their Christmas holiday and I was free to devote myself entirely, once again, to the affairs of the Mercury; to make arrangements for the continuance of *The Cradle* and to supervise the final rehearsals of the second production of the Mercury's repertory season.

On his return from his New Hampshire retreat Orson had brought back, besides the final text and designs for *Julius Caesar,* an edited copy of *The Shoemaker's Holiday,* with which I immediately fell in love and which we soon substituted, by common consent, for *The Silent Woman*—to be followed by *The Duchess of Malfi* and *Heartbreak House.* Dekker's Elizabethan domestic comedy was the perfect companion to Shakespeare's political melodrama: gay, colorful and democratic, it had a charming, nonsensical musical-comedy plot and more bawdry than Broadway was accustomed to seeing outside of burlesque houses.

We had known we would have to add actors to the company as the repertory increased, but *Shoemaker* called for more than we had anticipated. We ended up with seven additions to our weekly payroll. For Simon Eyre, the merry shoemaker, later Lord Mayor of London, we cast Whitford Kane, whom we had always thought of as one of the company; for his impossible wife, Marian Waring-Manley; to play the philandering Master Hammond, we invited Vincent Price, who had made a hit the year before as Prince Albert opposite Helen Hayes in *Victoria Regina;* Sybil, the busy maid, was Edith Barrett, of the great acting family of that name. (She and Vincent Price met at rehearsal and had their wedding party on our stage.) Ruth Ford, a protégée of Pavel Tchelitchew, played the ingenue, Jane; Fred Tozere was Sir Hugh Lacy; Alice Frost, a creamy blonde and one of the reigning queens of radio, played the beauteous Rose.

Once again the set design was Orson's, executed by Samuel Leve under Jean's supervision. Thanks to their joint ingenuity it was possible, by rotating the whole central section of the *Caesar* platform so that the fan-shaped rear ramp now faced the audience, to give the stage an entirely new shape with a minimum of movement and expense. The set itself suggested the stylized configuration of a sixteenth-century city: from materials that were intentionally plain and rough—natural wood, burlap and unpainted strips from used orange crates—it managed to create a stage picture that struck one observer as one-third Elizabethan, one-third Italian deep perspective and one-third workable nonsense.

A high burlap cyclorama enclosed the stage and concealed the tragic blood-red of our brick walls. We continued to use the *Caesar* forestage, now covered with cocoa matting; immediately upstage of it there were three framed inner stages, side by side, filling the entire width of the proscenium arch and each shut off by burlap curtains. The central one, when its curtain was open, represented a London street about ten feet wide running uphill and upstage between tall wooden houses in false perspective. The side stages were smaller: one represented the interior of the Guildhall, the other Simon Eyre's shop where he and his journeymen plied their trade and exchanged their earthy jokes. The whole thing had a feeling of lightness, simplicity, gaiety and style, "very much in the tradition of Palladio's theatre at Vicenza."

Our costumes were designed by Millia Davenport, my neighbor in New City. They were in period—heightened for dramatic and comic effect and made in solid, bright colors and plain materials—wool, jersey and felt rather than silk and brocade. More interested in men's than in women's costumes, she was assiduous in her measuring of male crotches and her codpieces (carefully tailored and personally adjusted) were among the more striking items of this generally lusty production.

Virgil Thomson was completing the score of *The River* for Pare Lorentz and he and Marc Blitzstein were also assembling background music for a documentary film of the Spanish Civil War, *The Spanish Earth,* for which Ernest Hemingway had written the narration. The music for *The Shoemaker's Holiday* was therefore assigned to another member of the family—Lehman Engel, who had conducted the orchestra and chorus for *The Cradle* and who was using our stage on Sunday afternoons for recitals of his New York Madrigal Society. Since we were playing in repertory he was forced to use the same limited instrumentation as Marc had used so effectively in *Caesar*—horn, trumpet, drums and Hammond organ. Faced with the necessity of adapting this combination to the requirements of a light-hearted, ingenuous comedy, he solved the problem by writing "an entire score of duets for trumpet and horn with occasional percussive folderol."

By mid-December these various elements had been brought together without too much difficulty or pain and we were ready for technical and dress rehearsals. This was one production in which there was to be no dramatic lighting—just general illumination with minor variations as the action moved from day to night and from one part of the stage to another. Spared the agony of all-night lighting sessions, our working hours remained reasonable and there was a relaxed air of confidence and affection about the whole production that was unlike anything I had experienced before with my protean partner.

ACT TWO

On Christmas Day we gave our usual sold-out evening performance of *Julius Caesar*. After the bravoes that greeted the
final call, Orson stepped forward and dropping his solemn Brutus manner, announced that, in honor of the festive season, the
Mercury was offering a small Christmas gift to its customers: at
midnight we would give the first preview of our next production—*The Shoemaker's Holiday* (applause and cheers) which
they were all invited to attend (more applause, whistles and
cheers). Since it would take about an hour and a half to make
the change-over, members of the audience were given the choice
of going out and refreshing themselves and returning, with
friends if they wished, on a first-come, first-served basis; or, if they
preferred, since we used no house curtain, they could remain in
their seats and watch the crew changing sets, which they might
find interesting. Amid renewed applause the worklights were
turned on, the crew invaded the stage and the central platform
began to pivot. About half the audience remained in the lighted
house and watched the city of London take form while the actors
and extras, in their dressing rooms, between hot dogs and hamburgers, were changing from the drab greens and faded black of
contemporary Rome into the bright, padded costumes of Elizabethan England. At 11:45, with the new set in place, and Jean
calling for her opening light cue, it was discovered that our two
electricians, who had gone out for a quick, added Christmas
celebration, had not returned. They were found, after a frantic
search of the neighboring bars, walking up Sixth Avenue in the
wrong direction. Hustled back to the theatre, hoisted onto their
platform and plied with cartons of black coffee, they applied
themselves to their switchboards under Jeannie's watchful eye.

At midnight exactly, with a fanfare by Lehman Engel, while
George Zorn tried to cope with the two or three hundred extra
persons who had poured in at the last moment from Times
Square, we began our first public performance of *The Shoemaker's Holiday*. Thrilled but rattled, at first, by unexpected
waves of laughter and applause, the company soon settled down
and went on to surpass itself. At 1:16 A.M. it was over and as the

theatre began to empty into Forty-first Street for the second time that night, we knew we had another hit.*

The Shoemaker's Holiday, which opened officially on New Year's Day (388 years to the day after it was first performed before Queen Elizabeth), "struck Broadway like a brisk wind." It was "the funniest jig of the season" and "the most entertaining theatrical event of the month."

> If there was any doubt after *Julius Caesar* that the Mercury is the liveliest drama household in this town, *The Shoemaker's Holiday* should dispel it.

Once again, Orson's direction was much admired:

> It is swift and certain with a pattern that is consistently gay, full of gusto and wit. The total effect is one of poetry that derives from a vital inner bounce, a festival surface and a love of life.

And, once again, the Mercury Company (with its new additions) was praised for its individual and ensemble work:

> The effect of spontaneity and fun rather than competition is a brilliant achievement.
> *The Shoemaker's Holiday* looks and sounds like spontaneous revelry, but it represents the hard work of this talented new group whose ambition is, in the word's best sense, theatrical. . . . The best of these jackanapes in droopy drawers and flapping codpieces is Hiram Sherman whose fingernail playing of low comedy won him a first night ovation.

One particularly bright star had emerged from the production—Hiram Sherman as the lewd journeyman, Firk. The *Times* hailed him as "a clown of the first order" and saw in him "the incarnation of the comic spirit of the play," thus vindicating

---

* *The Shoemaker's Holiday* was one of the shortest shows ever to be presented on Broadway. After it had shaken down, its playing time was reduced to one hour and nine minutes, without intermission. On one occasion a lone customer who lingered in the men's room returned to his seat and was astonished to find the theatre empty for what he assumed to be the start of the second act.

Orson's unwavering faith in this plump and reticent companion of his youth. By the same token it was undoubtedly Sherman's performance that caused raised eyebrows among members of the Catholic press, who protested the "coarseness of the language" and the "obtrusiveness of the codpieces." The only other objection came from the visiting English critic Ivor Brown, who admitted that he had enjoyed himself but felt that "in its preoccupation with boisterous fun" the Mercury had left out "a kind of lyrical tenderness and a sweet opportunity for song and dance." He claimed that we had given only the "strong meat" and omitted the "tender lettuce."

All in all, it was a triumph—the third in seven weeks. And the general attitude toward us was summed up in a piece that appeared in the *Times* the following Sunday:

MERCURY GOING UP

Although the success of the Mercury's *Julius Caesar* was an occasion for great rejoicing, the success of *The Shoemaker's Holiday* perhaps deserves more. Many promising movements in the theatre have disintegrated after an exhilarating beginning; many organizations have had one good shot in their arsenal.

Julius Caesar was produced only seven weeks ago and straightway became a resounding hit. An organization with less enthusiasm for producing would have been content to bask in success and take in dollars as rapidly as they came. But since November 12th the Mercury has employed its slack time of Sunday nights reviving Marc Blitzstein's *The Cradle Will Rock* while staging *The Shoemaker's Holiday*. It thus becomes a repertory theatre. More repertories have been destroyed by a hit than you can shake a stick at. But already the Mercury is mumbling about productions of *King Henry* IV (Parts 1 and 2) and *Henry* V in a consolidated version, Webster's *The Duchess of Malfi*, Shaw's *Heartbreak House*, Gillette's *Too Much Johnson* and Wilde's *The Importance of Being Earnest*. Although theatregoers have learned to let imposing announcements slip into one ear and out the other, there is every reason to believe that Orson Welles and John Houseman not only mean what they say but also have an ability to do it.

VIII

THE MERCURY came into being in mid-depression at a time when subsidy and deficit were obscure and dirty words in the theatre. Too late for individual millionaires' capricious benefactions (like those of the late Otto Kahn), too early for the calculated munificence of the foundations, we had to rely on our wits to survive. Having wrung a few thousand dollars from our friends to get us floated, we were left to sink or swim in the rough seas of the profit system. We chose to swim with one hand tied behind our back: by refusing to exploit our hits and by continuing to produce successes of which we could not possibly take advantage, we were playing a losing game with dice which we had loaded against ourselves.

Of our three hits, there was only one we could present outside the repertory structure to which we had committed ourselves. That was *The Cradle Will Rock*. Following the reviews of our first Sunday performance, both Marc and the Mercury had received offers—from labor organizations anxious to have the show played all over the country and from commercial producers eager to give it a Broadway run. Marc was of two minds. He wanted to be a hero in the labor movement but, after so many years of hardship, he was not averse to receiving a substantial weekly check as an Equity performer in addition to triple royalties for the book, lyrics and score of a commercial production.

By mutual consent we chose a Broadway run: the offer we accepted was that of a minor show-business figure named Sam Grisman, who was enjoying a brief opulence in the mid-thirties as co-producer of *Tobacco Road*. Among his precipitate investments, he had acquired the old Forty-eighth Street Theatre (where *Tobacco Road* had run for four years), redecorated it and rechristened it the Windsor. This was the new home into which we moved Marc's labor opera in the first week of 1938. We undertook to supply the show as performed that Sunday night at the Mercury. All other risks and expenses were Grisman's. The scale was to be the same as ours and profits were to be split fifty-fifty.

The Cradle never seemed as satisfying and dynamic at the Windsor as it had in the vastness of the Venice or the intimacy of the Mercury. There was something incongruous about its austere staging and radical sentiments in the garish luxury of a renovated Broadway playhouse. And just before we opened there, something happened that was worse than incongruous.

The Cradle was a passionately pro-union work. But the unionism it advocated was the new industrial unionism of John L. Lewis' CIO rather than the old-time craft unionism of the American Federation of Labor. Each night when Howard da Silva's hand went up and the fingers were folded, one by one, into a closed fist, his symbolic gesture provoked ringing applause from our left-wing audiences. It also received unfavorable attention from officials of the Musicians' Local #802—one of the staunchest bastions of craft unionism in the country. Now that *The Cradle Will Rock* was about to start a commercial run in a contract house controlled by the union, they demanded, as a minimum, the original Maxine Elliott orchestra of twenty-eight, which they grudgingly reduced, finally, to twelve musicians and a conductor. When Marc and I protested that this was a concert

performance and that we did not need, did not want and had no
intention of using anything but a piano, they replied that this
was our privilege but that it was the Union's business to enforce
the rules. It surprised them, they added, that an author whose
work showed such concern for union organization should object
to a minimal union orchestra for its performance. This was the
end of the conversation.

The Cradle ran for thirteen weeks; for thirteen weeks, eight
times a week, twelve union musicians with their instruments and
a contractor-conductor with his baton arrived at the theatre half
an hour before curtain time, signed in and descended to the
basement where they remained, engrossed in card games and the
reading of newspapers, while their composer colleague exhausted
himself at the piano upstairs. When the sounds of applause indicated that the show was over, they put away their cards, newspapers and racing forms, put on their hats and coats, picked up
their instrument cases, signed out and left the theatre. For this
they received, each Friday night, several hundred dollars more
than the entire cast and virtually doubled the running cost of the
show by their presence.

The Cradle was the first of my expansionist operations. The
second involved the exploitation of our first and strongest asset,
Julius Caesar. Within a few days of its opening we had been
approached by a number of Broadway managements, all excited
by the idea of a smash hit with no scenery and all eager to help
us milk our surprise success in a large Broadway house at
advanced prices. I refused, and they came back with a new
thought: that a second company be formed and sent out immediately on an extended road tour to take advantage of our
enormous publicity. We rejected this too, at first. Orson, in particular, saw himself as another Henry Irving or Edwin Booth,
leading his company on a triumphal tour of the hinterland, and
he wanted no interference with this vision. My own opposition to
the tour lasted two weeks. After that I found irresistible arguments in its favor.

This change of heart was attributable, in part, to megalomania. But, more directly, it stemmed from a growing realization that, for all our astonishing chain of successes, the Mercury was in serious financial trouble. Our advance sales continued heavy and, by supplying us with a continuous flow of ready cash, obscured the real danger of our situation. The cost of the *Shoemaker* production, though modest by Broadway standards, had absorbed the few thousand dollars of profits we had made since the opening of *Julius Caesar*. Our weekly gross was limited by the size of our theatre; our expenses were not. Our maximum intake at the Mercury, with every seat sold, was just under $6,000 a week. Our weekly cost including rentals, promotion, house staff, stage crew and an acting company that, with *Shoemaker* in the repertory, numbered over fifty, came to $6,500. With two smash hits in its theatre, the Mercury was going a little deeper into debt with each passing week. A way must be found to correct this absurd situation. The road tour of *Caesar* seemed to be it.

The best of our proposals came from Alex Yokel, producer of *Three Men on a Horse*. He offered us a five-thousand-dollar advance and a half-share of the profits after production costs had been paid. We accepted and began casting. For Brutus we engaged Tom Powers, for years a leading actor with the Theatre Guild; he lacked some of Orson's "high-souled nobility" but he had sincerity and authority. For Antony we chose Edmund O'Brien, who, at twenty-six, had played Shakespeare with John Gielgud, Maurice Evans and Katharine Cornell. Cassius was Herbert Ransom, a choleric, red-faced pillar of The Players' club; Caesar was Lawrence Fletcher and Cinna the Poet was played by Vincent Donohue, a pale skinny boy (who became a Broadway director and staged *The Sound of Music* shortly before he died). For the mob we detached a few of our own stalwarts, counting on them to take the talking parts and to drill local students and enthusiasts to follow their movements in the crowd scenes. Rehearsals were held on the empty stage of the National Theatre, two blocks down the street. It was while sitting in the darkened auditorium of that agreeable house (today the Billy Rose) watching our road company's first run-through, that another,

337

even more wildly expansionist notion began to form in my mind. I have never been able to decide whether it was wise or foolish, whether it aided the Mercury or helped to destroy it.

I was not a free agent. The situation which had begun to disturb me a month earlier was getting worse rather than better. We might be the darlings of New York and the smash hit of the theatrical season, but under the glitter of our three successes it was becoming evident that we were headed for bankruptcy. With our capital spent, no reserves, little coming in from the *Cradle,* nothing expected from the road company for some time and the need to finance the two new productions we had already announced—*The Duchess of Malfi* and *Heartbreak House*—I did not see how we could last out the season.

Convinced that what we were doing was far too important and exciting to permit any squalid, short-term financial impediments to check us on our sweeping forward march, I began to work on Orson with my new idea—which was to move the entire Mercury operation two blocks west for a couple of months to the much larger National Theatre. Since its orchestra floor was more than twice as big as the Mercury's we would finally be able to satisfy the carriage trade's clamor for our higher-priced seats; at the same time it would permit Sylvia to sell theatre parties and students' group tickets to her heart's content. At a conservative estimate we would be certain to come out several thousand dollars a week ahead; in ten weeks we could accumulate enough to pay for our new productions and carry us through to the end of the theatrical year.

As soon as this idea became known it was violently opposed by a voluble minority of the company headed by Hiram Sherman. They felt we were making a fatal mistake in abandoning our home so soon after occupying it, and that in attempting to increase our audience, we were, in fact, dissipating it. We were a repertory theatre, they argued. The more people we turned away the longer we would be able to keep *Caesar* and *Shoemaker* running. And if it meant carrying them over into our second year, so much the better: it would be a protection for a season that might not be as lucky or successful as the first.

These were sound arguments and I had already made them all to myself. In the circumstances I had no choice but to override them. However, since I was well aware of the dangers of the move and anxious to avoid the accusation that we were getting too big for our boots, I insisted with the management of the National that we retain our Mercury price scale, including our much advertised fifty-cent seats. Against all Broadway precedent I made them "split" their orchestra floor: the three hundred best seats in the house would sell at the regular price of $3.30 while the rest of the orchestra and the mezzanine would still be available at our original price of $2.20. The move was set for January 24th, four days after the opening of the road tour of *Julius Caesar* in Providence, Rhode Island.

This took place with Orson, Jeannie and myself present, in a howling blizzard that almost prevented us from getting our trucks into the theatre alley and unloaded on time. "Flung across a bare stage!" was a critic's phrase which Yokel had taken to his heart and used widely in his publicity. It never failed to provoke embittered merriment among the crews who, each time they entered or left a theatre, had to wrestle for fourteen hours with one of the heaviest productions ever sent out on the road—except possibly the Circus. Our basic platform, which Orson had insisted on reproducing exactly (and which cost Yokel more than three times as much as the original set), represented more than three thousand cubic feet of lumber, to which a series of rising ramps and stairs and wingpieces had to be added, traps dug, subterranean stairs installed and unusually heavy equipment hung in special places for the lighting effects that gave the production its special quality.

Leaving a trail of barn-red stagehouses in its wake, *Julius Caesar* was "flung across a bare stage" in Providence, Boston, Hartford, Washington, D.C., Cleveland, Chicago and Toronto to phenomenal reviews but only moderate business. This was due to the precipitate nature of the venture, which received none of the advance promotion and organized sales without which no road show can hope to survive. To make up for this lack of preparation, Yokel (a former press agent) tried various high-pressure selling techniques. He hired a famous circus advance man by the name of Ned Alford, whose working uniform was a matching chocolate-colored cutaway and bowler hat and whose publicity methods delighted us in theory but were not always successful in practice. Our own original *"Death of a Dictator!"* promotion was carried several steps further: the streets of each city we visited were bright with hundreds of huge colored posters showing a Mussolini-type tyrant in his death throes; hundreds of thousands of dummy tabloids were printed and distributed with huge headlines and lurid photographs of the assassination. Our fears that such selling methods might harm us with the critics proved groundless. Conservative Boston, our next stop after Providence, vied with New York in the extravagance of its praise:

> Shakespeare's *Julius Caesar* is an astonishing spectacle, the most extraordinary thing of its kind in the recent annals of drama . . . it is the freshest, most vital, most forceful, most completely compelling Shakespeare that we of this generation have yet seen.

So raved Elliott Norton, while others, the *Christian Science Monitor* among them, assured their readers that the "effectiveness of this production has not been exaggerated. Rather it has been underestimated . . . It should be seen and discussed not once but often, both as entertainment and portent."

Yet our business was not spectacular and Yokel, that simple and sanguine man, was bitterly disappointed. He must have dropped quite a lot of money on the tour; the Mercury for its part never received a penny beyond its first five-thousand-dollar advance.

January, 1938, was a fantastic month. *Shoemaker* opened on the 1st, *Cradle* on the 4th, the road company of *Caesar* on the 20th and, on the 24th, we moved to the National. After rehearsing all weekend to adapt our productions to its larger stage and auditorium, we opened our ten-week repertory engagement there with *Julius Caesar* followed two nights later by *The Shoemaker's Holiday*. Framed in by massive red towers such as we had designed for the road, *Caesar* seemed to benefit from the greater depth and space, while *Shoemaker* suffered slightly but not seriously from the loss of intimacy.

Gypsies that we were, we soon adjusted to our new home. We may have missed the shabby familiarity of our Mercury surroundings, but in most ways life was easier at the National. Orson, as usual, occupied the star dressing room, which he also used as his office. After their sheer three-story cell block, the company's dressing rooms seemed accessible and comfortable, and our new wing towers made entrances and exits less nerve-wracking than before. The extras still dressed in the basement, which was warm, well-lit and ratless. For myself and Augusta Weissberger an agreeable suite was found at the rear of the orchestra floor with a French window opening onto the long, curving alley that led from the stage door to Forty-first Street. The mounted policeman on the beat had a horse which regarded this area as its own private domain and spent hours at the glass door spying on my activities.

Business was excellent from the start. So, after their initial doubts, was the company's morale. Then, in mid-February, something happened that further justified our move. *The Cradle Will Rock* had been running for eight weeks at the Windsor to grosses that were good but not good enough. The cheap seats were all filled: there seemed to be no limit to the left-wing audiences Sylvia was able to muster. But the orchestra seats, even at our reduced prices, were not selling. This should have surprised no one: Marc's labor opera was hardly carriage-trade entertainment. Yet it was depressing, when I wandered over to the Windsor of an evening, to see the main floor half-empty and to think of those thirteen cardplayers in the basement.

After some weeks of this, Grisman became restless and, thinking it might help him with the agencies, insisted on reinstating the full Broadway price for the main floor. When I refused, he announced that he was invoking his stop clause to terminate our contract. With the Mercury lying dark seven blocks away this was precisely what I had been waiting for. We moved *The Cradle* back to Forty-first Street, where it played to what looked like full houses for the remainder of its thirteen-week run. The card-players may have found the Mercury basement less to their liking than that of the Windsor, but everyone else was happy to be home and, economically, it was better to be playing in our own theatre where the receipts, such as they were, were all ours.

So now during February and March, the Mercury had one hundred and twenty-four actors performing in four shows in three theatres. Our three New York shows were playing within two blocks of each other on West Forty-first Street. We renamed it Mercury Street, and without permission from the city, put up temporary signs to that effect on the corners of Sixth and Seventh Avenues and Broadway. And we engaged a young specialist in industrial graphics to design an elegant poster, headed WELCOME TO MERCURY STREET, in which each of our productions was clearly symbolized by small, stylized figures: fascist-military; renaissance-comic; a cradle in a treetop in a rising wind.

Our next scheduled show was Webster's *The Duchess of Malfi,* which, since we first started announcing it in the early days of Project #891, had acquired certain artistic accretions. One was a superb décor designed by Pavel Tchelitchew. Originally conceived as an offering of the Federal Theatre, it had extremely lavish scenery and costumes. There was one particularly striking rendering of a green satin peignoir to be worn by the doomed duchess for her murder: at the moment of maximum terror her long red hair was shown standing to a height of four feet above her head. When I asked Pavlik how he expected us to achieve this, he explained quite seriously that her wig must be so rigged that at the critical moment each hair, attached by a thin copper wire to an overhead baton, could be raised on a line manipulated from the fly floor high above the stage! Another commitment involved the role of the Duchess, which we had offered to that admirable actress Aline MacMahon. Now she was back from Hollywood and available.

Our first reading was held on the stage of the National following a performance of *Shoemaker.* It began at 10:15 P.M., and it was a disaster. With the exception of Welles himself, whose fantastic voice seemed ideally suited to Webster's extravagances, the actors seemed incapable of capturing the mood of the piece, which sounded muddled, verbose and in its wildest moments, merely foolish. Having failed to ignite in its early scenes, it dragged itself on through the night, growing more dreary and embarrassing as the hours went by. When it was finally ended, some time after 1 A.M., we thanked the cast and bade them goodnight. Then Orson and I held a brief, private meeting in his dressing room. There was no argument. *The Duchess of Malfi* joined *'Tis Pity She's a Whore* in the locked cupboard of our discarded loves.* We abandoned her with regret but with some relief. By dropping one production we were greatly helping our financial situation. But, beyond that, there was something about the piece itself, magnificent as it was in the wild poetry of its monstrous emotions, that was wholly out of tune with the current tone of the Mercury company and the "social-conscious" attitude of our fervent audiences. Pavlik snatched the drawings for which he had never been paid, and Aline MacMahon, not unnaturally, turned her back on us and refused the part of Hesione Hushabye in *Heartbreak House* when we offered it to her some weeks later.

With one less show to produce we postponed rehearsals for a while. We gave as our excuse that we were still waiting to hear from Bernard Shaw, to whom I had written requesting the rights to his play, and from whom I had received no reply. I wrote again, enclosing selected reviews of our shows. But the truth was that we were only too happy to continue basking for a few weeks longer in the sunshine of our miraculous success.

However, lest anyone accuse us of idleness, we did manage, during that time, to get ourselves involved in still another project: the recording, on phonograph records, of complete performances of Shakespeare's plays by Welles and the Mercury company. Since the invention of the long-playing disk, this has

---

* After twenty years I returned to *The Duchess* and produced it for the Phoenix Theatre in collaboration with Jack Landau, who had had a resounding success with the same author's *White Devil* the year before. Once again I failed.

become standard practice. I believe ours were the first to be made. I arranged to have them recorded at 78 r.p.m. and pressed by Columbia Records (with eight to ten heavy disks per album) and merchandised in association with Harper and Brothers, who put out accompanying volumes of the text edited and illustrated by Orson Welles at the age of seventeen and now reprinted from the original plates set up on the Todd School press five years before.

Using all the resources of radio—music, sound, crowd noises etc.,—Orson recorded *Julius Caesar, The Merchant of Venice* and *Twelfth Night.* The albums were praised but they never really sold. They were too long and expensive for private playing and, educationally, we were ahead of our time. The original editions were gradually sold out and no further pressings were made.

In spite of Lent, business remained wonderful at the National. Little by little, as the weeks went by, the specter of bankruptcy began to recede. And in my relationship with Orson this was a period of relative peace and affection. We had been far too busy, since the opening of *Julius Caesar,* to indulge in those spasms of hostility which so often followed the success of our projects. Tension continued (our relationship would have been unthinkable without it) , but during this winter of our content there were few of those ugly, neurotic scenes that had marked the period of our anxious beginnings and were to become increasingly frequent in the months ahead.

Though life was peaceful at the National, it was by no means uneventful. There was, for instance, the incident of the flood. We had a boy in the company named Arthur Anderson: he was thirteen, gangling, with a long neck and prominent Adam's apple, curly hair and a nice smile. As a successful child actor on radio (where Orson had discovered him) he contributed to the support of his widowed mother and was in every way an admirable youngster. He played a Cheapside urchin in *Shoemaker,* but his main contribution to our repertory was in *Julius Caesar,* in which he played the role of Brutus' page, Lucius, first in the orchard scene, then, later, in the tent before Philippi where he sang his troubled master to sleep. It was a lovely lyric interlude— a last moment of peace before the final, inevitable catastrophe.

Between his two appearances Arthur had a long, tedious wait, and it was here that he and the Mercury ran into trouble. Our first intimation that all was not well came when a chronic shortage of light bulbs was reported in the third-floor dressing rooms. The reason was soon discovered. Master Anderson, having played his orchard scene and finished his homework, had been conducting experiments to discover the shock-resistant powers of electric light bulbs: he had been hurling them out of his dressing room window against the bricks of the opposite wall and comparing the different kinds of pops they made. He was ordered to desist, and being an obedient boy, he did. Instead, he started a series of new experiments: standing on his dressing-room chair one Wednesday afternoon with a box of matches in his hand, he began testing the melting point of the little copper tongues located beneath each sprinkler valve.

Two floors below, on-stage, Brutus had just ascended the pulpit above the body of Caesar and was urging the crowd below to "be patient to the last." At that moment, unperceived by the audience, a few drops of rain began to fall. Intent upon the action of the play, assuming it was some kind of leak in the roof above the grid, Orson continued to address the crowd in a measured, reasonable tone:

> If there be in this assembly any dear friend of Caesar, to
> him I say that Brutus' love to Caesar was no less than his. If
> then that friend demand why Brutus rose against Caesar, this
> is my answer. . . .

The answer was never heard, for at that moment, what had been an accelerating drizzle turned to a heavy shower and then, within a few seconds, into a deluge of tropical rain. Brutus paused, looked up into the fly floor, glared questioningly into the wings, then turned back, as clouds of water began to envelop him and, in the sincere, clear-souled tones of the noble Brutus, urged the audience to remain in their seats and not to be alarmed. As the asbestos curtain began to fall and half the stage lights went out, he was seen running for shelter with the rest of the Roman citizenry through a solid sheet of falling water, while blasts of blue fire and showers of sparks flashed around them from the short-circuiting dimmer boards.

Alerted by the ringing of the fire bell, I rushed through the door that led backstage just in time to see our carpenter struggling with the handle that shut off the sprinkler system. Assured that there was no fire, I ran back, while others calmed the audience, to cancel the automatic call to the fire department. While I was dialing, I looked up and saw the mounted policeman galloping along the alley toward the stage door.

Two minutes later a pale, very frightened Arthur Anderson was brought into my office under guard. Appalled at the enormity of what he had done, Arthur's first instinct, when the water began to spout, had been to escape. Halfway down the alley he thought of his mother, stopped, trotted back to the stage door, slipped a coin into the pay phone and was whispering: "Hey, Mom, I'll be home early," when he was seized.

As soon as he realized he was not going to jail, Arthur became amazingly calm. He was sorry for what he had done. He had $184.82 in his personal savings account which he was placing at our disposal to pay for any damage he might have caused. I ordered him back to his dressing room, still under guard, to await his cue for the last scene. He asked if he might call his mother again and I said yes.

Meantime, on stage, the crew had replaced the fuses and mopped the stage floor and platforms. Ten minutes after the start of the shower I stepped out from under the rising asbestos and assured the audience that the show would resume where it had left off. There was a moment of darkness and a roar from the Hammond organ. Then as the lights dimmed up, Brutus, his hair slicked down as after a bath, his dark suit clinging damply to his body, was seen climbing slowly back into the pulpit above the drenched Roman mob. "Be patient to the last," he began—to loud applause.

On that same stage, some weeks later, a less comic incident occurred. The conspirators, when they attacked Caesar in the Senate, did so with heavy rubber daggers with aluminum-painted blades which they jabbed savagely from various angles into the dictator's dark-green coat. All except Brutus. Feeling that his final confrontation with the tyrant needed the reality of a gleaming blade, Orson used a bright steel hunting knife to deliver the decisive blow. For more than a hundred performances he had held its sharp point against the cloth that covered Joseph Holland's chest; then, as Caesar clung to him in his death agony, he masked the final thrust with a turn of his body.

One spring night, without either of them being aware of it, the blade went through the cloth and slipped quite painlessly into Joe Holland's chest and through an artery in the region of his heart. As Caesar fell at Brutus' feet the conspirators surrounded him. When they scattered again after the oath some minutes later one of them was seen to slip, recover himself and glance down, with a sudden look of apprehension, at the inert body of the dead dictator. This curious behavior was repeated during the scene with Marc Antony, which seemed to play faster and more nervously that night than usual. In the blackout that followed, amid the thunderous organ roar that followed Antony's "Cry havoc and let slip the dogs of war!" members of the cast were able to carry Joe Holland's inert body directly out the stage door and by taxi to the nearest hospital. He left behind him on the platform several pints of blood which, being roughly the same color as the stage floor, was not clearly visible from the front, but caused considerable inconvenience and dismay among the mob as it milled around the base of the pulpit. By the time the Cinna scene was over it had been pretty well spread around and was beginning to dry.

Joseph Holland was in a state of shock when he arrived at the hospital; he received transfusions and remained in bed for several days. He was admired and blamed for lying quite still for almost fifteen minutes while bleeding to death: in evaluating his heroism it must be remembered that the incision was quite painless and that neither he nor Welles nor anyone else was aware of what had happened until the blood began to ooze out from under him. Orson had a short, violent spasm of guilt. Then, when he learned that his victim was not in danger, he developed an angry conviction that the blame was entirely Joe's for making a wrong move and impaling himself on Brutus' stationary blade. Fortunately the incident coincided with the end of the road tour, and Larry Fletcher, the road-company Caesar, was rushed in to take Joe's place during his convalescence. We paid his hospital bills and he never sued us.

Another major event of that spring was the betrothal of Augusta Weissberger. When I had taken her into the Federal Theatre, two years before, she had been a barely competent secretary whom I had chosen from among several dozen applicants because she was the only one who was happy to work in Harlem. When we moved down to Thirty-ninth Street she followed us into the powder room of the Maxine Elliott, where she soon acquired such personal power over Orson and myself that by the time we left the project and formed the Mercury Theatre neither of us could exist without her. By the spring of 1938, when we arrived at the National, this virgin matriarch had, locked in her desk, formal documents, signed by Orson and myself, which gave her powers of attorney in such delicate dealings as contracts, leases, checks, deposits, loans and promissory notes. By indulging us in our habits of idleness, carelessness and helplessness in our personal affairs, she had enveloped us in a web that was no less binding for being entirely for our own good. Her widowed mother (from whom she inherited her pink cheeks, her goodwill and her energy) had, for years, been adding to her modest income by selling insurance to family friends: Orson and I found ourselves buying the best kind of life insurance from her in substantial amounts. Augusta's brother, Arnold, a graduate of Harvard Law School, had been working in the office of a corporation lawyer downtown: he left it for the dangerous adventure of theatrical law with Welles and myself as his first and only

clients.* The Weissberger tribal doctor happened to be an al-
lergist, the very man to help Orson with the hay fever and the
occasional asthma from which he suffered. The family banker, a
bald Irishman with a heart of gold, became our personal financier (very lenient with overdrafts) before acquiring the dubious
privilege of becoming official banker to the Mercury Theatre,
Inc. And now, suddenly, without warning, Augusta Weissberger,
having made us totally dependent upon her, was about to leave
us. She was giving herself to another!

Our fears were groundless. This new move in no way diminished her loyalty or blunted her zeal. The fiancé, Mortimer
Yolken, turned out to be an interior decorator. She married him
in time for him to decorate and furnish the gigantic duplex
which Orson had just rented on East Fifty-seventh Street and the
more modest apartment on West Ninth into which I moved later
that year. For the rest of our triumphal first season and then for
another two years—through our radio successes and theatrical
disasters—while we closed the theatre, moved to Hollywood,
drifted apart and finally broke asunder, Augusta remained
equally faithful to us both and continued to run our personal
affairs with garrulous discretion and emotional efficiency.

Our sojourn at the National was nearing its end and we were
about to start on our next production when I received a surprise
visit, one afternoon, from an unbelievably lovely young woman
with dark-red Irish hair, who arrived unannounced and claimed
she had been sent by one of Orson's former Dublin associates.
Her name was Geraldine Fitzgerald. Stunned by her beauty, I
asked her a few routine questions about her experience in the
theatre, to which she gave lying answers. Then, still bemused, I
led her to Orson's dressing room and left them together to talk

* He never regretted it. Within twenty years he and his partner, Aaron
Frosch, had become the most active theatrical lawyers in the business, with
an Anglo-American clientele that eventually included Rex Harrison, John
Gielgud, Huntington Hartford, Rebekah Harkness, Richard Burton, Elizabeth
Taylor and Igor Stravinsky.

about Dublin. An hour later he confirmed what I already knew—that we had found our Ellie Dunn in *Heartbreak House.**

> Some day we'll be producing a play in which an actor opens a door, a real door and walks in, sits down and begins to talk—and that, I imagine, will be the end of us.

Chubby Sherman's whimsy, uttered in an interview after his triumph in *The Shoemaker's Holiday,* was grimly prophetic—but not quite in the sense that he intended. Our setting for *Heartbreak House,* half ship, half living room, conformed to George Bernard Shaw's stage directions: it was the first solid scenery we had built, and it cost us a fortune since Orson, suddenly concerned with realism, insisted on genuine paneling indoors and real gravel cemented to the ground cloth for the exterior "so the footsteps will sound right." But though it had several real doors, *Heartbreak House* was not the immediate end of us. Rather, it became our fourth consecutive success of the season.

Mr. Shaw's royalty terms, which were stiff, reached us in mid-April. (With them came a typed note, signed G.B.S. in ink: "You would do well to have New York City printed under your street address. My eye was caught by the word Pennsylvania and I sent the envelope to that address. Needless to say it was returned here marked 'Unknown.'") By that time we were in rehearsal, Orson's daughter Christopher had been born and we had moved back into our own theatre.

We had announced in our manifesto that we would not play more than two shows in repertory at one time. It was decided,

---

* Years later Geraldine wrote: "I was very taken with Orson at first sight since he appeared to be so flatteringly, absolutely bowled over by me. He looked at me like Michelangelo's God looking at Adam and Eve before the fall. I had met you a few moments before and you looked at me as Michelangelo's God looks at Adam and Eve *after* the fall—seeing, I thought, only the inexperience, the ordinariness and the embarrassment I was feeling. I was afraid of you. I thought you didn't want me in your theatre and Orson did and that he had to overcome your objections before you let him hire me."

after much debate, that before *Heartbreak House* opened *Shoemaker's Holiday* would be dropped from the repertory. There was still a big untapped audience for the Dekker play and it seemed wise to save it for the following season when we might need it. *Caesar* was still selling out and could be counted on to carry the repertory until the hot weather forced us to close.

We were both in love with *Heartbreak House* but we knew the risks it entailed. Determined to avoid the stigma of stock casting, we found ourselves seeking actors, once again, from the outside. Of the ten characters in the play only four, including Orson, were from our own company. The rest, four of them ladies, formed an exotic group—a far cry from the austerity of our *Julius Caesar* casting six months before. For the star role of Hesione Hushabye (which Orson had half-offered in a fit of alcoholic enthusiasm to the aging Mrs. Patrick Campbell) we engaged Mady Christians.* I admired her beauty and skill but opposed her playing a part that seemed so entirely British; I deferred to Orson's insistence and was proved wrong. Her sister, Lady Utterwood, was played by an Australian—a sexy, middle-aged girl scout, the wife of a well-known New York architect. Brenda Forbes—a companion of Orson's on the Cornell tour— was Nurse Guiness; Geraldine Fitzgerald as Ellie Dunn got insufficient help from Welles and was shamefully treated by George Coulouris in rehearsal; her father was played by Erskine Sanford, a newcomer to the Mercury but not to the part of Mazzini Dunn, which he had created for the Theatre Guild eighteen years before. The Burglar was a dissolute and scholarly Englishman of whom we were all convinced that he was an unfrocked priest. Orson, with pounds of putty and clouds of white hair all over his

---

* Daughter of the long-time director of New York's German Theatre, Mady Christians had become a baroness and a successful actress in Germany before the Nazis; now she had just returned from Hollywood and a frustrated American movie career. Her appearance with the Mercury marked a turn in her fortunes. Six months later she was playing Gertrude to Maurice Evans' Hamlet and, after that, the name part in *I Remember Mama*. Unable to face two persecutions in a lifetime, she died after being investigated and blacklisted as a fellow traveler during the McCarthy purges.

face, played the octogenarian Captain Shotover. And it was in this makeup, with a huge beak of a nose against a pale blue sky, that he appeared on the cover of *Time* over the caption *"From Shadow to Shakespeare, Shoemaker to Shaw,"* accompanied by a five-page story headed MARVELOUS BOY.

It was a long, flashy piece, full of *Time*'s stylistic tricks and special angles—"troubled by his asthma, not troubled by his flat feet"; "with a voice that booms like Big Ben but a laugh like a youngster's giggle"; "his adolescent moon face slowly beginning to resemble a Roman emperor's"—and it was the first to give national circulation to the legends of Welles's gargantuan childhood and puberty. For the Mercury it marked the peak of the year's publicity, and if there was a note of warning in its concluding phrase—

> The brightest moon that has risen over Broadway in years, Welles should feel at home in the sky, for the sky is the only limit to his ambition—

I was too exhilarated to heed it.

The *Time* cover story was timed to coincide with the opening of *Heartbreak House,* and it was fortunate for all concerned that the Mercury did not fall on its face with its final presentation of the season. Two things had made me nervous: first, the probability of a critical backlash after so much extravagant praise and excessive publicity; second, the nature of the production itself. With the realistic performance of a very talky piece by a contemporary author we could not expect the explosions of enthusiasm that had greeted *Caesar* and *Shoemaker.* The best we could hope for were respectful reviews for a conventional but controversial play. And that is what we got.

> On a stage full of scenery, a well-directed company acts one of Mr. Shaw's most interminable plays with dramatic alertness.

> A capital production of one of Shaw's most difficult plays. The Mercury leaves Mr. Shaw no ground for complaint.

This was the tone of our best reviews. Others found the play tedious. Stark Young, our constant and ardent champion, was disappointed by the evening:

> For a moment I took it to be the production that was at fault. Presently I saw that the production was fair enough with some good performances and that the play itself was garrulous, unfelt and tiresome.

The company came off well on the whole. Mady Christians was praised for her "radiant sensibility"; Vincent Price was "humorous and distinguished, an abler actor than any of his previous performances have suggested." Geraldine was "a charming and sincere Ellie Dunn" with whom Richard Watts fell publicly in love.* Coulouris was widely admired as Boss Mangan. Orson's reception was more qualified: "intelligent and intelligible even when he is not more"; "a performance lacking the Shavian crispness expected of Captain Shotover but which in moments where power is needed is thrilling." Orson was disgruntled. For my part, I felt we were lucky.

Heartbreak House opened on April 29th, after a number of previews, and played in repertory with *Julius Caesar* to satisfactory business. *Shoemaker* was in moth balls for the summer and those of its cast who were not in other plays had been reluctantly removed from the payroll. In mid-May I attempted one final piece of manipulation. Since it seemed unlikely that the Shaw play would remain in the repertory during our second year, we decided to give it a month's straight run at the Mercury while we gave *Caesar* a closing fling at the National, replacing Orson, Coulouris and Hoysradt with members of the road company who were back in town. The maneuver was fairly successful and helped to pay off some of the heavy production expense of *Heartbreak House*. Still, summer was upon us: neither theatre was cooled and everyone was getting tired. We announced June 11th as a closing date for our first Mercury season.

* From Forty-first Street she went straight to Hollywood, where, within a year, she gave two beautiful performances—with Laurence Olivier in *Wuthering Heights* and Bette Davis in *Dark Victory*.

We parted with all the customary sentimentalities, wishing each other a happy summer and looking forward to a reunion within a few weeks. Our closing was marked by renewed encomiums in the press:

> The biggest Broadway news for 1937–38 was the Mercury Theatre. . . . To one new and adventurous group, the Mercury Theatre, has gone the lion's share of the year's success. . . . The liveliness that has marked the Mercury's race through the year may well be taken as the chief characteristic of the 1937–38 season.

But the most realistic appraisal of our first season was the one I wrote for the *Times* the day after we closed:

THE SUMMING UP

The Directors of the Mercury Theatre look over their

FIRST YEAR

One day last summer we sat down to write for *The New York Times* a piece about our hopes for the Mercury Theatre. . . . Now that our first season is over, it may be that we have attained enough of a perspective to compare our aim with our accomplishment; to find out how closely we have held to our original intention; to discover where we have taken a different road and why, and to note some of the things we have learned in the ten crowded months that have passed since we first committed ourselves in these columns.

Surprisingly enough, we have kept most of our promises and adhered quite closely to our original schedule. For seven months we have given our plays in repertory and we have discovered for ourselves what everyone told us before we started—that repertory in New York is an enormously expensive business. The technical cost of frequently shifting scenery is high, but we were prepared for that and we planned our productions accordingly. We spent a lot of money publicizing the details of a repertory system which the New York public (accustomed to the long runs of hit plays) continues to find vaguely incomprehensible and disturbing. We were prepared for that, too. What we were not prepared for was

354

the agony of deliberately slashing the run of our two most successful productions at the peak of the season to conform to our repertory schedule. With a chance to take advantage of our reviews, to split our company and play both shows in separate theatres and thus double our receipts, we decided that having announced repertory we would stick to it. In consequence *The Shoemaker's Holiday* closed to standing room after only sixty-four performances to make room for *Heartbreak House.*

After outlining some of our financial problems and apologizing for some of our apparent deviations from strict repertory operation, I summed up what I believed to be our main accomplishment of the season:

> We have played to around a quarter of a million people at an average price of slightly less than a dollar. Of these, twenty to thirty percent represents what is known as the "carriage trade"; forty percent represents collective audiences assembled in the form of theatre parties for modest profits by political, professional, labor and charity organizations; the rest represents window sales at various discounts, for we have distributed one hundred and twenty thousand students' and teachers' cards and we estimate that about one-third of our total audience has come from educational institutions of one sort or another.
>
> To sum up—we've produced a lot of plays. We've played to a lot of people. We've enjoyed it. We have plans—some definite, some still to be worked out. And we'll see you again in September.

Our books were atrociously kept, but certain things were quite evident about the operation of the Mercury Theatre. Through sheer luck with a dash of genius and by being incredibly quick on our feet, we had succeeded, during our first season, in keeping our heads just above water. With our fantastic record of four hits out of four, we had managed, with all our taxes and bills paid, to end the year with about half of what we started with. (This was not the way it appeared on the statement we presented to our stockholders, where our three existent productions were listed as assets at half their original cost. This showed us with a legitimate but fallacious profit of around twenty thousand dollars—and no cash.) With the few thousand dollars that were left, I must try and keep our organization alive through the fallow months of summer, pay our rents and finance the productions of our second season—at which time the rat race would begin again, with much expected of us and the odds heavy against our repeating anything like our recent ratio of success.

Having accepted our uncertain future as an inevitable fact of theatrical life, I tried to plan our 1938–39 season in what seemed a practical and economical way. To keep our theatre alight and maintain our identity as a repertory company, we had devised a production of *The Importance of Being Earnest* in which we would do for Wilde what we had already done for Labiche and Dekker. It was to be an elegant and economical Edwardian high comedy, perfect for our small theatre and for Chubby Sherman, Vincent Price and Brenda Forbes to follow up their success of the previous season in the company of two delicious young women still to be selected—one of them, possibly, Virginia Welles. In repertory with *Shoemaker* this would keep the Mercury in profits and public favor while we concentrated on the serious work of the season—the monster known as *Five Kings*. This was a stupendous project—a compressed and edited version of all the histories except *King John* and *Henry VIII*. It was to be in two parts, the first consisting of *Richard II, Henry IV* Parts 1 and 2, ending with *Henry V;* the second, covering the Wars of the Roses, included all three parts of *Henry VI* and *Richard III*. It was to be performed on successive evenings with the same cast, and Orson predicted—when he first announced it on the 374th anniversary of Shakespeare's birth—that it would be an unforgettable theatrical experience.

The performance of Shakespeare's historical plays in batches has become a commonplace of festival showmanship. In 1938 it was a bold and original notion. It germinated in Orson's mind as a hybrid—by *Caesar* out of *Shoemaker*—but secretly, I always believed, as a means of dealing a crushing blow to that English upstart Maurice Evans, Welles's only serious local competitor in the classical field, who had had the effrontery to follow his much acclaimed *Richard II* with a successful Falstaff—a part which Orson regarded (as he did every great classical role) as exclusively his own. *Five Kings,* by its sheer magnitude, would reduce Mr. Evans once and for all to his true pygmy stature.

For the creation of this colossus I had made what I felt to be a valuable alliance with the Theatre Guild. We would produce *Five Kings* jointly as a Mercury Production presented by the Guild on its subscription series the following winter. This would alleviate our financial burden and it would give Orson the time he needed to prepare such a massive and complicated work.

Satisfied with my arrangements, I drove into the Berkshires for a few days of peace with Mina at Chapelbrook in a world that seemed suddenly and magically free of anxiety and fear. In the flower garden outside her window, its feet bathed in white phlox, stood a new gray-green bronze statue, a Lachaise nude her brother Lincoln had given her. The water in the Baptist's Hole was dark brown and cool and there were wild strawberries in the woods. On the third morning, quite early, the phone rang: it was Augusta Weissberger and she asked me in a rather shaky voice if I had seen *The New York Times.* She then read me the lead item in Zolotow's theatre column in which it was announced that Hiram Sherman had signed with Max Gordon to star in a new topical revue by the author of *Pins and Needles,* to open in mid-September at the Music Box Theatre under the direction of George Kaufman.

I accepted this grim news as true the moment I heard it and I did not, then or later, call Sherman to verify it or to try and persuade him to change his mind. As I drove with a sinking heart between the turning tobacco fields and then down through Danbury and across the Bear Mountain Bridge toward Sneden's Landing, where Orson and Virginia, with their new daughter Christopher, were spending an uneasy summer, I found myself weighing the implications of his defection and trying to find an explanation for it.

Sherman had come to occupy a very special place with the

Mercury. Outside of Welles himself, his had been the outstanding personal success of the season. From our triumphal confusion he had emerged not only as our most versatile and valuable actor but also as the conscience of the company and the mainstay of its morale. Most important of all, he was Orson's oldest and closest friend.

Sherman was fully aware of our plans: he knew what his sudden leaving would do to the Mercury. Yet he must have been negotiating for days, even weeks, without saying a word to either of us. I began to question my judgment of our entire situation. In my anxiety to keep the Mercury afloat, had I misjudged the state of the company? It had seemed to me that morale was high. There was some resentment, I knew, over Welles's increasingly overbearing ways and some irritation over my arbitrary manipulation of the repertory, of which the premature closing of *Shoemaker* was just one example. Bemused by our continuing success, had I underestimated these murmurings? Was Sherman's departure a manifestation of this discontent? In his passionate devotion to the idea of a collective repertory company, had he, like Cassius, begun to wonder upon what meat his former friend was feeding that he was grown so great?

Or was there some more intimate and personal reason? Had he allowed himself to be swayed by his long, emotional relationship with his former teacher, Whitford Kane, with whom he shared an apartment on Fourteenth Street and who had supplied the only discordant note in *The Shoemaker's Holiday*. From the first reading he had taken exception to what he regarded as Welles's lack of respect, and this offense had turned to fury when he realized that as Orson was directing the play, it was no longer Simon Eyre, the happy Shoemaker, who was the star but his lewd journeyman, Firk. Torn between pride in his pupil and the wound to his aging actor's ego, had Whitford been pouring his Irish malice into Chubby's ear?

Later, still another much simpler explanation suggested itself: that for Sherman, as for so many of those who, at one time or another, worked with Orson and left him, the pace had become so wild, the mood so intense and violent as to be physically and mentally unendurable. Was Chubby, with his low threshold of fatigue and pain, merely the first of those who could not bear to stay around?

When I got to Sneden's Landing I found Orson lying limp and huge in a darkened room with his face to the wall. To him, Sherman's action was quite simply one of personal, malignant treachery: he was a Judas who could not forgive his master for having chosen him, an Iago jealous of his general's nobility. Loaded with so much guilt of his own and convinced that the whole world was in a conspiracy to destroy him, all that Orson could see in Chubby's desertion was yet another proof that, in the circle of his collaborators and intimates, there was not one who loved him, none he could trust, no one who was not waiting to stab him the moment his back was turned.

Some of this despair was histrionic, but coming, as it did, at a turning point in Welles's personal life, Sherman's perfidy hit him with exaggerated force. For the Mercury it marked the great divide between our halcyon days and the hurricane weather that followed. With Sherman gone, all plans for *The Importance of Being Earnest* were abandoned. Locked in his room, Orson refused to discuss the future. I spent two days in the theatre canceling our commitments and sending Augusta Weissberger off on a belated honeymoon before I retired to New City for a brief holiday with my mother.

I did not even reach Rockland County. I was over the bridge, driving along 9W, coming down the long hill that leads down into the village of Palisades, when I saw an oversized black limousine coming up the hill at high speed. As it approached, it began to sound its horn and I became aware of Orson's huge face sticking out of the window with its mouth wide open and of his gigantic voice echoing through the surrounding woods. I parked my Ford by the roadside and got into the limousine, which rushed on toward New York. Sherman was forgotten. Crossing the Washington Bridge and driving down Riverside Drive, Orson, in his sober Brutus pin-stripe, explained that we were on our way to the Columbia Broadcasting System on Madison Avenue, where he was about to receive a phenomenal offer—an hour's dramatic radio show once a week for ten weeks on which he could do anything he pleased.

I knew almost nothing about radio and did not listen regularly except to news. But I had listened the previous summer when Orson had done a four-part dramatization for a local station of Victor Hugo's *Les Miserables,* which he wrote and directed besides playing the part of the unfortunate Jean Valjean. Virginia and I had heard it together at Sneden's Landing and telephoned to him at the show's end to tell him how great he sounded. And indeed he did. Orson's voice, emerging from that small wooden box, whether he was reading poetry on Alex Woollcott's cultural program or being the voice of chocolate pudding or The Shadow, was awesome and unique.

I now sat in, as his partner, on his conference with Bill Lewis, vice-president in charge of programming at CBS, trying to look knowledgeable but understanding little of what was said. This much I gathered: the show was to be an hour long and broadcast nationally on Monday evenings; Orson was to have a free hand in the choice of material but would favor adventure—preferably familiar material in the public domain. It was intended as a prestige show of general appeal. The network's formula (all continuing radio shows had a formula) was that each of these stories would be introduced and narrated by Orson in the first person, while also playing the leading character. Under the title *First Person Singular* it was to be his show in every sense of the word: "Written, directed, produced and performed by Orson Welles."

There was talk about the orchestra and engineers, and about the studio from which the broadcast would originate (Orson insisting on Studio One and getting his way), all of which was Greek to me. One thing I did understand—and it filled me with a familiar tingle of alarm and excitement: the show was to go on the air on July 11th—in less than two weeks' time! Since this didn't seem to bother Orson, I kept my mouth shut until we were sitting in 21 two hours later celebrating the deal. Orson said it would be a tight squeeze but we could make it; he seemed to assume that I would be working with him. I reminded him that I knew less than nothing about radio. He said I'd better start learning in the morning.

Our first move, naturally, after the show had been announced, was to issue a manifesto in *The New York Times:*

> The Mercury has no intention of reproducing its stage repertoire in these broacasts. Instead, we plan to bring to radio the experimental techniques that have proven so successful in another medium, and to treat radio itself with the intelligence and respect such a beautiful and powerful medium deserves.

After that, I set to work to master the rudiments of a new art.

*　　*　　*

I came to radio during its short golden age, after it had been fully developed technically and before the advertisers and their agencies finally took it over and corrupted it. It was a brief period—three or four years in all—during which American radio drama created its own original forms and styles. Working in the single dimension of sound, it became a highly effective narrative medium which allowed full scope to the listener's imagination. In its time, it produced a number of valuable shows and a handful of creative directors: Reis, the sound engineer, the great innovator, who perfected many of the electronic devices (filters, echoes, etc.) that were entirely original with radio; Corwin, the poet-director; Fickett, the radio journalist; Cooper and Oboler, Robeson and Spear, the specialists in suspense. Welles was the only outstanding actor-director. All these men worked at high intensity and breakneck speed—as though eager to get the most out of their new medium before it was snatched out of their hands.

Next in importance after the director (and the engineer) was the radio actor. Here the medium called for a special kind of proficiency—a capacity for sight reading and instantaneous interpretation that brought to those who possessed it an income surpassed only by that of the highest-paid movie stars. These earnings were cumulative: they came from broadcasting a large number of shows day after day and week after week. Much of the successful radio actor's time was spent "bicycling" from one studio to another. On routine shows and serials this led to curious abuses: if the actor was wanted badly enough, he was permitted to arrive just in time for a single reading before going on the air. For *The Shadow,* in which Welles played the name part for a couple of years, he would be delivered in a taxi by one of his slaves just in time for the dress rehearsal. Having no idea what the episode was about, he would come up with some pretty strange readings. Often in the middle of a show he would have to change his whole attitude to meet some basic situation of which he had been unaware when he started.

There were a few programs of which this was not true: *The March of Time,* The Columbia Workshop, Corwin's Studio One and, later, Orson Welles's Mercury show—all these were rehearsed with infinite care by a picked group of performers who took great pride in their work and constituted the recognized élite of radio actors. Long before CBS made its offer, Welles was a high-ranking member of this chosen band. According to a colleague who had no reason to love him: "Welles raised the whole standard of radio acting. He carried the rest of the cast along with him and forced them through emulation to come up to his own level of intensity and color."

For Orson, as an actor, radio was a heaven-sent medium. With a vocal instrument of abnormal resonance and flexibility, uninhibited by that neurotic preoccupation with his own physical appearance that affected his stage performances, he was capable of expressing an almost unlimited range of moods and emotions. Entirely through his voice and the dramatic tensions it enabled him to create, he projected a personality on the air that soon made him one of the radio stars of his day and of which he took full advantage before an audience of several millions each week.

By agreement with the network, the first show of the series was to be *Treasure Island,* in which Orson, as narrator, would impersonate the boy hero grown up and, of course, the villainous Long John Silver. I spent several days holed up in my apartment on Sixty-first Street, reading radio scripts, then going through the book, marking it up, trying to reduce it—with scissors, paste pot and pencil—to a reasonable length. Being wholly without experience, I did little more than extract, abbreviate, compress and paraphrase the most exciting sections of Robert Louis Stevenson's work. It was still nothing like a radio show. Orson would drop in, between visits to the internationally famous ballerina with whom he was falling in love that summer, to see what I was doing and suggest rearrangements and changes. Then, less than a week before air time, he came rushing in one afternoon to announce that our plans were all changed. Instead of *Treasure Island* we were going to open with *Dracula,* to which we had just obtained the rights—not the corrupt movie version but the original Bram Stoker novel in its full Gothic horror.*

Augusta Weissberger, back from her curtailed honeymoon, was sent out for six copies of the book. Orson described his favorite scenes and departed. The next afternoon, two days before the start of rehearsal, he returned, and we started to go over what I had done. Around eight, taking along two copies of the book, several pads of lined paper, a pair of scissors, a handful of pencils and a paste pot, we moved over to Reuben's, two blocks away on Fifty-ninth Street. While we worked we dined, and then remained working after the table had been cleared—except for constantly renewed cups of coffee and cognac. By ten-thirty we had got through the first section: the Count had just been observed crawling, bat-like, down the sheer walls of his ancestral castle. Occasionally, an acquaintance passed by, paused for conversation and, receiving no encouragement, moved on.

As the after-theatre crowd began to arrive, we left the Carpathian Mountains, with Count Dracula in a catatonic condition, safely nailed in his coffin of polluted earth and on his way, in a drifting abandoned coal scow, to England. By this time there

---

* Orson had a particular theatrical fondness for Stoker, who had been Henry Irving's manager all through his great years at the Lyceum. There seems to be some foundation for the rumor that many of the physical and behavioral characteristics of the bloodsucking Hungarian count were modeled on those of his master—the star of *Richelieu* and *The Bells.*

was a pile of paste-stiffened paper on the edge of the table. Augusta was summoned from her bed to bring money. After she had left, with orders to start typing in the morning, we resumed work. I do not know if it was the sight and smell of food being devoured all around us or whether we were affected by the Count's desperate thirst for blood, but some time after midnight we ordered a whole new meal of our own—large steaks, very rare, followed by cheesecake and more coffee and brandy.

By three the place was empty again, but we did not notice it. We were now with the fly-eating lunatic in his Broadmoor cell, following his rising agitation during the great storm which drove the scow and its mysterious cargo of East European earth ashore on a deserted corner of the Cornish coast, where the Count, in the guise of a large gray wolf, leaped ashore and vanished into the woods.

It is Reuben's long-standing boast that it never closes. That night we were able to verify that claim. We saw the midsummer dawn come up over Fifty-ninth Street and continued our work, turning out gluey pages by the dozen and covering them with penciled zigzags, arrows and balloons as we moved relentlessly toward our climax. By now the last of the late revelers and scrambled-egg eaters had departed. Between six and seven, a team of cleaning women appeared with pails, mops and brooms. They worked around us, swabbing and scouring the floor under our feet. When they had gone we ordered eggs, bacon and a double order of kippered herring with coffee and orange juice. Then, just before nine, as a few early birds appeared for breakfast and the streets outside came to life, we nailed down the Count, with a burnt stake through his heart, and rose from our table. Three days later *Dracula* went on the air as the opener of what was to become a legendary radio series.

Our network supervisor on the show was a very tall, slender well-spoken executive by the name of Davidson Taylor. Trained for the ministry in a Kentucky seminary, suave, sincere, tactful and creatively permissive, he was literate and musically educated. Our theme music was his idea—the opening bars of Tchaikovsky's Piano Concerto No. 1 in B flat minor—which eventually

364

became something of a radio cliché. But in its day the use of a solo instrument as a signature was an innovation; it was skeptically received by the programming and sales departments, who had hoped for something more flamboyant and fanfarious as the intro to the network's major dramatic show.

It was thanks to Dave Taylor that we had the benefit of Bernard Herrmann and the superb CBS house orchestra on our show. Benny was the golden boy of music around CBS; egotistical, contentious, devoted and enormously well read, he managed, then and later, to combine a serious musical career with work for the mass media.* As a very young man he had become musical director of the CBS *Invitation to Music,* which, for a number of years, broadcast weekly a unique and fancy blend of classical and new and unfamiliar music. At the same time he composed and conducted regularly for the Columbia Workshop and for any other serious dramatic shows the network was presenting.

His first contact with Welles the previous year, in a broadcast of *Macbeth* of which Orson was the green guest director and star, had been a shambles. As musical director he had composed a score which he had had copied and placed before the orchestra at rehearsal. Orson arrived late, according to Herrmann, accompanied by an elderly gentleman in kilts—with a bagpipe. As soon as the reading began it became evident that the script was more than twice too long. By the time it had been cut there was no time for musical rehearsal. When Herrmann protested, Orson yelled, "No music! No music at all!" standing, as he always did, in the center of the studio at the main microphone, wearing earphones, which made it impossible for anyone to communicate with him on equal terms. To the bagpiper he said, "Every time I raise this hand, you come in and play!" To the trumpets and

---

* He became one of the world's leading film composers—working for Welles, Hitchcock, Truffaut and others while conducting regularly for England's Hallé and BBC Symphony orchestras. His U.S. conducting career was inhibited by his inability to be civil to the wives of board members and by a running feud with Arthur Judson, which kept him permanently out of symphonic jobs in this country.

drums he said, "Everytime I lift this hand, you play a fanfare!" And to the infuriated Herrmann, frozen on his podium in front of his assembled orchestra, he said, "Trust me, Benny! Just trust me!"

"And that's how we went on the air," reported Benny. "Every time Orson raised either hand, which he did frequently in the role of Macbeth, trumpets, drums and bagpipe came in fortissimo . . . and so did a whole lot of sound cues, including wind machines and thunder sheets."

Though both young geniuses had vowed never to work together again, Dave Taylor, with patient insistence, united them in a tempestuous but productive relationship that culminated, two years later, in the score for *Citizen Kane*. Amid screaming rows, snapping of batons, accusations of sabotage and hurling of scripts and scores into the air and at each other, they came to understand each other perfectly. More music was used by the Mercury show than by any other dramatic show on the air: out of fifty-seven minutes of playing time it was not unusual to have thirty-five to forty minutes of music.*

According to Herrmann, Orson was not a man for whom you could write original music, because of his tendency to change the show around up to the last moment. Since he never conformed to a preconceived outline, it was better to improvise with him:

> Welles' radio quality, like Sir Thomas Beecham's in music, was essentially one of spontaneity. At the start of every broadcast Orson was an unknown quantity. As he went along his mood would assert itself and the temperature would start to increase till the point of incandescence. . . . Even when his shows weren't good they were better than other people's successes. He inspired us all—the musicians, the actors, the

* It was not only with Welles that Hermann had scenes. His relations with his orchestra (which included such world-famous players as Harry Glanz on trumpet, Mitch Miller on oboe) were erratic, to say the least. I remember that one night, after a particularly stormy session, he flung his baton across the studio, dismissed the orchestra, then turned to me, gray with fatigue and fury. "I've known it! I've known it all along!" he muttered savagely. "There's a strong fascist element in the woodwinds!"

sound-effects men and the engineers. They'd all tell you they never worked on shows like Welles'. Horses' hooves are horses' hooves—yet they felt different with Orson—why? I think it had to do with the element of the unknown, the surprises and the uncomfortable excitement of improvisation.

Some of Orson's improvisation was extremely elaborate. Among the technical and electronic devices that were being perfected in those days, sound effects, which had started out as simple indications (footsteps, windows and doors opening and closing, cars starting, etc.), were taking on increasing complexity. Orson, determined to push this further than his competitors, spent hours experimenting with new devices and combinations. Long John Silver's wooden leg was easy, but for *The Count of Monte Cristo* the two actors who played the dungeon scenes were required to lie on the stone floor of the men's room and to speak into a special dynamic microphone set at the base of the toilet seat to achieve the right subterranean reverberation, while a second microphone, placed inside a toilet bowl at the other end of the building and constantly flushed, gave a faithful rendering of the waves breaking against the walls of the Chateau d'If.

In *A Tale of Two Cities* several hours of precious studio time were spent on the decapitation of Sydney Carton—the severing of the head and its fall into the basket. Various solid objects were tried under a cleaver wielded by one of the best sound men in the business: a melon, a pillow, a coconut and a leg of lamb. Finally it was discovered that a cabbage gave just the right kind of scrunching resistance. For Booth Tarkington's *Seventeen* (in which Orson played the hero in that curious whining falsetto which he habitually used for his portrayal of teenagers) he insisted on a real lawn mower whose blades trimmed acres of artificial grass matting spread over the studio floor. In *Beau Geste,* for the climactic Bedouin attack on the fort, Orson sent two engineers with microphones and hundreds of feet of cable onto the roof of the building together with four extras and a stage manager armed with guns and with orders to fire six rounds apiece every time he flashed a cue light from the studio. Now at last it sounded real—so real that within five minutes the building was invaded by uniformed police, who entered the studio demanding to know what the hell was going on. Orson, absorbed in his show, simply ignored them. When they became insistent— in order to gain time and to get his fusillade recorded—Orson turned suddenly, pointed an accusing finger at Vakhtangov and said, "There's the man who did it! Talk to him!" When that didn't work he summarily ordered the police out of the studio. It was not until the sergeant in charge made it clear to Dave Taylor and myself that he would arrest us all for illegal possession of firearms that Orson reluctantly recalled his men from the roof. But by then the attack had been recorded in duplicate on acetate disks.

Such episodes are comic in the telling: they formed part of the hysterical intensity amid which the show was produced each week with an obsessive perfectionism that gradually, over the summer, earned us a reputation for quality and imagination such as no dramatic radio series had quite achieved before. We adhered to the formula of first-person-singular narration but, within it, we invented all sorts of ingenious and dramatic devices; diaries, letters, streams of consciousness, confessions and playbacks of recorded conversations. (Some of these found their way, later, into films, which, till then, had generally avoided the use of narration as an aid to dramatic action.) And, gradually, though adventure continued to be the backbone of the show, we ventured into more varied and sophisticated material. *Dracula* and *Treasure Island* were followed by *A Tale of Two Cities* and *The Thirty-Nine Steps;* then came a show made up of three very different short stories—Sherwood Anderson's "I'm a Fool," "The Open Window" by "Saki" and Carl Ewald's "My Little Boy," which we had discovered in the Woollcott Reader. This was followed by John Drinkwater's *Abraham Lincoln,* Schnitzler's *Affairs of Anatol, The Count of Monte Cristo* and G. K. Chesterton's *The Man Who Was Thursday.*

We had no reader; the material was chosen by Welles and myself on the basis of contrast and personal preference with occasional suggestions from the outside. In each case we would discuss the tone and mood of the production and then I would go off and write it. Once again, as in the beginning of our partnership in the theatre, it was Orson who was the teacher, I the apprentice. But I learned quickly and once I had mastered the basic techniques and tricks, I wrote all our scripts—usually in bed, over a period of three to four days—and sent them over to Orson for his approval before they were mimeographed. Usually he accepted them with minor corrections but, once in a while, out of caprice or ego, or because he really felt he had a superior idea, he would make substantial changes, for better or for worse, before or during rehearsal.

Seated in the control room next to the engineer while he directed and performed, I was expected to monitor the show and pass on my impressions to Welles, who stood in the center of the studio on a raised podium where all could see him, with earphones clamped to his head through which he could hear everything, including himself. He also counted on me for the drastic, last-minute editing which took place every week just before air time, with the clock ticking over our heads, in an atmosphere of panic pressure.

It was a loose but viable collaboration and it worked with surprising efficiency. Within a few weeks ours had become the summer's leading dramatic program on the air—another bright feather in the cap of the Mercury. In my exhilaration over this new achievement I chose to ignore the change it was causing in our relationship.

Throughout my theatrical association with Orson over the past three and a half years, much of the intiative had been mine—strategically and artistically. While I never hesitated to acknowledge Orson's creative leadership, I had managed, consciously and not without effort, to maintain the balance of power in a partnership which, for all our frequent and violent personal conflicts, had remained emotionally and professionally stable. With the coming of the radio show (though my contribution to its success was substantial) this delicate balance was disturbed and, finally, destroyed. The formula "produced, written, directed and performed by Orson Welles" was one that I approved and encouraged. In the first place it was true: The Mercury of the Air *was* Orson's show. In the second, it was good showmanship and sound business to publicize and exploit one dominant, magnetic and salable personality. But its effect on our association and on the future course of the Mercury was deep and irreversible. From being Orson's partner I had become his employee: the senior member but, still, no more than a member of his staff.

In the beginning, because it was all so spontaneous and exciting and successful and because of our deep personal affection and continued professional need of each other, the change was barely perceptible. In the tensions of the following months, under the alternating extremities of great success and dismal failure, this growing imbalance in our partnership became the main cause of its final and inevitable dissolution.

That was still more than a year away. Meantime CBS had offered to continue the show for another twenty-six weeks if the problem of suitable air time could be solved. With the reopening of the theatre season, the Monday evening hour we had filled during the summer had become impossible. So had every other night of the week except Sunday, when the Mercury Theatre was dark. But Sunday night was dominated by the rival network's long-time popular favorite—Edgar Bergen with his puppet, Charlie McCarthy. For a while this looked like an insuperable obstacle. Finally, out of necessity and perhaps as an experiment in programming, Bill Lewis decided to run us against the puppet on the off-chance that we might attract a small part of his mass public in addition to our own limited but growing audience.

The last of our *First Person Singular* broadcasts before the name was changed to The Mercury Theatre of the Air was a work long dear to Orson's heart, but not to mine: G. K. Chesterton's *The Man Who Was Thursday*. This time, Orson said, he would write his own script: he wanted none of my cosmopolitan pussyfooting; this would be pure Catholic-Christian Chesterton as only he could understand and express it. Grateful for the rest, I agreed. Three days before air time I asked him for a script so as to have it mimeographed and distributed. The next afternoon he sent Augusta over with a copy of the novel, uncut and immaculate except for a few mysterious markings and some doodled sketches of the celebrated ballerina. On the day of the first rehearsal I found myself locked in a cell on the twentieth floor of the CBS building, with three copies of the book from which I hacked, pasted and dictated some sort of script, which was then rushed, sheet by sheet, to the typing pool below, where six carbon copies were made and hurriedly distributed to the cast upstairs in Studio One. There had been no time for dress rehearsal and halfway through the broadcast (which was lively but confusing) it became apparent that it was going to run between twelve and twenty minutes short. Radio actors and Welles in particular had remarkable control over time: his ability to extend or compress a script under stress was amazing. But even he could not stretch to an hour's length a show that was thirty percent short without some danger of losing his public. He made no attempt to slow down: he finished the show sixteen minutes before the hour. Then, without turning a hair, as his own master of ceremonies, he used the remaining time to thank his audience for their loyalty during the summer, and to give them a foretaste of pleasures to come. Without a word—since by that time he and I were so closely attuned that we could communicate, in a crisis, through panes of glass at considerable distance—I rushed downstairs to the library while he recited the funeral oration from *Julius Caesar* and returned with copies of *Jane Eyre, Oliver Twist* and *The Hound of the Baskervilles,* which I handed to Orson one by one, and from which he read dramatic excerpts with deep feeling and great variety until the hour was up and he was able to sign off with his customary "Obediently yours—Orson Welles." It was considered a bold stroke of promotion, a brilliant teaser for our next season's program on which we received congratulations from the sales and publicity departments of the Columbia Broadcasting System.

Such was our self-confidence and our blind faith in our own unlimited energy that, as we signed our new contract, we neither of us, for one instant, questioned the wisdom of trying to combine a weekly national radio show with the running of a full-scale repertory theatre in New York City.

IX

Neither welles nor I felt really alive unless we were doing a number of things at one time. Immediately after the broadcast of *Dracula,* the Mercury Theatre, which had been paralyzed since Sherman's defection, sprang back into furious life. Our first task was to reconstruct our wrecked program for the coming season: *The Importance of Being Earnest* was out; so was *The Shoemaker's Holiday,* in which Chubby had played an irreplaceable part. We found two substitutes for our repertory: the first was *Too Much Johnson,* an early twentieth-century American farce by William Gillette, which had been on our list for some time. It was not my favorite piece, but Orson assured me that, with a new production idea he had in mind, it would be funnier than *Horse Eats Hat.* The other was *Danton's Death,* on which we decided quite precipitately one afternoon at a radio rehearsal when Martin Gabel came into the control room, threw a black-and-orange book onto the formica console top and said, "Why don't you do this and let me play Danton?" The book was the collected works of Georg Buechner, including the Danton play, which we had often discussed as a vehicle for Orson. Now, suddenly, in spite of its obvious difficulties, it struck us as a brilliant notion—a contrast to the frivolity of *Too Much Johnson* and something we could sell to our politically minded theatre-party audience. We immediately announced a revised Mercury program: *Too Much Johnson, Danton's Death* and *Five Kings,* in that order.

Orson's production idea for *Too Much Johnson* consisted of two filmed interludes—both chases. The first, a prologue in which the leading characters and the basic situation (mistaken identity and a suspicion of cuckoldry) were introduced in a wild chase through the streets, parks and waterfront of New York City; the second, a comic manhunt through the Cuban jungle. Shooting began in mid-July with a cast that included Joseph Cotten, Arlene Francis, Ruth Ford, Virginia Welles, myself, a beetle-browed heavy from radio named Howard Smith and Augusta Weissberger, whose heaving bosom was occasionally substituted for Arlene's in close-ups requiring exceptional passion or terror. Our cinematographer was Harry Dunham, a fair-haired intellectual newsreelman recently returned from China—a friend of Paul Bowles and Virgil Thomson.

Dressed in rented Edwardian garments and accompanied by three horse-drawn cabs, we set out for our opening day's shooting in Central Park. Just before the first shot it started to pour. Orson felt this would add to the excitement of the chase. The horses and their drivers felt otherwise. Frightened by the rain, a rising wind and falling branches, they refused to budge. Scowling, in the shelter of a large tree, Orson, with his actors, awaited the passing of what, he assured them, was nothing but a summer shower. It turned out to be the beginning of the East Coast's worst hurricane in years and it lasted for two days.

Three days later he began again. Cecil B. De Mille was not more imperious or more reckless of human life than was Orson Welles, seated high astride the peaked roof of the Washington Market, urging Joe Cotten to greater efforts as he swung from eave to eave while the raging cuckold threatened him from above and the Keystone Cops, all twelve of them, including myself, in sugar-loaf helmets, waited for him on the cobblestones thirty feet below. Some days later I was torn from my bed, where I was trying to condense *A Tale of Two Cities* into fifty-seven minutes, rushed across the George Washington Bridge to the New Jersey Palisades, given a pith helmet and a tropical suit and instructed to fight a saber duel to the death with the outraged husband around a prop palm tree set on the very edge of a two hundred foot cliff. While we swung and hacked at each other and slithered in the loose gravel, Welles, Dunham and the camera crew, who were shooting up at us from the foot of the cliff in a shower of earth and stones, kept yelling "Closer! Closer!"—by which they meant closer to the edge of the precipice.

This was not the only cliff-hanging I was doing at the time. Between appearing in the film and writing and rehearsing our radio show each week I was trying to finance the new Mercury season. With incorrigible optimism I had hoped to eke out the summer and produce the Wilde play with what little remained of our original capital and then to use the profits of the repertory season to pay for our share of *Five Kings*. With our change of plans this scheme fell apart. Now we needed money for production and we needed it immediately. I could not or would not go to our original stockholders. After a triumphal season during which they had seen themselves described in the press as "beaming sponsors" and "Maecenases with a flair," I was embarrassed to tell them that their money was all gone. (From the start, our relations with our stockholders were peculiar. Personally, we were grateful to them for the generosity that had made the birth of the Mercury possible. But as business associates, our feelings toward them were as ambivalent as those of adolescents toward their parents. In Orson, particularly, those emotions were so intense as to make it virtually impossible for him to be civil to them on the rare occasions when he encountered them. While things were going well, he regarded them as parasites and exploiters, fattening on the successes wrung from his creative agony. When they began to go badly, this hostility was aggravated by shame and guilt: anticipating their reproaches, he developed a loathing for them such as one inevitably feels toward a benefactor whom one has disappointed or betrayed.) I preferred not to look for money there.

Instead, with help from Zorn and Arnold Weissberger, I devised what seemed an ingenious and fairly honest scheme: to cover the production costs of our second season I would go out and raise money exactly as though I were financing a regular commercial production with a capitalization of thirty thousand dollars against fifty percent of the entire season's possible profits. This in no way prejudiced our original stockholders and it gave the new investors a chance to spread their gamble over three productions without involving themselves in any of the basic risks of the Mercury Theatre. *Johnson* and *Danton* were to be financed at $10,000 apiece; the remaining $10,000 was to cover the Mercury's share of the production of *Five Kings*.

While I was still working this out, the filming of *Too Much Johnson* came to an end—or, rather, we had to stop shooting because there was no more money for film. What was already developed and printed was delivered in cans to the St. Regis Hotel, where Orson occupied an air-conditioned room for his hay fever and for the amours that were begining to play a large part in his life that summer. After a while it must have become difficult to use for that purpose: determined to do his own editing, he had moved in a Moviola, together with some film-cutting and splicing equipment, and given the floormaid a large bribe never to enter the room. As each day's rushes were brought in and run through the Moviola, they went to swell the rising pile of film that lay loosely coiled all over the floor. To reach the bed, the slaves, when they arrived to rouse Orson for rehearsal or for the radio show, had to wade knee-deep through a crackling sea of inflammable film. And on the nights when he was not on the air or with his paramour, Orson would sit for hours at the Moviola, laughing at his own footage while the slaves hunted vainly for the bits of film that would enable him to put his chases together into some kind of intelligible sequence. He also conducted desultory rehearsals of *Too Much Johnson*, which, by this time, amused him far less than the film he had shot but which we had already announced as our first production, opening in early September after a week's tryout at Stony Creek, Connecticut.

This was a small summer theatre operated by two of our lady apprentices. It was conveniently obscure; the appearance of the Mercury led by Orson Welles would make their season, cost us nothing and give us a chance to see our rather shaky farce before an audience. The film was not run on this occasion for lack of projection facilities. Also, because Orson had still not succeeded in cutting it together and, even if he had, the lab would not give us another print or release the negative until they had been paid.

Orson spent a week commuting between New York and Connecticut. I stayed in town writing the radio show (*The Thirty-Nine Steps* that week) and trying to raise money. But from what I heard from Jean Rosenthal and some of the actors, all was not rosy at Stony Creek. Summer theatre salaries were shamefully low in those days: for junior members they were barely sufficient to pay for a room and one meal a day. After the last dress rehearsal, Orson, before departing for New York, threw a party backstage at which he magnanimously presented the company and crew with two cases of champagne but forgot to order any food. Parched and desperate, they fell on the champagne, drank it all up in twenty minutes, then went swimming in Long Island Sound. Finding their rooms empty the following morning, search parties, fearing the worst, went looking for them and found them—having heroically saved each other from drowning—laid out like logs on the beach.

The account of this midnight swim was funnier by far than anything I saw on the stage the following night. Maybe I was tired and worried or perhaps I missed the lavish trimmings—the rich, multiple sets and costumes, the thirty-three-piece orchestra, the lady trumpeter and the regiment of Zouaves that had enlived *Horse Eats Hat*. On the small, dreary stage of the Stony Creek summer theatre I found *Too Much Johnson* trivial, tedious and underrehearsed, and I set myself firmly against its coming in as the opening production of the Mercury Theatre's critical second season. This led to an ugly scene with Orson, who secretly agreed with me but who needed to play out the sabotage scene to salve his pride.*

So once again we changed our program, which now read *Danton's Death* followed by *Too Much Johnson,* with *Five Kings* still in third place. And with this change our economic situation grew infinitely worse. *Danton,* a big and difficult show, could not possibly open till early October; this meant carrying a dark theatre and the entire Mercury organization, now back on full pay, for an additional, unproductive month. Despite the prestige of our successful radio show I had made little progress with my financing. For all our triumphs we remained an "art theatre"— poison to the smart money and the regular Broadway angels. It therefore came as a complete and happy surprise when I returned one afternoon from a routine visit to the United Booking Office with a commitment for ten thousand dollars from the most hardboiled outfit in show business: the syndicate headed by Marcus Hyman and Max Gordon, whose associates included the Shuberts and other, lesser Broadway sharks.

I never quite understood why they did it. It certainly wasn't largesse; perhaps they felt it was bread upon the waters that might return in the form of theatre bookings, a connection with a hot new producing organization, a possible future entry into the mass media. Anyway—there it was: a check for ten grand and few questions asked. A few thousand had already come in from individuals, attracted more by the flame of the Mercury's sudden fame than by any hope of profit from the three crazy shows we were announcing. More dribbled in during the next two months, including two thousand which I wrung by rather shady means from a bootlegger's son from Brooklyn on the promise that he would be allowed to work on the radio show. All in all, I raised seventeen thousand dollars, all of which—and more—was spent within two months on our production of *Danton's Death.*

* The only positive result of our Stony Creek tryout was that Katharine Hepburn appeared one night in the audience, saw Joseph Cotten, remembered him, and used him as her leading man in *Philadelphia Story* the following year.

Too Much Johnson was Orson Welles's first minor reversal in the theatre. The night it opened at Stony Creek he retired into his air-conditioned tent at the St. Regis, where he lay in darkness for a week surrounded by twenty-five thousand feet of film, ministered to by Augusta Weissberger and the slaves, rising from his bed only for the radio show or for one of his amorous sorties. The rest of the time he lay there, like a sick child, convinced that he was going to die, racked by asthma and fear and despair. Years later Vakhtangov still spoke with pity and horror of the spiritual flagellations he had witnessed in that twilit room, of "the self-vilifications and the remorse for what he had done to those around him . . . for the cruelty and moral corruption with which he reproached himself."

On the seventh day he rose from his bed and returned to the world, but his troubled emotional state continued to be reflected in his creative activity: it helped to explain the indecision and doubt that were beginning to infect his work in the theatre and it added to the difficulty we experienced as we tried to recapture our working rhythm at the Mercury and to restore the sense of continuity that had been snapped by our double change of plans. Our problem was aggravated by the vaguely looming mass of *Five Kings,* which, on account of its size, could not be performed on our own stage. As a result, by the end of summer, the Mercury Theatre, which had been the heart of our operation, our creative and sentimental home and our gateway to fame, had become an incubus rather than an inspiration, a chore to be disposed of before we could devote ourselves to the year's real accomplishment. It was in this dangerous mood that we approached the opening production of the Mercury's second repertory season.

Danton's Death had been written, just over a century before, by a boy who died at the age of twenty-four, leaving behind him this and two other more or less finished plays (*Leonce und Lina* and *Wozzeck*). Scribbled in a student's notebook in the attic of his father's house, where Georg Buechner was hiding from the police repression that swept Europe after the Congress of Vienna, it is a play of keen political and human insights—one that seemed to offer us scope for creative and experimental production and, at the same time, reflected significant aspects of the modern scene. Laid in that violent period of the French Revolution when it was making the transition from new-won liberty to dictatorship, it is a very young man's play with a fragmentary and defective structure. It had been seen in New York in 1927 when Max Reinhardt presented it (in an augmented version with vast crowd effects) as one of the great successes of his American season. This success, far from helping us, made our undertaking more hazardous: it conditioned Orson's approach to the play and influenced the nature of his production. Since Reinhardt had made a mass spectacle of it and Orson himself had already demonstrated his ability to handle crowd scenes, *Danton's Death* would be performed as a "drama of lonely souls and the mob," with the mob ever-present but rarely visible.

Except for such general notions, Welles came to the play unprepared and uncertain. He was a great improviser but he needed a strong structure (as in *Caesar*) or a brilliant texture (as in *Faustus*) around which to develop his inventions and variations. Both were missing in *Danton*. He brought to it, as he could not fail to do, intermittent genius, spasmodic energy and an occasional flash of vision, but none of that impregnable personal conviction that had carried him irresistibly through his first seven productions.

Casting, for all our disagreements, had always been an exhilarating and spontaneous process. That this was not true of *Danton* had to do with a basic flaw that weakened the entire structure of the new season's Mercury company.

The hero of Buechner's tragedy is a giant of a man: as a role, Danton calls for heroism, magnanimity, lethargy and great personal magnetism. I was confident that Orson had them all—until I discovered that he had no intention of playing the part, which he had already offered to Martin Gabel. We argued bitterly for two days, in the darkness of his air-conditioned hotel room and under the bright lights of Studio One. Orson maintained, not unreasonably, that he could not play Falstaff and Danton and direct both plays in addition to the radio show. Since when, I objected, had we conducted our affairs reasonably? The show needed him and he must do it. Finally, in an unsatisfactory compromise, he agreed to appear in the brief but flashy role of Saint-Just, in which he could be replaced without damage when the *Five Kings* rehearsals began—or whenever the ballerina summoned him, I might have added.

Meantime we had begun to reassemble what was left of the Mercury Company. Chubby and Whitford were gone; so were Vincent Price and Edith Barrett (married and off to California); Mady Christians was playing the Queen in Maurice Evans' *Hamlet;* Norman Lloyd was getting ready to play Johnny Appleseed in a Broadway musical. George Duthie was sick and Orson, predictably, had decided he did not want Joseph Holland around.

One of my first calls had been to the company's leading malcontent, George Coulouris. When I informed him that he was about to cap his series of Mercury triumphs with the great role of Robespierre, he took it coolly and asked who would be playing Danton. I told him—

"Gabel."

"Martin Gabel?"

"Martin Gabel."

The silence that followed should have alerted me, but I said cheerfully that I was sending over the script. Two days later Coulouris informed me that he found the part monolithic and the play turgid. I told him to go to hell.

After I hung up I remembered that Sokoloff, who had created the role for Reinhardt, was in Hollywood, where he had just played with Paul Muni in *Zola.* We called him and he was interested. After hearing him talk I began to worry about his English; Orson reminded me that I had worried about Mady Christians.

Finally we had only seven carry-overs from previous Mercury shows—not counting the slaves and the extras. Gabel was with us again; so were Joe Cotten, Eustace Wyatt, Ruth Ford, Ross (formerly Ted) Elliot, Erskine Sanford and Arlene Francis, whom we cast as Danton's mistress.* Most of the extras were still around: they had kept alive during the summer as Keystone Cops and Cuban peons; now, as they prepared to go back underground as Parisian sans-culottes, I added a few new faces, principally female, of which the most vividly remembered is that of a lovely child named Betty Garrett, from the Neighborhood Playhouse, whose arms and legs were perpetually covered with bruises incurred while repelling sexual attacks in the basement. (She was also frequently covered, rather more mysteriously, with bright patches of violet ink.) Most of our female apprentices had gone back to college: in their place we had two new male slaves —Howard Teichmann from Wisconsin and Richard Baer from Princeton, both of whom soon achieved positions of importance in the Mercury hierarchy.†

Teichmann may be exaggerating when he claims that during the final rehearsals of *Danton's Death* he was required to stay in the theatre for thirteen days and thirteen nights without a break. It is true that the show was prepared in an anxious mood that fluctuated between uneasy inertia and almost unbearable tension. It was rehearsed, almost from the first day, in a set of which the dominant element was a huge, curved wall, formed entirely of human faces that filled the rear of the stage from the basement to the grid. Called on to execute this in a hurry and at reasonable cost, Jean Rosenthal went out and bought five thousand unpainted Halloween masks, each of which was colored by hand and glued onto a curved, stiffened canvas cyclorama by rotating crews of assistants, volunteers, slaves, wardrobe women, secre-

---

* Once again the Mercury acted as marriage broker. Arlene and Gabel found each other on stage on a "Directoire" sofa that resembled a bathtub and, in due course, came together in what has proved to be one of the most durable marriages in show business.

† Howard Teichmann became a successful writer for radio and theatre (*The Solid Gold Cadillac*) before becoming administrator of what remains of the great Shubert theatrical empire. Richard Baer (later Barr) is president of the League of New Theatres, producer for Edward Albee of *The Zoo Story, Who's Afraid of Virginia Woolf, A Delicate Balance* and other successful plays including *The Boys in the Band*.

taries, visitors—anyone who could be persuaded or pressured into joining in the loathsome task. When finished and lit, it was an effective and active device that suggested different things to different people: in one light it was "the hydra-headed mob, impersonal but real, omnipresent as a reality," in another "it looked like a huge canopy of staring faces which gave the strange ominous effect of a rigid dance of death." At the climax of Danton's self-destruction, blood-red lights were thrown upon it; during Robespierre's midnight meditation it turned to vicious, steely gray, which made it seem, for a moment, "as though the whole pile of skulls was about to fall upon him and stone him to death." In the last scene, as Danton and his followers went to their execution, this whole rear wall opened up and revealed a narrow slit against a bright blue sky topped by glittering steel. At the final curtain drums rolled and the blade of the guillotine flashed down through the slit as the lights blacked out.

In front of this wall, starting immediately behind the fore-stage, was a yawning pit thirty feet long and twenty wide, hacked out of the center of the stage floor we had so lovingly and proudly rebuilt the year before. Out of this hole, rising in steep steps from the basement, like a miniature Aztec pyramid, was a four-sided structure the center of which was occupied by an elevator shaft through which a small platform traveled up and down, descending to the basement to unload and rising to a maximum height of twelve feet above the stage. This was successively used, at various levels, as a rostrum, a garret, an elegantly furnished salon, a prison cell and a tumbril until, in the final scene, it rose slowly to its full height to become the raised platform of the guillotine.

It was a brilliant conception but mechanically it was a horror. The only kind of elevator we could afford was a swaying, rickety, man-driven contraption. When I complained to Jean of its instability she explained that it was precisely this flexibility that made it safe. We spent days trying to make it stop at the right places; dozens of hours lighting it at its various levels. When it was all set and lit, it looked wonderful; it was also constricting and exceedingly dangerous.

The actors might have been less conscious of their physical problems if they had been more assured in their action. *Danton* was a play of many scenes and for most of the company it was difficult to create characters out of such brief, fragmented episodes. In the rehearsals I attended (between working on the weekly radio shows and trying to track down investors) it seemed to me that Orson was working with less patience and intimacy than usual. This was particularly evident in his work with Martin Gabel. In *Caesar* there had been mutual understanding and faith between them: none of that was evident now. Gabel was aggressive in his insecurity: he knew he was not ideally cast and that Orson should have been playing Danton. This suspicion hung between them, unspoken and corrosive, all through rehearsal. It was something only Welles could have dispelled: unconsciously competitive and vaguely annoyed at himself for having refused to play the part, he did little to help Gabel overcome his natural handicaps.

For Vladimir Sokoloff (with whom we all fell in love and who entertained the company with anecdotes of Reinhardt and Stanislavski) Welles had that awed and childlike respect which he showed for theatrical figures whom he admired. Most of Robespierre's great scenes were solos—orations and soliloquies. Orson let him play them exactly as he had played them in German for Reinhardt. It was very impressive and the company used to applaud at each rehearsal, but it made it more difficult for Sokoloff to assimilate the part in English than if the scenes had been restaged and redirected. He worried about his speech and requested and received hours of special coaching—to no perceptible effect.

With the extras herded in the basement and emerging only for occasional street scenes during which they sang Blitzstein's updated version of *"La Carmagnole,"* Orson was less painstaking and demanding than he had been in *Caesar*. He turned them over to the stage management and to Marc Blitzstein for musical and sound effects. Indeed, for a time, Marc seemed to be the only completely content and confident person in the organization. Besides the crowd sounds, he had composed some Mozartian harpsichord music and two vocal numbers: an "Ode to Reason" and a duet entitled "Christine" to be sung by Joseph Cotten and Mary Wickes. Then, suddenly, midway through rehearsal, he was seized with a deep anxiety which he lost no time passing on to Orson and myself and, in due course, to the entire company.

In forming the Mercury we had always counted on the solid support of an assured and loyal public—the organized, left-wing, semi-intellectual audiences that consisted predominantly of the Communist Party, its adherents and sympathizers. It was they who had been our main support during the various runs of *The Cradle Will Rock,* who had encouraged us during the early, shaky previews of *Julius Caesar* and who had already bought up the numerous previews on which we hoped to hone the ragged edges of *Danton's Death.*

Ever since the great night of *The Cradle,* Marc Blitzstein had constituted himself our political counsellor. He came to me now, ten days before our first scheduled preview, in a state of extreme agitation. In producing *Danton's Death* at this time, he explained, we were all guilty of a serious and dangerous error: perhaps we should cancel the production immediately. I said this was a hell of a time to tell me and pressed him for an explanation—which Marc now gave me straight from the cultural bureau of the Party: with the Moscow trials still fresh in people's minds and the Trotskyite schism growing wider by the day—couldn't I see the inescapable and dangerous parallel? To the politically uneducated and even to some of the younger emotional members of the Party, Danton, the hero of the Revolution, who had raised and commanded the armies of the young republic, would inevitably suggest Trotsky, while his prosecutor, the incorruptible, ruthless Robespierre, would, equally inevitably, be equated with Joseph Stalin.

When I smilingly minimized his fears he informed me, rather white around the gills, that unless we did something drastic to bring our production into line, our theatre parties (on which it was customary to receive a small deposit on signing and the rest a few days before the performance) would all be canceled. We might even be picketed. Having wiped the smile off my face, he suggested that a meeting be held as soon as possible with V. J. Jerome to discuss the matter.

In the days that followed we held a number of meetings, two of them in Stewart's Cafeteria on Union Square. I remembered Mr. Jerome from the MacLeish symposium, but I hardly knew him. As the result of these meetings we became better acquainted: I visited him at his apartment, where tea was served by an English spinster, his sister; he came to my new, half-furnished apartment on Ninth Street, where we ate some of my mother's *neufs en gelée*. But over *Danton's Death* we were deadlocked. To placate him, we removed a few of the more obvious Trotsky-Stalin parallels. In exchange, the Party agreed not to boycott us: they merely withheld their support. When we needed them desperately after our mixed notices in the capitalist press they did nothing to help us survive.

These negotiations took place amid rising anxiety and tension. Night after night, and sometimes all night, Welles went through the motions of rehearsal—endlessly shifting the order of scenes and the sequence of speeches. Each time such a change was made it called for a complete rerouting and relighting of that entire section of the play. The wall of faces, effective as it was, was horribly difficult to light; each of its five thousand rounded masks seemed determined to get itself into the light. If one single lamp was moved, even slightly, to accommodate an actor's changed position on the stage, it was likely, a moment later, to illuminate a hundred masks behind him.

Days and nights went by and nobody left the theatre. Mattresses were dragged into the aisles to take care of our twenty-four-hour shifts. Jeannie grew smaller and grayer. Still Orson would not stop. He drove himself and the company with no sense of time, to no apparent purpose and with no perceptible feeling. It was as though he expected, by continuously increasing the pressure, to strike some new well of inspiration that would save us all.

Our mood matched that of the world around us. If anyone, in a moment of restlessness, turned on the small radio that George

Zorn kept in the rear of the box office, it was to hear increasingly alarming news: Hitler's armies poised for invasion, Prague vowing resistance, France mobilizing, the British fleet massing in the North Atlantic. In mid-September, while Neville Chamberlain, with his umbrella, was flying between London and Munich to insure "peace in our time," a strange cloud of tragi-comic madness seemed to hang over the Mercury and its inmates.

There was an evening, a week before our first preview, when Orson suddenly announced that the script still wasn't right and he was going to do something about it. Calling the cast together on the stage, he explained that he was sending them home early (it was then after 11:00 P.M.) while he spent the night doing a final and definitive rewrite. He called a rehearsal for ten the next morning, and a moment later the theatre was empty except for Orson, Blitzstein, the slaves and myself. Vakhtangov was sent out to the Astor for cigars and Wilson to 21 for a bottle of brandy. By 1:30 A.M. no work had been done, and I went upstairs to the projection room for a nap while Orson, Marc and Teichmann discussed the Spanish-American War as a subject for a musical. At three I descended and suggested we get back to *Danton's Death*. Orson said no. He was going to do the rewrite by himself. It was better that way. He knew exactly what must be done. I offered to stay with him. He said he could work better alone in his room at the St. Regis. Vakhtangov went off to find him a taxi and they left.

I told Teichmann to cancel the next morning's rehearsal and to call the St. Regis at noon for instructions. Vakhtangov answered in a whisper. He said Orson had worked all night but still wasn't done. We called again at five and again Vakhtangov answered. He said Welles would be working all through the night and wanted the cast called for noon of the next day—at which time he would read them the new script. Rosenthal was to be there, also Augusta with two expert typists.

At twelve the cast assembled, refreshed from its first real sleep in two weeks. At one-thirty Welles arrived, smiled wanly as he crossed the stage and vanished into his dressing room, the slaves following to help him remove his coat and make final preparations for the reading. Seconds later an agonized howl was heard. Then Dick Baer, followed by Wilson and Vakhtangov, came flying out, rushed across the stage and out the stage door onto the street. Finally, Orson himself appeared, his eyes rolling, wringing his huge hands, patting himself all over and announcing in a sepulchral voice that the script on which he had worked for two nights and a day had been left in the cab which brought him from the St. Regis. There was no copy. After an hour had been spent calling police stations and trying to trace the missing cab, rehearsal resumed exactly where it had left off thirty-nine hours before.

Five nights later we had our first real disaster. The night had started badly. The Longchamps Restaurant next door, to which Orson owed several hundred dollars, had refused to release his double steak and triple pistachio ice cream (which he was in the habit of eating, seated in the aisle, while conducting rehearsal) unless they were paid for in cash, and no one in the theatre was able or willing to advance the necessary sum. Augusta Weissberger, hastily summoned from home, took care of that. Then Zolotow of the *Times* called on the box-office phone to ask if we were still going to open when we said we were. I said yes. When I got back into the theatre the run-through had begun. There was a crowd of citizens on the forestage—assorted couples, spies, drunks, market women, hawkers, agitators and lynchers—all calling for "death for those with no holes in their coats." Off stage, in the basement, they were singing *"La Carmagnole."* Then as the street scene faded—behind it, slowly rising out of darkness into light—the elevator platform came into view, revealing a delicate, civilized, eighteenth-century drawing-room scene, all silk and elegance and laughter—three men and two women drinking tea to the soft playing of a harpsichord. It had just cleared the level of the stage, swaying gently as was its wont, when it was shaken by a slight tremor, barely perceptible from the front but enough to make the actors glance at each other. For a few seconds it continued to rise—a charming sight. It had almost reached its mark when it stopped, shuddered (so that a tea cup fell off the table and smashed) and began to sink— slowly at first, but gathering speed as it vanished from sight. There was a silence that seemed eternal, then a girl's scream followed by a crash that shook the theatre. More screams and a man's groan. It came from Erskine Sanford, whose leg was broken; the rest were shaken but unhurt.

Jean Rosenthal, after examining the debris and determining the cause of the crash, which she said would never occur again, asked for three days to repair and reconstruct the elevator. So once again I called Zolotow of *The New York Times* and the rest of the press, canceled two previews and postponed our opening for the third time—"due to technical problems." Sanford was replaced, and Orson continued to rehearse while morale deteriorated.

Our preview situation was becoming a disgrace. Torn between my reluctance to lose the income we so desperately needed and my aversion to giving performances that could only result in bad word of mouth, I postponed one preview after another—five in all. Finally we could delay no longer. Sylvia Regan had begged me not to lose this one—a full house sold to a friendly middle-class group that had seen all our shows and would forgive our imperfections. The elevator had been tested and pronounced safe. There were still a few minor adjustments to be made, but Jeannie, standing over her reeking, oil-smeared mechanics as they tinkered with the cables and gears of what looked like some primitive, medieval siege engine, assured me that all would be well by curtain time. They were still tinkering when the cast came in at half-hour and Jeannie looked troubled. At nine they were still struggling and Welles insisted we cancel. Thinking of the $750 we would have to refund and didn't possess, I refused.

The audience was friendly when I appeared before the curtain at 9:15, spoke smilingly of "technical difficulties" and begged their indulgence. When I went back through the curtain Jeannie said she needed another twenty minutes. At 9:40, to keep them in patience, Welles and Gabel, wearing the tight silk breeches and high neck-pieces of their late-eighteenth-century costumes, went out on the forestage and performed the tent scene from *Julius Caesar*. There was applause and all was well for another twenty minutes; then they began to get restless again and started to clap and to stamp their feet. Orson came out of his dressing room and yelled that we should give them their money back and send them home. I said we didn't have it and he went back inside and slammed the door. Again I asked Jeannie how long. She was looking gray and she said fifteen minutes. Beyond the curtain the clapping and stamping was getting louder. Once again, I went out. I told them how grateful we were for their patience—so grateful that we were now giving them two alternatives. They could leave now, if their patience was at an end (and I couldn't blame them), and keep their present preview tickets, which would be honored at the box office at any time during the run of *Danton's Death*. Or, having waited this long, they could, if they preferred, remain in their seats and witness the performance, which we had every intention of beginning any minute now. I had not quite finished formulating my offer when I felt myself poked in the back. Turning, I saw a small hand protruding through the crack in the curtain, holding out a card on which I could make out the scrawled message:

SORRY NO SHOW TONIGHT—JEAN

With perfect sang-froid I turned back to the audience, concluded my offer, leaped the short distance from the forestage to the orchestra floor, walked quickly up the aisle, and ordered the doorman to open all doors including the safety exits. Returning to the edge of the stage, I vaulted up, faced the audience and raised my hand for silence. "A vote has been taken," I declared quietly, "and the sentiment of this house is overwhelmingly in favor of returning on another night." I wished them goodnight, then slipped back through the curtain onto the stage, from where I listened anxiously to the receding sound of voices as the house rapidly and peacefully emptied. Hardly were the lights out and the doors bolted when the phone rang in the box office. It was Sam Zolotow of the *Times* calling to inquire if this meant still another postponement. I told him yes.

We did give two perfectly smooth previews on the following

nights, which were Friday and Saturday. Our press opening was now set for Wednesday, November 3. It could not take place any sooner because over the weekend we had to do our regular weekly radio show which, on this particular Sunday, was *The War of the Worlds,* better known as *"The Men from Mars."*

The Mercury had been on the air four months; *The War of the Worlds* was our seventeenth broadcast. With the start of the theatre season, since Welles and I could no longer do the entire show by ourselves, we had increased our personnel by two. Our first addition was Paul Stewart, a Broadway and radio actor with ambitions to be a director, who now became our associate producer. The other was an extremely tall, spindly, hollow-eyed, earnest young man by the name of Howard Koch, who, after having had a play performed by the Federal Theatre in Chicago, had abandoned his law practice and arrived in New York with his wife and two children to earn his living as a writer. He was helpless, literate, and in desperate need. This qualified him for association with the Mercury, and I put him to work immediately on a trial basis at fifty dollars a week, which I raised to sixty after he had proved himself. And as aide and liaison I gave him Ann Froelich, who had been typing our scripts during the summer. She was an emphatic, pretty girl from Smith College with fine, ash-blonde hair, a rasping voice and a delicious smell of fading spring flowers.

Even with our augmented staff everyone was perpetually overworked and we rarely managed to get even a half-jump ahead of ourselves. Shows were created week after week under conditions of soul- and health-destroying pressure. But between us we had gradually worked out a system—a sort of chaotic routine which was supposed to survive the eccentricities of our leader. As general editor of the series I chose the material with Welles and, when possible, discussed the tone and general form of the show and its casting possibilities. I then laid it out roughly and turned it over to Koch and Annie, who would have a first draft ready by Wednesday night, when Orson was supposed to read it but seldom did, particularly during the last month's rehearsals of

Danton's Death. On Thursday Paul would put the show through
its first paces, rehearsing it all day with a skeleton cast while Koch
and I made whatever adjustments and changes seemed needed in
the script after we had heard it spoken. Late in the afternoon,
without music and with only rudimentary sound, we would make
an acetate recording of the show. From this record, played back
later—sometimes much later—that night, Orson would give us
his reactions and revisions, which we would accept or dispute. In
the next thirty-six hours the script would be reshaped and re-
written, sometimes drastically. Saturday afternoon there was another rehearsal, with sound—with or without Welles. It was not
until the last day that Orson really took over.

Sundays, at eight, we went on the air. Beginning in the early
afternoon—when Bernard Herrmann arrived with his orchestra
of high-grade symphony players—two simultaneous dramas were
unfolded each week in the stale, tense air of CBS Studio One: the
minor drama of the current show and the major drama of
Orson's titanic struggle to get it on. Sweating, howling, dishev-
eled, and singlehanded he wrestled with chaos and time—always
conveying an effect of being alone, traduced by his collaborators,
surrounded by treachery, ignorance, sloth, indifference, incompe-
tence and—more often than not—downright sabotage. Every
Sunday it was touch and go. As the hands of the clock moved
relentlessly toward air time the crisis grew more extreme, the
peril more desperate. Often violence broke out, which time and
the experience of more than twenty shows had not tempered.
Scripts and scores still flew through the air, doors were slammed,
batons smashed. Scheduled for six—but usually nearer seven—
there was a dress rehearsal, a thing of wild improvisations and
irrevocable catastrophes.

After that, with only a few minutes to go, there was a final
frenzy of correction and reparation, of utter confusion and
absolute horror, aggravated by the gobbling of sandwiches and
the bolting of oversized milkshakes. By now it was less than a
minute to air time—

At that instant, quite regularly week after week, with not one
second to spare, the buffoonery stopped. Suddenly out of chaos,

the show emerged—delicately poised, meticulously executed, precise as clockwork, smooth as satin. And above us all, like a rainbow over storm clouds, stood Orson on his podium, sonorous and heroic, a leader of men surrounded by his band of loyal followers; a giant in action, serene and radiant with the joy of a hard battle bravely fought, a great victory snatched from the jaws of disaster—which, in a sense, it was. For what Orson accomplished each week in those eight terrible hours was quite extraordinary.

In his present tortured mood he was functioning better in the bright lights and frantic atmosphere of Studio One than in the theatrical penumbra of Forty-first Street. He may have appeared faltering and confused on the home stage of the Mercury, where he could fall back on the escapes of postponements and cancellations; on the radio show, with the hands of the electric clock moving relentlessly toward air time and his ineluctable confrontation with an audience of several millions—he was at his very best.

The War of the Worlds formed part of our general plan of contrasting shows. No one, as I recall, was particularly enthusiastic about it. But it seemed good programming—following *Julius Caesar* (with the original Mercury cast and commentary by Kaltenborn* out of Plutarch), *Oliver Twist* (in which Orson played both the boy Oliver and the villainous Fagin), *Eighty Days Around the World*, *The Heart of Darkness*, *Jane Eyre* and before *Life with Father*, which was to be our next show—to throw in something of a scientific nature. We thought of Shiel's *Purple Cloud*, Conan Doyle's *Lost World* and several other well-known works of science fiction before settling on H. G. Wells's twenty-year-old novel, which neither Orson nor I remembered at all clearly. It is just possible that neither of us had ever read it.

Actually it was a narrow squeak. The men from Mars barely escaped being stillborn. Late Tuesday night—thirty-six hours before the first rehearsal—Howard Koch called me at the theatre. He was in deep distress. After three days of slaving on H. G.

* H. V. Kaltenborn was a leading news commentator of the day, distinguished for his clipped, pedantic speech.

Wells's scientific fantasy he was ready to give up. Under no circumstances, he declared, could it be made interesting or in any way credible to modern American ears. Koch was not given to habitual alarmism. To confirm his fears, Annie came to the phone. "You can't do it, Houseman!" she whined. "Those old Martians are just a lot of nonsense! It's all too silly! We're going to make fools of ourselves! Absolute idiots!"

We were not averse to changing a show at the last moment. But the only other script available was an extremely dreary version of *Lorna Doone* which I had started during the summer and abandoned. I reasoned with Koch. I was severe, I taxed him and Annie with defeatism. I gave them false comfort. I promised to come up and help. When I finally got there—around two in the morning—things were better. They were beginning to have fun laying waste the State of New Jersey. Annie had stopped grinding her teeth. I worked with them for the rest of the night and they went on through the next day. Wednesday at sunset the script was finished.

Thursday, as usual, Paul Stewart rehearsed the show, then made a record. We listened to it rather gloomily, between *Danton* rehcarsals, in Orson's room at the St. Regis, sitting on the floor because all the chairs were still covered with coils of unrolled and unedited film. He was dead tired and thought it was a dull show. We all agreed that its only chance of coming off lay in emphasizing its newscast style—its simultaneous, eyewitness quality.

All night we sat up—Howard, Paul, Annie and I—spicing the script with circumstantial allusions and authentic detail. Friday afternoon it was sent over to CBS to be passed by the network censor. Certain name alterations were requested. Under protest and with a deep sense of grievance we changed the Hotel Biltmore to a nonexistent Park Plaza, Trans-America to Inter-Continent, the Columbia Broadcasting Building to Broadcasting Building. Then the script went over to mimeograph and I went back to the theatre. We had done our best and, after all, it was just another radio show.

Saturday, Paul Stewart rehearsed with sound effects and without Welles. He worked for a long time on the crowd scenes, the roar of cannon echoing in the Watchung Hills and the sound of New York Harbor as the ships with the last remaining survivors put out to sea.

Around six we left the studio. Orson, phoning from the theatre a few minutes later to find out how things were going, was told by one of the CBS sound men, who had stayed behind to pack up his equipment, that it was not one of our better shows. Confidentially, the man opined, it just didn't come off. Twenty-seven hours later, quite a few of his employers would have found themselves a good deal happier if he had turned out to be right.

On Sunday, October 30, at 8:00 P.M., E.S.T., in a studio littered with coffee cartons and sandwich paper, Orson swallowed a second container of pineapple juice, put on his earphones, raised his long white fingers and threw the cue for the Mercury theme—the Tchaikovsky Piano Concerto No. 1 in B Flat Minor. After the music dipped, there were routine introductions—then the announcement that a dramatization of H. G. Wells's famous novel, *The War of the Worlds*, was about to be performed. Around 8:01 Orson began to speak, as follows:

WELLES

We know now that in the early years of the twentieth century this world was being watched closely by intelligences greater than man's and yet as mortal as his own. We know now that as human beings busied themselves about their various concerns they were scrutinized and studied, perhaps almost as narrowly as a man with a microscope might scrutinize the transient creatures that swarm and multiply in a drop of water. With infinite complacence people went to and fro over the earth about their little affairs, serene in the assurance of their dominion over this small spinning fragment of solar driftwood which by chance or design man has inherited out of the dark mystery of Time and Space. Yet across an immense ethereal gulf minds that are to our minds as ours are to the beasts in the jungle, intellects vast, cool, and unsympathetic regarded this earth with envious eyes and slowly and surely drew their plans against us. In the thirty-ninth year of the twentieth century came the great disillusionment.

It was near the end of October. Business was better. The war scare was over. More men were back at work. Sales were picking up. On this particular evening, October 30th, the Crossley service estimated that thirty-two million people were listening in on their radios. . . .

Neatly, without perceptible transition, he was followed on the air by an anonymous announcer caught in a routine bulletin:

ANNOUNCER

. . . for the next twenty-four hours not much change in temperature. A slight atmospheric disturbance of undetermined origin is reported over Nova Scotia, causing a low pressure area to move down rather rapidly over the northeastern states, bringing a forecast of rain, accompanied by winds of light gale force. Maximum temperature 66; minimum 48. This weather report comes to you from the Government Weather Bureau. . . . We now take you to the Meridian Room in the Hotel Park Plaza in downtown New York, where you will be entertained by the music of Ramon Raquello and his orchestra.

At which cue, Bernard Herrmann led the massed men of the CBS house orchestra in a thunderous symphonic rendition of *"La Cumparsita."* The entire hoax might have been exposed there and then—but for the fact that hardly anyone was listening. They were being entertained by Charlie McCarthy.

The Crossley census, taken about a week before the broadcast, had given us 3.6 percent of the listening audience to Edgar Bergen's 34.7 percent. What the Crossley Institute (that hireling of the advertising agencies) deliberately ignored, was the healthy American habit of dial twisting. On that particular evening Edgar Bergen, in the person of Charlie McCarthy, temporarily left the air about 8:12 P.M. E.S.T., yielding place to a new and not very popular singer. At that point, and during the following minutes, a large number of listeners started twisting their dials in search of other entertainment. Many of them turned to us—and when they did, they stayed put! For by this time the mysterious meteorite had fallen at Grovers Mill in New Jersey, the Martians had begun to show their foul leathery heads above the ground, and the New Jersey State Police were racing to the spot. Within a few minutes people all over the United States were praying, crying, fleeing frantically to escape death from the Martians. Some remembered to rescue loved ones, others telephoned farewells or warnings, hurried to inform neighbors, sought information from newspapers or radio stations, summoned ambulances and police cars.

The reaction was strongest at points nearest the tragedy—in Newark, New Jersey, in a single block, more than twenty families rushed out of their houses with wet handkerchiefs and towels over their faces. Some began moving household furniture. Police switchboards were flooded with calls inquiring, "Shall I close my windows?"; "Have the police any extra gas masks?" Police found one family waiting in the yard with wet cloths on faces contorted with hysteria. As one woman reported later:

> I was terribly frightened. I wanted to pack and take my child in my arms, gather up my friends and get in the car and just go north as far as we could. But what I did was just sit by one window, praying, listening, and scared stiff, and my husband by the other sniffing, and looking out to see if people were running. . . .

In New York hundreds of people on Riverside Drive left their homes ready for flight. Bus terminals were crowded. A woman calling up the Dixie Bus Terminal for information said impatiently, "Hurry please, the world is coming to an end and I have a lot to do."

In the parlor churches of Harlem, evening service became "end of the world" prayer meetings. Many turned to God in that moment:

> I held a crucifix in my hand and prayed while looking out of my open window for falling meteors. . . . When the monsters were wading across the Hudson River and coming

into New York, I wanted to run up on my roof to see what they looked like, but I couldn't leave my radio while it was telling me of their whereabouts.

Aunt Grace began to pray with Uncle Henry. Lily got sick to her stomach. I don't know what I did exactly but I know I prayed harder and more earnestly than ever before. Just as soon as we were convinced that this thing was real, how petty all things on this earth seemed; how soon we put our trust in God!

The panic moved upstate. One man called up the Mt. Vernon Police Headquarters to find out "where the forty policemen were killed." Another took time out to philosophize:

I thought the whole human race was going to be wiped out —that seemed more important than the fact that we were going to die. It seemed awful that everything that had been worked on for years was going to be lost forever.

In Rhode Island weeping and hysterical women swamped the switchboard of the Providence *Journal* for details of the massacre, and officials of the electric light company received a score of calls urging them to turn off all lights so that the city would be safe from the enemy. The Boston *Globe* received a call from one woman who "could see the fire." A man in Pittsburgh hurried home in the midst of the broadcast and found his wife in the bathroom, a bottle of poison in her hand, screaming, "I'd rather die this way than that." In Minneapolis a woman ran into church screaming, "New York destroyed, this is the end of the world. You might as well go home to die. I just heard it on the radio."

The Kansas City bureau of the AP received inquiries about the "meteors" from Los Angeles; Salt Lake City; Beaumont, Texas; and St. Joseph, Missouri. In San Francisco the general impression of listeners seemed to be that an overwhelming force had invaded the United States from the air—was in process of destroying New York and threatening to move westward. "My

God," roared an inquirer into a telephone, "where can I volunteer my services, we've got to stop this awful thing!"

As far south as Birmingham, Alabama, people gathered in churches and prayed. On the campus of a Southeastern college—

> The girls in the sorority houses and dormitories huddled around their radios trembling and weeping in each other's arms. They separated themselves from their friends only to take their turn at the telephones to make long-distance calls to their parents, saying goodbye for what they thought might be the last time. . . .

There are hundreds of such items, gathered from coast to coast. At least one book* and quite a pile of sociological literature have appeared on the subject of "the invasion from Mars." Many theories have been put forward to explain the "tidal wave" of panic that swept the nation. Two factors, in my opinion, contributed to the broadcast's extraordinarily violent effect. First, its historical timing. It came within thirty-five days of the Munich crisis. For weeks, the American people had been hanging on their radios, getting most of their news over the air. A new technique of "on-the-spot" reporting had been developed and eagerly accepted by an anxious and news-hungry world. The Mercury Theatre of the Air, by faithfully copying every detail of the new technique, including its imperfections, found an already enervated audience ready to accept its wildest fantasies. The second factor was the show's sheer technical brilliance. To this day it is impossible to sit in a room and hear the scratched, worn, off-the-air recording of the broadcast without feeling in the back of your neck some slight draft left over from that great wind of terror that swept the nation. Even with the element of credibility totally removed it remains a surprisingly effective broadcast.

Beginning some time around two when the show started to take shape under Orson's hands, a strange fever seemed to invade the studio—part childish mischief, part professional zeal. First to

* *The Invasion from Mars,* by Hadley Cantril, Princeton University Press, from which many of the above quotations were taken.

feel it were the actors. I remember Frank Readick (who played the part of Carl Phillips, the network's special reporter) going down to the record library and digging up the recording of the explosion of the *Hindenburg* at Lakehurst. This is a classic reportage—one of those wonderful, unpredictable accidents of eyewitness description. The broadcaster is casually describing the routine landing of the giant dirigible. Suddenly he sees something. A flash of flame! An instant later the whole thing explodes. It takes him time—a full second—to react at all. Then seconds more of sputtering ejaculations before he can make the adjustment between brain and tongue. He starts to describe the terrible things he sees—the writhing human figures twisting and squirming as they fall from the white burning wreckage. He stops, fumbles, vomits, then quickly continues. Readick played the record to himself, over and over. Then, recreating the emotion in his own terms, he described the Martian meteorite as he saw it lying inert and harmless in a field at Grovers Mill, lit up by the headlights of a hundred cars, the coppery cylinder suddenly opening, revealing the leathery tentacles and the terrible pale-eyed faces of the Martians within. As they began to emerge he froze, unable to translate his vision into words; he fumbled, retched, and then after a second continued.

A few moments later Carl Phillips lay dead, tumbling over the microphone in his fall—one of the first victims of the Martian ray. There followed a moment of absolute silence—an eternity of waiting. Then without warning, the network's emergency fill-in was heard—somewhere in a quiet studio, a piano, close on mike, playing "Clair de Lune," soft and sweet as honey, for many seconds, while the fate of the universe hung in the balance. Finally it was interrupted by the manly reassuring voice of Brigadier General Montgomery Smith, Commander of the New Jersey State Militia, speaking from Trenton and placing "the counties of Mercer and Middlesex as far west as Princeton and east to Jamesburg" under martial law! Tension—release—then renewed tension. Soon after that came an eyewitness account of the fatal battle of the Watchung Hills; then, once again, that lone piano was heard—now a symbol of terror, shattering the dead air with its ominous

399

tinkle. As it played on and on, its effect became increasingly sinister—a thin band of suspense stretched almost beyond endurance.

That piano was the neatest trick of the show—a fine specimen of the theatrical "retard," boldly conceived and exploited to the full. It was one of the many devices with which Welles succeeded in compelling not merely the attention, but also the belief of his invisible audience. *The War of the Worlds* was a magic act, one of the world's greatest, and Orson was the man to bring it off.

For Welles, as I have said, was, first and foremost, a magician whose particular talent lay in his ability to stretch the familiar elements of theatrical effect far beyond their normal point of tension. For this reason (as we were discovering to our sorrow on Forty-first Street) his productions required more careful preparation and more perfect execution than most; like all complicated magic tricks, they remained, till the last moment, in a state of precarious balance. When they came off they gave, by virtue of their unusually high intensity, an impression of the greatest brilliance and power; when they failed—when something in their balance went wrong or the original structure proved to have been unsound—they provoked a particularly violent reaction of unease and revulsion. Welles's flops were louder than other men's. The Mars broadcast was one of his unqualified successes.

Among the columnists and public figures who discussed the affair during the next few days (some praising us for the public service we had rendered, some condemning us as sinister scoundrels), the most general reaction was one of amazement at the "incredible stupidity" and "gullibility" of the American public, who had accepted as real, in this single broadcast, incidents which in actual fact would have taken days or even weeks to occur. One explanation of our success lay in the fact that the first few minutes of our broadcast were strictly realistic in time and perfectly credible, though somewhat boring, in content. Herein lay the great tensile strength of the show; it was the structural device that made the whole illusion possible. And it could have been carried off in no other medium than radio.

Our actual broadcasting time, from the first mention of the

meteorites to the fall of New York City, was less than forty minutes. During that time men traveled long distances, large bodies of troops were mobilized, cabinet meetings were held, savage battles fought on land and in the air. And millions of people accepted it—emotionally if not logically.

There is nothing so very strange about that. Most of us do the same thing, to some degree, most days of our lives—every time we look at a movie or a television show. Not even the realistic theatre observes the literal unities; films, TV and, particularly, in its day, radio (where neither place nor time existed save in the imagination of the listener) have no difficulty in getting their audiences to accept the telescoped reality of dramatic time. Our special hazard lay in the fact that we purported to be not a play, but reality. In order to take advantage of the accepted convention, we had to slide swiftly and imperceptibly out of the "real" time of a news report into the "dramatic" time of a fictional broadcast. Once that was achieved—without losing the audience's attention or arousing their skepticism—once they were sufficiently absorbed and bewitched not to notice the transitions any more, there was no extreme of fantasy through which they would not follow us. If, that night, the American public proved "gullible," it was because enormous pains and a great deal of thought had been spent to make it so.

In the script, *The War of the Worlds* started extremely slowly—dull meteorological and astronomical bulletins alternating with musical interludes. These were followed by a colorless scientific interview and still another stretch of dance music. These first few minutes of routine broadcasting "within the existing standards of judgment of the listener" were intended to lull (or maybe bore) the audience into a false security and to furnish a solid base of realistic time from which to accelerate later. Orson, in directing the show, extended these slow movements far beyond our original conception. The interview in the Princeton Observatory—the clockwork ticking monotonously overhead, the woolly-minded professor mumbling vague replies to the reporters' uninformed questions—this, too, was dragged out to the point of tedium. Over my protests, lines were restored that had been cut at earlier rehearsals. I cried there would not be a listener left. Welles stretched them out even longer.

He was right. His sense of tempo, that night, was infallible. When the flashed news of the cylinder's landing finally came—almost fifteen minutes after the beginning of a fairly dull show—he was able suddenly to spiral his action to a speed as wild and reckless as its base was solid. The appearance of the Martians; their first treacherous act; the death of Carl Phillips; the arrival of the militia; the battle of the Watchung Hills; the destruction of New Jersey—all these were telescoped into a space of twelve minutes without overstretching the listeners' emotional credulity. The broadcast, by then, had its own reality, the reality of emotionally felt time and space.

At the height of the crisis, around 8:31, the Secretary of the Interior came on the air with an exhortation to the American people. It was admirably spoken—in a voice just faintly reminiscent of Franklin Delano Roosevelt's—by a young man named Kenneth Delmar, who later grew rich and famous as Senator Claghorn.

THE SECRETARY

Citizens of the nation: I shall not try to conceal the gravity of the situation that confronts the country, nor the concern of your Government in protecting the lives and property of its people. However, I wish to impress upon you—private citizens and public officials, all of you—the urgent need of calm and resourceful action. Fortunately, this formidable enemy is still confined to a comparatively small area, and we may place our faith in the military forces to keep them there. In the meantime placing our trust in God, we must continue the performance of our duties, each and every one of us, so that we may confront this destructive adversary with a nation united, courageous, and consecrated to the preservation of human supremacy on this earth. I thank you.

Toward the end of this speech (circa 8:32 E.S.T.), Davidson Taylor, supervisor of the broadcast for the Columbia Broadcasting System, received a phone call in the control room, creased his lips, and hurriedly left the studio. By the time he returned, a few minutes later, pale as death, clouds of heavy smoke were rising from Newark, New Jersey, and the Martians, tall as skyscrapers, were astride the Pulaski Highway preparatory to wading the Hudson River. To us in the studio the show seemed to be progressing splendidly—how splendidly Davidson Taylor had just learned outside. For several minutes now, a kind of madness had been sweeping the continent: it was somehow connected with our show. The CBS switchboards had been swamped into uselessness, but from outside sources vague rumors were coming in of deaths and suicides and panic injuries by the thousands.

Taylor had orders to interrupt the show immediately with an explanatory station announcement. By now the Martians were across the Hudson and gas was blanketing the city. The end was near. We were less than a minute from the station break. Ray Collins, superb as the "last announcer," was choking heroically to death on the roof of Broadcasting Building. The boats were all whistling for a while as the last of the refugees perished in New York Harbor. Finally, as they died away, an amateur short-wave operator was heard, from heaven knows where, weakly reaching out for human companionship across the empty world:

2X2L Calling CQ
2X2L Calling CQ
2X2L Calling CQ
Isn't there anyone on the air?
Isn't there anyone?

Five seconds of absolute silence. Then, shattering the reality of world's end—the announcer's voice was heard, suave and bright:

ANNOUNCER

You are listening to the CBS presentation of Orson Welles and the Mercury Theatre of the Air in an original dramatization of *The War of the Worlds,* by H. G. Wells. The performance will continue after a brief intermission.

The second part of the show well written and sensitively played —but nobody heard it. It recounted the adventures of a lone sur-

vivor, with interesting observations on the nature of human society; it described the eventual death of the Martian invaders,
slain—"after all man's defenses had failed by the humblest thing
that God in his wisdom had put upon this earth"—by bacteri-
ological action; it told of the rebuilding of a brave new world.
After a stirring musical finale, Welles, in his own person, delivered a charmingly apologetic little speech about Halloween
and goblins.

I remember, during the playing of the final theme, the phone
starting to ring in the control room and a shrill voice through the
receiver announcing itself as belonging to the mayor of some
Midwestern city, one of the big ones. He was screaming for
Welles. Choking with fury, he reported mobs in the streets of his
city, women and children huddled in the churches, violence and
looting. If, as he now learned, the whole thing was nothing but a
crummy joke—then he, personally, was on his way to New York
to punch the author of it on the nose! I hung up quickly. For we
were off the air now and the studio door had burst open.

The following hours were a nightmare. The building was suddenly full of people and dark-blue uniforms. Hustled out of the
studio, we were locked into a small back office on another floor.
Here we sat incommunicado while network employees were
busily collecting, destroying, or locking up all scripts and records
of the broadcast. Finally the Press was let loose upon us, ravening
for horror. How many deaths had *we* heard of? (Implying they
knew of thousands.) What did *we* know of the fatal stampede in
a Jersey hall? (Implying it was one of many.) What traffic
deaths? (The ditches must be choked with corpses.) The suicides? (Haven't you heard about the one on Riverside Drive?) It
is all quite vague in my memory and quite terrible.

Hours later, instead of arresting us, they let us out a back way
and we scurried down to the theatre like hunted animals to their
hole. It was surprising to see life going on as usual in the midnight streets, cars stopping for traffic, people walking. At the
Mercury the company was still rehearsing *Danton's Death*—
falling up and down stairs and singing the *"Carmagnole."* Welles
went up on stage, where photographers, lying in wait, caught

him with his eyes raised to heaven, his arms outstretched in an attitude of crucifixion. Thus he appeared in a tabloid the next morning over the caption, "I Didn't Know What I Was Doing!" *The New York Times* quoted him as saying, "I don't think we will choose anything like this again."

We were on the front page for two days. Having had to bow to radio as a news source during the Munich crisis, the press was now only too eager to expose the perilous irresponsibilities of the new medium. Orson was their whipping boy. They quizzed and badgered him. Condemnatory editorials were delivered by our press-clipping bureau in bushel baskets. There was talk, for a while, of criminal action.*

Then gradually, after about two weeks, the excitement subsided. By then it had been discovered that the casualties were not as numerous or as serious as had at first been supposed. One young woman had fallen and broken her arm running downstairs. Later the Federal Communications Commission held some hearings and passed some regulations. The Columbia Broadcasting System made a public apology. With that the official aspects of the incident were closed.

Of the suits that were brought against the network—amounting to over three-quarters of a million dollars for damages, injuries, miscarriages and distresses of various kinds—not one was substantiated. We did settle one claim, however. It was the particularly affecting case of a man in Massachusetts, who wrote:

> I thought the best thing to do was to go away. So I took three dollars twenty-five cents out of my savings and bought a ticket. After I had gone sixty miles I knew it was a play. Now I don't have money left for the shoes I was saving up for. Will you please have someone send me a pair of black shoes size 9B!

* It was during this crisis that Arnold Weissberger first proved his worth as a lawyer. There was a small clause in the contract, accepted by CBS, that absolved us from all legal liability resulting from the content of our show. Claims of all sorts, from miscarriages to mental anguish, that had been sent over to us by the Network's lawyers, were returned to them for disposal.

We did. And all the lawyers were very angry with us.

So obsessive had our rehearsal pattern become on *Danton's Death* that on the night following the *Mars* broadcast we were back in the Mercury Theatre checking light cues with Jean Rosenthal at three in the morning. We had spent half the day closeted with CBS network executives, the other half being cornered by the press in unlikely places. That evening there had been a preview of *Danton* which had not gone badly: in my hazy condition it almost seemed as though Sokoloff was becoming comprehensible and Gabel dynamic. Orson still had a few changes he wanted to make; he rehearsed the cast for two hours after the show; then we got down to light changes. At 3:20 A.M. our chief electrician, who had been doubled up over his dimmers for seven hours, fainted and fell off the switchboard. He was revived and placed in a taxi. As it went off down Forty-first Street a phone began to ring in the box office. It was Sam Zolotow of the *Times*. He said he was sorry to hear about the electrician and hoped it wasn't serious. I said no. He asked if this meant another postponement. I said no and goodnight.*

At our opening night performance of *Danton's Death*, mingling with the press, the fashionables and intelligentsia, Marc Blitzstein identified Earl Browder, secretary of the American Communist Party; Joe Freeman, leader of the Trotskyites; and Jay Lovestone, head of still another dissident Marxist sect, all seated within a few yards of each other. The performance was good—the best we had given so far—but the audience was restless.

Mina Curtiss was giving a party for the cast in her downtown apartment, but I did not go down there until after everyone had left. I sat in Bleeck's waiting for the reviews. *The New York Times* was first and from what I could gather from Sam Zolotow's

* I discovered later who the informer was: it was one of our most dedicated extras, who received a couple of dollars every time he slipped Sam Zolotow a bit of hot, preferably bad news.

furtive reading over the phone, Atkinson liked us a lot. I heard the words—

> Overwhelming. . . . A worthy successor to *Julius Caesar* and *Shoemaker's Holiday*. . . . Mr. Welles's real genius is in the theatricality of his invention. . . . Using the script as a ground plan of a show he knows how to impregnate it with the awe and tumult of a theatrical performance. . . . By the wizardry of lighting he gives the broken narrative a fluid progress across the stage and at times a dazzling brilliance. . .

I have always suspected that Brooks Atkinson, anticipating the reactions of his colleagues, went out of his way to help the Mercury that night. Our notices were not disgraceful, but there was little in the papers the next day to encourage anyone to visit the Mercury Theatre while *Danton's Death* was playing there. "For the Mercury the honeymoon is over" was the general tone of the reviews. Our friends on the weeklies were particularly severe. Stark Young wrote of the play that except for a few "flair-flashes" it was a pleasant bore more suited to the Little Theatres of a decade ago than to the Mercury. Joseph Wood Krutch felt that the production was "as much a parody of Mr. Welles's methods as the play itself seems a parody of post-war German pessimism." Gabel did better than I expected. He was praised for "an impelling performance. . . . Sturdy, full-blooded, defiant." On Sokoloff opinions were divided. One admired his "ravaged asceticism," another the "wonderful, quivering simplicity of a pedantic demagogue." Others found him merely unintelligible. Rosamond Gilder gave us credit in the *Theatre Arts Monthly* for an experimental production such as "only the lucky few who were able to travel when Russia and Germany still had creative theatres have had opportunities to enjoy." *Variety*, more hard-boiled, warned that "if the Mercury's Wonder Boy hopes to retain his legit prestige, he will have to give his best to the theatre, not his second best."

By the end of our first week it had become apparent that nothing could save us—not even the men from Mars. The ticket agencies ignored us; half of our theatre parties were canceled;

our faithful, lower-middle-class semi-intellectual audience was conspicuous by its absence. After twenty-one performances we threw in the sponge—not just for *Danton's Death* but for the Mercury Theatre. It all happened so quickly and quietly that we never knew what hit us. Even now it is difficult to explain how one single setback (which by the law of theatrical averages was long overdue) could have annihilated an organization with such a fantastic record of unbroken success and acclaim. We had planned, operated and sacrificed to form a repertory theatre capable of withstanding just such hazards; at the first intimation of failure, without the slightest gesture of resistance, we lay down and died.

We were broke. With the ruinous cost of all those incessant, all-night rehearsals and the endless postponements that had meant carrying the entire company and staff at full salary for two months beyond our original opening date, we had spent every cent of the money I had raised with such difficulty for our entire season. (For several weeks, now, we had been regularly issuing checks, on the theory that it was all right for them to bounce once, or even twice, but that they should be made good the third time.) But it was not money, or the lack of it, that destroyed us. It is always possible to find money—somewhere, somehow, for something you really want to do. And I have always believed that if we had really wanted to save the Mercury Theatre that winter, we could have done so. If we had dropped everything else (including *Five Kings*) and used our radio money to restore to health the repertory theatre to which our life had been dedicated the year before, there is no doubt in my mind that we could have done it. The truth is—we were no longer interested. In the grandiose and reckless scheme of our lives, the Mercury had fulfilled its purpose. It had brought us success and fame; it had put Welles on the cover of *Time* and our radio show on the front page of every newspaper in the country. Inevitably, any day now, the offers from Hollywood would start arriving. It was too late to turn back and we did not really want to.

In mid-December, a few days before Christmas and three weeks before we started rehearsing *Five Kings,* we abandoned the theatre and liquidated the organization. George Zorn became company manager for *Five Kings* and Senber its press agent, working with the Guild's publicity department.* And I found a subtenant for the Mercury: a left-wing Yiddish workers' theatre group known as ARTEF, which had achieved considerable success over the past year with a nineteenth-century Russian play, *The Recruits,* and two autobiographical plays by Maxim Gorky. Before they could move in, we had to restore the stage floor we had wrecked for *Danton's Death.* Through the window of my projection-booth office I saw the work started, then moved to the Empire Theatre building into a two-room suite on the third floor formerly occupied by Jed Harris.

So now (though the electric sign over the door remained untouched until the building was pulled down to make room for a parking lot after the war) the Mercury Theatre was no more. Like the Oceanic it had lasted a little over a year; like the Oceanic it had flown too near the sun, and when the wax melted, no one was surprised. There was no moaning at the bar when we departed.

> After a giddy trip to the Moon the Mercury has come to earth with a rude crash and the gods of last year's theatre have become mortal men again. Sic transit gloria dramatis!

So began our obituary in *The New York Times.* It attributed the eclipse of the Mercury to the cost of repertory and the egotism of its directors. And it ended on a note of regretful affection:

> Let us hope that the Mercury continues to represent Hobo-hemia in the theatre—not too sensible and never dull!

In his admirable book, *The Fervent Years,* Harold Clurman has made his appraisal of the Mercury: he concedes "a dash of originality, a boyish zip"; he refers to our "newfangled bohemianism," to our "fundamental lack of seriousness" and to our

---

* Senber has always claimed that in lieu of his last week's salary from the Mercury he and his bride of two weeks received a secondhand vacuum cleaner from the theatre that never worked.

"delightful capacity to turn easily from our presumed path with a genial what-the-hell." He also describes us as sensational but not controversial. "The Mercury was safe. It trod on no toes but rather kicked the seat of traditions for which our reverence is more advertised than real."

There is some truth to this analysis of our attitude, which he contrasts with the more consistent dedication of his own Group, who looked to the theatre for a chance "to live full lives unified by disciplined moral and intellectual codes" and "to provide for its members what society failed to provide."

The Group Theatre's life was considerably longer and, in many ways, more significant than ours: through its development of the "Method," its influence on American acting has been, for better or worse, dominant for a quarter of a century, first in the theatre and then in films and television. Yet, today, the Mercury's program and structure, together with certain aspects of our theatrical behavior, come rather closer to the current needs and hopes of the American theatre than the more intense and far less flexible tenets of the Group. Personally and collectively the Group was more "social-minded" and held far more radical social views than ours—which were virtually nonexistent. Yet in the theatre it was we who were the radicals, they who were conservative and conventional. The Group's productions were consistently and obstinately naturalistic: almost without exception they worked inside the proscenium arch in the obsolescent tradition of realistic scenery and the fourth wall. And in their business practices (which were no more stable than ours) they blindly followed the most traditional and arthritic practices of the capitalist, commercial theatre that they condemned.

With the exception of *Waiting for Lefty* (which, though written and performed by Group members, was originally a New Theatre presentation) and *My Heart's in the Highlands* (produced for a limited run at Clurman's insistence out of the profits of *Golden Boy*) all Group Theatre plays were produced on Broadway under Broadway conditions and at Broadway prices. While we were riding the furious waters of the mid-thirties—blown by winds of change from WPA to Mass Media, from the

Imperial to the Lafayette, from Shubert Alley to Harlem and back to Thirty-ninth Street, from the Maxine Elliott to the Venice and, finally, into our own shabby playhouse on Forty-first Street—the Group's directors were cooling their heels in the Shubert offices, humbly waiting for a theatre in which to present their latest play when they had finally raised the money to produce it on Broadway terms. They who, of all people, should have striven to achieve the flexible status of a permanent low-priced People's theatre were condemned by their directors to play intermittently for the carriage trade at prices that were higher and for runs that were even more precarious than ours.

In our very different ways—together with the Neighborhood, the Provincetown, Eva Le Gallienne's Civic Repertory and the ubiquitous and protean Theatre Guild—we represented the leading attempts at continuity in the American theatre over the past half-century. Of all these, the Mercury Theatre was the shortest lived but, in its final influence, perhaps not the least important.

X

For two weeks after the Martian broadcast the fate of the Mercury Theatre of the Air hung in the balance while executives of the Columbia Broadcasting System tried to make up their minds whether they were proud or ashamed of us. Then, just before Thanksgiving, the Campbell Soup Company came through with an offer of commercial sponsorship at prime time and at such a figure that the network was suddenly very proud of us indeed.

Accompanied by Ward Wheelock, head of the agency that represented them, Orson and I, in our most conservative suits and stiff collars, journeyed to Camden, New Jersey, and spent several hours with the president of Campbell Soups and his leading executives. Dutifully we made our tour of the plant, saw hecatombs of dead chickens and huge, bubbling vats of tomato and pea. At noon, in the executive dining room, we smacked our lips over the thin, briny liquid of which we were about to become the champions. After lunch there was a formal meeting around a long, gleaming table with pads and pencils that so awed us that Orson and I—all four hundred pounds of us—sat down with perfect solemnity in the same chair. A few days later (just about the time *Danton* closed) the deal was consummated and announced: The Mercury Theatre of the Air had become The Campbell Playhouse.

This time we were really in the big money. Orson himself, depending on the size of the cast and the cost of royalties, stood to make between $1000 and $1500 a week. But there were disadvantages. After the first excitement had worn off and we began preparations for the new series, it became apparent that our life with Campbell's Soups was going to be less agreeable than when we were our own masters. Previously our only worries had been over the quality of the broadcast and the problems of getting it on the air: now we were concerned with "format" and with adjusting to the commercials that riddled the broadcast. Welles, in addition to being "producer, writer, director, star and narrator" of the Campbell Playhouse now became its leading salesman: he assumed the role of a sophisticated world traveler who, having savored all the greatest broths and potages of the civilized world, still returned with joy and appreciation to Campbell's delicious chicken-and-rice, tomato and pea. Also, since the agency felt we should enliven our own classic tastes with more popular fiction, elaborate negotiations now had to be conducted for the radio rights to current best sellers. This was also true of our casting. Gone were the happy days of our tight little stock company: each week, after endless bickering with agents and studios, one or more greater or lesser movie stars were brought in to brighten the show. While Orson was struggling with *Five Kings,* most of this added work devolved upon Paul Stewart and myself aided by Howard Koch and a flock of slaves and piece-workers, including, on one occasion, the poet W. H. Auden, who received one hundred dollars for an "extraction" of *Pride and Prejudice.*

The Mercury Theatre of the Air came to an end on December 4th and the Campbell Playhouse was launched five days later. Our opening show was Daphne du Maurier's *Rebecca,* with Margaret Sullavan as the unnamed heroine, Welles as the romantic

hero with a secret tragedy in his past and Agnes Moorehead as the
dreadful Mrs. Danvers. It was a resounding success, and it was
followed by the inevitable *Christmas Carol,* in which Orson
played Scrooge and, if I remember rightly, Tiny Tim.

*   *   *

To tell the story of *Five Kings* is like trying to record the terminal stages of a complicated and fatal disease. The name of our
disease was success—accumulating success that had little to do
with the quality of our work but seemed to proliferate around
the person of Orson Welles with a wild, monstrous growth of its
own.

Published around this time and almost lost in the whirlwind
of publicity that swirled around Orson's name, a *New Yorker*
"profile" had come out. It was better researched than the *Time*
cover story, with a fuller background and a more perceptive view
of the twenty-three-year-old Wonder Boy in the first fevered flush
of his rising fame.* Among the elements the writer had diagnosed as decisive in Welles's life was the divorce of his parents:
the beautiful, passionate mother who died young and the Chicago society playboy after whom, in his heyday, "a restaurant, a
race horse and a cigar had been named." This friend of musicians, artists and writers was also an inventor of useless gadgets
(an unbreakable picnic set that splintered at a touch, a homemade aeroplane that flew only when towed by the family car)
and a bon vivant who, before killing himself in a Chicago hotel
room, had cut a wide swath on three continents. Through him,
vicariously, while still in his early teens, Orson had "sampled the
wine, women and song of London, Paris, the Riviera, Singapore,
Tokyo and the island of Jamaica."

Those of us who were close to Orson had long been aware of

---

* There was a sentence in the profile which both Welles and I found
offensive, though for different reasons. Russell Maloney had written of the
Mercury operation that "if Welles is the inspiration of the group, Houseman is the brains. He is thirteen years older than Welles, heavy-set with receding hair and a weakness for check jackets and suede shoes."

the obsessive part his father continued to play in his life. Much of what he had accomplished so precociously had been done out of a furious need to prove himself in the eyes of a man who was no longer there to see it. Now that success had come, in quantities and of a kind that his father had never dreamed of, this conflict, far from being assuaged, seemed to grow more intense and consuming. Having demonstrated his superiority as an artist and a public figure, he must now defeat his rival on his own ground—that of Champagne Charley, the man about town.

This helped to explain the growing wildness and the conspicuous extravagance of Orson's behavior that winter. It was as though he was determined to bury the ghost of Richard Welles, once and for all, under the mass of his own excesses. Each meal was a feast; his consumption of alcohol was between one and two bottles of whisky or brandy a night; for his new apartment, which had a living room the size of a skating rink, he acquired furniture so huge that it had to be hoisted by a crane through the double windows; his sexual prowess, which he was inclined to report in full statistical detail, was also, apparently, immense. This dissipation reached its climax during *Five Kings* and contributed to that calamity. It conditioned the atmosphere in which the production was prepared and helped to give the entire venture the tone of grotesque horror with which it is associated in my memory.

It was, at best, a difficult and unwieldy project. To make it possible I had had to do some ingenious and tricky manipulation. From the day Orson first suggested it as a Mercury production, it had been apparent that it was far beyond our means. I knew that the Theatre Guild was having a difficult time finding five new productions a year for its subscribers. Early in May 1938, in the pride of our four successive triumphs, I offered to help them out. I visited Warren Munsell, their general manager, and explained that since our own theatre was too small to hold this colossus of ours, we would consider an association with the Theatre Guild for its production and presentation the following winter. He was interested enough to arrange a meeting with my old friends and enemies, Lawrence Langner and Theresa Helburn. Strong in my position as head of the town's most successful new producing organization, I must have given a convincing impression of self-assurance. Within a week we had a deal. The first half of *Five Kings,* which included a fragment of *Richard II,* the two parts of *Henry IV* and *Henry V,* was to be presented on its subscription series by the Guild as a Mercury production directed by Orson Welles. If successful it was to be followed by a second evening—all three parts of *Henry VI* and *Richard III*—to be rehearsed during the run of the first. All artistic decisions were ours; so was the budget of forty thousand dollars, of which the Mercury would contribute five in cash and five in services, with the Guild supplying the balance. The two things they kept asking me were how long the performance would run—to which I had no answer—and how we expected to produce a hundred-thousand-dollar show for forty thousand dollars. Since my estimate was based on the wildest of guesses, I could only reply that the Mercury had its own way of doing things which I was not prepared to reveal.

So a joint announcement was given to the press and *Five Kings* was placed on the Guild's New York schedule, with a two weeks' preliminary engagement in Boston. Seven months later, Orson began to grow a beard for the part of Falstaff, and soon after Christmas we started to rehearse in the ballroom of the Claridge Hotel off Times Square, then moved onto the various empty stages that the Guild was able to procure for us around town. Gone were the days when we could insist on working in a full set on our own stage and Jeannie did the impossible to satisfy us. Orson raged—not without reason. For if ever a play needed ideal physical conditions to rehearse in, this was it. I have always believed that if Welles could have put on *Five Kings* under the same circumstances and with the same dedicated preparation as he devoted to *Julius Caesar,* it could have been one of the memorable events of the modern theatre. His production scheme was brilliant—a viable theatrical solution to the problem of moving an historical play with multiple locations through an infinitely varied and mobile pattern of continuous, progressive action.

The Cradle Will Rock ("oratorio" version): Peggy Coudray (Mrs. Mister) and John Hoysradt (Dauber) with Marc Blitzstein at the eviscerated piano.

John Houseman and Marc Blitzstein in conference.

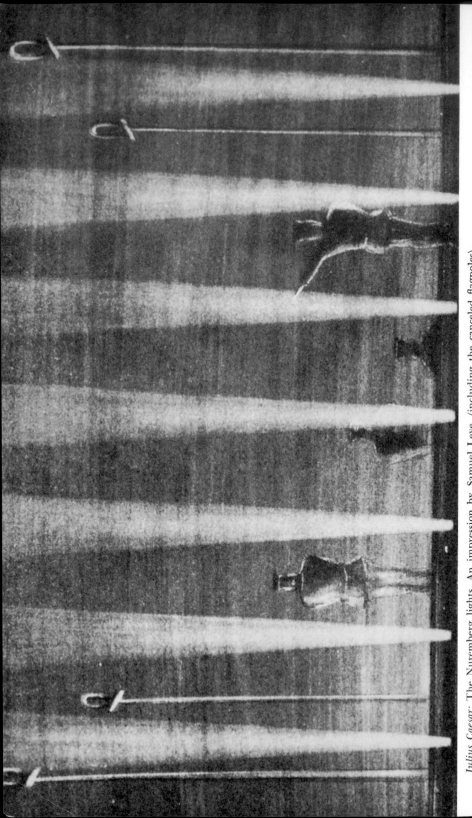

Julius Caesar: The Nuremberg lights. An impression by Samuel Leve (including the canceled flagpoles).

Julius Caesar: George Coulouris as Antony. " 'Friends, Romans, countrymen' sounded on his tongue like a rabble-rousing harangue uttered for the first time."

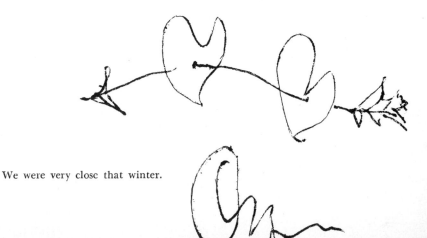

We were very close that winter.

Julius Caesar: Norman Lloyd (right) as Cinna the Poet, with Joseph Cotten, Ross Elliot and the Mercury's three stage managers—Richard Wilson, Walter Ash and William Alland (alias Vakhtangov).

Julius Caesar: (Act I, Scene 2) : Cassius and Brutus.

Julius Caesar: Brutus and Portia.

The Shoemaker's Holiday: Among those standing are Stefan Schnabel (third from left), followed by George Duthie, Edith Barrett, Vincent Price, Marian Waring-Manley, George Coulouris, Whitford Kane, Ruth Ford, Alice Frost, Joseph Cotten, Fred Tozere (bearded); kneeling are Ross Elliot, Arthur Anderson, William Alland, Francis Carpenter, Jack Berry, Norman Lloyd, Hiram Sherman.

OPPOSITE

Hirman Sherman as *Firk*—a "jackanapes in droopy drawers and flapping codpiece whose fingernail playing of low comedy won him a first-night ovation."

Heartbreak House: Left to right, Brenda Forbes, Eustace Wyatt, Orson Welles, Mady Christians, John Hoysradt, Phyllis Joyce, Vincent Price, Geraldine Fitzgerald, Erskine Sanford and George Coulouris.

Danton's Death: Saint-Just and Fouqu (Orson Welles and Eustace Wyatt) .

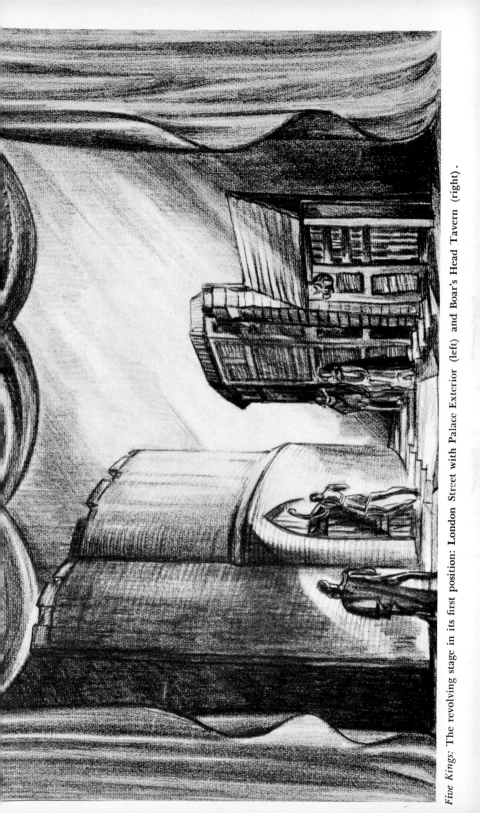

Five Kings: The revolving stage in its first position: London Street with Palace Exterior (left) and Boar's Head Tavern (right).

Five Kings: **The revolve in its second position: A chamber in the Palace with Hotspur (John Emery), The King (Morris Ankrum), Northumberland (Erskine Sanford) and others.**

Falstaff and Prince Hal (Orson Welles and Burgess Meredith).

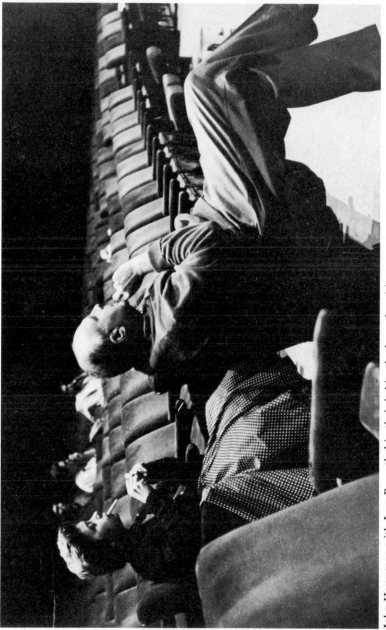

John Houseman with Jean Rosenthal in their habitual rehearsal position.

CBS Studio One with sound equipment in the foreground. Orson Welles, 23rd is second from right.

Native Son: Canada Lee as Bigger Thomas.

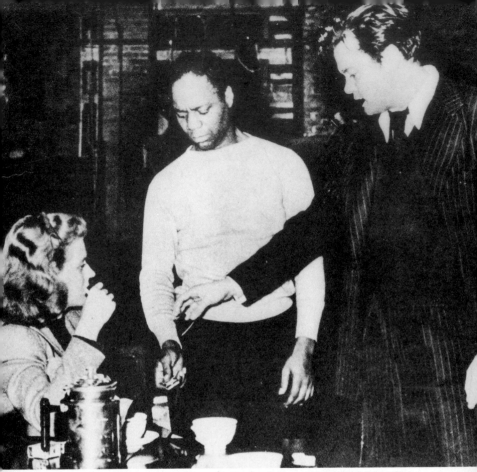

Native Son: Anne Burr, Canada Lee and Orson Welles in rehearsal.
(New York, February 1941)

Herman Mankiewicz during the writing of *Citizen Kane.*
(Victorville, April 1940)

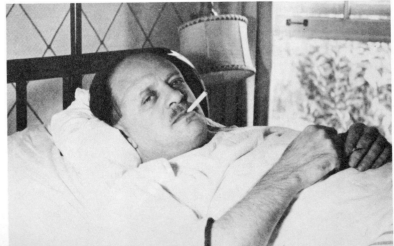

John Houseman.

Photographs of A. E. Astin and Frederick Ashton by Lee Miller; the group photograph of Pavel Tchelitchew, Aline McMahon, Orson Welles and the author by George Platt Lynes; photographs of Federal Theatre productions by WPA photographic service; photographs of Four Saints in Three Acts *by White Studios; of Mercury productions by Van Dam, White Studios, Alfredo Valente and Richard Tucker; photographs of the author by A. Brant of Sinaia, Rumania, Sybil Day of London, Bromhead of Bristol, England, and John Claxton.*

I wish to thank all those who lent and granted permission for the use of these materials and especially the Theatre Collection of the New York Public Library (Astor, Lenox and Tilden Foundation), without whose help no research on contemporary American theatre is possible.

To execute it, Jean came up this time with a young designer named James Morcom who had worked as Nat Karson's assistant at the Radio City Music Hall. As in *Shoemaker*, the basic materials were burlap and wood—but far more massive and grand. For diversity—so that the scenery could be used at all possible angles—it was double-faced with thin veneer cut into narrow slats and stained a light blue-gray without shadowing or paint of any sort. With changes of light these wooden surfaces took on an appearance of lightness and gaiety or somber mass, depending on the intensity and color of the illumination. No effort was made to suggest real materials.

At the center of the production was a large revolving platform, thirty feet in diameter, which kept circling like a lazy Susan without blackouts or visible sceneshifts in a great variety of forms throughout the play's thirty-two scenes. The scenery was divided into two main elements: London and the battlefields. A basic castle setting with huge rounded walls towered over one third of the revolving stage. The tavern set occupied another third. Running between them was a ramped street with an open court at one end and a narrow alley at the other. Within these three revolving structures the actors would move from one scene to another in full view of the audience. A characteristic transition was that in which Prince Hal is summoned from the Boar's Head to appear before his father in the palace. By revolving slowly with accompanying light changes it would be possible to keep him continuously in view as he left the tavern, walked up the crowded alley into the castle and through the anteroom into the failing King's presence in the council chamber. For the battle scenes the whole stage would turn around as the actors marched or fought over a series of ramps and platforms which, in different arrangements and at accelerated speeds, became the Field of Shrewsbury for the English wars and Harfleur and Agincourt for the wars in France. Though mechanical problems reduced much of its final effectiveness, it was a dynamic theatrical concept.

Costumes—codpieces and all—were once again designed by Millia Davenport. They were made of somewhat richer materials than *Shoemaker*, but they had the same simple dramatic quality.

The music was Aaron Copland's. (We had given Virgil Thomson an advance to compose a score for us; he waited four months for a script, then left for Paris.) Aaron did a professional job but he, too, suffered from a lack of communication with the director, and *Five Kings* was not one of his happiest theatrical experiences.

The company was the largest we had assembled since Federal Theatre days—forty-two, with seven doubles and four stage managers. Among the newcomers was Robert Speaight (fresh from his London success as Beckett in *Murder in the Cathedral*), whom we used as narrator of the connective material—the Chorus and the Hollingshead Chronicles. Morris Ankrum came from Pasadena to be our Bolingbroke, John Emery was Hotspur and Burgess Meredith (who had scrawled his name on a contract at 1:00 A.M. on the *Ile de France* just before sailing with Franchot Tone and two girls to spend Christmas in Paris) was Prince Hal, to which he brought a warmth and an energy that I have never seen equaled in the part, even by Laurence Olivier. Our unfrocked priest played the part of the Ancient Pistol, and one of the better "skullers" from burlesque, Gus Schilling (whose wife, a celebrated stripper known as the "Ball of Fire," we tried to press into the part of Doll Tearsheet) was an earthy, vernacular Bardolph.

Rehearsals were undisciplined and desultory from the start. It was *Danton* all over again—without the tension and with a lot more alcohol. Welles had known the Histories from childhood and played in them at Todd School; now he seemed unable to organize either his material or himself. Like a magician who is unsure of his act, he masked his insecurity with procrastinations and diversions. And this time I was of little help to him. Wholly involved in the Campbell Playhouse and the logistics of *Five Kings*, I attended few of his early rehearsals, and at those I was made to feel uneasy and unwelcome. The reports I received were increasingly disturbing. Some came from the directors of the Theatre Guild. Orson had announced that he did not want them at rehearsal: when either of them defied this interdiction, a bottle of scotch, especially kept for that purpose, was produced and Orson would call a break and entertain the cast with jokes and anecdotes until he or she had withdrawn.

Welles had always been a prolific raconteur. Now, as one of his devices for evading rehearsal, he gave his fancy free rein. His stories were of two kinds. There were the sagas of travel and adventure in distant places. These were vaguely based on truth and included encounters with Isadora Duncan in Paris, with fighting bulls in Spain and with the Glaoui (pronounced "Glowy") in his fortress-palace in the mountains of Morocco. There was also an Oriental cycle: a perilous caravan trip, which Orson led at the age of six across the Gobi Desert, and a case of silver leprosy diagnosed as fatal by the entire medical profession until a Japanese specialist in Tokyo (the world's leading leprosy expert) after staring at Orson's arm—the one that bore the mark of the dread disease—had finally scrubbed it with soap and water and removed the aluminum from a freshly painted radiator which Orson had leaned on in a whorehouse in Singapore.

Then there was the other kind—the fantasies that were invented on the spot out of sheer exuberance or to cover up some particularly outrageous piece of behavior. One night Welles burst into rehearsal, more than two hours late, in a new, extravagantly tailored dinner jacket, and announced that the Mob was after him: a gorgeous creature, the wife of a celebrated gangster, had been seized with lust for him; he had possessed her in Harlem, then fled, with the husband and his torpedoes in hot pursuit. Baer and Teichmann were sent to mount guard before the building while rehearsal got under way.

Another time, he was not two but four and a half hours late. Everyone knew where he had been—to Chicago to spend the night with the ballerina. With all regular flights grounded for the journey back, he had secured a place in a small, crowded private plane, where he found himself sitting beside the pilot. The flight was a nightmare: visibility nil, lightning bolts, downdrafts and swirling rain. The passengers, in panic, begged the pilot to turn back, but the wretched man admitted he was lost— somewhere over the northwest portion of New York State. They cruised about for two hours, the passengers moaning and praying. And then it happened. A huge downdraft sent them plunging earthward, and as they finally leveled, the clouds parted briefly. The pilot screamed and his hands froze on the controls. Orson looked and gasped, for rising high *above* them were the waters of Niagara Falls. How Orson swung into action and swept the worthless pilot from the controls; how he seized the stick, gunned the motor and slowly, slowly lifted the brave little plane above the roaring waters of the Falls—all this was described in vivid and fascinating detail. When they were finally out of danger, and not till then, Orson relinquished the command to the amazed and grateful pilot. That was the end of the story, and no one in the theatre said a thing. Then Orson topped himself. "Believe me, I was scared!" he said, as he finally went to work.

Halfway through rehearsals, in addition to my deteriorating relations with Welles and the directors of the Guild, I found myself facing money troubles—the worst so far. We had gone into *Five Kings* without a cent in the bank and still owing money on *Danton*. When the Guild demanded that we put up the balance of our ten thousand dollars, I did not have it. The big money from the radio show was only just beginning to come in and Orson himself was deep in debt. In desperation I turned to one of our stockholders—the sorrowful contractor with the red eyes. Out of the goodness of his heart he lent us several thousand dollars and the heat was off till we got to Boston in the middle of February. There the real horror began.

Having no stage of our own, we had decided to hold all technical rehearsals in the Colonial Theatre, where I derived some sentimental comfort from finding the walls still red from our Boston engagement of *Julius Caesar*. By day, while an enormous crew occupied the stage, assembling and installing the great mass of our scenery, Orson rehearsed in lobbies and underground. At night, after the construction gang had quit, he and his troupe, half-costumed and armored, swarmed all over the unfinished set, while the prop department made experimental firings of our two huge mortars (seven feet long and fifteen inches in circumference), loaded with real gunpowder, and showers of flaming arrows. After midnight, light rehearsals began and continued till dawn. For two nights Virginia Welles appeared in a strange, sad attempt to recapture the past and stood in with the stage managers as she had at the Maxine Elliott during our long, happily remembered light rehearsals of *Faustus* and *The Cradle Will Rock*. On the third morning she left for New York and, in due course, for Reno.

Over the weekend, we started a run-through. The first few hours were encouraging; Miss Helburn was seen to smile. Although Burgess Meredith had complained all through rehearsal that he never got to work with Welles, the scenes between Prince Hal, Falstaff and the hangers-on had that exciting quality of closeness that Orson sometimes achieved with his male actors. The set was impressive and the transitions looked as though they might work. But since, by 3 A.M., we had got through less than a quarter of the play, it was still too early to tell. We advanced no further the next night and only slightly further, under pressure, the night after that.

By now two things had become evident: first—that, once again, we were about to suffer for our poverty. To drive our lazy Susan we had an electric motor that worked less well than it should have. It had two speeds, but even in high it did not turn fast enough to let the actors move through the scenery at their normal pace. When we tried to accelerate it, it had an alarming way of jumping into reverse, whirling at twice its forward speed and hurling masses of scenery into the orchestra pit. Second—we were faced with what everyone had known for days but hoped that a miracle of energy and inspiration would suddenly correct: the fact that the second half of *Five Kings* had, literally, never been staged.

On our third day in Boston Orson came to me and announced that we would have to postpone our opening. There was nothing unusual in this request: we had postponed *Macbeth* three times, *Horse Easts Hat* twice, *Faustus* four times, *Julius Caesar* once and *Danton's Death* five times. Unfortunately, those days were over. I explained to Orson—as I had frequently over the past month—that we were now in the commercial big time with the Theatre Guild subscription involving tens of thousands of people and specific theatre bookings. I pointed out that plenty of big shows were not ready when they opened out of town and that if the worst came to the worst I could probably force the Guild to give us another out-of-town engagement—as long as we paid for it. By this time Orson was in a panic. He had assumed he would get his postponement as he always had before. Thwarted and betrayed, his face streaming with tears and sweat, he turned his full rage against me. In that moment I was his father and every other enemy he had ever known. I was a yellow son-of-a-bitch—a whore—a crooked bastard who had sold him out to the Guild— milked and exploited him and then left him holding the bag! As I turned to go, he tore a telephone from the wall and threw it after me.

Such scenes took place almost daily during the final agony of *Five Kings*. Not all were ugly; some were extremely funny—like the night I tried to murder him. During the scenes in the Boar's Head Tavern, Orson, inside his hundred pounds of soaking padding, drank large quantities of steaming mulled wine. This, as he carefully explained to our property man, could be achieved by inserting the tip of a red-hot poker into the tankard. The prop man pointed out that he had no way of heating the poker— a brazier on stage being against the rules of the Fire Department. He suggested that steam could be created by slipping a small lump of dry ice into the wine. Orson categorically forbade its use. The man explained that the lumps were harmless and the smoke dangerous only in large quantities. Welles ordered him to heat the poker.

At 11:30 on the night of one of our final run-throughs the prop man came to me in fear and asked what he should do about Falstaff's steaming tankard. I had just arrived from New York and knew none of the background.

"Dry ice," I said.

"But, Mr. Houseman . . ."

I had other cares at the moment. An hour later I was sitting in the orchestra, begging Jeannie to make the turntable move faster and thinking how wonderfully good Orson was as the Fat Knight. Suddenly he stopped in the middle of a line. I watched him as the realization came to him that the steaming tankard from which he was noisily gulping was ice cold! With a fierce yell he summoned the prop man onto the stage. "Front and Center!" he yelled "Front and Center!" Then indicating the thin wisp of smoke, Orson demanded to know what caused it. "Dry ice," whispered the prop man, and as Orson moved upon him (all three hundred and forty pounds of him, including padding) he added quickly, "Mr. Houseman said . . ."

That was all Orson needed. He flung the tankard from him. He clutched at his belly and groaned. Then, staggering down to the edge of the stage, he singled me out in the darkness and pointed a long, pale finger at me.

"You've done it! You've killed me! For months you've wanted to destroy me—and now you've done it! You've poisoned me!"

Shaken by terrible spasms, he started back upstage, turned to shout "Killer! Poisoner!" then reeled and fell groveling to the floor, muttering "Poisoned! Poisoned!" and crying for milk. Someone arrived with a bottle of it and held it to his mouth. Orson gulped it down like a man dying of thirst, then spewed it up till the stage all around him was white with it. After that, still groaning piteously, he was helped off the stage and driven back to the Ritz-Carlton, having achieved his real objective, which was, once again, to avoid rehearsing the second half of the play.

We traveled to New York together in silence the next morning for the Campbell Playhouse, returned the same evening and re-hearsed all through the night and the weekend. And on Monday, February 27, at 8:00 P.M., without ever having had a complete dress rehearsal, *Five Kings* opened to a theatre filled with The-atre Guild subscribers. It ran, with two intermissions, till one in the morning. One third of the audience vanished at the first intermission; another third left during the next two and a half hours. Some had suburban trains to catch, others were exhausted; others, especially those down front, fled in terror of the explo-sions, flaming arrows and chunks of solid wooden scenery which our revolving stage, jumping into reverse, kept hurling across the pit into the orchestra. Those who remained and applauded (their ranks swollen by the arrival of Gertrude Lawrence accompanied by the actors with whom she was touring in *Susan and God*) were thanked in a speech which Orson, still wearing the flesh of Falstaff, delivered from the stage at the final curtain. Among them were the directors of the Theatre Guild, who had watched the show in gloom and terror. The next day's press did little to cheer them up. According to *Variety*—

> Orson Welles has bitten off a big chunk and he will have to do a lot of chewing during the try-out.

"Bold and ingenious," wrote a local critic, but added—

> What might have been a tour de force jumps so fast from one thing to another as to be a non-sequitur de force. *Five Kings* covers Shakespeare as a two-day Cook's Tour covers England.

Another found the outline of the story clear but the depth of characterization missing. Still another felt that the acting had an enthusiasm that was infectious, found Meredith eloquent and Welles's Falstaff deserving of the highest praise "outwardly satisfying, inwardly persuasive" but declared that the revolving stage must be tamed. "Like Ole Man River it still keeps rollin' along." The one thing they all agreed on was that the show was not ready for Broadway.

Even more painful than the reviews were the crew bills that were now presented to the directors of the Guild. With overtime and all-night rehearsals on golden hours, they amounted to over fifteen thousand dollars and carried us more than twenty thousand dollars over our original budget. In sessions that were less noisy but no less grim than my scenes with Welles, the Guild directors held me personally responsible for the disaster. They began by demanding that we pay our share of the overage: I assured them with profound sincerity that we did not have a nickel. All-night rehearsal must cease, they insisted. I told them that Welles was incapable of working by day and that their only chance of getting the show they hoped for was to let him function in his own way as he had in *Julius Caesar*. I explained how fine was the line between success and failure in Orson's shows. They were not appeased and in their mouths that morning "genius" became a dirty word. Finally, under protest, they agreed to carry *Five Kings* as far as Philadelphia. But, from now on, if Welles wanted all-night rehearsals he must pay for them himself, in cash—which he did, during the next ten days, to the tune of several thousand dollars, borrowed against his future radio earnings.

Five Kings was shortened by forty minutes during its Boston run. Slowly the show was finding itself; scenes were staged that had been ad-libbed on opening night, and a dramatic form began to appear. Technically, too, it was smoothing out, though the accursed lazy Susan, for all Jean's tinkering, still held up transitions and slowed down the battle scenes.

As their exhaustion diminished and as more of the audience remained to applaud, the spirits of the company rose. So much so that during our second week in Boston, Welles and Meredith decided the time had come to give Robert Speaight (that earnest Anglo-Catholic Marxist) * a taste of sporting life in America. A company party was organized after the show and girls brought over from the Old Howard Burlesque. When I arrived from New York the next morning the manager of the Ritz-Carlton suavely suggested that the gentlemen of the company might prefer to move to a more remote wing of the building for their next revel; he also presented me with a bill for fourteen hundred dollars for broken glass and the furniture they had tossed through a twelfth-story window.

We played Washington, then Philadelphia. The Chestnut Street

---

* Speaight's ordeal on opening night had been almost beyond human endurance. Since Orson had changed all his positions at the last moment without telling Jeannie, he spoke his narrations in pitch-darkness while a bright light illuminated the spot where he had previously stood. By the time he moved into the light, it was gone—over to the position he had just left. To add to his humiliation, as he was making his final, groping exit along the apron of the stage, a nice old lady in the front row handed him a note and asked him to be sure and give it to Burgess Meredith.

Theatre, into which the Guild had booked us, was a large, old-fashioned theatre with a raked stage. It had only a slight tilt but it was enough to ruin us; it meant not only leveling and resurfacing the whole stage to receive our turntable, but also rebuilding the forestage to meet a local fire law that forbade construction of any sort downstage of the fire curtain. Our opening had already been postponed from Monday to Tuesday; while a crew of carpenters and masons was toiling on stage with lumber, asbestos and sandbags, a second, even more grievous disaster hit us below stairs. Philadelphia's electric current, we discovered, was not as other currents were. For technical reasons which I never even tried to understand it was found to be incompatible with the wretched little motor that drove our turntable. Back and forth rushed Jeannie's friends, the electrical experts, from New York, New Haven and Camden. By Tuesday afternoon no suitable mode of conversion had been discovered. If we opened that night it would be with a revolving stage that was turned by hand. I called the Guild and pleaded with them. They were adamant. We must open that night or not at all.

One of my persistent nightmares, for years, was a vision of those two dozen heavy, elderly men, working in relays, crouched in the bowels of the theatre, naked to the waist, sweating, cursing and grunting as they struggled with the gears and handles of the great iron windlass while, overhead, loaded with the full weight of its tower, palace and tavern, our lazy Susan ground its uneven, agonizingly slow way around the stage. Our actors, who had only just become accustomed to moving through the spinning sets from one scene to another, now found themselves forced to do it all in grotesque slow-motion, pausing between steps and speeches to let the scenery catch up with them while the play died under their feet.

Once again the curtain fell long after midnight with only a small remnant of the audience present. Our Boston reviews had been paeans of praise compared to what we received in the City of Brotherly Love. By Wednesday noon a new converter had been found, adapted and installed—too late. For at eleven that morning Lawrence Langner had officially informed me in the lobby of the Warwick Hotel that the Guild was withdrawing its sponsorship of *Five Kings* and that the Mercury would be solely responsible for all expenses incurred from that time on. *Variety* had been keeping the profession supplied with bulletins of our progress. From Boston it had informed its readers:

> It is common knowledge that Guild officials have been burning for weeks at the practices of the Welles-Houseman combine
> . . .

On March 22nd it reported:

KINGS BENT IN PHILLY

> *Five Kings* will fold at the end of the week and is in doubt thereafter. There is talk of opening on Broadway without Guild participation. But that is viewed as an outside possibility. From Mercury sources it was indicated that Houseman favors holding the show off Broadway at this time but Welles wants to rehearse it this week and bring it in the week after that.

Variety was right, as usual. Now, suddenly, much too late, a frenzy had seized the Wonder Boy. Determined that his show must not die, he was up at dawn, rehearsing all day, replacing actors, pouring in his radio money, trimming and vitalizing *Five Kings* for its New York opening in the same way as he was accustomed to pull his radio show together each week in its final hours. Between rehearsals he was busy on the phone, making personal appeals in all directions (including a flight to Illinois to anticipate a $20,000 trust fund he was to receive at the age of twenty-five), begging the world not to let a masterpiece perish for lack of a few thousand dollars and a few more days of work.

In this desperate attempt to salvage *Five Kings* he received no help from me. I watched its final agony with indifference, almost with relief at the thought that it would soon be dead and buried and out of the way. I saw no hope for the show in its present form: its flaws were too deep, its wounds beyond any possibility of cure. One day, perhaps, at another time, in some other place,

Five Kings might rise from its ashes, but I knew that I would not be there to see it.*

If *Danton* marked the death of the Mercury Theatre, it was during *Five Kings* that my association with Welles moved irrevocably toward its predictable end. Fatigue, humiliation, mutual reproaches and, through it all, our growing inability to communicate except in anger—all these were having their cumulative and corrosive effect on an association from which all affection seemed to have been drained and only self-interest (expressed at the moment by our weekly radio show) remained to hold us together.

Soon after *Five Kings* opened in Philadelphia I went to New York for a rehearsal of the Campbell Playhouse. Before returning I spent an hour with Robert Edmond Jones, who had written to ask if I would be interested in directing a new American opera for which he was designing the settings. I had asked him if he could wait a few days for my answer. The next morning, from my hotel room in Philadelphia, I called and accepted his offer. I did not tell Orson of my decision and when he read about it in *The New York Times* he said nothing about it either.

I was present the following Saturday when *Five Kings* closed ignominiously after a two weeks' run from which the Guild's subscribers stayed away by the thousands. Still, Welles would not accept defeat. The scenery—all seventeen tons of it—was shipped to New York, where it was held in demurrage for several days at great expense while Orson made his last desperate bids for backing. Finally, he was forced to have it unloaded in a theatrical warehouse, where it lay, with the rest of the Mercury scenery, piling up storage charges for the next twenty years. As a final token of defiance Orson announced that he was retaining his beard and would not shave it off until he had appeared as Falstaff on a New York stage.

---

* *Five Kings* was reborn not once but twice. First in Dublin in 1960, in a somewhat shorter version but with an almost identical pattern of inadequate preparation and dismal failure and, again, some years later, as *Chimes at Midnight* (*Falstaff* in the U.S.) —a shamefully underestimated film.

Living at opposite ends of town, Orson and I saw little of each other that spring except on Fridays when the Campbell Playhouse went on the air. Howard Koch, followed by Annie, had gone off to Hollywood on the strength of the men from Mars. Since it was too late in the season to break in a new writer, I was, once again, with help from Howard Teichmann, writing most of the scripts, whose production, during the crises of *Five Kings,* had been left increasingly in the competent hands of Paul Stewart. As a reward for his services, Welles, soon after his return to New York, dismissed him before a studio full of people for trying to take over the show in his absence. Formerly this would have provoked one of our more ghastly scenes: it was a measure of our estrangement that I had no reaction at all—except that when Stewart left the studio, I went with him. Orson finished the broadcast alone. Then, at three in the morning, he appeared—as I knew he would—at Stewart's apartment, prostrate with remorse, and begged him to return to the show. He did, and we continued to broadcast, week after week, at varying levels of imagination and energy until the end of the radio season.

*   *   *

I may have been lucky or shrewd in my choices, but I have never directed an opera from which I did not get some sort of stimulating and satisfying experience. *The Devil and Daniel Webster* was no exception. It was my first work alone in the theatre since *Hamlet* and, in my eagerness to recover my own identity, I had agreed to direct it without hearing the music. I knew the story by Stephen Vincent Benét: the confrontation between Webster and the Devil to whom one of his New Hampshire constituents had committed the criminal folly of selling his soul. To save the man Webster agrees to plead his case before a ghostly jury of the damned—twelve of the blackest traitors in the country's history. Under the flood of his eloquence even those lost souls are moved to pity, and the man gets to keep both his farm and his soul. The music, when I heard it the following week, performed by the composer, Douglas Moore, seemed effective, melodious and conventional—a far cry from the disingenuous novelties of *Four Saints* and the intoxicating risks of everything I had been involved in for the past three years. I accepted this limitation with a sense of relief.

My collaborators were men whose work I admired: Fritz Reiner was our conductor; Eugene Loring, creator of Aaron Copland's *Billy the Kid,* was my choreographer. Even more important—and my main reason for doing the production in the first place—was the presence of Robert Edmond Jones.

For years he had been an illustrious figure in the American theatre; histories of the contemporary stage were filled with his designs: *Macbeth, Hamlet, The Jest* for the Barrymores, Stravinsky's *Oedipus, The Man Who Married a Dumb Wife,* O'Neill's *Desire Under the Elms* and, more recently, *The Iceman Cometh.* He was an imaginative, vulnerable man with a diffident manner and a will of iron, which (as I discovered later when we worked together under difficulties on his exquisitely beautiful *Lute Song*) he was prepared to enforce with a wide variety of sinuous emotional wiles. This time I found him a joy to work with in his double capacity of designer and artistic adviser to the American Lyric Theatre.

This was an ephemeral outfit, formed around a bonanza of a quarter of a million dollars made available by a musical millionaire from Cincinnati for an operetta based on the life and music of Stephen Foster. To get himself a prestigious New York production he had agreed that some part of his money be used for a second evening of new American works: those selected were *The Devil and Daniel Webster* and a ballet, *Filling Station,* already performed in Hartford by Lincoln Kirstein's Ballet Caravan, with sets by Paul Cadmus and music by Virgil Thomson.

After the angry chaos of *Five Kings,* it was a pleasure to be working among friends under humane conditions on a project that carried no possibility of catastrophe or triumph. For five weeks the St. James Theatre, where we were rehearsing, became an oasis in which I found temporary shelter from Orson's burning sun.

The opera was short and easy to stage. It called for energy and style, and it presented one major theatrical challenge—a complete, instantaneous transformation from the yard of a New England farmhouse to the ghostly courtroom and back again. Bobby and I wrestled with the problem and solved it with partial success. I was less successful with the diction of my singers who, since they were performing in their native tongue, should, I felt, be intelligible. Though I had the forceful aid of Bobby Jones's wife, the celebrated Margaret Carrington (who had worked with John Barrymore on his preparation of *Hamlet*), our Daniel Webster, for all his fine baritone voice, never achieved more than an indication of rhetorical brilliance.

We gave our first performance the week the 1939 New York World's Fair opened. It was well received as a minor work with "an engagingly native quality":

> Fanciful, sentimental, idiomatic . . . it has a popular pulse and the quality of the vernacular and it shows American artists in admirably coordinated efforts in the direction of a real American theatre.
> Delightful entertainment admirably staged, full, vivid and, if you please, native . . . Here was not only a plank and a tune but a dramatic stage. Here were singers who could act.

The Stephen Foster operetta, which opened the following night, was a predictable disaster and marked the end of the American Lyric Theatre.

Throughout rehearsals of the opera I had continued to write and supervise the Campbell Playhouse which, by now, was an almost automatic operation that made few emotional demands upon any of us. With the passage of weeks the fever of my relations with Welles had abated; we were living in a sort of Indian summer from which the clouds of disaster had temporarily lifted. Success in show business is largely a matter of momentum: the Mercury's initial impetus had been enormous and had not been seriously reduced by our recent theatrical failures. Since *Five Kings* had not been seen in New York, it had not dimmed Welles's luster in the world of the mass media. The radio show was a success—critically and in soup sales—and there was every indication that the soupmakers would continue it after the summer layoff. In mid-May negotiations had begun with RKO for a film contract. By early June, Welles had been offered and had accepted the most glorious deal ever given, up to that time, to an individual by a major Hollywood studio. He was to receive one hundred thousand dollars for one film a year—to be produced, written, directed and performed by himself, on a subject of his own choosing, with no artistic interference by the studio and the right to refuse to show the film to anyone until it was finished. Such authority was unheard of, even among veteran directors, and no other studio would have given him such a contract. But RKO was a maverick operation, the victim of a long series of financial manipulations and changing managements from Joseph Kennedy's to Howard Hughes's. Its present interim and insecure boss—a former sales manager named George Schaeffer—had little to lose and a lot to gain by putting a good many of his eggs into the hands of the Wonder Boy of Broadway and Radio, who just might come through with a winner for him.

In the excitement of the new contract and the exhilarating prospect of fresh worlds to conquer, the rancors and miseries of recent months were hastily buried in a shallow grave. A year, almost to the day, after he had invited me to work with him on the radio show, Orson asked me to go with him to California to help with the film. I said yes. A week later, immediately after the last of the Campbell shows, he left, still wearing his beard and stopping over in Chicago for what was possibly the most ludicrous venture of that whole phantasmagoric year. For a very large sum of money he had agreed to make a four-a-day personal appearance for one week at the largest vaudeville house in the Middle West. Following in the footsteps of Sarah Bernhardt, Ethel Barrymore and other stage luminaries who had performed capsulated drama on vaudeville stages, he had decided on an abbreviated version of William Archer's *The Green Goddess,* a melodrama made famous by George Arliss, which we had done on the Campbell Playhouse.

Since I disapproved of the whole project and had things to

take care of in New York, I saw only the last performance, in which Orson, in a rented Hindu garment with a bejeweled turban, a mud pack for makeup and an incredible accent, was supported by a troupe consisting of Wilson, Vakhtangov and Baer in pith helmets and plain turbans and a girl whom I had never seen before in white riding breeches. The audience was puzzled and apathetic. On the way back to our hotel, Orson stopped the cab for a moment and pointed to an alley leading to the rear entrance of a hotel in the Loop. "That's where they brought my father out—feet first," he said.

We were met by photographers at the Los Angeles airport—Orson, myself and Dick Baer, who was now acting as secretary, valet and major-domo. We lived for some weeks at the Chateau Marmont on Sunset Boulevard, then moved into a mansion in Brentwood, complete with swimming pool, a huge luminous jukebox, palm trees and a distant view of the Pacific Ocean.

Here Orson resided for several months, tended by Alfalfa the midget chauffeur and Charles the butler (the original of Raymond in *Citizen Kane*), a sinister and idle figure, whose only accomplishment was making soggy crêpes Suzette. Soon by plane, train, car and hitchhiking, the entire entourage arrived: Arnold Weissberger; Albert Schneider, once Orson's agent and now his manager; Herbert Drake, formerly of the *Herald Tribune* drama desk and now publicity director for the Mercury enterprises; also a full contingent of slaves, from whose presence Orson seemed to derive security and comfort in a strange and hostile town. They descended like locusts, occupying every room in the house and, when those were all filled, camping in the cabanas that surrounded the pool. Here at night, under the bright reflectors, we would listen to the latest news of the Danzig crisis and feel the war coming closer from seven thousand miles away.

Orson's position in the film colony was a peculiar one. Hollywood was still a closed society whose social, financial and professional structure, though subject to constant shifts, remained basically rigid and unchanged. By the members of this established order Welles's coming was awaited with suspicion, envy and a perplexity which Orson did nothing to allay. Soon after our arrival rumors began to circulate about the strange all-male population of the house in Brentwood. (Virginia was in Nevada and Augusta remained in New York.) These spread following our first public appearance at a Hollywood "gala premiere" at Grauman's Chinese Theatre. In the line of purring limousines, each with its cargo of celebrated and carefully selected couples, was an aging open Lincoln with Alfalfa at the wheel and Orson and me, with Arnold Weissberger sandwiched between us, in the back. The news of Welles's well-publicized heterosexual prowess seemed not to have reached the Pacific Coast: it was as a "queer" that he was taunted one night in the Brown Derby by Big Boy Williams, a bully-boy polo player, who tried to provoke Orson to one of those trials-by-combat-in-the-parking-lot that were still an atavistic part of Hollywood night life and ended up by cutting off his tie with a steak knife.

But most of our time was spent at the studio, where we sat hour after hour in battered leather armchairs running one film after another. Like many young directors of that era it was from John Ford that Orson seemed to learn the most. Between films we wandered around the sound stages and talked about *Heart of Darkness*, which Orson had just announced—with considerable fanfare and without consulting me—as his first picture.

We had done this Conrad story with only moderate success on the Mercury Theatre of the Air, and while it was a wonderful title, I never quite understood why Orson had chosen such a diffuse and difficult subject for his first film. I think, in part, he was attracted by the sense of corroding evil, the slow, pervasive deterioration through which the dark continent destroys its conqueror and exploiter—Western Man in the person of Kurtz. But, mainly, as we discussed it, I found that he was excited by the device—not an entirely original one—of the Camera Eye. Like many of Orson's creative notions, it revolved around himself in the double role of director and actor. As Marlow, Conrad's narrator and moral representative, invisible but ever-present, Orson would have a chance to convey the mysterious currents that run under the surface of the narrative; as Kurtz, he would be playing

434

the character about whom, as narrator, he was weaving this web of conjecture and mystery.

The attractions were obvious; so were the difficulties. In this double quest—for the body of Kurtz rotting in the Congolese jungle and for the soul of Kurtz as he moved toward his final moral destruction at the heart of darkness—Joseph Conrad had used all sorts of subtle literary devices; the evil that destroyed him was suggested and implied but never shown. In the concrete medium of film no such evasion was possible. Kurtz's life and the actions that led to his downfall must be dramatized and shown on the screen.

Orson was aware of this, but he had not given it much thought. He had ideas about Kurtz as a young man rather like himself, with a fiancée who was rather like Virginia. And Dick Baer was sent down to the County Museum to make a survey of all the primitive races of the world—their customs, peculiarities and habits, with the idea of creating a "composite native." Beyond that, it was left to me to develop Welles's ideas into some kind of first-draft motion-picture script.

I was an editor and an adapter rather than a writer. On our radio show, over the past year, I had taken finished texts of varying qualities, condensed and translated them successfully into another medium: it had been one of my virtues as an adapter that I managed to retain much of the quality and texture of the original works—including *Heart of Darkness*. But in this new venture I was a failure. Frightened by the necessities of an unfamiliar medium, worried by the ambivalence of my own feelings for Orson and in my anxiety to give him what he wanted, I found myself unable to give him anything at all. And Orson, who was beginning to have his own doubts about the project, had the satisfaction of feeling that he had, once again, been betrayed.

I was spared further embarrassment by the owners of Campbell Soups, who, when they renewed their option, insisted that the Playhouse continue to be produced under their direct supervision in New York City. This complicated Orson's life, but it suited me admirably. Feeling that I had no real place in Welles's movie career and that our Indian summer was drawing to a close, I proposed the following arrangement: I would reside in New York and take charge of the Campbell Playhouse—arguing with agency men, getting the scripts written and watching preliminary rehearsals. Once a week Orson would come in for the broadcast. He agreed, and I flew back to New York where, with the war now seemingly inevitable, my mother had arrived from Paris and moved into the back room of my Ninth Street apartment.

With the new DC–3's, commutation to California had become painful but possible. Orson would come in on the Thursday night flight, drive straight to the studio, where he would listen to a recording of the previous day's rehearsal while eating a second breakfast. We rehearsed all day, went on the air at 8:00 P.M., and then again at 10:00 P.M. for the Pacific Coast. Between broadcasts we ate large dinners during which we talked about the next week's show and the film. If our talk was not ended, I would drive to Newark with him; twice I flew to California and returned the following night, by which time every member of the organization had taken me aside to tell me that there was still no script for *Heart of Darkness*. This did not seem to bother Orson: he was busy making tests of his camera-eye technique—his first experience of shooting film under professional studio conditions. He claimed he would be able to absorb much of this experimental footage into the body of the film. I didn't see how.

By mid-November, when Campbell relented and I moved back to California, the vultures were beginning to hover. With the war and the uncertainties of European business, George Schaeffer was losing his nerve. He asked Orson to postpone *Heart of Darkness* and start with a less ambitious film. Orson, who had already spent a large part of his first hundred thousand dollars, switched without protest but without enthusiasm to *The Smiler with a Knife,* an English potboiler in the Hitchcock manner, written by the poet Cecil Day Lewis under the pen name of Nicholas Blake. Orson gave me the book to read and asked me to work on it. Against my better judgment I tried for two weeks between radio shows, then gave up. Since I knew he was working on it himself, and had, in addition, given it to Herman Mankiewicz, an experienced film writer, to see what he could do with it, I was not unduly disturbed at my failure. Besides, I was convinced that he never had the slightest intention of making it.

By now another crisis was forming. When the Campbell Playhouse moved to Hollywood, Orson had decided that he wanted his regular New York actors with him. Most of them were earning so much in radio that they could not afford to move to the Coast for one show a week. This was no problem, said Welles, and he instructed Schneider to put them all under contract at RKO on a film salary in addition to what they would be earning on the radio show. Ray Collins, Everett Sloane, Agnes Moorehead, Paul Stewart, George Coulouris (finally forgiven) and Joseph Cotten (fresh from his success with Kate Hepburn in *The Philadelphia Story*) – they all arrived and were welcomed with a huge party in the Brentwood manor. Their faith in their leader was slightly shaken when they learned that *Heart of Darkness* had been canceled. Not canceled, Orson assured them, only postponed. Besides, there were parts for all in *The Smiler with a Knife*.

A week before Christmas, with no progress evident on *The Smiler*, a staff meeting was held in an upper room of Chasen's Restaurant in Beverly Hills. Present were Schneider, Drake, Baer, Wilson, Vahktangov, our new California secretary (a dark girl with wonderfully long, narrow, crimson nails) and myself. My position at such meetings was equivocal: I had little to say about Welles's film activities, yet I remained president of the Mercury and Orson's partner. Both Drake and Schneider were jockeying for position, hoping to move into my place, yet neither dared take the first step. I condoned their maneuvers: when the time came for me to quit, I wanted no adhesions to hinder my going.

As usual, when there was something unpleasant to discuss, small talk, jokes and the inevitable anecdotes occupied the first part of the meal. It was not until after the steaks Brizzola that we got down to the real subject of the meeting—a notification received that morning from RKO that, after December 31st, the studio would pay no further salaries until a final script had been okayed and a firm shooting date set for Orson's film. This raised the urgent problem of what to do with our New York actors.

Orson would not admit it was a problem. If RKO didn't pay them, he would.

"But, Orson—"

"Pay them!".

"We can't, Orson. We haven't got the money."

This from Schneider. Orson looked at him. In preparation for this distasteful conversation he had absorbed more than his normal quantity of alcohol. His eyes were bloodshot, his face damp and white.

"What the hell have you done with it?"

"Orson—"

"You're supposed to be my manager. . . . What have you done with it? Answer me! Where's it all gone?"

Schneider, an emotional man, bowed his head and stared at what was left of his steak. Orson, having scored this initial success, turned to the rest of us.

"I work myself to the bone for this money and you sons-of-bitches piss it away! And you don't tell me! Not one of you has the decency . . ."

At this moment two of Chasen's waiters entered to remove the steak dishes. They retired quickly; but in the fifteen seconds they were in the room I had made up my mind. At other times, in such a crisis, I would have used the waiters' incursion to halt the debate. Then, the next day, I would have taken each of our actors apart, explained the situation to them and given them a week's notice. They would have gone home quietly, disappointed but somewhat richer through their visit, and waited to be called back when the film was ready—if something else had not come up for them in the meantime. One day, probably on the next radio show, Orson would have noted their absence and made a scene. But his pride would have been spared. Not this time. As soon as the waiters had left I asked him what he intended to do about his actors. Orson looked at me sharply.

"What would *you* do?"

438

"Tell them the truth for once."

"I don't lie to actors. I've never lied to an actor in my life! You're the one who lies! That's why they hate you! You're a crook and they know it! Everybody knows it! Everybody—"

I had wanted my *Götterdämmerung* and now I had it. As I rose from the table, collecting my papers and laying my napkin down carefully beside my plate, Orson picked up one of the four burning sterno dish heaters that had been left on the table and threw it at me. It missed me by a yard and landed at the foot of a drawn window curtain behind me. Another flaming object flew by me as I moved toward the door, which had opened and in which I could see Dave Chasen, frozen with horror, staring at the flames that were beginning to lick at his curtains. Two more blazing sternos followed me across the room. The last one crashed against the side of the door as I went through it and began to descend the stairs. Behind me I could hear Orson on the landing yelling "Crook!" and "Thief!" after me, his voice becoming fainter as I walked through the half-empty restaurant and out into the street.

I went back to my apartment, took the phone off the hook and went to bed. The doorbell rang twice in the night. The first time it was the girl with the red nails and the second time it was Orson and I did not answer it. At dawn a four-page telegram from him was delivered. That afternoon I started to drive east. Crossing the Arizona desert by night, I listened on my car radio to Orson in the last Campbell Playhouse I had written. I drove fast, without stopping for sleep, filled with the initial exhilaration that I have always felt following the destruction of something that had once been supremely important in my life. At dusk I arrived, somewhat sobered, in La Luz, New Mexico, where Mina was spending the winter. And the next day I wrote two letters. The first, formal and typewritten, was to Orson:

> . . . Nothing that has happened recently affects the very deep affection I have for you and the delight I have found in my association with such a talent as yours. Every word I wrote to you in New Hampshire more than two years ago con-

tinues to be true for me. And it is this feeling, mainly, that prompts me to do what I am now doing. We have been through too much together and have had too much excitement and too much joy for me to let our partnership follow the descending curve of misunderstandings and mutual dissatisfactions along which I see it so clearly moving. What happened the other night merely brought to a head a situation I have seen growing worse for some time—the situation of my false position with the Mercury.

For the fact that this has come about, I believe circumstances are to blame. For the manner in which it has happened I accept, personally, a good deal of the fault. However that may be—it is true that in the past year my position with you and with the Mercury has become something between that of a hired, not too effective manager, a writer under contract and an aging, not so benevolent relative. Besides, there has been something between us, lately, which instead of being intense and fruitful merely succeeds in embarrassing and paralyzing us both.

So I am going back to New York. Nothing would make me happier than, one day, again to produce plays together. I have no illusions—the theatre will never be as wonderful for me again as it was during those four years with you and I need not tell you that the Mercury continues to be my first love. It is simply that the present situation is hopeless and must be changed at once for both our sakes.

Next time you are in New York, let's have dinner together. Love—

J.

The second, in longhand, was to Virgil Thomson in Paris. It was the first time I had written to him since the previous summer. Apart from his personal annoyance over the delays of *Five Kings,* he had not approved, for some time, of the direction in which the Mercury was going. Now, like a man sucking at a sore tooth, I described our theatrical reverses of the past year:

> . . . Failures that were sometimes honorable, sometimes idiotic and ignominious—but constant and uninterrupted! Looking back, I can see now how dearly we paid for our first

success, our entry into the big time, our publicity-inflated personality—Orson's and the theatre's. We paid for it in many ways: in our personal relations and loyalties; in our changing public image, with audience-friendliness being replaced by audience-challenge; in our own creative work where feelings of grandeur and what-is-expected-of-the-Mercury completely supplanted the simple desire to put on a good show. I allowed Orson (and the fault is mine as much as his, since by failing to control and influence him, I was betraying my most useful function in the Mercury) to use the theatre as an instrument of personal aggrandizement. . . . *Five Kings* fell on its face (though it contained notable things and was often wonderful to look at and gave Orson a chance to be a magnificent Falstaff) not just through lack of time and technical inadequacies, as Orson likes to tell himself, but because it was a half-baked, impure idea, in which size and competitive "notions" took the place of love and thought.

It smashed the Mercury. We started the year fertile, successful, happy, foolish perhaps, but in love with ourselves and each other and the theatre and the public. We ended it, tired to the point of sickness, full of hatred and distrust of each other, of our audience, of our theatre—weary and full of fear and loathing for the whole business of producing plays together in the theatre. And it left me, personally, without the fervor and, worst of all, without the love and faith which, during its brief, brilliant career, was the essential quality of the Mercury and before that of Project #891 and before that of the Negro Theatre and before that of our *Four Saints.* . . .

In its place we have had publicity in unbelievable quantities, snowballing to the point where Orson has become a public figure only less frequently and massively projected into the news and the national consciousness than Franklin D. Roosevelt, N. Chamberlain and A. Hitler. This new fame has grown in inverse proportion to the success of our recent artistic endeavors. It is unrelated to our work. In fact, it is just about fatal to our work. It is an appetite that grows as it is fed: in a creative artist, it becomes a compensation and a substitute for creation. For an artist in the theatre the danger is particularly great. The immediate test of his work is public response: if he finds that public response can be stimulated by monkeyshines, then the necessity for, even the interest in, creative work inevitably dwindles. That is the main reason why, for seven months now, a picture (under one of the most magnificent contracts ever granted an artist in Hollywood) has been "about to be made," talked of, wondered about, defended, attacked, announced, postponed, reannounced in thousands of publications with hundreds of thousands of words—without the picture itself (either on paper or even in Orson's own mind) having got beyond the most superficially and vaguely conceived first draft.

If and when it does get made, I shall not be there to see it. Because—not suddenly but after much painful communion with myself—I have decided to end my association with Orson.

If yours is the first letter I have written since the break, it is because you are one of the few—perhaps the only one since you were there from before its beginning—capable of understanding just how much of an uprooting the dissolution of this artistic marriage means to me. It was you who gave me my first taste of work-in-the-theatre-by-those-who-have-faith-in-and-love-for-each-other; I know that you have regarded the direction I have taken with the Mercury and with Orson—if not with disapproval, then certainly with doubts. You have always disliked the notion of work produced on schedule and under compulsion—compulsion of any kind, whether of ambition or desperation or greed or real estate or anything else. And you were right when you warned me that neither creative work nor human values could stand up under the kind of pressure to which Orson and I were subjecting them. . . .

It is my great virtue that I can impart terrific initial acceleration to any project to which I am a part; it is my great weakness that I am unable (or unwilling) to control its speed once it is under way. Instead, there comes a day when I suddenly find myself disliking the direction in which it is moving and sick from the speed which I have helped to impose upon it. At that instant, having made quite sure right along that there is a safety-hatch open and working, I hurriedly abandon ship. That is what I have just done. I am not proud of myself but, being what I am, I had no choice. I am fond of Orson still and I retain much of my admiration for his talent: but

our partnership is over for good and with it an exciting
chapter of my life. It has been very wonderful and very painful
and I am very glad that it is ended. . . .

Reviens donc! What are you doing in Europe, with a war
on, that is half as important as returning home to influence
the cultural life of your time? L'Amérique a besoin de toi.
Moi surtout . . .

Je t'embrasse,
John

Virgil did not return until six months later, when he left Paris
a week ahead of the Germans with fourteen pieces of luggage
containing his scores, his collection of paintings and his new
Lanvin suits. But I felt better, having written to him, and
drove on East, two days later, through a snow-white desert, which
I recognized in the newsreels five years later when it became the
scene of the world's first atomic explosion. Four days after that I
was in New York.

Back in my apartment on Ninth Street with my mother as my
house guest, divided between relief at my liberation and an almost unbearable sense of loneliness, I set about trying to fill the
sudden vacuum in my life.

I owned a play which I was hoping to produce before the end
of the theatrical year. The script was Howard Koch's, begun
some time before with his friend John Huston, who had abandoned it for film writing and left it to me, as its producer-director, to finish with Howard. It dealt with the last tragic years of
Woodrow Wilson's presidency—from his triumphal departure for
the Paris Peace Conference to the dark months, after his stroke,
when everything he had worked for was being destroyed. The
parallel with the present world situation was inescapable and
called for an immediate production. Casting was my main problem: with no clear notion of where I would find the money to
produce it, I began sending the script around to middle-aged
stars on both coasts. While I was waiting for their replies I got an
urgent phone call one evening from Augusta Weissberger asking
me to call Orson immediately at a California number. I said no,

but if she wished she could give him mine. It was five in the morning when he called from Chicago, between planes: would I meet him for lunch at 21?

It was the first time we had seen each other since the night of the flaming sternos. After three dozen oysters, some jokes, sentimental amenities and an overwhelming display of charm, Orson came to the point. Things were getting grim at RKO: with *Heart of Darkness* still on the shelf and *The Smiler with a Knife* stalled, the miraculous contract had three and a half months to run and there was no film in sight. There was one faint glimmer of hope: Herman Mankiewicz had come up with a project—little more than a notion, but an exciting one. If it could be developed into some sort of screenplay in the next ten weeks, the situation might still be saved.

Mankiewicz was notoriously unreliable: I asked Orson why he didn't take over the idea and write it himself. He said he didn't want to do that. Besides, Mank had asked for me to work with him. In the name of our former association Orson urged me to fly out, talk to Mankiewicz and, if I shared his enthusiasm, stay and work with him as his collaborator and editor till the script was done. It was an absurd venture, and that night Orson and I flew back to California together.

ACT THREE

TO THE MEMORY OF
HERMAN MANKIEWICZ

XI

HERMAN MANKIEWICZ was a legendary figure in Hollywood. The son of a respected New Jersey schoolteacher, one of a brilliant class at Columbia, he had fought the war as a Marine, worked for the *World* and the *Times*, collaborated on two unsuccessful plays with two otherwise infallibly successful playwrights, George Kaufman and Marc Connelly, come to California for six weeks to work on a silent film for Lon Chaney and stayed for sixteen years as one of the highest paid and most troublesome men in the business. His behavior, public and private, was a scandal. A neurotic drinker and a compulsive gambler, he was also one of the most intelligent, informed, witty, humane and charming men I have ever known.

His career would have been inconceivable anywhere but in the motion-picture business. At $2,000 to $3,000 a week, he had served B. P. Schulberg at Paramount, Louis B. Mayer at MGM and Harry Cohn at Columbia. But since to employ him was to incur his contempt and deadly hate, he had goaded them, one by one, into barring him from their lots until, finally, there was

447

nowhere left for him to go. Of the two million dollars he had earned, nothing was left except debts. Of his numerous credits as writer and producer there were not more than half a dozen he was prepared to acknowledge: his work on the early Marx Brothers pictures; *Laughter,* which he had produced with Harry d'Arrast as director; and *Million Dollar Legs,* with which he had bamboozled the entire industry (and delighted the intelligentsia of the Western world) by producing the first American surrealist film with W. C. Fields, Ben Turpin, Jack Oakie and a Polish bombshell named Lyda Roberti. Reduced to utter penury, with the bailiffs camped on the lawn, he had demeaned himself to the extent of writing a couple of our radio scripts, which I had edited rather harshly. Then, in his mid-forties, in twelve and a half weeks, for a few thousand dollars, he wrote *Citizen Kane.*

Out of our work together on that script a friendship was born that lasted until his death. For thirteen years, during my comings and goings in California, the house on Tower Road, in which he lived with his wife Sarah, a beautiful, indestructible Jewish madonna,* and their three children, Don, Frank and Johanna, became for me what the Poors' house had been on the South Mountain Road. Throughout those years he was, variously, my collaborator, my father, my wayward son, my counsellor and a source of inexhaustible stimulation, exasperation and pleasure.

In late February, 1940, when I returned with Orson to California, Herman Mankiewicz was flat on his back in a cast with a triple fracture of his left leg. (His account of the accident was more than an hour long and was another surrealist movie in

---

* Sympathy and pity were felt in the upper echelons of Jewish movie society for the main victim of his excesses, the beloved and faithful Sarah. Mank knew this and it infuriated him. On his return to the studio after one of his more horrendous escapades, a colleague, out of politeness, asked after Sarah. Mank looked puzzled and uncomprehending. Then, after a moment, with a flash of recognition, "You mean Poor Sarah? Oh, she's fine! I'll tell her you asked." It was around this time that he wrote to the head of the Beverly Hills Police Department suggesting that a curfew be rung and the streets cleared in the interest of public safety during the five minutes it took him to drive every evening from Romanoff's Bar to his house on Tower Road.

itself.) I sat by his bedside and listened while, between grunts, feverish stirrings and panic calls for Sarah, he outlined his notion for a film. It was something he had been thinking about for years: the idea of telling a man's private life (preferably one that suggested a recognizable American figure), immediately following his death, through the intimate and often incompatible testimony of those who had known him at different times and in different circumstances.

In one of its earlier versions, the subject of this prismatic revelation had been a celebrated criminal like John Dillinger, whose personality and motivations were to be discovered successively, though not necessarily chronologically, through the eyes of his doting mother, the brother who hated him, a member of his gang, his childhood sweetheart, the FBI man who trailed him on his final flight and the woman who had lived with him for the last month of his life before turning him in for the reward. Then, while talking with Orson one day, an infinitely better idea had come to him. As a former newspaperman and an avid reader of contemporary history, he had long been fascinated by the American phenomenon of William Randolph Hearst. Unlike my friends of the Left to whom Hearst was now the archenemy, fascist isolationist and labor baiter, Mankiewicz remembered the years when Hearst had announced himself as the working man's friend and a political progressive. He had also observed him as a member of the film colony—grandiose, aging and vulnerable in the immensity of his reconstructed palace at San Simeon. By applying his "prism" notion to a figure of such complexity and stature and adding to it the charisma inherent in the public and private personality of Orson Welles, the possibility of a rich and unusual movie became apparent.

Welles, in his desperate search for a film subject, had snapped at it instantly. So did I when I heard it. After Mank and I had talked for several hours and Sarah had sent dinner up to the room, I phoned Orson from his bedside and told him I was ready to try. He arrived with a magnum of champagne, and we talked on until Sarah threw us out. The next day—no longer as president but as a writer—I made a deal with Mercury Productions for a period of twelve weeks. At Mank's insistence and remembering how badly I myself had worked with Orson peering over my shoulder, it was clearly stated in the agreement that we would do our work without interference. Welles would be shown what there was of the script after six weeks; the rest of it, if he decided he wanted to continue, when we were finished. It was felt by everyone, especially Sarah, that our only hope of getting such a difficult script done in such a limited time* was to move Mankiewicz out of his natural habitat—away from distractions and temptations of all sorts. The retreat chosen for us was a guest ranch in the Mesa country near Victorville at the top of the Cajon Pass.

Two days later, we set out for the San Bernardino Mountains in a small caravan that consisted of a studio limousine containing Mankiewicz, prone and protesting in the back seat, with a trained nurse and two pairs of crutches in the front, and a convertible driven by myself, containing a secretary, a typewriter and three cases of stationery and research material. That night the limousine departed and the next day we went to work.

The Campbell Ranch was owned and run by an intellectual couple, both lawyers, from Los Angeles. Our life was austere but comfortable; the food monotonous but adequate; the climate temperate, dry and perfect for work, with no distractions for a hundred miles around. Since we were there between seasons we had the place almost to ourselves during the week: weekends were crowded and there were musicales, symposia and folk dancing at night, from which we were excused on account of Mank's leg. He and I shared a bungalow with two bedrooms and a living room which we used as a study. His nurse was a long-suffering German body whom Mankiewicz summoned at all hours of the day and night for unnecessary services. The secretary, discovered and briefed by Sarah, was a patient, efficient, nice-looking English girl named Rita Alexander, married to a refugee recently arrived from Europe. No pair of internal rev-

---

* Under the luxurious, highly organized studio system of the day it was not uncommon for a script to be prepared over a period of from nine to eighteen months by five or six different writers.

enue agents could have been more diligent in their daily inspection of Mank's room for intoxicants. This precaution proved unnecessary. With no family to make him feel guilty, no employer to hate and no one to compete with except an incomprehensible, cultivated, half-gentile hybrid with a British upper-class accent, the mental and emotional energy which had been squandered for years in self-generated conflicts and neurotic disorders was now concentrated on the single task of creating our script. After so many fallow years his fertility was amazing.

We started with the image of a man—a giant, a tycoon, a glamor figure, a controller of public opinion, a legend in his own lifetime—who had entered the world with all possible advantages, exploited them to the full, yet failed to achieve most of what he really wanted from life—including love. As we talked we asked each other how this man had got to be the way he was, made the choices he did. In the process we discovered what persons were associated with him; we learned what brought them together and what he did with them and to them over the years. In deciding who was qualified, personally and historically, to tell his story and reflect his image, in selecting the "prisms" which would most clearly reveal the parts from which we must finally create a whole, we found the dramatic structure of the film gradually asserting itself.

By trial and error we reduced the number of principal witnesses to five—each with different attitudes and subjective versions of the events of this man's life: the lawyer-guardian, who had observed him with exasperated and impotent disapproval in childhood, at the height of his fortunes and in his final, predictable collapse; his manager, who followed him with slavish and admiring devotion from the beginning of his career through his greatest triumphs and down again; the friend who understood him better than anyone else and who, for that reason, finally split with him; his mistress, whom he came closest to loving and who, through no fault of her own, helped to destroy him and finally left him; the servant, who saw only the ruin and the folly and the lonely end.

In the brouhaha that preceded and followed the first Hollywood press showings of *Citizen Kane,* amid the accusations and denials, the massive pressures and the truculent refutations, the whole question of Kane's identification with Hearst became wildly confused. The truth is simple: for the basic concept of Charles Foster Kane and for the main lines and significant events of his public life, Mankiewicz used as his model the figure of William Randolph Hearst. To this were added incidents and details invented or derived from other sources.

The main parallels are obvious. Both Kane and Hearst, as young men, entered the newspaper field by taking over a dying metropolitan daily into which each poured his inherited treasure at the rate of one million dollars a year. The calculated sensationalism, the use of patriotism as a circulation builder—these form part of the Hearst legend to which were grafted anecdotes from other giants of journalism, including Pulitzer, Northcliffe and Mank's first boss, Herbert Bayard Swope. Kane's political career and Hearst's are similar: Hearst ran on a reform ticket for mayor and then for governor of New York. (According to journalistic legend he had two special editions of the *Journal* ready to go to press on election night—one headed HEARST WINS, the other FRAUD AT POLLS.) He was defeated (not, like Kane, following a sex scandal) as proof of the American political axiom that money and power cannot, by themselves, win the people's vote. Both Hearst and Kane had unsuccessful first marriages; both took up in middle age with blonde young women whose professional careers (in different fields) they obstinately and vainly promoted in a tradition of American tycoons that includes McCormick, Brulatour and Samuel Insull. Both Hearst and Kane saw their empires collapse in the Depression. Both ended their days in extravagant and tedious retirement. Xanadu, the ultimate American vision of heaven on earth, was directly modeled after Hearst's San Simeon, which Mank had personally observed and which he now recreated in all its exorbitant folly, complete with private zoo, motorcade picnics, oversize Renaissance fireplaces and jigsaw puzzles.*

* This is where the film ran into trouble. It is unlikely that anyone would have bothered about the obvious parallels in the public lives of

With the single exception of Susan Alexander whose situation, though not her personality, clearly resembled that of Marion Davies, our "witnesses" had no individual equivalents in the life of William Randolph Hearst. Bernstein (to whom we gave some of the characteristics of Everett Sloane, who would be playing the part, and the surname of Orson's guardian, a music-loving doctor from Chicago) was the prototype of the shrewd, unquestioningly loyal business manager. Jed Leland, Kane's best friend, was superficially modeled after Ashton Stevens, the drama critic, a long-time friend of Hearst and, incidentally, of Orson's father. Thatcher, the guardian-lawyer-banker, was a wholly fictitious personage, to whom Mank added, mainly for his own amusement, overtones of J. P. Morgan, including a recent newsreel in which the haughty financier had been subjected, during a Congressional investigation, to the humiliation of being photographed with a midget on his knee.

This seemingly irrelevant clip was typical of the use he made throughout the script of newsreel material—real, reconstructed and imagined.* Assembled in staccato *March of Time* style and first shown as a summary of the fabulous career of Charles Foster Kane immediately after his death, many of those clips were repeated later in the body of the film, no longer as newsreels but as part of Kane's personal story. From this constant cross-fertilization between myth, fact and fiction the film acquired much of its vitality and dimension.

Hearst and Kane, but with the invasion of Xanadu a particularly sensitive nerve was touched. Not only Mankiewicz but every male and female columnist in Hollywood, not to mention actors, directors and film executives by the dozens had been entertained at San Simeon and had witnessed the embarrassing boredom of their aging unmarried hosts. To expose this in a movie seemed unethical, ungrateful and dangerous. Hearst, even in his decline, remained a powerful national figure: by uttering shrill cries of hypocritical indignation, the industry and the press were protecting themselves from the wrath to come.

* In our search for related material we became veritable magpies: the *Reporter*'s first interview with Susan Kane in a sleazy bar in Atlantic City was based on a recent interview with Evelyn Nesbitt Thaw in the run-down nightclub where she was performing.

Throughout our work on the screenplay of what later came to be called *Citizen Kane,* we had one special advantage: we were not working in a vacuum, developing a script for some absent producer; we were—and we never for one instant forgot it— creating a vehicle suited to the personality and creative energy of a man who, at twenty-four, was himself only slightly less fabulous than the mythical hero he would be portraying. And the deeper we penetrated beyond the public events into the heart of Charles Foster Kane, the closer we seemed to come to the identity of Orson Welles.

Orson was aware of this. Far from resisting the resemblance, he pushed it even further when he came to shoot the film. Between young Kane and young Welles there is more than a surface likeness: in the dramatized person of Charles Foster Kane, "Champagne Charley" was finally able to realize extravagances that far exceeded anything achieved in life by Richard Welles and his precocious son. Kane's fury, too, was of a special and recognizable kind. A vague aura of violence surrounded the Hearst legend: there was the persistent rumor of the fatal shooting, in a jealous rage, of a well-known Hollywood director on a yacht off the Malibu coast. We made no reference to that episode in our script. We did not need it. The wanton, wordless, destructive fury which Kane wreaks upon the inanimate objects in his wife's room when he realizes that she has left him was taken directly from our recent scene in the upper room at Chasen's. During its filming, Orson reproduced with frightening fidelity the physical gestures and the blind agony of rage with which he had hurled those flaming sternos against the wall. The cuts he received on his hands on both occasions were, I was told, almost identical.

Our days and nights on the Campbell Ranch followed a reassuring routine. Mankiewicz wrote and read half the night and slept in the morning. I got up early, had my breakfast in the main house so as not to disturb him, then went riding for an hour—my first contact with a horse since the Estancia Santa Maria. After that, while I waited for him to come to life, I would

454

edit the pages Mank had dictated the night before, which the secretary had typed at dawn. At nine-thirty Mank received his breakfast in bed. An hour later, having made an enormous production of shaving, washing, and dressing himself on one leg, he was ready for work. This consisted of going over yesterday's material, arguing over changes and seeing how the new scenes fitted into the structure of the whole and affected the scenes to come.

The wranglers' daughters who served us our meals were frightened by our shouting, but we enjoyed our collaboration. Once Mank had come to trust me, my editing, for all our disagreements, gave him more creative freedom than his own neurotic self-censorship. We argued without competitiveness or embarrassment till the middle of the afternoon. At that time Mank, who suffered great pain from the knitting bones in his leg, would retire for his siesta while the secretary and I went over her notes on the day's talk. At six Mankiewicz rose, ready and eager for the great adventure of the day, when I would drive him and his crutches to a railroad bar known as The Green Spot, where we slowly drank one scotch apiece and watched the locals playing the pinball machines and dancing to the Western music of a jukebox. Once a week we visited the only movie, then returned to The Green Spot for dinner. Other evenings we worked until around ten, when I became sleepy from the mountain air. From my bed, through the closed door, I could hear Mank's voice as he continued his dictation, interrupted by games of cribbage which he had taught our devoted secretary.

We were not entirely incommunicado. Sarah drove up every other week to satisfy herself that all was well, and seemed astounded to discover that it was. Orson telephoned at odd hours to inquire after our progress. On the appointed day, at the end of six weeks, he arrived in a limousine driven by Alfalfa, read a hundred pages of script, listened to our outline of the rest, dined with us at The Green Spot, thanked us and returned to Los Angeles. The next day he informed the studio that he would start shooting early in July on a film which, at the time, was entitled *American*.

The script grew harder to write as it went along. We had started with a clear, objective outline of the Kane story—a linear record of the significant public and private events in his life, from the cradle to the grave. In the screenplay these events were briefly reviewed in the introductory March of Time, then revealed through the testimony of successive witnesses delving into memories that were shaped and colored by the bias of their own personal relations with Kane. Their testimonies followed each other in vaguely chronological order; they also crisscrossed, overlapped, anticipated and bled into each other. This gave the film its particular quality; it also created a structural problem that grew more serious with each new day's work. The richer and the more varied the sum of the testimonies became, the harder it got to keep them in manageable order. After each testimony it became necessary to go back into the script and make changes to conform to the new and sometimes seemingly contradictory events and situations that had just been revealed. Since our witnesses frequently appeared in scenes that took place before their own testimony began and stayed in the action long after their own story had ended, these multiple adjustments became increasingly delicate and complicated as the script developed.

Finally, after ten weeks, we were done. Raymond, the butler, had spoken his last snide word, and ROSEBUD had been reduced to ashes in the incinerator at Xanadu. The script was more than four hundred pages long—overrich, repetitious, loaded with irrelevant, fascinating detail and private jokes, of which we loved every one. We spent two more weeks going through the pages with machetes—hacking away, trimming, simplifying, clarifying its main dramatic lines and yelling at each other all the time. Above all, we worked on the connective tissue, substituting sharp cinematic cuts and visual transitions for what, in the first version, had too often been leisurely verbal and literary expositions. And, for the twentieth time, I reorganized the March of Time, which had become my special domain, to conform to what now appeared to be significant facts in the life of Charles Foster Kane.

Our peace was disturbed, during that last fortnight, by the news that was coming in night and day over the radio. The "phony war" was over: Hitler's invasion of Belgium and France had begun. Mank could not bear to be away from the half-dozen newspapers he was in the habit of reading each day. We extended our working hours. Then one evening, from The Green Spot, I called the studio and ordered the limousine for the next day. Mank's leg was almost healed, but he clung to his invalid's privileges. He lay alone, groaning, in the rear seat of the limousine and I followed in the convertible as we made the reverse journey through the Cajon Pass, down the steep curves of the San Bernardino Mountains, between the vineyards and orange groves of Azusa, through the slums of Los Angeles to the RKO studio in Hollywood, where, before returning Mankiewicz to Poor Sarah, we solemnly presented Orson with a screenplay whose blue title page read:

AMERICAN

by

Herman Mankiewicz

That night, in the lobby of the Chateau Marmont, I listened incredulously to the crackling, fading short-wave broadcast of the capitulation speech by the King of the Belgians.

In the days that followed, there were moments when I regretted my decision to return to New York as soon as my work on the script was done. The whole mood of the Mercury unit was changed: Orson was working, once again, with a concentrated, single-minded intensity that I had not seen since the first year of the Mercury. Eager to show me what he was doing, he took me first to his art director's room, its walls covered with hundreds of production sketches, some by Welles himself, in which all our notions of the past three months had begun to find form and substance. He introduced me to Gregg Toland, one of the industry's top cameramen, who had come to him and offered to work on his film. They were making tests that day and the next for the part of Susan Alexander. Having no one in the Mercury company who could play it and determined to use no familiar faces Orson was working with two contract girls from the studio.

One was Lucille Ball, the other a reddish blonde named Winter, who later resumed her real name of Dorothy Comingore. After work we drove around the back lot and then over to the old Pathé lot in Culver City, to look at standing sets. Orson was full of ideas—most of them wonderful.

I stayed on for three days waiting for the script to be mimeographed and breathing the dizzying air of an excitement of which I no longer felt myself a part. On the fourth day I asked for a studio car to drive me to the station in Pasadena. I spent my first night and day on the Santa Fe Superchief going over the screenplay (on which Welles's name was now prominent) and re-reading a novel to which Mank and I had decided to try and obtain the dramatic rights—Richard Wright's *Native Son.*

Mankiewicz stayed on at RKO throughout the making of *Citizen Kane,* as it came to be called, torn between his enthusiasm over the way Welles was shooting it and his indignation (which grew as he realized what a great picture it was going to be) at Orson's tacit, at first, and then quite open assumption of writing credit on the film. It was a brawl I had seen coming and of which I was determined to have no part. When I returned to Los Angeles six weeks later to do a pilot broadcast with Fredric March for CBS, it had already erupted and would continue to rage, from beyond the grave, for another thirty years.*

Citizen Kane is Welles's film. No one else could have made it. The dramatic genius that animates it and the creative personality with which it is imbued are wholly and undeniably Orson's —just as, in another medium, *The War of the Worlds* owed its final impact to his miraculous touch. But he did not write either of them.

Long before "auteurism" became part of the critical film jargon, it had been generally accepted that a script (no matter how complete, detailed or brilliant) is only the first stage in the creative process of film making. In *Kane,* Welles's direction of his own and the other actors' performances, his pacing, his strong,

* If Pauline Kael's fifty-thousand-word introduction to the published text of the screen play does not finally settle it, nothing will.

personal visual concept (including his brilliant use of Toland's deep-focus photography), his original use of superrealistic sound (which he brought over from radio), his audacious cutting and, above all, the theatrical vitality with which he filled every frame of the film—all these add up to make it one of the world's recognized masterpieces. But it could never have been made without Mankiewicz' screenplay.

It is no denigration of Welles's talent to observe that, throughout his career, he has functioned most effectively and created most freely when he was supported by a strong text. Mankiewicz supplied him with such a structure in a screenplay of which the conception, the form and the texture were his and his alone. I did no more than any skilled and sympathetic editor or producer is expected to do; Orson, in the half-dozen "revised" and "finally revised" scripts that were ground out of the RKO mimeographing machines, did no more than a creative director is accustomed to do before and during the shooting of a film.

Since no one has ever disputed Welles's cinematic authorship of *Citizen Kane* and since its success and fame, like that of *The War of the Worlds,* was overwhelmingly his—how explain the furious malignance with which he has attempted to deny both Koch and Mankiewicz the writing credits to which they were so clearly entitled? It is always difficult to fathom an ego like Orson's, to understand the alchemy through which any project in which he was even remotely involved became automatically and wholly his own. For this reason he was genuinely surprised and disturbed when, in place of gratitude, his collaborators expressed an unreasonable desire for personal credit. When, like Koch or Mankiewicz (both of whom profited greatly from their collaboration with Welles), they persisted in their demands, he regarded their attitude as disloyal and treacherous.

Writing was a particularly sensitive region of Orson's ego. It was a form of creativity in which he had never excelled but in which he refused to concede defeat. His ability to push a dramatic situation far beyond its normal level of tension made him a great director but an inferior dramatist. His story sense was erratic and disorganized; whenever he strayed outside the solid structure of someone else's work, he ended in formless confusion. But this was something his ego would not acknowledge. It was also something which, for more mundane reasons, he could not afford to admit. "Written, produced, directed and performed by Orson Welles" was the wording of his contracts with the mass media: it justified the amount of money and the degree of artistic freedom which he was able to demand and obtain from his employers. For anyone else to receive credit—particularly a writing credit—on one of his productions not only diminished him personally but threatened the entire fiction of his superhuman capacity. After the notoriety he had achieved with *The War of the Worlds,* how could he let it be known that a $60-a-week scribbler had, in fact, been responsible for the script? Following a year of false starts and international suspense over his entrance into motion picutres, how could he acknowledge that his first film was based on the work of a well-known Hollywood hack?*

During the two weeks I spent in California later that summer, preparing and rehearsing my radio show for CBS, I spent most of my time at RKO. Still more deeply concerned with Orson's work than with my own, I watched him shooting his film and sat with him one night through a forty-minute rough-cut of his first month's work on what was clearly going to be an extraordinary motion picture. Once again I was astounded at the instinctive mastery, the sureness with which he moved into a new medium and shaped it to his own personal and original use.

It was during that fortnight that I made my final contribution to *Citizen Kane.* Along with the Mercury actors, Bernard Herrmann had arrived from New York to work on the score, including the opera in which Susan Kane makes her ill-fated debut in the opera house her husband has built for her. Benny had decided not to use a scene from a standard opera but to create one

---

* Welles's position was extreme but not unique. In addition to normal credit-snatching, instances of directors and producers who become so deeply involved in a show that they feel entitled to share in its writing credit are sufficiently common for the Screen Writers' Guild to have devised a whole set of rulings for the protection of their members. Under the current rules Welles could not possibly have claimed a writing credit for his contribution to *Citizen Kane.*

that would conform to the cinematic requirements of the sequence. He decided, for reasons of his own, that it should be a French opera and asked me to write him a text. Remembering my father's bathroom recitations, I assembled a potpourri from Racine's *Athalie* with some added lines from *Phèdre*. It did not make too much sense; as sung by an unknown soprano, lip-sinc'd by Dorothy Comingore, it was barely intelligible; but, around it, Orson, with his particular genius, had built one of the great visual sequences of his film. I was not present when he shot it, for by that time I was back in New York and finished for good with Charles Foster Kane though not, quite yet, with Orson Welles.

* * *

I had signed a contract for the fall to be one of two writers on the Helen Hayes weekly dramatic radio show. Free of money worries, I was now able to devote myself once again to the theatre. I was making little progress with my Wilson play: several well-known actors were interested in the part but, as usual, I was finding it difficult to raise money. With the U.S. entry into the war drawing ever closer, regular Broadway angels were reluctant to finance a play that was growing more controversial with every passing week.* Besides, I had already transferred my own excitement to the dramatization of Richard Wright's *Native Son,* which, by this time, had become a national best seller and to which I now owned the producing rights.

Soon after it appeared, while we were still in Victorville, Mankiewicz and I had become interested in adapting the novel to the stage. Having learned that Wright was in Mexico, I asked a visiting friend to call upon him and stake our claim. She found

---

* It was produced a year later by Otto Preminger and received respectable reviews, but ran aground on the reefs of public opinion, which, in New York, by the end of 1941, was overwhelmingly for our entry into the war. We sold it years later to Darryl Zanuck for his epic *Woodrow Wilson,* where it furnished the only vital scene in the film—the final bitter confrontation between Henry Cabot Lodge and the dying President.

him by the side of a pool in Cuernavaca and learned that arrangements had already been made for Paul Green to dramatize
the work. I was disappointed, but it was a reasonable choice:
Green was the first white playwright to write sympathetically of
Negro life in the South. (We had done two of his one-acters as
exercises with the Negro Theatre in Harlem and *In Abraham's
Bosom,* starring Rose McLendon, had won a Pulitzer Prize in
1927. More recently *Evenin' Sun Go Down* had been done on the
same New Theatre night as Odets' *Waiting for Lefty.*) I had my
own personal doubts as to Green's suitability for the task: *Native
Son* was a violent, revolutionary work that did not accord with
Green's perceptive and sensitive but essentially Southern, rural
attitude toward the race problem in America.* However it was
done, and the next best thing was to try and secure the producing rights. With my record in the Negro Theatre this was not
difficult, and, in July, Paul Reynolds informed me that Wright
was returning from Mexico and would go directly to North
Carolina to work with Green on the play script.

I was there when Wright arrived—a surprisingly mild-man-
nered, round-faced, brown-skinned young man with beautiful
eyes. It was only later, when I came to know him better, that I
began to sense the deep, almost morbid violence that lay skin-
deep below that gentle surface. At that first meeting I was surprised—not altogether agreeably, having read his books—by the
blandness with which he recounted the shameful story of his
return to his native land. At Brownsville, at the border, a Texan
customs inspector had pawed through his baggage, suspiciously
examined and criticized his manuscripts and books ("Where's

---

* My doubts would have been even graver if I had known of Green's attitude as reflected in the three "stipulations" which he described years later
to the editor of *Black Drama*—"one being that I would have freedom to in-
vent new characters and make editorial story changes where necessary, another being that I could make the Communist slant in the book comic when
I felt like it." The third was that, though Wright would not be writing any
of the damatization, he would "come and be with me during my dramatizing work—this last being necessary for discussion purposes as I went along."

462

your Bible, boy?") and demanded to know where he got the money for travel and clothes. On the train that carried him across the South he had, of course, been denied access to the dining car, and the black waiter carrying his meal to the Jim Crow chair car was stopped as he passed through the train and forbidden to serve a nigger on dining-car china with white men's linen and silver.

I spent a day with him and Green, listening to Paul's ideas for the play. I watched Dick Wright for his reactions: I saw nothing. But my own apprehensions rose sharply. Paul Green was a man who sincerely believed himself free of racial prejudice. His action in inviting Wright to live in his home during their collaboration was an act of some courage—even in an academic community like Chapel Hill. Throughout his stay, according to Dick, he could not have been more courteous, thoughtful and hospitable in his treatment of his black guest. But having granted him social equality, he stopped. From the first hour of their "discussions" it became clear that he was incapable or unwilling to extend this equality into the professional or creative fields. Whether from his exalted position as veteran playwright and Pulitzer Prize-winner or from some inate sense of intellectual and moral superiority (aggravated by Wright's Communist connections), Paul Green's attitude in the collaboration was, first and last, insensitive, condescending and intransigent. No less disturbed than Wright by the injustices and cruelties of the racial situation in America, he was in total disagreement with him as to its solution. The basic and radical premise of Wright's novel—that only through an act of violence could a Negro like Bigger Thomas break through the massive and highly organized repressive structure by which he was surrounded ("The most I could say of Bigger was that he felt the *need* for a whole life and *acted* out that need; that was all") was something that Green absolutely refused to accept—morally or artistically. Resenting what he called Dick's existentialism, he attempted, till the day of the play's opening—through madness, reprieve, suicide, regeneration and other "purging" and sublimating devices—to evade and dilute the dramatic conclusion with which Wright had consciously and deliberately ended a book in which he wanted his readers to face the horrible truth "without the consolation of tears."

When I left them to their uneasy collaboration, Green estimated it would take him less than two months for a first draft. Until then there was nothing I could do but tamp down my apprehensions and start making arrangements for an early production, so as to profit from *Native Son*'s continued presence on the best-seller lists. I called Mankiewicz to tell him of my progress. Instead, I had to listen to his ambivalent ravings about "Monstro" (his latest name for Welles) whom he alternately described as (1) A genius shooting one of the greatest films ever made. (2) A scoundrel and a thief who was now claiming sole credit for the writing of *Citizen Kane*. Infected by his indignation, I sat down and wrote a letter to Orson in which I informed him that if anyone but Mank was to get credit for the script of *Kane* it would be me, and that I was prepared to enforce my claim through the Screen Writers' Guild on the basis of my writer's contract with Mercury Productions. The next morning I tore the letter up.

Five or six weeks later I got a call from Richard Wright in North Carolina saying that Green's first draft had gone to the typist and that he would be returning to New York. I asked him to wait till I had a chance to read it, but he said there was nothing more he could do. He sounded so discouraged that I told him I would be down the next day and drive him back. Knowing my mother's passion for motoring, I invited her to drive with me through country she had never seen. We arrived in Chapel Hill at night, and the next morning I met with Wright and Green, who seemed satisfied with his work. Richard said nothing, but on the way up I sensed enough to ask him with some impatience why, if he was so disturbed, he had not spoken up and given me a chance to provoke a confrontation. Wright, who had quit the Party but remained a disciplined Marxist, replied that under no circumstances would he risk a public disagreement with a man like Paul Green. There were too many people on both sides anxious to enjoy a dogfight between a successful black intellectual and a white Southern writer of progressive reputation—an avowed "friend" of the Negro people.

It was getting dark when we reached Washington, D.C. We had agreed to go on through to New York, but we were famished and we decided, now that we were out of the South, to stop for something to eat. We parked the car on an avenue facing the White House and the three of us went into a cafeteria on the corner which, at that hour, was almost empty. We had served ourselves and were about to sit down when the manager came up and informed us quietly but firmly that no colored were allowed. I asked him if that was the law. He said it was. I began to yell at him: in that case why had my friend been allowed to serve himself? He said that was a mistake and he was sorry. I asked where we were to eat the food we had paid for. He said he would gladly take back my friend's food and refund the money. I refused. My mother had begun to express her cosmopolitan views on racial equality when Dick, who had not said a word, started for the exit with his tray and we followed him. It was a warm night, and the three of us sat on the curb and ate our supper while Dick explained to my mother that he was accustomed to this sort of thing, which would never change until the entire system was changed. We left our trays on the sidewalk when we were finished and as we got back into the car and headed North, we saw the man from the cafeteria picking them up.

Some days later a "first rough working draft" arrived—a hundred and forty pages long. Structurally it stayed fairly close to the book, which Wright had consciously written in dramatic scene form. ("I wanted the reader to feel that Bigger's story was happening *now* like a play upon a stage or a movie on a screen.") But the "editorial changes"—the additions and modifications—exasperated me. Among the former was a wholly invented, Dostoievskian police "reenactment" scene for which I saw no necessity in a script that was already overlong. Among the modifications was the blending of the dead girl's Communist boyfriend with the left-wing labor lawyer who finally undertakes Bigger's defense. Even more serious in my opinion was the changed moral attitude that pervaded the script, leading inevitably to a total betrayal of Wright's intention in the closing scene. This was the scene of which Wright had written:

> At last I found how to end the book; I ended it just as I had begun it, showing Bigger living dangerously, taking his life in his hands, accepting what life had made of him. The lawyer, Max, was placed in Bigger's cell at the end to register the moral—or what I felt was the moral—horror of Negro life in the United States.

This final facing of the terrible truth of his life was distorted, in Green's version, by giving Bigger "lyric" delusions of grandeur in which he saw himself as "a black God, single and alone."

> BIGGER
>
> Ring the bells! Beat the gongs! Put my name on the hot wires of the world—the name of Bigger, Bigger—the man who walked with God—walked this earth like God—was God!

During the final fade-out a priest in a white surplice "with a great book in his hand" intoned *"I am the Resurrection and the Life."*

I called Wright as soon as I had read it and told him of my anger. He asked me to call or write to Paul Green and explain how I felt and why. I tried, and it was like talking to a stone wall. Some weeks later a revised script arrived. It was down to reasonable length; the Dostoievskian reenactment was gone and the lawyer, Boris Max (rechristened Paul), had been restored to life. But the basic flaw—the distortion of Wright's book—remained. In his final moments in the death cell, Bigger now burbled of the watermelon-patch back home until "the murmuring throb of an airplane motor" offstage caused "his voice to burst from him in a wild, frenzied call"—

> BIGGER
>
> Fly them planes boys—fly 'em! Riding through—riding through. I'll be with you! I'll—
>
> GUARD
>
> He's going nuts.

BIGGER

(Yelling, his head wagging in desperation)

Keep on driving! To the end of the world—Smack into the face of the sun!

(Gasping)

Fly 'em for me—for Bigger—

(The sound of the airplane fades away and now the death chant of the prisoners comes more loudly into the scene. In the dim corridor at the rear, the white surplice of a priest is discerned . . . They start leading him from the cell. As of its own volition the door to the little death house opens and a flood of light pours out. Bigger with his eyes set and his shoulders straight, moves toward its sunny radiance like a man walking into a deep current of water. The guards quietly follow him, their heads bent down.)

PRIEST'S VOICE

(Intoning from the shadows)

I am the resurrection and the light.

THE END

I urged Wright to repudiate what I considered a deliberate betrayal of his work. I told him I had no intention of producing the play in its present form. Dick continued to be distressed but repeated that he preferred not to see it produced than to risk a public disagreement with Paul Green at this time. There was nothing more I could do. My option ran for three and a half months longer. I put the script away in a drawer, swallowed my disappointment and turned back to my radio work.

*   *   *

The Helen Hayes Show was produced for Lipton Tea by the advertising agency of Young and Rubicam. Like most agencies they fussed more over their commercials than over the text of the broadcasts. As a result, Terry Lewis and I, who were each responsible for writing two shows a month, had unusual freedom:

she did most of the contemporary American stories, while I took care of Europe and the classic material, which I adapted to the amazingly flexible personality of our star. Of the ten or more shows I did that season, I remember only two: between the scenes of Laurence Housman's *Victoria Regina,* with which Miss Hayes had enchanted Broadway audiences for three years, I inserted unfamiliar extracts from the Queen's letters and diaries. And I wrote a new version of the *Joan of Arc* story for her, using only authentic material from the trial and contemporary chronicles and emphasizing the tragic similarity between France's present occupation by the invading Nazis and by the British five centuries earlier.

For my own pleasure and Virgil Thomson's (who had returned and was now music critic of the New York *Herald Tribune*) I produced and directed for the CBS Radio Workshop a shortened version of Euripides' *The Trojan Women.* It was our first collaboration since *Hamlet*—an experiment in dramatic sound in which music was used not for transitions or sound effects but continuously, as part of the dramatic action, for the coloration and support of the human voice. The women's parts (Joanna Roos as Cassandra, Mildred Natwick as Hecuba and Zita Johann as Andromache) were cast "for speaking voices of high, middle and low timbre" and the music was orchestrated (mostly for solo instruments—flute, clarinet and English horn) "for pointing up this contrast as well as for aiding identification and giving to each of the solo lines the expressive content of the speech."* It was a fascinating experiment that I would have liked to pursue. But *The Trojan Women* was the last radio show I directed for some time.

One morning around Thanksgiving I awoke in my raised red-velvet bed and raged at the thought that I owned one of the hottest theatrical properties in the world and was prevented from doing anything with it by a peculiar combination of Southern moral prejudice and black, Marxist scruples. I called up Dick Wright and asked him to come over to Ninth Street for lunch. I

* *Virgil Thomson* by Virgil Thomson.

assured him that I understood those scruples but that as his producer and director I refused to accept them. I had reexamined the book and Green's dramatization of it: the revised version was structurally sound; wherever it followed the novel it was usable; where it deviated, as in the absurd final scene, it was reparable by returning to his own original text. Dick asked if we would let Green know what we were doing. I said no. I wanted Wright's help in the restoration, but it would be done entirely on my authority as producer and I would assume full responsibility for it.

Almost every morning, for three weeks, he came over from Brooklyn Heights (where he lived in the basement apartment of a house that was also inhabited by Oliver Smith, Paul Bowles and Wystan Auden) and we would work our way through the scenes, transfusing the blood of the novel back into the body of the play. We had a good time, and when we were done I had the script retyped and took it with me to California, where I was flown at the invitation of David Selznick, who was looking for an associate producer to help to run his studio while he rested after his triumphs with *Gone with the Wind* and *Rebecca*. I listened to him talk for four hours, then drove to RKO, where Dick Wilson ran the work print of *Citizen Kane* for me. That night, in my first spasm of enthusiasm, I did what I had vowed I would never do again. Over dinner I gave Orson the new script of *Native Son* and asked him if he would like to direct it as a Mercury production.

He called me in New York two days later and said yes, very much, as soon as he had seen *Citizen Kane* through its releasing pains—probably in mid-February. My feelings were mixed by this time. I had set my heart on directing this one myself. But I was anxious to end my theatrical association with Welles on a note of triumph and I felt that with the strong text of Wright's book to support him, his direction of *Native Son* would be more dramatic than mine. I gave Wright the news and he was delighted. So was Paul Green.

Meantime I found myself unexpectedly involved in a curious venture with, of all people, the Theatre Guild. Once again

Lawrence Langner and Theresa Helburn had to suffer my hateful presence—this time at the insistence of Philip Barry, who, with *The Philadelphia Story*, had become their most successful playwright and could not be denied.

The play he wanted me to direct for him was a variation of a script he had given me to read two years earlier under the title *The Wild Harps Playing*. It was a frail, whimsical, vaguely poetic piece (a love child among his more mundane commercial plays) about the final, visionary hours of a poor little rich Irish girl dying of a mysterious, incurable ailment. He had laid it aside when he could not get it produced, then returned to it after the huge success of *The Philadelphia Story* and tried to fortify it with elements of contemporary political significance. He rechristened his heiress *Liberty Jones* and related her decline to the presence of three villainous figures who were clearly identifiable as the three totalitarian powers. From their unholy conspiracy she was saved by an upstanding juvenile who vaguely suggested the United States of America. In the process of change it had turned into a musical with songs and ballets. This is what finally induced me to undertake it. Raoul Pène duBois did the sets and costumes, Paul Bowles the music and as choreographer and principal dancer I used Lew Christiansen, who had done *Filling Station* with us the year before. With every ingenue in New York competing for the role of Liberty Jones, Nancy Coleman won out by a nose over Dorothy McGuire, who, brokenhearted, accepted the name part in *Claudia* and became a star overnight.

I had as good a time as I could with a production that I was directing without real conviction or hope of success. We went through the usual stages of nervousness in New Haven, made the usual meaningless changes and played to Guild subscribers in Philadelphia and then in New York without arousing either indignation or enthusiasm. The critics were mild but kind and *Liberty Jones* was still running when *Native Son* went into rehearsal late in February.

My relationship with Orson was quite different from what it had been, but this made it easier for us to be together. Throughout rehearsals of *Native Son* he was happy, overbearing but exciting to work with. With Jean Rosenthal (who was beginning to make her reputation on the outside) and, once again, Jimmy Morcom (on leave from Radio City), he worked out a production in which, behind a vast permanent brick-painted portal, ten wagon stages of various sizes moved past and around each other with never more than a few inches to spare. It took thirty-five stagehands to move them but they worked without a hitch. And for once we had no money problems. Since *Kane,* Hollywood was suddenly full of operators eager for a piece of the action—Orson's action. Two of them, in the hope of becoming his partners in future film ventures, put up the money for *Native Son* to the tune of fifty-five thousand dollars.

Casting was a pleasure. The Mercury regulars—those who had not stayed in California after *Citizen Kane*—were reassembled: Ray Collins (who played Max, the lawyer), Everett Sloane, Paul Stewart, Erskine Sanford, Jack Berry and Richard Wilson. Our new faces included Philip Bourneuf from the Federal Theatre, Frances Bavier, Joseph Pevney and Anne Burr, a complete unknown chosen in an open audition, as the girl. For our black actors we turned to old friends from the Lafayette: Evelyn Ellis, Helen Martin, Rena Mitchell, Bootsie Davis, Wardell Saunders and Canada Lee, a former prize fighter and nightclub owner who had played Banquo for us in *Macbeth* and whom the role of Bigger Thomas made a Broadway star.

For our script we used the text Wright and I had worked on: the few changes we made in rehearsal were all returns to the book. Dick came regularly and appeared to enjoy himself. Then one day I got word that Paul Green would be in New York for the final run-throughs. He appeared in the theatre one evening, sat in silence and left without a word after the last scene. The next morning, the day of our first preview, we held a meeting: Green, Wright, Paul Reynolds and I, joined by Welles, who was rehearsing downstairs and whom I summoned at a dramatic moment. Green insisted that we reinstate his version—particularly the final scene. I told him it was much too late for that and, besides, we had no intention of being parties to the distortion of a work we admired. Richard sat silent beside his agent, who now informed us that Green's second draft (credited to Paul Green and Richard Wright) was already in the publisher's hands. I suggested to Green that he get it back and change it to conform to the acting version. Green was furious. There was talk of enjoining the performance, which I knew he could not do, all the more since not one word was spoken on that stage that was not Wright's—particularly in the last scene, where we had gone back word for word to the book. When Orson began to howl at him, Green got up and left, and I have never seen him again. After our successful opening I called his publisher and pointed out the absurdity of the situation. But it was too late to do anything about it, and as long as it remained in print, Harper and Brothers continued to circulate a version of the play that was radically different from what had been performed on the stage of the St. James Theatre.

At the final preview of *Native Son* two sets of pickets appeared on 44th Street. One, from the conservative Urban League, was protesting the squalor of the book and the bad light in which it put the Negro people. The other represented a small, purist faction of the intellectual Communist Party, which could not forgive Richard Wright for having defied Party orders and refused to rewrite certain sections of his book at their behest. They left after an hour and did not reappear on opening night, which took place (without a single postponement) on the night of March 24th as a Mercury Production presented by Orson Welles and John Houseman.

> Mr. Wright and Paul Green have written a powerful drama and Orson Welles has staged it with imagination and force. These are the first things to be said about the overwhelming play that opened at the St. James last evening but they hardly convey the excitement of this first performance of a play that represents experience of life and conviction in thought and a production that represents a dynamic use of the stage.

This from *The New York Times*. Approval came from widely different quarters—for Canada Lee, for Welles and for the production. Burns Mantle in the *Daily News* gave us four stars and was impressed by the "symphonic binder of sound" (an improved variant of the ill-fated street noises in *Julius Caesar*) that held the multiple scenes of our intermissionless show together. The *Christian Science Monitor* approved. The *Daily Worker* was enthusiastic:

> In comparison, all the productions of the current season seem dim and ancient chromos. The theatre, that slumbering giant, tears off its chains in this production. From the theatrical point of view it is a technical masterpiece. As a political document it lives with the fire of an angry message.

Stark Young found Canada Lee's performance the best he had ever seen from a Negro player. And of Orson he wrote:

> *Native Son* also gains by the thunderous and lurid theatre methods of Mr. Welles. In my opinion Mr. Welles is one of the best influences our theatre has, one of its most important forces . . . His talent begins with the violent, the abundant and the inspired-obvious, all of which make for the life of the theatre-art as contrasted with the pussyfooting and the pseudo-intelligence and the feminism that has crept into this theatre of ours.

What reservations there were came mostly from those whose admiration for the book led them to question the wisdom of dramatizing it:

> In trying to bring *Native Son* to the stage the Mercury has done better than might be expected with the impossible . . . The production achieves something and the almost unbearable suspense of Wright's novel.*

> *Native Son* is a vivid evening in the theatre, a tragic case of a morally mangled victim of society and circumstance. All the same the play lacks the richness and subterraneous power of the book as well as its essential meaning. We do not get

---

* John Mason Brown in the New York *Post.*

473

the novel's down-pressing, unanswerable charge against the white race for crushing and crippling the black one.*

The critic of the *Journal American*, loyal to his angry master, William Randolph Hearst, detected "propaganda that seems nearer to Moscow than Harlem" and reminded readers that Richard Wright had been a staff member of the *Daily Worker* and the *New Masses* and had approved the Soviet trials. "It may be that his idea of justice has been warped to acquit Party members of any charge but execute everybody else."

Native Son was a hit and did excellent business. It needed to, for with its large cast and three dozen stagehands it was as expensive to run as a musical. After 114 performances, with the coming of the hot weather, Orson's Hollywood backers decided to close it.† By then Welles and I were both living in California—Orson preparing *The Magnificent Ambersons* and I as vice-president of David O. Selznick Productions.

I was on the Coast when I received a note, forwarded from Ninth Street:

Dear John Houseman:

I am sorry that we did not get a chance to have a drink and a talk a little before you left for Hollywood . . .

The object of this letter is to try to express to you my gratitude for the enormous help you gave me with *Native Son*. If it had not been for your willingness to give so generously of your time, I doubt gravely if *Native Son* would have ever seen the boards of Broadway. It was a little shameful and ridiculous that you could not have gotten public credit for that help, but that would have meant my dragging into the open those all-too-touchy relations between Paul Green and me, and I was seeking, above all, to keep any word of dissension out of the public press.

I enjoyed immensely working with you, and if our days in

* Louis Kronenberger in *P.M.*

† It reopened in the fall in a more economical version that played New York, Chicago, and major Eastern cities for the better part of a year.

this world are long enough, perhaps we shall meet again under more favorable circumstances.

Give my regards to your mother.

As ever,
Dick Wright

*   *   *

David O. Selznick, when I went to work for him in the spring of 1941, was at the peak of his success. Within two years he had produced *Gone with the Wind,* the most costly and profitable film made up to that time, and followed it up with *Rebecca,* Alfred Hitchcock's first American picture—also a winner. He was a dynamic, flamboyant, spoiled, utterly egotistical man. Compared with Orson he was semieducated and uninspired, but he had an infallible, instinctive sense of the motion picture business with its strange blend of blatant romanticism and commercial preoccupation. By inheritance and marriage he was an organic part of the Hollywood establishment. His father (the S. of Essanay) was one of the notorious early freebooters in the business.* His brother, Myron, was the first of the great manipulating talent agents who virtually invented the high-pressure power-plays that were to dominate the motion picture and, later, the radio and television businesses for years to come. Finally, through his dynastic marriage to the handsome and brilliant Irene Mayer, he had acquired the head of MGM as a father-in-law and future business associate. For all his arrogance and exasperating self-indulgence, he was a man of intelligence and considerable charm—a typically Hollywood combination of oafishness and sophistication. We remained friends long after I stopped working for him—on a superficial, male, competitive basis that usually consisted, when we met, of comparing our

---

* There was a well-founded Hollywood legend that Louis Selznick was once offered a quarter of a million dollars a year by his more successful competitors William Fox and Adolph Zukor if he would guarantee to stay out of the country and stop messing up their business.

weight and the beauty and talent of our respective mistresses.
(He once tried to bet me a hundred dollars that, within a year,
"his" would be making fifty thousand dollars more per picture
than "mine.") If I found the time I spent in his service frustrat-
ing and disappointing, it was my own fault for having misunder-
stood the basis on which he had engaged me.

I was under the impression that what Selznick needed, while
he rested on his laurels and watched the money roll in, was
someone to keep his studio active and to produce pictures in his
place with his advice and protection and the benefit of his producing organization. I could not have been more mistaken. David
O. Selznick had not the slightest intention of letting anyone
produce pictures in his studio except himself.

His vanities and extravagances were personal and neurotic but
unlike Orson's, they did not affect the conduct of his business.
Even in this, the period of his highest success, the operation of his
studio remained reasonably economical. He continued to occupy a
small section of RKO's Pathé lot in Culver City: his personal
bungalow was luxurious but not extravagant—with just enough
room for the three secretaries who were on call for twenty-four
hours of the day and night. The rest of the organization, operating in quarters that were anything but grandiose, consisted of
some dozen persons, of whom the most important, by far, was the
vice-president and general manager, Daniel O'Shea. Jesuit-edu-
cated, a former lawyer and a shrewd negotiator, he was charged
with administering and exploiting the properties—human and
literary—that David O. Selznick had accumulated in the four
years of his independent operation. The former included Ingrid
Bergman (recently imported from Sweden), the De Haviland
sisters—Olivia and Joan Fontaine—Alan Marshall and, later,
Joseph Cotten; also William Cameron Menzies (the industry's
top production designer), Alfred Hitchcock and a number of
lesser figures whom he had under exclusive contract—a form of
indenture which permitted him to lease them out to other producers, with or without their consent, at huge profits, of which
they never saw a cent.

Negotiations for literary properties, which played an essential part in Selznick's operation, were conducted by Danny O'Shea, but the creative task of discovering and sewing them up ahead of the competition was entrusted to his two story departments—East and West. The former was run from New York by Kay Brown, who had achieved considerable national publicity with her "discovery" of *Gone with the Wind* and *Rebecca* before they became best sellers. The West Coast department, which concerned itself mainly with material in the public domain, was run by a brilliant, neurotic malcontent of Russian origin by the name of Val Lewton.* The son of Nazimova's sister, he had begun life as a journalist in Connecticut and a writer of popular fiction, of which he had published several million words under various names before his hand froze one day and he found himself suddenly incapable of writing another line. He found his way, somehow, into motion pictures and into the service of David O. Selznick, for whom he had mixed feelings of adoration, envy, fear and resentment but for whom he fulfilled a very special and important function in which I soon found myself involved.

There was a curious system prevalent in Hollywood at the time—a gentlemen's agreement among motion picture producers regarding the registration of works in the public domain. Designed to protect studios from unfair competition by fly-by-nights, it gave each major producer the right to register up to one hundred titles in which he was interested as possible productions. Once registered, he could retain his exclusive stake in the work for three years, and for twelve months beyond that if he could prove that he had already invested time and money in its development. Two of Selznick's biggest successes at MGM had been *David Copperfield* and *A Tale of Two Cities*. This whetted his appetite for the classics, and when he went into business on his own he became the great specialist of the "reserved" list, which

---

* He found his vocation some years later when Selznick dissolved his organization and Lewton became a producer of low-budget "C" pictures for RKO. Here, at absurd prices, he produced a number of suspense and fright pictures (of which *The Cat People* was the first) that made him a critics' favorite and one of the most vital picture makers in the business until his death of heart failure at an early age.

he used not only as a source of story material for his own pictures, but also as a speculative market in potential properties for other people. With Val Lewton's erudition and excellent taste, coupled with his own acute business sense and his ability to foretell the direction in which the business was going, he had built up a list of "reserved" titles that was the envy of the trade—an envy that David used as a basis for all kinds of lucrative transactions and manipulations.*

My first assignment for Selznick was on one of his properties in the public domain—Charlotte Brontë's *Jane Eyre.* I had begun working on it during rehearsals of *Native Son.* As usual, David was in a hurry: he had sent Robert Stevenson—a new English writer-director whom he had under contract—to New York to work on it with me. The day after the opening we flew to the Coast together, and five weeks after that, with Stevenson doing most of the work, we finished it and presented it to our leader, only to discover that he had not the slightest intention of producing it. Danny O'Shea began offering it around, together with the services of Joan Fontaine and Robert Stevenson, at a price so fabulous that it was not until the war boom a year later that he was able to sell it to Darryl Zanuck at 20th Century-Fox. (It was made in my absence with Joan Fontaine as the nubile Jane, Orson Welles as Mr. Rochester and a troupe of moppets that included Margaret O'Brien, Peggy Ann Garner and Elizabeth Taylor.)

My second assignment was to work with Alfred Hitchcock. It was no secret that all had not been roses between him and David during the making of *Rebecca,* to which Hitch had attempted to apply the very personal creative methods that had made him world-famous. These methods were profoundly repulsive to David O. Selznick, who belonged to the school of the well-made, producer-controlled, strictly-adhered-to shooting script and who,

---

* Years later, when I came to produce Shakespeare's *Julius Caesar* at MGM, it was discovered that David O. Selznick had it locked up on his "reserved" list and had no intention of surrendering it. He did, finally, for a price—in exchange for the use of two "hot" MGM stars he needed and the acquisition by MGM of two properties which they never filmed.

besides, was determined on this, Hitch's first American picture, to assert his producer's position of power. With the success of *Rebecca* all had been forgiven, but a residue of hostility and suspicion remained. I was instructed to use my British background, as well as my cultivation and charm, to establish good personal relations with Hitch and to cajole and encourage him into conceiving and preparing an "original" screenplay for his second American film.

In the course of this delicate mission I developed a relationship with Hitch and Alma, his wife, that lasted through all the years I lived in California and beyond. I had heard of him as a fat man given to scabrous jokes—a gourmet and an ostentatious connoisseur of fine wines. What I was unprepared for was a man of exaggeratedly delicate sensibilities, marked by a harsh Catholic education and the scars from a social system against which he was in perpetual revolt and which had left him suspicious and vulnerable, alternately docile and defiant. He was an entertaining and knowledgeable companion: books and paintings, dogs, houses and politics all occupied a place in his life. But his passion was for his work, which he approached with an intelligence and an almost scientific clarity to which I was unaccustomed in the theatre.

Rebecca had been a distasteful experience for him. Anxious to get started on a new and more individual film, he came up with a notion for a picaresque spy story—a U.S. version of *The Thirtynine Steps*—with a transcontinental chase that moved from coast to coast and ended inside the hand of the Statue of Liberty. He called it *The Saboteur,* and we outlined it to Selznick, who thought it was terrible but gave us the go-ahead—the quicker the better.

Working with Hitch really meant listening to him talk— anecdotes, situations, characters, revelations and reversals, which he would think up at night and try out on us during the day and of which the surviving elements were finally strung together into some sort of story in accordance with carefully calculated and elaborately plotted rhythms. His listeners on this project were Joan Harrison (an able, well-tailored English blonde who had been his assistant in London), Peter Viertel (an apprentice writer in Selznick's stable whose first novel had just been published), occasionally Alma (who had been one of the highest-paid continuity writers in English silent pictures before she married him) and myself.

My own enjoyment of the work was diminished by the secret knowledge that I would have nothing to do with its production, since David had every intention of selling it outright, together with Hitchcock's services as a director, to the highest bidder. Long before the script was finished, negotiations for its sale began: appointments were set up with various studio heads to which I accompanied Hitch, feeling rather like a pimp, while he did his stuff—outlining the subject of his film, its locales, its principal characters and its flashiest moments. Hitch was divided between humiliation over these performances and the pleasure he always felt at trying out his gimmicks on a new audience. But there was one aspect of these visits that infuriated him: the knowledge that David O. Selznick's asking price for the package, including Hitch's services as a director, represented a profit—to Selznick—of around three hundred percent! This grievance over what he quite rightly regarded as the exploitation of his talent became so deep that it finally affected the quality of the picture. *The Saboteur* was sold to an independent producer who had paid so much for the property that he was forced to economize on the making of the film. It was less conscientiously produced than any of the other Hitchcock pictures. But David made a net profit of over a hundred thousand dollars on the transaction.

My next activity for David O. Selznick was something I was delighted to do. Ingrid Bergman was between pictures and someone (Selznick or Kay Brown or, perhaps, Ingrid herself) suggested that she was a natural for the name part in Eugene O'Neill's *Anna Christie*. David asked me what I thought of the idea and if I would be interested in directing it at the Biltmore Theatre in downtown Los Angeles. I suggested, instead, that we do it at the Lobero in Santa Barbara, which had an excellent stage and a quality audience. Within twenty-four hours Selznick had converted my idea into a gala summer theatre season which he asked me to direct.

Anna Christie was our opening production, with Bill Menzies as designer and my old friend Kate Lawson as technical director. J. Edward Bromberg (of the Group Theatre) gave a fine, non-Scandinavian performance as the father, and Ingrid was a joy to work with. She was eager, passionate, well-prepared, and she gave me everything I asked for except the feeling that Anna was sick and corrupted and destroyed; one had the conviction that beneath her period skirt her underclothes were starched, clean and sweet-smelling. It was a success—with a real Hollywood, Selznick-promoted opening, and after a week we moved it to San Francisco, where we played for another two weeks before Ingrid had to return to Culver City to begin *Dr. Jekyll and Mr. Hyde* with Spencer Tracy.

The night of our San Francisco opening I was taken to Izzy Gomez' bar (supposedly the scene of *The Time of Your Life*), where I encountered William Saroyan surrounded by characters from his works. I asked him if he had a new play we could do in Santa Barbara. He said he'd just had an idea—a one-act piece called *Hello Out There* which he'd finish by the end of the week and send to me. He did, and we went into rehearsal with it a week later.

Our second production at the Lobero was a new play by Enid Bagnold—*Lottie Dundass*—with Geraldine Fitzgerald in the name part, Faith Brook as the girl she strangled and May Whitty as her mother. It never quite worked—either in Santa Barbara or, later, in England. Our third was a very full evening: *The Devil's Disciple* preceded by *Hello Out There,* which I directed, in which the boy was played by Harry Bratsberg and the girl by a completely unknown young actress whose name Selznick had just changed from Phyllis Walker to Jennifer Jones. In the Shaw play Alan Marshall played Dick Dudgeon (and came close to being strangled in the last act when the noose slipped); Janet Gaynor was his wife and June Lockhart the waif; Cedric Hardwicke, who also directed, played the show-stealing part of General Burgoyne. It was a creditable theatrical season for which I was rewarded with the second vice-presidency of David O. Selznick Productions. Another assignment I undertook for Selznick that summer was less rewarding. He and Irene had grown very close that year to Henry and Clare Luce, who, in turn were deeply involved with Chiang Kai-shek and his wife. Eager to play a role in public affairs, Selznick had placed the full resources of his studio behind the nationwide drive for funds which the Luces were conducting on behalf of the Generalissimo and what appeared, at the time, to be the Chinese national government. As part of this campaign I produced and directed a coast-to-coast all-star radio show in which Shirley Temple made a tearful appeal on behalf of the children of China.*

In October familiar faces appeared on the RKO Pathé lot where Orson Welles was beginning to shoot *The Magnificent Ambersons*. We had done it in the Mercury radio show: Booth Tarkington had been a close friend of Orson's father and the Middlewestern scene at the turn of the century was very close to his heart. I watched him shoot part of the opening sequence—the long approach through the industrial streets to the family mansion, the slow move up the grand staircase into the glittering ballroom of the Amberson home. In its rough-cut, before it was edited to meet the requirements of a normal-length feature picture, it was one of the most extraordinary film sequences I have ever seen.

It may have been Orson's presence on the lot, sharply reminding me of the creative excitement in which I no longer had a part, that finally stirred me to revolt against the well-paid, tranquil, irrelevant life I was leading as vice-president of David O. Selznick Productions. But the discontent had been there for

---

* On the negative side I managed to dissuade Selznick from a scheme of which he was particularly enamored: through Central Casting he proposed to engage several dozen Oriental extras, dress them in aged coolie suits, load them into buses and ship them across the country. On the outskirts of each major city they would be unloaded, supplied with appropriate props, including rice bowls, and marched through the streets to collect contributions to the Chinese nationalist cause.

months, running deep under the immediate frustrations of my career; and it had to do, in part, with the state of the world.

Beginning with *Panic,* through my two years on the Federal Theatre and during the rise and fall of the Mercury, I had become accustomed to relating my theatrical activity to the historical movements of the time. On WPA this participation had been immediate and inescapable. The Great Depression had created problems that were urgent and all-inclusive: on the Negro Theatre and, later, on Project #891 we were reminded daily, by friends and enemies alike, that our work was an essential part of the social and political life of our day. Some of this sense of involvement was carried over into the Mercury, where it directly affected our choice of subjects and our methods of operation. Then, gradually, as the Depression receded and international events replaced domestic crises on the front pages of our newspapers, this participation became less satisfying. Germany's persecution of the Jews, the Moscow trials, the Spanish Civil War, the successive threats against Austria and Czechoslovakia culminating in the enervating suspense of Munich—these formed a mounting tide of tension to which no positive creative response was possible and to which our theatrical activity could no longer be directly related. (For me, in particular, this confusion was aggravated by my European background: having no clear feelings of national loyalty I was torn by a number of sentimental adhesions which pulled me this way and that on a purely subjective and sentimental basis.) The Nazi-Soviet pact leading to the invasion of Poland, the stress of the "phony" war followed by the fall of France and the threatened invasion of Britain—each had its cumulative traumatic effect, from which I had been partially protected by the constant, furious pressures of the Mercury operation and the personal crises of my deteriorating relations with Orson Welles. When these ceased, I found myself suddenly alone and vulnerable. In the security of Culver City I felt myself slipping back into one of those dark moods of inertia and self-doubt of which I had thought myself forever free.

My outward circumstances were different: I was making more

money than I had ever made in my life; I had a substantial reputation and a well-organized mechanism of work. But under the surface there was the old frightening sense of isolation, of being hopelessly adrift while I waited (with not the faintest idea of when or from where it was coming) for some great new wind to arise and fill my drooping sails.

Late in November I received a call from my friend Pare Lorentz. He had just arrived to make a movie for RKO, where George Schaeffer, his courage restored by the artistic success of *Citizen Kane,* had decided to try his luck with another maverick film maker. Pare had followed *The Plough That Broke the Plains* and *The River* with a film about childbirth in the Chicago slums—*The Fight for Life.* He was now at work on his most ambitious project—a dramatic documentary about the condition of the U.S. industrial worker with special emphasis on the economic and emotional effects of the production line. He called it alternately *Ecce Homo* and *Name, Age and Occupation,* and he had already shot several tens of thousand feet of industrial footage in Detroit.

I was fond of Pare, impressed by his films and, even more, by his passionate and comprehensive historical sense about the United States of America. He asked me to help with the script and casting of his new project, and I leapt at the chance. D.O.S. was away, but I pointed out to Danny O'Shea that he would be saving close to ten thousand dollars by loaning me out during the idle holiday season. He agreed, and I went to work with Pare the next day. It was not the great wind I was waiting for, but I had the sense, once again, of participating in the realities of the world.

Pare and I had a chronic problem—socially and professionally. He wanted to talk all night and I insisted on working by day. I soon tired of wasting half my best hours waiting for him to come to life. So we reached a modus vivendi: we would spend the afternoon, dinner and the first part of the night together; then I would go home to sleep while Pare spent the rest of the night typing or talking to someone else. In the morning I would find

4 8 4

his pages, go over them and do some writing of my own until after noon, when he finally appeared. It worked less well than my collaboration with Mankiewicz; Pare's feeling for his material was entirely subjective and personal and he was having difficulty reconciling his documentary approach to the requirements of this, his first full-length dramatic film. We were making slow progress when Pare decided one night that the moment had come for a trip to New York to discover some of those unknown faces he was determined to use in his picture. We flew East together and, for a week, we interviewed scores of males between the ages of twenty-five and thirty-five. We chose two of them, and RKO put them under contract. (Neither of them appeared in Pare's film, which was never made. They both went off to the war: one was killed at Iwo Jima; the other, Robert Ryan, returned and became a star.) Then we went back to California by rail, hoping to get some work done on the way. In Chicago, during the usual long wait between the Twentieth Century Limited and the Chief, we stoppped off at the Blackstone Hotel; in the lobby Pare encountered Willian Benton, who assured us over drinks that we did not understand the real feelings of the country: the Middle West was solidly isolationist; Charles Lindbergh was a popular hero; Roosevelt would never get us into war, no matter how hard he tried. We left him to catch our train, talked and fell asleep. The next day, around noon, speeding through Western Kansas, we heard the news of Pearl Harbor over the radio in the club car and stayed there for the rest of the day and night drinking and listening to the news with mixed feelings of exhilaration and terror.

A week later I was flying East on a Government priority. In a telegram from Washington, Robert Sherwood had asked me to meet him in the State Department building, where he introduced me to a tough, white-haired charmer named William Donovan who asked me if I would undertake the organization and programming of the Overseas Radio operation for the Coordinator of Information. We were starting from scratch, Bob explained, with no equipment or personnel and no clear notion of what form U.S. wartime propaganda should take. I said yes, of course, and asked for a few days to wind up my affairs in California. When I informed David O. Selznick of my new assignment he praised me for my patriotism, then notified me by registered letter that my contract still had eleven weeks to run, which he expected me to complete when the war ended.

Early in January 1942, I was back in New York meeting my new colleagues—Joseph Barnes, James Warburg, Edd Johnson—and helping to set up the Overseas Operation of what came to be known as the Office of War Information. While we waited for our shortwave transmission equipment to arrive and began to recruit the multilingual personnel that was to broadcast the Voice of America in twenty-seven languages to the four corners of the earth, I had a chance to look back over the twelve crowded years that had passed so quickly since the collapse of the Oceanic Grain Corporation and to consider my future.

For all my continuing fantasies I had few illusions about myself. I had been born into an era of prodigious mutations in which my floating, eclectic energy had proved an effective substitute for the creative originality I lacked and the social and cultural identity that my hybrid birth and divided upbringing had denied me. It was an age of improvisation, of violent change and drastic readjustments to which I was uniquely suited. With my limited equipment and my total absence of ties I had scurried through the confusions of the Great Depression into the heart of an astonishing number of creative projects, in each of which I had played an important, and sometimes an essential, part. At the time, these operations had seemed accidental and unrelated, the results of adroit maneuvering and prodigious luck. Now, in my fortieth year, as the shape of my life became clearer and its varied achievements seemed finally to come together into some sort of recognizable form, I was finding it necessary to make certain ironic reevaluations.

I had always thought of my British public school education with sentimental affection and a vague sense of absurdity: I had been carefully and conscientiously prepared for leadership in a world to which I would never belong and in which, as it turned out, there was no one left to lead. Now, a quarter of a century

486

later, I found myself wondering if some remnants of that training had not made possible my successful administration of two particularly difficult projects for the Federal Theatre of the WPA. Of my years in the international grain business nothing remained but hateful memories buried in the glamorous agitations of my new theatrical career. Yet where else could I have acquired the material experience, the nerve and ability to assume and pursue the calculated risks without which my maverick artistic enterprises and collaborations (including the Mercury) might never have seen the light of day?

Finally I reflected with some amusement that without my mother's obstinate, mystical belief in the value of foreign tongues (four of which had been crammed down my throat before I was old enough to object) I would not be embarking, with my usual combination of shuddering panic and reckless self-assurance, on this, my latest and strangest adventure—as Chief of radio propaganda for the United States Government in the Second World War. As I received my civil service appointment in the name of *Jacques Haussmann* (whose naturalization papers, filed in 1936, had not yet come through) no one—least of all myself—seemed to question the propriety of placing the Voice of America under the direction of an enemy alien of Rumanian birth who, as such, was expressly forbidden by the Department of Justice to go near a shortwave radio set.

Index